Medical Office Procedures

Sixth Edition

Karonne J. Becklin, MEd., CMA

Anoka Technical College, Anoka, MN

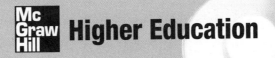
Higher Education

Boston   Burr Ridge, IL   Dubuque, IA   Madison, WI   New York   San Francisco   St. Louis
Bangkok   Bogotá   Caracas   Kuala Lumpur   Lisbon   London   Madrid   Mexico City
Milan   Montreal   New Delhi   Santiago   Seoul   Singapore   Sydney   Taipei   Toronto

Higher Education

MEDICAL OFFICE PROCEDURES, SIXTH EDITION

Published by McGraw-Hill, a business unit of The McGraw-Hill Companies, Inc., 1221 Avenue of the Americas, New York, NY 10020. Copyright © 2006, 2003, 1996, 1992 by The McGraw-Hill Companies, Inc. All rights reserved. No part of this publication may be reproduced or distributed in any form or by any means, or stored in a database or retrieval system, without the prior written consent of The McGraw-Hill Companies, Inc., including, but not limited to, in any network or other electronic storage or transmission, or broadcast for distance learning.

Some ancillaries, including electronic and print components, may not be available to customers outside the United States.

This book is printed on recycled, acid-free paper containing 10% postconsumer waste.

6 7 8 9 0 QPD/QPD 0 9

ISBN 978–0–07–319100–3
MHID 0–07–319100–0

Publisher, Career Education: *David T. Culverwell*
Senior Sponsoring Editor: *Roxan Kinsey*
Managing Developmental Editor: *Patricia Hesse*
Senior Marketing Manager: *James F. Connely*
Senior Project Manager: *Sheila M. Frank*
Senior Production Supervisor: *Kara Kudronowicz*
Lead Media Project Manager: *Audrey A. Reiter*
Media Technology Producer: *Janna Martin*
Senior Coordinator of Freelance Design: *Michelle D. Whitaker*
(USE) Cover Image: © *PictureArts/CORBIS*
Lead Photo Research Coordinator: *Carrie K. Burger*
Photo Research: *Pam Carley/Sound Reach*
Supplement Producer: *Brenda A. Ernzen*
Compositor: *Carlisle Communications, Ltd.*
Typeface: *10.5/14 Guardi Roman*
Printer: *Quebecor World Dubuque, IA*

The credits section for this book appears on page 350 and is considered an extension of the copyright page.

www.mhhe.com

Contents

Preface v

To the Student ix

Part 1   The Administrative Medical Assistant's Career 1

Chapter 1   The Administrative Medical Assistant 2
Chapter 2   Medical Ethics, Law, and Compliance 28
Chapter 3   Computer Usage in the Medical Office 53

Part 2   Administrative Responsibilities 77

Chapter 4   Telephone Procedures and Scheduling 78
Chapter 5   Records Management 110
Chapter 6   Written Communications 133
              Simulation 1 159

Part 3   Patient Records 163

Chapter 7   Patient Medical Records 164
Chapter 8   Insurance and Coding 190
Chapter 9   Billing, Reimbursement, and Collections 222
              Simulation 2 251

Part 4   Practice Finances and Management 253

Chapter 10   Practice Finances 254
Chapter 11   Office Management 276
              Simulation 3 301

Appendix A Introduction to NDCmedisoft™ 303

Appendix B HIPAA Overview 330

Glossary 340

Index 351

Working Papers .... WP 1

Preface

The medical profession is complex and demanding. The typical physician rarely has time to attend to the administrative responsibilities of the office. Successfully performing the work of an administrative medical assistant requires a foundation of procedural knowledge as well as continuing education to keep up to date with technology, including computerization skills and new computer software. This sixth edition of *Medical Office Procedures*, a well-known and widely used textbook, provides the required background for the responsibilities of the administrative medical assistant. To prepare students for the greatly increased use of technology in the medical office, this revision places increased importance on the computerization of routine tasks and of communications.

Job opportunities in the medical field continually change with varying degrees of education and specialization. This textbook allows for the integrated application of office procedures skills and knowledge in the classroom through the use of simulation techniques. Students learn to perform the duties of the administrative medical assistant under realistic conditions and with realistic pressures that require them to organize the work and set priorities.

■ What's New?

- NDCmedisoft™ exercises have been updated to Version 9.
- HCFA 1400 has been changed to CMS 1500.
- Appendix A which contains an introduction to NDCmedisoft™ has been updated to Version 9.
- Appendix B contains an eight-page HIPAA overview
- Instructions for restoring the data file that is used in the NDCmedisoft™ exercises have been added to the inside front cover of the text.
- Glossary terms have been updated.

■ Organization of the Text

The sixth edition is divided in four parts containing eleven chapters. Part 1 introduces the administrative medical assistant's career, defining the tasks, describing the work environments, and introducing medical ethics and medical law as they apply to the administrative medical assistant. Specific administrative responsibilities are introduced and applied in Part 2. These include scheduling patients by telephone or in person, records management, and medical communications. The use of the computer is emphasized in each of these topics. In Part 3, procedures for preparing and organizing patients' charts and bills/insurance are discussed. Part 4 concerns practice finances and office management.

■ Chapter Overview

Each chapter provides background information and current procedures in a clear, comprehensive presentation. Photographs, figures, and tables are included to enhance the learning process. The chapters also contain the following elements to ensure that students grasp the key points:

- *Objectives.* A description of the most important concepts and abilities that can be acquired by studying the chapter.
- *Introduction.* An orientation to the chapter's key concepts.
- *Key Terms.* An alphabetic list of important vocabulary words. Key terms are printed in boldface and defined when introduced in the text.
- *Projects.* Within each chapter, students are directed to complete projects at frequent intervals so that they can immediately put into practice the concept just studied. Records and correspondence that the student creates in these individual projects are used later in the simulations, where they illustrate the complexity of the administrative medical assistant's responsibilities. The scheduling and financial projects can be established using the NDCmedisoft™ software. The written communications and charts can be completed using any word processing software.
- *Chapter Summary.* The key concepts associated with each chapter objective are summarized.
- *Thinking It Through.* Questions that require the student to apply the knowledge gained by studying the chapter for correct answers.

■ Simulations

A two-day simulation appears at the end of Part 2; three-day simulations appear at the ends of Parts 3 and 4. The text provides instructions for the completion of the simulation. In each simulation, the student listens to the *Simulation Recordings* that accompany the program. The recordings contain the conversations between Linda Schwartz (the doctor's administrative medical assistant, with whom the student will identify) and Dr. Karen Larsen, various patients, and other office callers. (*Note:* The student may use the simulation recordings individually, or they may be assigned for use by the class as a whole. A complete transcript of the Simulation Recordings appears in the *Instructor Manual and Key*.)

■ Student Resource Materials

In the *Working Papers* section at the back of the text, forms, medical histories, handwritten drafts, incoming correspondence, and other communications needed to complete the projects and the simulations are provided.

Additional *Project Resource Materials* are provided on the Student CD that accompanies the program. The CD contains patient information forms and statements, as well as the letterhead for the physician's practice used in the projects and simulations.

■ Special Features

Additional features are included in *Medical Office Procedures* to provide more information, practice new skills, or permit students to extend their knowledge through Internet research and computer applications:

Compliance Tips. These hints on ensuring compliance with correct billing and coding practices are located in the margins near the related chapter topics.

Internet Activities. Each chapter's projects contain optional Internet activities that describe relevant Web sites and direct the student to use the Internet to research and report their findings. The goal of the activities is to extend the student's knowledge of the selected topics and to learn to use the Internet as a research tool.

NDCmedisoft™ Applications. Many projects and parts of the simulations can be completed with the use of a patient billing software program, *NDCmedisoft™ Advanced: Patient Accounting*, which is free to adopters of *Medical Office Procedures*. The Student Data Disk that accompanies the program contains the sample medical practice with which the students work. Basic instruction in using NDCmedisoft™, which must be studied before students work through the activities, is contained in Appendix A: Introduction to NDCmedisoft™.

Information on ordering and installing *NDCmedisoft™ Advanced: Patient Accounting* is contained in the *Instructor Manual and Key* that accompanies the program. To use the software and the NDCmedisoft™ activities, the following equipment and supplies are needed:

- 400 MHz or greater processor speed

- 128 MB RAM

- 500 MB available hard disk space

- CD-ROM 2x or faster disk drive

- Windows 98, ME, NT, 2000, or XP operating system

- *NDCmedisoft*™ *Advanced: Patient Accounting* Version 9 (free to adopters)

- *Medical Office Procedures* Student Data Disk

- Blank, formatted 3.5" floppy diskette

- Printer

■ Instructor's Materials

Instructor's materials include an *Instructor Manual and Key* and a CD. The manual provides answers to the *Thinking It Through* questions in the text, teaching suggestions, resources for insurance information, correlation charts for SCANS, the National Health Care Skill Standards, the 1997 AAMA Role Delineation Study Areas of Competence, and the AMT competencies. It also includes information on ordering and installing *NDCmedisoft*™ *Advanced: Patient Accounting* software.

The instructor's CD includes PowerPoint® Presentations highlighting the main points of each chapter and an ExamView® Pro Test Generator.

■ Acknowledgments

For insightful reviews, criticisms, helpful suggestions, and information, I would like to acknowledge Nenna Bayes (Office Technology and Medical Office Systems, Ashland Technical College) and Janet I. Boring Seggern (Lehigh Carbon Community College). Alison Cable, RN, assisted with medical technical support.

Karonne J. Becklin

To the Student

You have chosen a fascinating, challenging profession. The field of health care is growing at a rapid pace, providing many opportunities for the trained professional. Welcome to an educational program designed to prepare you for immediate and long-range success as an administrative medical assistant. In this course, you will use *Medical Office Procedures* not only as a source of practical information but also as an instrument for realistic practice in applying what you have learned.

■ Practical Information

Every topic that you will study in this course is directly related to one or more of many administrative tasks in the medical office. In Part 1 of this textbook, you will learn about career opportunities available to you, the work environments, the qualifications needed in order to succeed, and medical law and ethics as they apply to the medical administrative assistant. Computer usage is also introduced in Part 1. After studying and absorbing this information, you should be better able to set your sights on the job that is best suited to your interests, qualifications, and ambitions.

In Part 2, you will learn how to work with patients in an efficient, effective manner dealing with scheduling, records management, and communications. As an administrative medical assistant, you will be required to work with patients' records and reimbursements. Part 3 will help you become thoroughly acquainted with medical records and patient billing and health insurance. Practice finances and management will be presented in Part 4 introducing you to the various financial records that are a part of the medical office and to office management topics.

■ Realistic Job Training

Throughout the chapters, you will be asked to apply your newly acquired knowledge—not simply to tell how or why you would use the information on the job. You will then repeatedly apply the information throughout the text.

As you complete the designated projects within the text, you will accumulate many of the medical records and correspondence needed in the simulations that occur after Parts 2, 3, and 4. You will be asked to assume the role of Linda Schwartz, an administrative medical assistant. During each simulation, you will handle various tasks assigned by the physician, the patients, and other office callers.

During the simulations, you will be expected to listen carefully to recorded conversations between Linda Schwartz and the doctor, the patients, and other office callers. With some instructor guidance, you will perform your duties in an appropriate manner.

You will be performing a variety of closely related administrative medical office tasks in the simulations: answering the telephone, scheduling appointments, taking messages, transcribing dictation, filing, preparing bills, and so on. You have occasion to use various resources, such as dictionaries, reference books, and medical references, just as you would use in an office. Thus, you will gain proficiency in performing a wide range of administrative activities and in coping with a variety of problems and pressures in the medical office. All these activities will help you strive to organize work, set priorities, relate one task to another, and manage time. After completing these simulations, you will find that you are well prepared for the transition from classroom to office.

At the end of each chapter, you will find a chapter summary, list of key terms, and thinking it through (critical thinking) activities that will help you better understand your chosen profession and its responsibilities.

■ Supplies

Starting with Part 2, you will be "working" for Dr. Karen Larsen, a family practitioner. As directed, save your work from the chapter projects. This work will form the basis for your "office files." In the simulations, you will use and add to these files.

Essential patient data and forms are provided either in the working papers or on the CD that is a part of this text. You will also need the following supplies:

- File folder labels and 31 file folders.
- A ring binder or a file folder to serve as your appointment book if you are not using the NDCmedisoft™ computer software.
- An expandable portfolio to serve as your file cabinet. All your office files can be stored in this portfolio.
- Paper for printing.
- Computer disks to store the projects as directed.
- Miscellaneous items—rubber bands, a note pad, pens, pencils, paper clips, and so on.

Karonne J. Becklin

PART

1

The Administrative Medical Assistant's Career

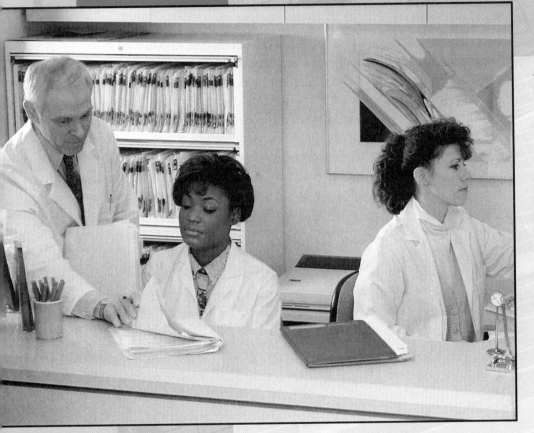

CHAPTER 1
The Administrative Medical Assistant

CHAPTER 2
Medical Ethics, Law, and Compliance

CHAPTER 3
Computer Usage in the Medical Office

Welcome to *Medical Office Procedures!* This program has been written specifically to provide you with the skills and knowledge you will need to succeed. In Part 1, you will learn about the role of the administrative medical assistant, legal and ethical aspects of the job, and the use of computers in the medical office.

CONSIDER THIS: Physicians' offices, hospitals, clinics, and other employers hire administrative medical assistants. *In what type of medical setting do you intend to pursue employment?*

The Administrative Medical Assistant

OBJECTIVES

After studying this chapter, you will be able to:

1. Describe the tasks and skills required of an administrative medical assistant.
2. List three personal attributes essential for an administrative medical assistant.
3. Describe the employment opportunities in various medical settings and specialties.
4. Define five of the positive work attitudes that make up the work ethic of an administrative medical assistant.
5. Describe the professional image of the administrative medical assistant.
6. List three advantages of professional affiliation and certification.
7. Describe the elements of good interpersonal relationships with patients and others within the medical office.

INTRODUCTION

As sophisticated technologies, improved medications, and new treatments are introduced into the health care industry, the opportunities for rewarding careers in medical offices increase. These changes also pose new challenges for health care professionals. Legal and ethical issues abound. Following procedures that comply with government regulations concerning patients' privacy is also critical.

Because of rapid changes and the increasing complexity of the industry, continuing education is necessary to succeed in performing the role of an administrative medical assistant. Equally important is exhibiting the personal attributes and work ethic that contribute to the smooth and efficient operation of the medical practice.

KEY TERMS

Study these important words, which are defined in this chapter, to build your professional vocabulary:

AAMA	assertiveness	empathy	initiative	self-motivation
AAMT	certification	flexibility	maturity	tact
accuracy	confidentiality	good judgment	problem-solving	team player
administrative	dependability	honesty	professional image	thoroughness
medical assistant	efficiency	IAAP	punctuality	work ethic
AMT				

1.1 TASKS, SKILLS, AND PERSONAL ATTRIBUTES

Medical assistants are medical office professionals who capably perform a number of tasks in a wide variety of settings. Administrative tasks are those procedures used to keep the offices in medical practices running efficiently. Clinical tasks are those procedures the medical assistant may perform to aid the physician in the medical treatment of a patient. A comprehensive list of the administrative and clinical tasks and skills required of the medical assistant is shown in Figure 1.1 on pages 4–5.

This textbook concentrates on administrative responsibilities, which involve the personal traits and technical skills required in most medical office careers. Throughout the text, the **administrative medical assistant** is often referred to as the "assistant," rather than by the full title.

■ Administrative Medical Assisting Tasks

The administrative medical assistant is a professional office worker dedicated to assisting in the care of patients. To effectively perform all the required tasks, an assistant must be proficient in a number of skills.

The major categories of tasks performed by an administrative medical assistant are:

- Front desk procedures
- Scheduling
- Records management
- Administrative duties
- Billing and insurance

Front Desk. The administrative medical assistant greets patients and other visitors, such as family members. The assistant also verifies personal data about patients, explains the fees that will be charged for services, collects payments, and guides patients through their medical office encounters.

Scheduling. The administrative medical assistant answers the telephone; schedules appointments, either by phone or in person; and forwards telephone calls according to office procedures.

Records Management. The administrative medical assistant creates and maintains patient medical records (sometimes referred to as *charts*); stores and retrieves the records for use during encounters with physicians; and files other kinds of documents.

Administrative Duties. The administrative medical assistant opens and sorts incoming mail, composes routine correspondence, and transcribes physicians' dictation. The assistant also maintains the physicians' schedules,

FIGURE 1.1 AMA Role Delineation Study Areas of Competence (1997) Correlation Chart

ADMINISTRATIVE

Administrative Procedures

Perform basic clerical functions.

Schedule, coordinate, and monitor appointments.

Schedule inpatient/outpatient admissions and procedures.

Understand and apply third-party guidelines.

Obtain reimbursement through accurate claims submission.

Monitor third-party reimbursement.

Perform medical transcription.

Understand and adhere to managed care policies and procedures.

* Negotiate managed care contracts.

Practice Finances

Perform procedural and diagnostic coding.

Apply bookkeeping principles.

Document and maintain accounting and banking records.

Manage accounts receivable.

Manage accounts payable.

Process payroll.

* Develop and maintain fee schedules.

* Manage renewals of business and professional insurance policies.

* Manage personnel benefits and maintain records.

CLINICAL

Fundamental Principles

Apply principles of aseptic technique and infection control.

Comply with quality assurance practices.

Screen and follow up patient test results.

Diagnostic Orders

Collect and process specimens.

Perform diagnostic tests.

Patient Care

Adhere to established triage procedures.

Obtain patient history and vital signs.

Prepare and maintain examination and treatment areas.

Prepare patient for examinations, procedures, and treatments.

Assist with examinations, procedures, and treatments.

Prepare and administer medications and immunizations.

Maintain medication and immunization records.

Recognize and respond to emergencies.

Coordinate patient care information with other health care providers.

GENERAL (TRANSDISCIPLINARY)

Professionalism

Project a professional manner and image.

Adhere to ethical principles.

Demonstrate initiative and responsibility.

Work as a team member.

Manage time effectively.

Prioritize and perform multiple tasks.

Adapt to change.

Promote the CMA credential.

Enhance skills through continuing education.

Communication Skills

Treat all patients with compassion and empathy.

Recognize and respect cultural diversity.

Adapt communications to individual's ability to understand.

Use professional telephone techniques.

Use effective and correct verbal and written communications.

Recognize and respond to verbal and nonverbal communications.

Use medical terminology appropriately.

Receive, organize, prioritize, and transmit information.

Serve as liaison.

Promote the practice through positive public relations.

Legal Concepts

Maintain confidentiality.

Practice within the scope of education, training, and personal capabilities.

Prepare and maintain medical records.

Document accurately.

Use appropriate guidelines when releasing information.

Follow employer's established policies dealing with the health care contract.

Follow federal, state, and local legal guidelines.

Maintain awareness of federal and state health care legislation and regulations.

Maintain and dispose of regulated substances in compliance with government guidelines.

Comply with established risk management and safety procedures.

Recognize professional credentialing criteria.

Participate in the development and maintenance of personnel, policy, and procedure manuals.

* Develop and maintain personnel, policy, and procedure manuals.

FIGURE 1.1 *(continued)*

Instruction

Instruct individuals according to their needs.

Explain office policies and procedures.

Teach methods of health promotion and disease prevention.

Locate community resources and disseminate information.

* Orient and train personnel.

* Develop educational materials.

* Conduct continuing education activities.

Operational Functions

Maintain supply inventory.

Evaluate and recommend equipment and supplies.

Apply computer techniques to support office operations.

* Supervise personnel.

* Interview and recommend job applicants.

* Negotiate leases and prices for equipment and supply contracts.

* Denotes advanced skills.

which involves keeping track of the time required for office encounters with patients, meetings, and conferences as well as coordinating patients' hospital admissions and surgical procedures.

Billing and Insurance. The administrative medical assistant codes or verifies codes for diagnoses and procedures; processes and follows up on insurance claims and patients' bills; assists with banking duties; guides patients to available financial arrangements for payment; and maintains financial records.

■ Administrative Medical Assisting Skills

The work of an administrative medical assistant, which requires many technical and personal skills, is interesting and varied.

Communication Skills. The assistant must understand and use correct English grammar, style, punctuation, and spelling in both writing and speaking. These skills enable the assistant to handle correspondence, medical records, and transcription, and to interact well with other staff members, patients, and other medical personnel.

Mathematics Skills. The assistant must have good math skills to be able to maintain correct financial records, bill patients, and order and arrange payment for office supplies.

Organizational Skills. Controlling the sometimes hectic pace of work requires the assistant to have the skills of managing time and priorities.

COMPLIANCE TIP

The administrative medical assistant plays an important role in ensuring that the medical office's procedures comply with government regulations concerning patients' records. These rules include keeping patient information private and following guidelines for release of this information. Chapter 2 presents information on how to stay in compliance.

Systematic work habits, the willingness to take care of details, and the ability to handle several tasks at the same time are essential. Scheduling, updating and maintaining records, and keeping an orderly office require strong organizational skills.

Computer Skills. A basic understanding of a variety of technologies and the ability to use computers with mastery are essential workplace skills. Computers are used in every kind of health care setting for many different tasks. Computer programs handle word processing, financial spreadsheets, databases, and charts and visuals for speeches and presentations. With these programs, the assistant may handle billing, scheduling, account updating, records management, and other tasks.

Wireless technologies allow health care professionals who are away from their offices or hospitals to contact staff members and computers from any distance. Voice-recognition technology enables the physician to dictate notes using voice commands. The use of e-mail to communicate is as widespread as telephone communication, both within the medical practice and among medical practices, hospitals, and insurance companies. Chapter 3 discusses computer skills.

To assist effectively in patient care, the medical assistant must be able to:

- Use computers to process claims and bills and perform other routine financial tasks.
- Use computers to edit, revise, and generate documents.
- Use computers to scan and send documents to other locations.
- Use computers to communicate through e-mail within and outside the workplace.
- Research and obtain information from computer sources such as the Internet.

Knowing how to use basic technologies such as copiers and fax machines has long been a requirement for every office professional. Continuing to develop computer skills and learning new technological applications are keys to effectiveness and career advancement for administrative medical assistants.

Interpersonal Skills. Excellent interpersonal skills often come from a genuine desire to work with people. This desire and these interpersonal skills are essential for the administrative medical assistant, who is usually the patient's first contact with the medical office. That contact sets the tone for the patient's visit and influences the patient's opinion of the physician and the practice.

The assistant skilled in positive communication with patients is warm, open, and friendly. Patients appreciate attention and concern—for their schedules and their comfort. Effective interpersonal skills involve looking directly at the person being spoken to, speaking slowly and clearly, and listening carefully. Respect for and openness to the other person are often shown by a pleasant facial expression and a genuine, natural smile. At the heart of interpersonal skills is sensitivity to the feelings and situations of other people.

■ Administrative Medical Assisting Personal Attributes

In addition to essential office skills, the success of the administrative medical assistant depends on a positive attitude toward work and a cheerful personality. *Personality* has been defined as the outward evidence of a person's character. Many aspects of personality are important in dealing with patients and other medical professionals.

Because patients entering a health care setting may be anxious, fearful, or unwell, most of them value a friendly, pleasant personality as the most important attribute of a medical assistant. The qualities discussed here are components of a pleasing personality and are useful professional and personal skills.

Genuine Liking for People. A genuine enjoyment of people and a desire to help them are keys to success in a medical assisting career. These qualities are expressed in the way you communicate with people through speech and in your body language.

Because patients may sometimes worry that they will be viewed only as numbers and notes on their patient charts, it is important that they feel recognized as individuals. In communicating with patients, your warmth and attentiveness help to reassure patients and signal your desire to help.

FIGURE 1.2

The administrative medical assistant enjoys working with people. *How do assistants show their care and concern for patients?*

Looking directly at the patient and listening with attention communicate acceptance of the person. A pleasant facial expression, a natural smile, and a relaxed rather than rigid body posture are all body language signs that express openness and acceptance.

While these qualities are critical in dealing with patients, they are also attributes that contribute to a spirit of cooperation with associates and managers.

Cheerfulness. The ability to be pleasant and friendly is an asset in any career. Lifting patients' spirits helps build goodwill between them and the physician. A pleasant assistant can frequently head off difficulties that occur when patients become worried, anxious, or irritable.

EXAMPLE

It is five o'clock, normal closing time for the office. The doctor is behind schedule because of several difficult cases, and there are two patients yet to be seen in the waiting room. One of the patients approaches the assistant.

Patient: I've been waiting a long time to see the doctor. How much longer will I have to wait?

Despite feeling tired at the end of the day and ready to go home, the assistant remains cheerful and explains the situation without frustration.

Assistant: Dr. Larsen has had several difficult cases today that have caused this delay. She will see you next, but it may be another 20 to 30 minutes.

Empathy. Many of the personal traits needed to be a successful medical assistant spring from **empathy**, a sensitivity to the feelings and situations of other people. Empathy enables you to understand how a patient feels because you can mentally put yourself in the patient's situation. Everyone has had some personal experience with an illness or with not feeling perfectly well. Reminding yourself of how you felt and of how you wanted to be treated in that situation will help you to treat patients with kindness.

EXAMPLE

Assistant: Mr. Strauss, I realize you are not feeling well after your surgery yesterday. Would you feel more comfortable lying down while you wait?

Understand that nervous patients may not be listening clearly to your instructions. Offering to repeat them and answering questions is another example of empathy.

GO TO PROJECT 1.1 ON PAGE 25

1.2 EMPLOYMENT OPPORTUNITIES

The U.S. Department of Labor predicts that the demand for medical assistants will grow much more quickly than the average rate for all occupations through 2005. There are many organizations, institutions, and companies that operate in areas within or closely related to health care. Workers familiar with the health care environment are of value and in demand.

A thorough education in technical skills and the development of good interpersonal skills help ensure a successful career for administrative medical assistants. Because the health care industry is booming, a well-trained medical assistant has a wide variety of opportunities in many different settings.

■ Physician Practice

The most common place of employment for the administrative medical assistant is in a physician practice. The majority of physicians are associated with a group practice, in which space, staff, and physical resources such as equipment and laboratory facilities are shared. A group practice may consist of physicians who are all generalists or who all have the same specialty, or of a combination of generalists and specialists.

There are many advantages to both doctors and patients in these larger practices. Doctors may better control spiraling overhead costs of operating an office. Such practices also give new physicians the opportunity to join an established practice and to acquire new patients to add to their clientele. Because of the large volume of patients, the administrative medical assistant may specialize in a particular task area, such as patient scheduling, or may perform a variety of duties.

Some administrative medical assistants work in a small office where one or two physicians practice. The assistant acts as the doctor's right hand, taking care of all administrative tasks. Working in a small office gives the assistant a great deal of responsibility, variety in the tasks to be done, and an opportunity to develop close ties with patients and with the physician.

There are job opportunities for assistants in a wide range of practices. Many such medical specialties are listed and defined in Figure 1.3 on page 10. In addition to these specialties, the American Medical Association (AMA) lists 170 other specialties. Many of the specialties on this expanded list are surgical practices related to the specialties shown in Figure 1.3. However, there are also specialties that deal with new areas, such as undersea and aerospace medicine. Other specialties reflect the increased use of new technologies to treat illness. Interventional radiology is an example of such a specialty; it uses tools guided by radiologic imaging to perform procedures that are less invasive than those required with surgery.

FIGURE 1.3 Medical Specialties and Subspecialties

Allergy: An allergist diagnoses and treats adverse reactions to foods, drugs, and other substances.

Anesthesiology: An anesthesiologist maintains pain relief and stable body functions of patients during surgical procedures.

Dentistry: A dentist is concerned with the care and treatment of teeth and gums especially prevention, diagnosis, and treatment of deformities, diseases, and traumatic injuries. Subspecialties include:

An **endodontist** specializes in root canal work.

A **forensic** dentist applies dental facts to legal issues.

An **oral surgeon** specializes in jaw surgery and extractions.

An **orthodontist** straightens teeth.

A **pedodontist** provides dental care for children.

A **periodontist** specializes in gum disease.

A **prosthodontist** specializes in dentures and artificial teeth.

Dermatology: The dermatologist diagnoses and treats diseases of the skin and related tissues.

Emergency Medicine: An emergency room physician provides immediate treatment of accidents or illnesses.

Family Practice: A family practice physician provides total health care for the family.

Gynecology: A gynecologist is concerned with the diseases of the female genital tract as well as female endocrinology and reproductive physiology.

Internal Medicine: An internist diagnoses a wide range of non-surgical illnesses. Subspecialties include:

Cardiovascular Medicine: A cardiologist diagnoses and treats diseases of the heart, blood vessels, and lungs.

Endocrinology: An endocrinologist diagnoses and treats endocrine gland diseases.

Gastroenterology: A gastroenterologist diagnoses and treats diseases of the digestive tract and related organs.

Gerontology: The gerontologist treats the process and problems of aging.

Hematology: A hematologist diagnoses and treats diseases of the blood.

Immunology: An immunologist diagnoses and treats symptoms of immunity, induced sensitivity, and allergies.

Infectious Disease: A specialist in infectious disease diagnoses and treats all types of infectious diseases.

Nephrology: A nephrologist diagnoses and treats disorders of the kidneys and related functions.

Oncology: An oncologist diagnoses and treats cancer.

Pulmonary Disease: A pulmonologist diagnoses and treats lung disorders.

Rheumatology: A rheumatologist is concerned with the study, diagnosis, and treatment of rheumatic conditions.

Neurology: A neurologist diagnoses and treats disorders of the nervous system.

Obstetrics: An obstetrician provides care during pregnancy and childbirth.

Occupational Medicine: A specialist in occupational medicine works with companies to prevent and manage occupational and environmental injury, illness, and disability, and to promote health and productivity of workers and their families and communities.

Ophthalmology: An ophthalmologist cares for the eyes and the vision.

Orthopedics: An orthopedic surgeon or orthopedist provides treatment of the musculoskeletal system.

Otorhinolaryngology: A physician in otorhinolaryngology specializes in the diagnosis and treatment of illnesses of the ears, nose, and throat (ENT).

Pathology: A pathologist investigates the causes of disease using laboratory techniques.

Pediatrics: A pediatrician specializes in the comprehensive treatment of children.

Physical Medicine/Rehabilitation: A physiatrist evaluates and treats all types of disease through physical means, such as heat.

Plastic Surgery: A plastic surgeon repairs and reconstructs body structures through surgical means.

Psychiatry: A psychiatrist diagnoses and treats mental, emotional, and behavioral disorders.

Radiology and Nuclear Medicine: A radiologist uses radioactive materials to diagnose and treat disease.

Thoracic Surgery: A thoracic surgeon uses surgery to diagnose or treat diseases of the chest.

Urology: A urologist diagnoses and treats diseases of the urinary tract.

■ Clinics

The administrative medical assistant may be employed by a clinic. A clinic may specialize in the diagnosis and treatment of a specific disorder: back pain, headache, mental health, or wound treatment, for example. Many clinics have a number of specialties within one building. The specialties may be related so that the patient moves from department to department for extensive examination and specialty consultations.

■ Hospitals and Medical Centers

Hospitals and the large physical complexes that make up medical centers employ many administrative support personnel, particularly those skilled in specific medical office management tasks. Assistants may work in the admissions department in several different areas of a hospital or medical center—the main admitting office where patients are received for a stay in the hospital, admissions to the emergency room, or admissions for patients in same-day surgery clinics. Departments such as patient education, insurance, billing, social services, and medical records also need skilled and knowledgeable assistants. Career opportunities for assistants in these facilities will continue to grow along with technological advances that have increased the ways in which patients are diagnosed and treated, as well as the rapidly growing size of the aging population.

■ Care Facilities

There are many facilities specializing in the short-term care of patients recovering after hospital stays. There are also patients who enter rehabilitation centers to improve the functioning of their back, arms, legs, hips, or hands. Other facilities provide long-term care for patients with chronic mental or physical illnesses. All of these facilities rely on skilled personnel who understand patients and their care.

■ Insurance Companies

The health care industry is subject to great pressure because of high health costs and the reality that people are living longer and often require greater care as they age. Insurance companies and government health insurance programs must ensure that claims from health care providers are correct and complete. They employ administrative medical assistants who are skilled in handling medical documents and understand medical procedures. Assistants may work for:

- Large insurance companies specializing in health care, such as Blue Cross and Blue Shield, and CIGNA.

- Government-sponsored programs such as Medicare and Medicaid.
- Other insurers, some of which are sponsored by clubs, unions, and employee associations.
- Managed care organizations.

All of these groups have complex needs and require the handling of tasks such as completing and checking reports received from doctors, coding diagnoses and procedures, adjusting claims, sending payments of claims, and renewing contracts.

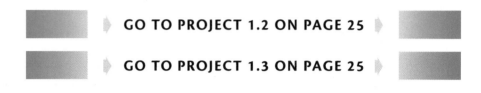

▶ **GO TO PROJECT 1.2 ON PAGE 25** ▶

▶ **GO TO PROJECT 1.3 ON PAGE 25** ▶

1.3 WORK ETHIC AND PROFESSIONALISM

Positive personality traits are developed into habits and skills that help the administrative medical assistant deal effectively with tasks and with people. These habits and skills, which form a **work ethic**, greatly enhance employees' value in any medical work setting.

■ Work Ethic

Employers responding to research surveys about employees rank certain habits and skills the highest. These habits and skills make the employee valuable to the practice. They are also often predictors of success in a medical office setting.

Accuracy. Because even a minor error may have consequences for a patient's health, physicians rank **accuracy** as the most important employee trait. Although physicians may give exact instructions, they may not oversee tasks to completion. The physician counts on the assistant to perform tasks with complete correctness, including constant attention to detail.

Thoroughness. The careful and complete attention to detail required for accuracy is known as **thoroughness**. The thorough assistant produces work that is neat, accurate, and complete. This trait involves:

- Listening attentively.
- Taking ample notes.
- Paying attention to details such as who, when, why, where, and how.
- Verifying information.
- Following through on details without having to be reminded.

Dependability. The administrative medical assistant who finishes work on schedule, does required tasks without complaint, even when these may be unpleasant, and always communicates willingness to help is said to be a dependable employee. **Dependability** is related closely to accuracy and thoroughness. The dependable assistant:

- Asks questions and repeats instructions to avoid mistakes.
- Asks for assistance with unfamiliar tasks.
- Enters all data, such as insurance claim information and lab values, carefully.
- Takes clear and complete messages.

Efficiency. Using time and other resources to avoid waste and unnecessary effort is the defining mark of **efficiency**. An efficient administrative medical assistant plans the day's work in advance, makes a schedule for completion, and assembles the materials and resources necessary to complete the tasks. Efficiency also includes the organizational ability to divide large and complex tasks into smaller, more manageable components.

Flexibility. The ability to adapt, to change gears quickly to respond to changing situations, interruptions, and delays is **flexibility**. The flexible assistant is able to respond calmly to last-minute assignments, to meet deadlines under pressure, and to handle several tasks at once. The ability to grasp new situations and new concepts quickly is an important aspect of flexibility. Being able to implement new ideas and good suggestions with self-confidence is a mark of flexibility.

FIGURE 1.4

The administrative medical assistant shown here is completing an insurance claim form. *How can assistants ensure accuracy in their work?*

Good Judgment. The quality of **good judgment** involves the ability to use knowledge, experience, and logic to assess all the aspects of a situation in order to reach a sound decision. Frequently, good judgment is expressed by the administrative medical assistant who knows when to make a statement and when to withhold one. For example, choosing the right time and the right words when making a suggestion to an employer or to other staff members shows good judgment. It may also be good judgment to decide that the suggestion should not be made because, based on your experience, the suggestion will not be accepted.

Honesty. Telling the truth is **honesty**. It is expressed in words and actions. It is the quality that enables the physician to trust the administrative medical assistant at all times and in all situations. The trustworthy assistant understands the serious nature of the physician's work and the confidential nature of the patient's dealings with the physician. The assistant can be trusted not to reveal any of a patient's data, any conversations, or any details, which must always remain confidential. The honest assistant is also quick to report mistakes without attempting to cover them up or to blame others. Finally, honesty is central to the integrity that allows the assistant to effectively represent the profession.

Initiative. To take action independently is to show **initiative**. The administrative medical assistant works with certain routine administrative activities every day. Dealing with these often requires the assistant to take action without receiving specific instructions from the physician. The assistant's ability to move work forward and to resolve issues by using initiative is a valuable skill in a busy office.

Initiative also involves making unsolicited offers of help that mark a valued employee, one who goes beyond the job's regular responsibilities. For example, offering to stay late to help the physician or coworkers finish extra work is always appreciated. To give patients additional help, you may offer to telephone for a taxi after an appointment, obtain a wheelchair when needed, write out instructions, or send a reminder card before the next appointment.

Problem-Solving Ability. **Problem-solving** involves logically planning out the steps needed to accomplish a job. Asking for advice when appropriate and acting wisely also demonstrate the ability to solve problems effectively. The administrative medical assistant who is adept at solving problems also has a basic understanding of the goals and requirements of the work environment.

Punctuality. Being on time—**punctuality**—is important for the administrative medical assistant because of the physician's schedule and the need to complete routine duties before patients arrive. A medical office is often open for the staff a half hour before patient appointments. This is not a time for employees to use in getting from home to work. It is a time to be used for planning the day's work, organizing tasks, and greeting patients who may arrive before the start of business hours.

Self-Motivation. The quality of **self-motivation** is expressed by a willingness to learn new duties or procedures without a requirement to do so. The administrative medical assistant who helps with work that needs to be done and learns new aspects of job responsibilities is self-motivated. Alertness is an aspect of self-motivation. This alertness enables the assistant to see and undertake jobs that need to be done and to anticipate the patient's and the physician's needs.

Tact. The ability to speak and act considerately, especially in difficult situations, is known as **tact**. Working with people in ways that show you are sensitive to their possible reactions helps to achieve the purpose at hand smoothly and without giving offense. Tactful manners and speech create goodwill with patients and with other staff members.

Being a Member of the Team. Those who have the positive attitude of a **team player** are generous with their time, helping other staff members when necessary. A good team player observes stated office policies and quickly learns the unwritten rules of office life, such as:

- When it is acceptable to sit at another employee's desk. – NEVER
- Whether it is acceptable to eat or drink at your desk. – NEVER
- How to time a break and determine how long it should be. – you'll be told.
- When and in what manner it is acceptable to converse with coworkers.

Being a good team player also involves the simple courtesies: avoiding personal activities and phone calls; knocking before entering an office, even if the door is open; being careful about sharing details of your personal life in ordinary polite conversation; and avoiding the use of profanity and coarse language. Team players, moreover, are always careful to observe confidentiality by not discussing patients or commenting in any way about them or about any other staff members.

Assertiveness. **Assertiveness** is the ability to step forward to make a point in a confident, positive manner. In some ways, assertiveness is the result of having acquired many of the habits, attitudes, and skills discussed here. Administrative medical assistants who are accurate, dependable, and honest, who understand and perform tasks with intelligence and good judgment, are confident employees. They are able to step forward and contribute to a more efficient, more cordial work environment. Assertiveness is always a positive force. It is unlike aggressiveness, which is a hostile and overbearing attitude. Assertiveness assumes that the assistant not only is competent but also has established cordial and cooperative working relationships.

■ Professional Image

Few professions are as much respected as the medical profession. It is a profession that has an image of health, cleanliness, and wholesomeness. If you choose to work in a health care setting, your appearance and bearing must reflect this image. Patients expect your positive personality and pleasing manner to be reflected in your appearance through healthful habits, good grooming, and appropriate dress.

Being in style, as advertisements and magazines define style, is not the same thing as projecting a **professional image**. Style is about reflecting a personal vision of who you are in the way you act, dress, and fix your hair. In the workplace, however, you reflect not your own personal vision but the employer's preferences about how the practice should be seen by patients and the community.

Physical Attributes. Good health is the result of maintaining good posture, eating a properly balanced diet, getting sufficient rest, and exercising regularly. These good health habits show in the energy of your body when you move, walk, or communicate; in the healthful glow of your skin; in the alertness and clarity of your eyes; and even in the shine of your hair.

Habits that promote good health are essential to maintaining a professional image. These habits of good health are complemented by good grooming habits. Although cleanliness is the basis of good grooming, grooming means more than cleanliness. A daily bath or shower, the use of deodorant, regular dental care along with daily dental brushing and flossing, and a neat overall appearance are all elements of good grooming. Also included in good grooming habits are the following:

- Nails should be manicured so that the hands look cared for. Employees should avoid bright or unusual nail polish colors and

FIGURE 1.5

The administrative medical assistant projects a professional image. *What habits, grooming, and dress styles show professionalism?*

stenciled nails. Nails should not be so long that they pose a threat to others or interfere with working at the keyboard.

- Hair requires frequent shampooing and should be arranged in a conservative style that will not require a great deal of attention during working hours.
- Male employees should shave daily or have neatly trimmed facial hair.
- Perfumes or colognes are acceptable if the fragrance is light. Powerful fragrances may be irritating to patients and others.
- Makeup should be used moderately.
- Clothes must always be freshly laundered and pressed. If you are required to wear a white uniform, it must be kept *snow* white and should never be worn over dark underclothes. If street clothes are worn in the office, they should be simple and should fit well. Tight or revealing clothes are not appropriate.
- Shoes should be comfortable and in good repair.
- Jewelry and hair ornaments are not good accompaniments to uniforms. Jewelry that is worn with street clothes in the office should be small and unobtrusive. Large bangles and bracelets with dangling parts are often noisy and get in the way of work.

Maturity. Many administrative and personal skills contribute to the achievement of **maturity**. And maturity *is* an achievement. It takes great determination to acquire and to practice the attitudes, habits, and skills that contribute to maturity.

Emotional and psychological maturity is not dependent on age. It is made up of many aspects of personality and of many skills. The mature person is able to work with supervisors and under pressure, even in unpleasant or frustrating conditions. The mature person sees a job through and gives more than is asked. Maturity enables a person to gather and use information to make good decisions. Maturity is reflected by independence of judgment as well as by ambition and determination. As maturity becomes evident in the administrative medical assistant, it inspires the confidence of managers, patients, and coworkers.

■ Professional Growth

Successful administrative medical assistants enjoy an enviable professional status. They are eligible, once they complete specific requirements, to join several different national associations. By passing examinations, medical assistants may become certified. **Certification** is the indication given by certain associations that a person has met high standards and has achieved competency in the knowledge and tasks required. Through continuing education, seminars, conferences, and the chance to meet other professionals in the field, these organizations provide opportunities to grow as office professionals and to advance in a chosen career.

AAMA. The American Association of Medical Assistants **(AAMA)** is a major nationwide organization. The AAMA recommends to the Commission on Accreditation for Allied Health Education Programs (CAAHEP) those formal education programs that have met AAMA curriculum standards. Further, the AAMA sponsors the national certification examination for medical assistants. The examination tests the accomplishment of competencies outlined in Figure 1.1. These are known as the DACUM competencies; *DACUM* is an acronym that stands for **D**eveloping **A** Curricul**UM**. This examination is reviewed before being given by the National Board of Medical Examiners (NBME). Those who successfully pass the examination are certified and receive the designation of Certified Medical Assistant (CMA).

The AAMA requires CMAs to be recertified every five years. This practice ensures that medical assistants keep up with developments in the field. There are hundreds of continuing education courses sponsored by the AAMA to help assistants keep current and become recertified.

Although medical assistants need not be certified to be employed as assistants, certification improves the chances of career advancement and provides motivation for continued professional growth.

AMT. The American Medical Technologists **(AMT)** is another nationwide organization offering certification for medical assistants. Successful completion of this examination earns the credential of Registered Medical Assistant (RMA).

AAMT. The American Association of Medical Transcription **(AAMT)**, a nationwide organization, promotes professional standards and growth for those who have a special interest in transcription and wish to be certified. The Medical Transcription Certification Commission (MTCC) offers an examination through the AAMT for those who would like to become Certified Medical Transcriptionists (CMTs). The examination is objective, comprehensive, and job-related. The certification is valid for three years, after which recertification is required. Although the AAMT does not offer courses, it does provide materials for independent study.

Even with the use of voice-recognition technology, medical transcriptionists will continue to be in demand. The technology cannot yet handle all the nuances of English. The transcriptionist's skill in English usage, grammar, and style ensures the competent editing and correction of materials. Taking advantage of certification and opportunities for continued study in this field, as in medical assisting, helps in career advancement.

IAAP. The International Association of Administrative Professionals **(IAAP)**, until recently known as Professional Secretaries International (PSI), is a worldwide organization working with employers to promote excellence. This organization sponsors a comprehensive examination. Successfully completing the examination earns the designation of

American Association for Medical Transcription
100 Sycamore Avenue
Modesto, CA 95354-0550
Phone: 800-982-2182
Web site: www.aamt.org
E-mail: aamt@aamt.org

American Association of Medical Assistants
20 North Wacker Drive,
Suite 1575
Chicago, IL 60606-2963
Phone: 800-228-2262
Web site: www.aama-ntl.org
E-mail:
  membership@aama-ntl.org

American Medical Technologists
710 Higgins Road
Park Ridge, IL 60068-5765
Phone: 847-823-5169
Web site: www.amt1.com

International Association of Administrative Professionals
10502 NW Ambassador Drive
P.O. Box 20404
Kansas City, MO 64195-0404
Phone: 816-891-6600
Web site: www.iaap-hq.org
E-mail: service@iaap-hq.org

Certified Professional Secretary (CPS). The organization, which maintains chapters all over the country, makes professional contacts easy. The IAAP provides study materials and information about available review courses. A new certification examination, to qualify for the title of Certified Administrative Professional (CAP), is now available.

There are companies that offer salary incentives to those who become certified secretaries. In this area, as in all other areas of most professions, certification improves the chances for advancement.

GO TO PROJECT 1.4 ON PAGE 25

1.4 INTERPERSONAL RELATIONSHIPS

The administrative medical assistant is usually the first person that patients meet when they come to the doctor's office. The way in which the assistant receives and welcomes patients establishes the tone of the visit and can give patients a positive feeling about the doctor and the treatment.

The responsibility to make patients feel that they are important and that enough time is available to them for treatment is of major concern for the medical assistant. Although the office may be busy, and both the doctor and the patients may want to speak to the assistant at the same time, the assistant must remain calm, reassuring, and pleasant to everyone.

■ Taking Care of Patients

Greeting a patient by name, if possible, contributes to making that patient feel important. If you are away from the desk when a patient arrives, acknowledge the patient with a smile or greeting.

Every person is to be shown the same degree of respect and concern without regard to race, age, gender, or socioeconomic situation. Every doctor's office accepts patients who receive care for a nominal fee or even completely free. The physician's aim in all cases is the same: to make the person well in the shortest possible time. The assistant's aim in all cases is to treat all patients with the same amount of sympathy, concern, and attention.

■ Familiarity

A physician may choose to establish a less formal tone in the office in order to make patients feel more comfortable. Even when this is the case, the office is still a professional setting. Certain ways of expressing familiarity, either with the physician or with the patients, are not appropriate.

The doctor should always be referred to and spoken to by title and last name: "Dr. Larsen will see you now." This courtesy is observed even if the physician and the administrative medical assistant are relatives or have a personal relationship. Conversation in front of patients should never indicate anything other than a professional relationship.

Patients may have preferences about the way they are addressed. It shows respect to address the patient by the appropriate title and last name: "Mr. /Mrs. /Ms. /Miss /Reverend /Lopez." If a patient wishes to be addressed in some other way, as by a first name or nickname, that patient will invite you to do so.

EXAMPLE

Assistant: Mrs. Haynes, Dr. Larsen is ready to see you now.

Patient: Thank you, Linda, but please call me Margaret. I'm not used to being called Mrs. Haynes.

■ Social Relationships

In many offices the policy discourages, or may even forbid, a social relationship between a patient and a staff member. Such a policy reflects the physician's belief that these relationships are not consistent with a professional atmosphere and may interfere with the proper medical management of the patient's case. Under no circumstances should you make a social engagement with a patient without first checking office policy and discussing the situation with your employer.

■ Conversation With Patients

If the administrative medical assistant has to spend considerable time with a patient, the patient is the one who decides whether or not to start a conversation. If the patient wishes to talk, the patient should also choose the subject. The assistant should listen and respond courteously. General subjects such as the weather, sports, hobbies, or local events may be ideal conversation topics. Try to avoid controversial topics, such as politics or religion. Keeping the conversation to general topics should also ensure that you are never in a situation where you argue with a patient or try to persuade a patient that a certain view is correct.

Because the patient identifies the administrative medical assistant with the doctor, the patient also believes that the assistant carries the doctor's authority. For this reason, the assistant should never offer a patient medical advice or comment on the patient's treatment. Very few patients have a substantial knowledge of medicine, anatomy, or physiology. They may easily misunderstand a remark made by the assistant, especially if the remark contains a technical term. If the patient seeks advice or asks a question related to treatment, the medical assistant should respond tactfully: "That is a question the doctor should answer for you. Be sure to ask about that during your examination."

Difficult Patients. The best test of interpersonal skills may be the successful handling of difficult, unreasonable, or unpleasant patients. The patient's self-control may be undermined by the pain and worry that accompany the illness. Dealing with those patients who may be short-tempered or irritable requires the medical assistant to show patience, understanding, and restraint. Calmly repeating instructions to an uncooperative patient may be difficult, but it may prevent having to ask a patient to redo a procedure or task or having to repeat the instructions later.

EXAMPLE

> **Assistant:** Mr. Rosen, here are the instructions for the x-ray you are going to have on Monday. Let me go over them with you again to make sure you understand them and to see whether you have any questions. If you think of any questions at a later time, you may call me. I have written my name and telephone number here and will be happy to help answer your questions.

Sometimes, a patient who has had to wait a long time to see the doctor may become restless or impatient. In such instances, the medical assistant should make some gesture of attention. Introduce a general topic of conversation or offer the patient some reassurance that you are aware of the lateness of the schedule and thank the person for understanding.

There are times when a patient may become angry. A mistake in an insurance payment, a long wait to see the doctor, or even the patient's physical pain or discomfort may trigger an outburst of bad temper. The medical assistant must remain calm and courteous. A gentle tone and soothing voice sometimes help to calm a patient. Never argue. Politely offer to help correct a situation in any way you can. The offer by itself may help to eliminate the patient's anger.

Every patient should leave the doctor's office with a feeling of goodwill. Frequently, the medical assistant will have an opportunity to talk to the patient as the patient prepares to leave the office. Calling the patient by name, if possible, and extending a pleasant good-bye will have beneficial results. A patient who leaves the office on a positive note may tell others about a good experience with the staff.

Terminally Ill Patients. If a patient whom you know to be terminally ill engages you in conversation, be sensitive to the situation by avoiding certain questions that you might ordinarily ask, such as "How are you?" Try to keep the conversation short and on a general topic.

FIGURE 1.6

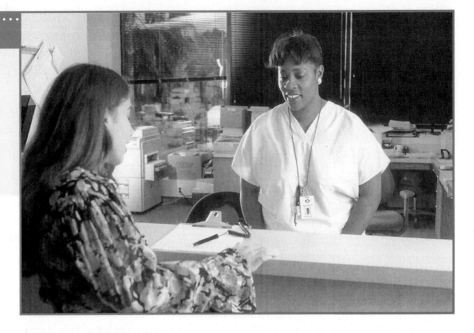

■ Confidentiality

Maintaining the **confidentiality**, or privacy, of patients' medical information is a legal requirement. A doctor who gives information about a patient without a patient's permission, except to another doctor, can be prosecuted under the law, and the doctor's license may be revoked. Similar legal requirements and penalties apply to employees in the doctor's office.

Medical Histories. Medical histories of patients contain a great deal of confidential information, not only about the patients but also about their families and perhaps other contacts, such as friends. Employees may not disclose any information about a patient's illness, personal history, or matters relating to family or others.

Confidentiality about medical records is also to be observed in any conversations the medical assistant has with the patient. It is not the medical assistant's place to share with the patient the doctor's diagnosis or prognosis. The doctor is the sole judge of what information is to be given to, or withheld from, the patient. The assistant must refuse to discuss the patient's case and should refer the patient to the doctor for information.

Many people other than the patients themselves may ask the medical assistant for information about a patient's case. There are some patients who are curious about other patients whom they may know or may have seen in the doctor's office during their own visits. There are some curious patients who may try to obtain personal information about the doctor, staff, or other patients. Friends or relatives of a patient may inquire about the doctor's opinion, the method of treatment, or the duration of the illness. A courteous but firm refusal, such as "I'm sorry, but that information is confidential," should prevent further attempts to get information.

COMPLIANCE TIP

The responsibility for confidentiality extends beyond the office environment. Neither a patient's name nor any other information should ever be mentioned outside the office. A patient may not wish to tell family members or business associates that medical care is needed. The doctor's specialty may be an indication of the disease for which the patient is being treated, and the patient may not wish this to be known.

Record Security. The medical assistant must be aware of the location of the front desk and of various work areas in relation to public spaces, such as the lobby or waiting room. Location is important in safeguarding the confidentiality of records because they may be read if left where other patients, staff members, or visitors can see them. Because patient records, schedules, and billing information are now often computerized, the locations of computer screens at the front desk and in work areas are also important. Sensitive information should not remain on the screen when you need to be away from the desk.

In areas close to the waiting room or lobby, caution should also be exercised in conversations, whether over the telephone or face to face. Conversations between a patient and the assistant or among employees may easily be overheard.

In general, nothing that happens in the office should be repeated at home or to friends. A patient can sometimes be identified by the circumstances of the case or by some other detail, even when the patient's name is not mentioned.

There is wisdom in the adage "What you see here, what you hear here, must remain here when you leave."

■ Cultural Diversity

People's beliefs, value systems, and language, and their understanding of the world, grow out of the culture into which they were born and in which they were raised. It is important to understand that just as the elements of your culture are formative for you, so the cultures of others are formative for them. Although each culture is different, no one culture is better than, or superior in any way to, any other culture. However, it is important to understand that people in cultures different from yours may express themselves and present themselves in a different way from what your own culture has taught you to expect. Be respectful of people of all cultures and backgrounds. Never assign patients to stereotypes that are racial, ethnic, or religious. Always treat each person as an individual.

Language Barriers. Although most aspects of other cultures do not present barriers, a great cultural barrier may occur when the patient and staff do not speak the same language. The ideal solution is to be able to speak to a family friend or relative who accompanies the patient and can act as an interpreter. If this is not possible, you may want to have several foreign language phrase books on hand in the office. Sometimes, using drawings and hand signs will help. Following are guidelines for communicating with patients who do not speak English:

- Speak slowly and clearly.
- Do not raise your voice above an ordinary conversational tone. Speaking louder does not improve understanding.

- Use simple words, not technical terms.
- Be brief.

Another form of language barrier may occur in the office when the assistant must deal with patients who are deaf. If no one in the office understands and uses sign language, the assistant should rely on a pad to write instructions or directions for the patient. It is a good idea to ask patients in writing to confirm their understanding of what you have written.

■ Nonpatients

All visitors to the doctor's office should be treated courteously. Often, a patient's friend or relative may accompany the patient.

Visitors on business, such as pharmaceutical company sales representatives, call on the office frequently. The doctor may not wish to allow time for these people in the schedule and may ask the administrative medical assistant to do so. The assistant usually will get information on the product, obtain samples, and keep the business cards on file. Some offices schedule a specific time each month when the doctors give representatives an opportunity to present materials.

EXAMPLE

Sales representative: I'm here to see Dr. Larsen about ordering a new antibiotic from my company.

Assistant: Dr. Larsen has scheduled the first Monday of each month from noon to 2 P.M. as the time she will see sales representatives. Shall I enter your name on the calendar for next month?

There may be other visitors who take up the doctor's time unnecessarily, and most doctors appreciate an assistant who screens them and tells them that the doctor is not interested.

 GO TO PROJECT 1.5 ON PAGE 25

Chapter Projects

PROJECT 1.1　Brainstorming for an Interview

Imagine that you have the opportunity to interview a number of administrative medical assistants about their jobs. What information would you like to learn from them? With a partner, brainstorm a list of questions to ask the medical assistants. Divide your list into questions about tasks, skills, and personal attributes. Be prepared to discuss your findings in class.

PROJECT 1.2　Internet Research: Employment

Using the Internet, research and describe three available positions for administrative medical assistants. If possible, locate the job opportunities in your geographical area by visiting the Web sites of your state's department of labor and those of local newspapers.

PROJECT 1.3　Medical Specialists

Match the terms for the medical specialists shown in Figure 1.3 to their definitions on Working Paper 1 (WP 1) located in the back section of this text-workbook. Be prepared to discuss your answers in class.

PROJECT 1.4　Internet Research: Professional Organizations

Using the Internet, research the Web sites of the AAMA, AMT, AAMT, and IAAP. Write down the student membership requirements of each and the advantages of belonging to each.

PROJECT 1.5　Work Ethic and Interpersonal Relationships

On WP 2 in the back section of this text-workbook, match each of the terms in Column 2 with its definition in Column 1.

-homework　1·3 &1·5

CHAPTER SUMMARY

1. The administrative medical assistant has responsibilities in these five areas: front desk procedures, scheduling, records management, administrative duties, and billing and insurance. These tasks require communication, mathematics, organizational, computer, and interpersonal skills.

2. Three personal attributes essential for an administrative medical assistant are a genuine liking of people, cheerfulness, and empathy.

3. Employment opportunities for medical assistants are increasing in physician practices, clinics, hospitals and medical centers, care facilities, and insurance companies. Assistants may be employed by physicians in general practice, such as family doctors, or by specialists, as in an orthopedic group practice.

4. The habits and skills that make up the work ethic of an administrative medical assistant are:

   - Accuracy: the ability to be correct, clear, and thorough.

   - Dependability: the ability to be relied upon to fulfill instructions and to complete tasks on time.

   - Efficiency: the ability to use time and other resources in such a way as to avoid wasted effort.

   - Flexibility: the ability to respond quickly to changed situations, last minute assignments, and delays; the willingness to accept and implement new ideas.

   - Honesty: the ability to always tell the truth and to own up quickly to mistakes.

5. The professional image of the medical assistant is that of a friendly, capable person who inspires confidence. From the assistant's manner, speech, posture, and appearance, patients and others have the impression of someone who is mature and dedicated to competent service.

6. Certification frequently influences an employer's opinion favorably and contributes to career advancement. Professional growth is fostered by the need to be recertified, by continuing education programs, by seminars and conferences, and by the opportunity for contact with others working in the same profession.

7. Administrative medical assistants treat patients, physicians, coworkers, and others with courtesy, maintaining a calm, pleasant, reassuring manner. They do not reveal confidential information and have a professional relationship with the physicians, coworkers, and other visitors to the office.

KEY TERMS

The following terms appear in **boldface** type in this chapter. Administrative medical assistants must know the meaning and the correct use of each of these terms. Can you recall what each term means? Refer to this chapter or to the glossary for any terms you need to review.

AAMA	honesty
AAMT	IAAP
accuracy	initiative
administrative medical assistant	maturity
AMT	problem-solving
assertiveness	professional image
certification	punctuality
confidentiality	self-motivation
dependability	tact
efficiency	team player
empathy	thoroughness
flexibility	work ethic
good judgment	

THINKING IT THROUGH

These questions cover the most important points in this chapter. Using your critical thinking skills, play the role of an administrative medical assistant as you answer each question. Be prepared to present your responses in class.

1. What qualities and skills are needed by the assistant who is responsible for the front desk? Why are these critical skills?

2. How can imagining yourself in someone else's situation help you develop empathy for patients?

3. Do you think that assistants working in various medical settings have the same type of assignments? Might some employers assign assistants a single task or related tasks, such as processing insurance claims, while in other settings the assistant is likely to perform a variety of tasks?

4. Why is it important to be a team player in the office?

5. What qualities project a professional image in an administrative medical assistant?

6. An assistant is asked by another employee why the assistant decided to meet the requirements to become certified. What might the assistant answer?

7. How should an assistant communicate with non-English-speaking patients?

CHAPTER

2 Medical Ethics, Law, and Compliance

INTRODUCTION

Daily news headlines reflect legal and ethical questions: Should life support be ended for a patient when there are no signs of brain function? May a patient sue the physician for an unsuccessful treatment? When may a health care provider refuse to treat a patient? All consumers of health care services are interested in these legal and health care issues. As health care professionals, administrative medical assistants have an even greater interest in such issues. Understanding the legal and ethical aspects of health care helps them act according to the highest professional standards. Such knowledge also helps assistants resolve issues of confidentiality and patients' rights.

KEY TERMS

Study these important words, which are defined in this chapter, to build your professional vocabulary:

abandonment	contributory	fraud	informed consent	registration
arbitration	negligence	Good Samaritan Act	liability	release of
assault	defensive medicine	Health Insurance	licensure	information
authorization	deposition	Portability and	litigation	settlement
battery	ethics	Accountability Act	malpractice	statute of
bioethics	etiquette	(HIPAA)	medical practice	limitations
compliance	express consent	implied consent	acts	subpoena
				summons

All professions, as well as people's lives, are governed by standards of conduct. The standards of conduct that grow out of one's understanding of right and wrong are known as **ethics.** The medical ethics that govern the health care professions are usually found in written policies or codes for each profession. These standards are not laws. A person acting within the law may nevertheless do something that is not ethical. A person may also do something right, or ethical, and at the same time may break the law. Ethics are statements of right and wrong behaviors that hold members of the profession to a high degree of behavior.

■ Principles of Medical Ethics

Hippocrates, a Greek physician who lived during the fifth and fourth centuries B.C., is called "the father of medicine." He made the first statement of principles governing the conduct of physicians. This statement, known as the Hippocratic oath, is the foundation of modern medical ethics. In part, the oath requires the physician to pledge the following:

> I will follow that method of treatment which, according to my ability and judgment, I consider for the benefit of my patients, and abstain from whatever is deleterious [harmful] and mischievous. . . . Whatever, in connection with my professional practice or not in connection with it, I may see or hear in the lives of men which ought not to be spoken abroad, I will not divulge, as reckoning that all such should be kept secret.

Today, physicians follow the principles of medical ethics developed by the American Medical Association (AMA). It is easy to see from reading the code, shown in Figure 2.1 on page 30, that these principles can be traced back to the Hippocratic oath. The code requires physicians, among other rules, to practice high standards of patient care, to respect patients' rights, to treat patients with compassion, and to safeguard patient confidences.

■ The Medical Assistant's Ethical Responsibility

Most other associations that regulate health care professions also have stated codes of ethics to set levels of competence and patient care. The American Association of Medical Assistants (AAMA) has developed the Code of Ethics and Creed, shown in Figure 2.2 on page 31. Because the administrative medical assistant is considered an agent of the physician while performing tasks related to employment, the AAMA code is based on AMA standards.

"DOCTOR'S"

Medical assistants, in their role and within the boundaries of their job responsibilities, are also required to treat all patients with respect, to maintain confidentiality, to improve knowledge and skills, and to contribute to the community. In addition, they are advised to merit the respect of the public and of the medical profession. The creed emphasizes the qualities of effectiveness, loyalty, compassion, courage, and faith.

■ Bioethics

The area of **bioethics** deals with the ethics of medical treatment, technology, and procedure. Advances in the sciences, rapid developments in technology, and new kinds of treatment have dramatically increased the number of bioethical issues and questions. Agreed-upon professional guidelines in these areas may still need to be established. These issues are associated with abortion, the definition of death, patients' rights, and types of medical care. The response to bioethical issues may require a restatement or a new application of existing ethical guidelines.

Issues. Because physicians have always faced life-and-death situations, they have always also faced difficult decisions. Today, their ethical responses have been made even more difficult by the increased power of

FIGURE 2.2 American Association of Medical Assistants Code of Ethics and Creed

Code of Ethics

The Code of Ethics of AAMA shall set forth principles of ethical and moral conduct as they relate to the medical profession and the particular practice of medical assisting.

Members of AAMA dedicated to the conscientious pursuit of their profession, and thus desiring to merit the high regard of the entire medical profession and the respect of the general public which they serve, do pledge themselves to strive always to:

A. Render service with full respect for the dignity of humanity;

B. Respect confidential information obtained through employment unless legally authorized or required by responsible performance of duty to divulge such information;

C. Uphold the honor and high principles of the profession and accept its disciplines;

D. Seek to continually improve the knowledge and skills of medical assistants for the benefit of patients and professional colleagues;

E. Participate in additional service activities aimed toward improving the health and well-being of the community.

Creed

I believe in the principles and purposes of the profession of medical assisting.

I endeavor to be more effective.

I aspire to render greater service.

I protect the confidence entrusted to me.

I am dedicated to the care and well-being of all patients.

I am loyal to my physician-employer.

I am true to the ethics of my profession.

I am strengthened by compassion, courage, and faith.

Reprinted with the permission of the American Association of Medical Assistants.

technology and scientific knowledge. Consider the ethical aspects of these questions:

- What rights are involved with using a human fetus?
- Should genetic engineering—the altering of cells to produce physical traits or to eliminate disease—be encouraged? Suppose one of the outcomes is the cloning of a human being?
- How should scarce, usable body organs be fairly allocated throughout the United States?
- When is it acceptable to remove a patient from life support? Who makes that decision?

The ability to create, sustain, or end life is a major concern for individuals and for society. Many people who fear that their lives may be sustained without their consent have made living wills. In a living will, a person states clearly the intent to refuse certain life-sustaining measures and specifies the length and the methods of these measures. Should that person become unable, at some point, to make that decision, some other person may be appointed to carry out the requirements of the will. The person's wishes may also be stated with regard to organ donation. The living will, which is valid in most states, is one response to a bioethical issue.

Moral Values. The link between moral values, or concepts of what is good, and professional behavior is shown in ethics by the use of words such as *compassion, honesty, honorable,* and *responsibility.* The primary ethical obligation of the physician is to put the benefit of the patient first. Moral values may dictate that physicians take certain actions and refrain from others. For example, considering the patient's well-being, the physician may agree to perform an abortion. However, every physician also has the right, based on his or her moral views, to refuse to ever perform abortions. Physicians also make moral choices about treatment based on how the treatment will benefit the patient. Some patients may request a particular treatment for their illness. A physician may ethically refuse to use the requested treatment if it does not meet the recognized standard of acceptable care.

Many times, physicians find moral values contained within the laws of the state where they practice; these laws must be obeyed. For example, violence to children must be reported in many states. However, even if the law does not require this notification, the physician must respond ethically to report such cases. The physician's own belief system, good judgment, and decision-making skill all contribute to the ethical practice of the profession.

■ Etiquette

Etiquette is defined as those behaviors and customs that are standards for what is considered good manners. While codes of ethics specify standards for capable patient care, *etiquette* is a broad term for behaviors that mark courteous treatment of others.

Frequently, an employer's rules of etiquette are found in the policy and procedures manual of the medical practice. Examples of good manners in the office include:

- Dressing appropriately to show respect for others and for the profession.
- Using proper forms of address for both the physician and patients.
- Cheerfully greeting all who visit the office.
- Using good telephone techniques.
- Observing the use of polite everyday phrases: "Please," "Thank you," "Excuse me."

Etiquette forms the basis of effective communication and fosters satisfying interactions in all cultures and in all settings. Using good manners and following those aspects of etiquette that may be unique to the workplace help create a pleasant environment in an efficient office.

 ▶ **GO TO PROJECT 2.1 ON PAGE 49** ▶

2.2 MEDICAL LAW

Law is a set of rules made and enforced by a recognized authority. For example, federal, state, and city laws require some actions and forbid others. Law protects citizens and helps society to work smoothly. Physicians and other health care professionals may be affected by the law—both criminal and civil statutes. The law, then, as it applies to standards of acceptable care, is known as *medical jurisprudence,* or *medical law.*

■ Law and the Right to Practice

Medical law regulates the right to practice and the granting of various licenses and certifications. Each state governs the practice of medicine within its borders through laws known as **medical practice acts.** These acts:

- Define *medical practice.*
- Explain who must be licensed to give health care.
- Set rules for obtaining a license.
- State the duties imposed by the license.
- Cover the grounds on which the license may be revoked.
- List the statutory reports that must be sent to the government.

Medical practice acts also protect users of health care services. To do this, the acts set forth the penalties for practicing medicine without a valid license. The acts also define *misconduct,* including conviction of a felony, such as insurance fraud; unprofessional conduct, such as sexual behavior with a patient; personal or professional incapacity, such as mental illness; inappropriate use, or overprescribing, of drugs. The penalty for such acts may be the suspension or revoking of a license.

Licensing. The license to practice medicine, called **licensure,** is granted by a board established in each state. Licenses are issued to applicants once they have completed the educational requirements and have successfully passed an examination. Licenses may also be issued as a result of reciprocity, the recognition by one state of another state's requirements for licensure. Those who have passed the examination given by the National Board of Medical Examiners receive licenses from the state through what is called *endorsement.*

Relicensure is required either annually or every other year. Those who hold licenses may be relicensed by paying a fee and providing proof, such as certificates of course completion, that they have met continuing education requirements.

Certified Specialization. The American Board of Specialties determines the competency of, and then certifies, those doctors who intend to practice a medical specialty. The board requires additional academic in-hospital training in which the medical student, known as a *resident,* concentrates on a specialty and takes a comprehensive examination. Fulfilling the requirements, the candidate becomes *board-certified.* This certification is an essential minimum standard of competence in a particular medical specialty.

Narcotics Registration. A physician in clinical practice who will have occasion to prescribe or dispense drugs must register for a permit. This **registration** issued by the registration branch of the Drug Enforcement Administration (DEA) grants these permits, which must be renewed annually.

■ The Physician's Practice

In today's complex health care environment, the physician's practice has many elements of both a health service and a business, such as providing good patient care, scheduling, performing billing and insurance procedures, hiring and training staff, and maintaining the physical resources of the office, such as equipment and the office premises. Every part of the practice is affected by legal and ethical considerations.

Because the physician's primary responsibility is to practice an acceptable standard of patient care, the laws, responsibilities, and ethical considerations that surround the physician-patient relationship are of great importance.

Contracts. The relationship between the physician and the patient starts when the patient comes to the physician for care. The contract is implied; it is not expressed in either words or writing. The physician does not say "I am here to offer you care." The patient does not say "I am requesting care." The patient usually comes with a complaint, and the physician treats it. The physician's behavior, in having a practice open to patients, and the patient's behavior, in coming to the physician's office, together establish an implied contract. At times a written, or express, contract is provided, and both physician and patient sign a document. The physician may provide a standard written contract to allow a patient to pay for services over an extended period of time, for example.

Once the physician-patient relationship is established, the physician is legally required to:

- Possess the ordinary skill and learning commonly held by a reputable physician in a similar locality. The patient has the right to believe that the physician is so qualified. Accordingly, the physician's license should be displayed in the office.

legally required

(handwritten annotation:) Legally Required

(handwritten annotation:) on test

(handwritten annotation:) Not Legally

- Use his or her learning, skill, and best judgment for the benefit of the patient.
- Preserve confidentiality.
- Act in good faith.
- Perform to the best of his or her ability.
- Advise against needless or unwise treatment.
- Inform and advise the patient when the physician knows a condition is beyond his or her scope of competency.

The physician is not legally required to:

- Accept as patients all those who seek his or her services.
- Restore a patient to the same condition that existed before illness occurred.
- Obtain recovery for every patient.
- Guarantee successful results from an operation or a treatment.
- Be familiar with all possible reactions of patients to various medicines.
- Be free from errors in complex cases.
- Possess the maximum amount of education possible.
- Continue care after a patient discharges himself or herself from a hospital, even if harm could come to the patient.

In the physician-patient relationship, the patient also has certain responsibilities. The patient must give the information necessary for the physician to make a correct diagnosis; follow the physician's instructions and any orders for treatment, provided that these are within the bounds of similar standards of care for physicians who practice in that area of medicine; be, in general, cooperative; and pay for all services rendered.

Consent. When a patient comes to a physician's office for treatment, that patient's consent to treatment, like the contract itself, is not stated outright. This **implied consent** applies to routine treatment only. For more complicated procedures, especially surgery, diagnostic tests, and x-ray treatments, it is important to have **express consent.** The patient may express consent either in writing or orally. It is standard practice for the patient to give written consent by signing a special consent form before any special procedure is performed. An exception to this practice is the patient who is incapable of giving consent when an emergency requires immediate action. Express consent is important to avoid later lawsuits or, even more seriously, criminal accusations.

When oral consent is acceptable, it may be given in a telephone conversation provided that the call is a three-way conversation involving the patient and two office personnel. Both office employees then must sign as witnesses to the conversation in which the patient expressed consent.

There is another aspect of patient consent, whether implied or express. The patient must give **informed consent.** Informed consent means that the patient has had the illness or problem explained by the physician in simple, understandable language. The patient has also been given options for treatment, with the individual benefits and risks of each, along with the physician's prognosis. In other words, the patient has been given enough information to make a knowledgeable decision. A sample consent form is shown in Figure 2.3.

Adults who are *legally competent* are able to give informed consent. The law requires that in order to be competent, a person must have attained legal *majority* (adult age as defined by law) and must be of sound mind. When a patient is not able to give consent, that consent must be given by the next of kin, the legal guardian, or a court-appointed guardian.

CONSENT FOR INFLUENZA (FLU) VACCINE
Office of Karen Larsen, MD

Purpose of the Influenza Vaccine

Influenza is a highly contagious respiratory tract infection. Symptoms may include chills, fever, headache, cough, sore throat, and muscle aches. Generally, the illness lasts several days to a week or more. The flu may be severe or even life-threatening for some people.

Each year the influenza vaccine is updated because viruses that cause the flu often change.

Influenza Vaccine

The flu vaccine contains inactive (dead) influenza viruses selected by the U.S. Food and Drug Administration. Because it is an inactive virus vaccine, the vaccine will not give you the flu.

Protection from the flu vaccine develops within 2 weeks after receiving the vaccine and may last up to a year.

Risks and Side Effects

The risk of the flu vaccine causing serious problems is very small. Mild side effects may include soreness, redness, and swelling of the injection site; fever; and muscle aches. If any side effects occur, they may begin upon receiving the vaccine injection and last 1 to 2 days.

NOTE: People who have an allergy to eggs, chicken, or chicken feathers should **not** receive the influenza vaccine. Also people who currently have an active infection should not receive the vaccine.

If you have any questions or concerns, please check with your physician before receiving the flu vaccine.

Freedom of Consent

The influenza vaccine is a voluntary injection. You are free to deny this consent.

Patient's Consent

I have read this form. I understand the purpose of the influenza vaccine and the risks and benefits of the vaccine. I have expressed any questions or concerns about the flu vaccine to my physician.

_____   _____
Patient receiving the vaccine (Please print)   Date of birth

_____   _____
Signature of patient or guardian   Date

FIGURE 2.3

Informed Consent Form

Those who have not reached the adult age required by law, and are therefore minors, may give legal consent in certain cases:

- A minor who is in the military service.
- A minor who is living away from his or her parents and is managing his or her own financial affairs.
- A college student who is living away from home.
- A minor who is married or divorced.

The kinds of care that minors may usually consent to are:

- Pregnancy tests.
- Prenatal care.
- The diagnosis and treatment of a sexually transmitted disease.
- The diagnosis and treatment of alcohol or drug abuse.

Although there is no one consent form required by law, the informed consent that the patient signs should usually contain the following:

on consent form

- The name of the patient and the date.
- The name of the procedure to be performed.
- The name of the physician performing the procedure.
- An explanation of the procedure.
- A statement of risks and benefits.
- A statement that the patient signs to signify understanding of the procedure and the information given in the form.
- The patient's signature.
- The signature of a witness (optional) testifying to the patient's signature.

In addition to written, informed consent for procedures, there are other reasons for obtaining patient consent. For example, if a physician wishes to videotape a patient visit or procedure for training purposes, the physician must obtain the patient's written consent. An example of this type of consent form is shown in Figure 2.4 on page 38.

COMPLIANCE TIP

The assistant should always bring to the physician's attention any confusion noticed in a patient about directions or any lack of understanding. If the patient has questions, the assistant should inform the physician. Alertness on the part of the assistant will help to ensure informed consent.

FIGURE 2.4

Consent for Videotaping
Form

CONSENT FOR VIDEOTAPING

I, _____Anita Melendez_____ , give my consent for the videotaping of my appointment with Karen Larsen, MD, including medical history and examination on
this date.

I understand that I have a right to private, confidential medical consultation
and treatment, and I voluntarily waive that right so that the videotape may be
used for teaching purposes at the University Medical School.

I am in agreement that my medical history, which is related to the taped
examination, may be disclosed during the described use of the videotape for
teaching purposes.

I further understand that at any future time I may request in writing that certain
parts or the entire recording may be deleted and not used.

Signature _____Anita Melendez_____   Date _____7/10/20--_____

Witness _____Joanne Diaz_____   Date _____7/10/20--_____

▶ **GO TO PROJECT 2.2 ON PAGE 49** ▶

2.3 MEDICAL LIABILITY AND COMMUNICATIONS

Liability means legal responsibility. In many areas of life, people are liable, or
legally responsible, for actions (or nonactions) and their consequences. The
owner of a home may be liable for an injury caused to a guest in the home.

Physicians have liability in their roles as providers of health care and
as owners of a practice. In general, physicians are responsible not only for
the quality of the care they give to patients but also for:

- *The safety of employees.* An office policy and procedures manual will often contain regulations that relate to observing state laws for safety, including the handling of discarded waste and hazardous materials.
- *The safety of the premises.* Rules that help ensure protection from injury, theft, and fire need to be specified. This is important not only for patients and employees but also for the safety of records.

Physicians, wishing to protect themselves from lawsuits brought by patients, sometimes practice **defensive medicine.** This means that physicians order additional tests and follow-up visits to confirm a diagnosis or treatment result. The physician's liability as it relates to patient care is discussed below.

■ Malpractice

Malpractice is the improper care or treatment of a patient by a physician, hospital, or other provider of health care as a result of carelessness, neglect, lack of professional skill, or disregard for the established rules or procedures. In spite of vigilance on the part of the physician and the office staff, accidents may occur during treatment. Some patients may be dissatisfied with the care they have received. In cases such as these, a patient may file a malpractice suit against the physician. A patient who files a suit is required to prove that there is an injury, as the law defines *injury,* and that the physician's inadequate care was the direct cause of the injury.

■ Termination

As discussed earlier, the contractual agreement between the patient and the physician calls for the physician to furnish care to the patient for a particular illness as long as care is required. At times, a physician may choose to terminate, or end, the physician-patient relationship because a patient does not follow treatment instructions, or because the patient has stated (either orally or in writing) an intent to seek care from another physician. The physician may also terminate the relationship if the patient fails to pay for services.

The physician is required to notify the patient of the decision to terminate and to allow the patient a reasonable amount of time to obtain another physician. The notification should be in the form of a letter, sent to the patient, that states why the physician is ending the relationship, the date of the termination, and the physician's willingness to continue treatment temporarily if the patient needs further care.

After a withdrawal letter has been sent, the physician should provide the patient's name to the administrative medical assistant who schedules appointments. If the patient calls and requests an appointment, the call should be transferred to the physician, who will explain to the patient what needs to be done to reestablish care.

■ Abandonment

Unless the patient is discharged in an appropriate way, either because the treatment was completed or because the physician followed the procedure for termination, the patient may sue the physician for **abandonment.** Good documentation is essential to proving that the physician did not abandon the patient.

EXAMPLE

> Notations in patient medical record:
>
> 4/6/—   Patient cancelled appointment. Rescheduled for 4/13/—.
>
> 4/13/—   Patient did not show up for follow-up appointment.
>
> As a precaution, patients should be notified of any absences of the physician from the office—for vacation, conferences, emergencies. The name and telephone number of the substituting physician should be made available to patients. The assistant may post a notice of the physician's absence or mail a notice to patients. The notice or letter should be kept on file.

■ Assault and Battery

The clear threat of injury to another is called **assault.** Any bodily contact without permission is called **battery.** In medical law, *battery* is interpreted to include surgical and medical procedures performed without the patient's consent or procedures that go beyond the degree of consent that was given.

EXAMPLE

> A badly damaged uterus is removed during exploratory surgery even though the patient had not signed a consent for the removal.
>
> In this example, even though the procedure may have been in the best interest of the patient, the physician may be sued for battery. Unless a physician acts in a grave emergency, he or she may well lose a suit in court as a result of not having proper patient consent.

■ Fraud

An intentionally dishonest practice that deprives others of their rights is called **fraud.** Depending on the laws of the state where the physician practices, the penalty may range from reprimand to the revoking of a license.

A wide range of activities is included under the definition of fraud. Such activities include:

- Making false statements to a patient about the benefits of a particular drug or treatment.

- Falsifying diplomas or licenses.
- Submitting false or duplicate claims for payment to the federal government or an insurance company.

■ Litigation

The bringing of lawsuits, or **litigation,** against the physician is not uncommon. Many lawsuits arise out of civil law. Civil law deals with crimes against persons committed by other persons or institutions, such as the government or a business. While criminal law handles the actual commission of a crime, civil law gives a person the right to sue. For example, a physician may be convicted of battery in a criminal court and then may be sued by the patient in civil court for injuries resulting from the battery. The civil court may decide to award the patient a certain amount of money for the injuries.

One common type of civil suit that patients may bring is for malpractice. However, the law also covers many other aspects of the physician's practice, such as the hiring process, drug testing of employees, equal opportunity, sexual harassment, fair labor laws, and workers' compensation.

Steps in Litigation. Once a lawsuit is begun, there are several steps involved in resolving it:

- *Summons.* A written notice—the **summons**—is sent to the person being sued (the *defendant*) ordering the defendant to answer the charges made. The summons is sent by the court along with a copy of the complaint filed by the other party (the *plaintiff*).
- *Subpoena.* A **subpoena** is a legal document in which the court orders that all documents relevant to the case be delivered to the court. A subpoena may also require any person who has information related to the case to appear in court.
- *Deposition.* A sworn statement to the court before any trial begins, and usually made outside of court, is called a **deposition.**

The Physician's Response to Litigation. Complete, accurate documentation is critical in physician-patient disputes. The documentation may provide the physician with evidence of **contributory negligence.** A patient's refusal to have tests, x-rays, or vaccinations, or a patient's failure to follow the physician's instructions, may be considered contributory negligence. The physician's notations in the patient record, made at the time of the patient's actions, would protect the physician against a later claim that reasonable precautions had not been taken. Any contact by telephone or letter regarding laboratory or x-ray reports should also be indicated.

EXAMPLE

Notation in patient's medical record:

3/12/— Patient refused to have chest x-ray. Patient did accept medication.

Alternatives to Trial. The complaint may be heard in court at a trial. However, the case may also be resolved through settlement or arbitration. In a **settlement,** the plaintiff and the physician's insurance company reach an agreement and the case does not go to court. In **arbitration,** through a process fair to both sides, an *arbitrator* (an unbiased third party) is chosen. This person, rather than a judge, hears evidence and helps both sides to resolve the dispute or makes a decision if the two sides cannot agree. Because the defendant and the plaintiff agree beforehand to abide by the arbitrator's decision, the arbitration also ends the case before it reaches court.

Statute of Limitations. A law that sets a time limit for initiating litigation is called a **statute of limitations.** This time limit varies from state to state. The time span during which a lawsuit for malpractice may be brought may begin when the claimed negligence first occurred, when the claimed negligence was first discovered, or when the physician-patient relationship ended. In pediatric cases, the time span may begin after the patient reaches majority. When children are treated, physicians should retain records long enough to cover this span of time. Information about particular state laws is available from state offices and their Web sites.

Good Samaritan Act. The purpose of a **Good Samaritan Act** is to protect the physician from liability for civil damages that may arise as a result of providing emergency care. Because there are minor variations from state to state, the medical assistant's role in emergency situations is defined by the state in which the assistant is employed.

■ Medical Communications—Access to Information

All information a patient gives a physician is confidential. Administrative medical assistants who process physicians' correspondence and work with patients' records are authorized to read this information. However, no patient information may be conveyed to anyone outside of the practice without permission from the patient. Under the federal law known as the *final privacy rule,* patients must provide a general consent to the sharing of information for the purposes of carrying out treatment or submitting insurance claims. They must also provide written **authorization** for specific items that are not covered by the general consent.

Patients have the right to see their medical records. Preferably, this is to be done with the physician's participation so that the information can be interpreted for the patient in a meaningful way. The physician must always be notified when patients request to review their records.

Release of Information. It is often necessary to release information from patients' medical records to insurance companies, other medical facilities, or other physicians. These releases are connected to patient care, proper treatment, and accurate billing. The strictest confidentiality must be maintained while providing requested data. The medical office follows a procedure to make sure that the party asking for the data has the right to receive it and that proper authorization to release the information has been granted.

The administrative medical assistant can ensure the proper transfer of information by following the office's procedure carefully, double-checking the source and validity of the request, and verifying that the patient has given permission in writing to release the information. This written permission is in the form of an authorization for **release of information,** sometimes simply called a *release*. The authorization for release of information must meet several legal requirements in order to be valid. A sample authorization form is shown in Figure 2.5 on page 44. The release must contain:

- The name of the facility releasing the information.
- The name of the individual or facility requesting and receiving the information.
- The patient's full name, address, and date of birth.
- The specific dates of treatment.
- A description of the information to be released.
- The signature of the patient.
- The date the form was signed.

Helping to Ensure Confidentiality. The assistant can help to protect confidentiality by:

- Avoiding any conversation, either in person or on the telephone, with a patient or others, about any aspect of treatment, patient records, or financial arrangements. When speaking on the phone, also avoid using the caller's name or the name of any patient.
- Being careful when calling patients about test results—never leaving a message on the answering machine or with any other person except to request a return call from the patient.
- Always keeping documents shielded from view in areas where fax machines, copy machines, and printers are located.
- Always removing documents from these areas and shredding them, rather than putting materials in the trash.
- Protecting computerized records and other information. Do not leave information showing on any unattended screen. Be careful of access to the network if the computer shares programs and data files.

COMPLIANCE TIP

The physician's office may only forward information about a patient that is part of the patient's care in that office. Information about patients that comes from hospital or clinic records cannot be forwarded by the physician's office. Such information must be requested from the source that generated it.

FIGURE 2.5

Authorization for Release
of Information Form

AUTHORIZATION TO RELEASE MEDICAL INFORMATION

Original Authorization MUST be attached to the patient's permanent medical record. A copy of this Authorization should be attached to forwarded medical record.

DATE: _____

TO: Karen Larsen, MD
       2235 South Ridgeway Avenue
       Chicago, IL 60623-2240
       312-555-6022, 312-555-0025 fax

RE: Patient name _____
       Patient street address _____
       Patient city, state, ZIP _____
       Patient telephone _____
       Patient date of birth _____

The undersigned hereby requests and authorizes Karen Larsen, MD, to release to (INSERT NAME OF RECIPIENT OF PATIENT RECORDS) or any of his/her/their assigned representatives, copies of any and all records and documents regarding the undersigned's past and current medical treatment, medical condition(s) and medical expenses. The information to be released includes any and all medical and hospital records currently within your possession, including, but not limited to, any and all x-ray films, pathology slides, laboratory reports, medical histories, consultation reports, prescriptions, medical correspondence, consent forms, employment information, and billing information.

In addition to authorizing the release of the above stated medical records and documents, the undersigned expressly authorizes Karen Larsen, MD, to release the following information to the designated individual or entity: (Please initial the items below for release, if appropriate)

_____ Psychiatric information _____ Drug/Alcohol information _____ HIV-related information

The physician is instructed to comply with this request by providing *copies* of my records only, with the understanding that my original medical record will be maintained within the possession of Karen Larsen, MD.

A copy of this authorization **shall not** be used in lieu of an originally signed authorization.

This authorization may be revoked by the undersigned at any time by a written notice to the physician except to the extent that action has already been taken.

This authorization will expire sixty (60) days from the date of this request OR _____ (specify other date) and will be null and void thereafter.

_____   _____
            Signature of patient   Date

Patient is a minor, or patient is legally unable to sign because _____

_____   _____
         Signature of authorized person   Date

_____   _____
        Print name of authorized person   Relationship to patient

Disclosure statement: This information is being disclosed to you from records whose confidentiality is protected by federal and state law. Federal and state law prohibit you from making any further disclosure of this information without the specific written authorization of the person to whom it pertains, or as otherwise permitted by law.

■ Exceptions to Confidentiality

Under some circumstances, the physician is required to file reports containing confidential information to state departments of health or social services. These are called *statutory reports.* The government needs this information to protect the health of the whole community. Each state has its own requirements for statutory reports. Each state is responsible for making and enforcing the laws related to the reports it needs. Examples of circumstances requiring statutory reports are:

- Births.
- Deaths.
- Abuse of a child, a vulnerable or elderly adult, or a battered person. State law requires teachers, physicians, and other licensed health care workers to report cases of suspected abuse. It is also true that any private citizen may, at any time, file a complaint with a protective agency.

- Injuries resulting from violence, such as gunshot or stab wounds, or any other evidence of criminal violence.
- Occupational illnesses, such as chemical poisoning.
- Communicable diseases, including acquired immune deficiency syndrome (AIDS), hepatitis, neonatal herpes, Lyme disease, rabies, and sexually transmitted diseases.
- Cases of food poisoning.

■ Transmission of Information Electronically

In today's medical practice, it is very common to transmit information electronically. To ensure that health information is protected from misuse, a federal law, the **Health Insurance Portability and Accountability Act,** or **HIPAA** (pronounced hip-uh), regulates how electronic patient information is stored and shared. (See Appendix B: HIPAA Overview on pages 330–339 for a summary of HIPAA, including the HIPAA Privacy Rule.) The administrative assistant must be conscientious about the following:

- If information is faxed, the assistant should carefully check the fax number and then call to confirm receipt.
- The assistant should use a cover page for the fax, requesting the return of the information if it has reached the wrong person.
- Do not send confidential information by e-mail. Most e-mail networks are not secure.

▶ **GO TO PROJECT 2.3 ON PAGE 49** ▶

2.4 MEDICAL COMPLIANCE PLANS AND SAFEGUARDS AGAINST LITIGATION

Medical practices must take steps to reduce the risk of accusations of fraud and abuse when submitting claims to insurance companies and federal agencies such as Medicare. The processes involved in coding and billing are complicated, and there is much room for error. Although many errors are not intentional, medical practices are required to show their resolve to behave with **compliance,** or adherence, to rules and regulations.

To assist in this process of ensuring that procedures are in compliance, the Office of the Inspector General (OIG), an agency of the U.S. Department of Health and Human Services (HHS), has issued *Compliance Program Guidance for Individual and Small Group Physician Practices.* This voluntary plan is a positive step toward helping physicians protect themselves and their practices from violations related to claims and reimbursements. Using the guidance provided by the OIG, physicians can develop an effective compliance plan for their practices.

COMPLIANCE TIP

To comply with the HIPAA Privacy Rule, medical offices must give each patient a copy of their Notice of Privacy Practices at the patient's first encounter. The written notice explains how patients' information may be used or disclosed and describes their privacy rights. Patients must then sign an acknowledgment showing that they have read and understand the document.

There are specific risk areas in practices that a medical compliance plan addresses:

- *Coding and billing.* The risks include billing for services not rendered, submitting claims for equipment or medical supplies that are not reasonable, and double billing, which results in duplicate payment.
- *Reasonable and necessary services.* The practice must offer the patient only necessary procedures and treatments that meet Medicare's definitions and may not offer more complex and more expensive methods when simpler, less expensive alternatives exist.
- *Documentation.* Great care is to be taken in entering data and maintaining and retaining all information related to treatment, claims, and reimbursements.
- *Improper inducements, kickbacks, and self-referrals.* Neither the physician nor anyone on staff may accept payment for awarding contracts or for purchasing anything *(inducements)*. Neither may anyone knowingly offer, pay, solicit, or receive bribes to influence getting business that is reimbursable by federal government programs *(kickbacks)*. The physician may not refer a patient to any health service with which the physician or any member of the physician's immediate family has a financial relationship *(self-referral)*.

■ The Medical Compliance Plan

The major purpose for creating and implementing a compliance plan within the practice is to prevent the submission of erroneous claims or unlawful conduct involving the federal health care programs.

The OIG *Program Guidance* suggests seven basic elements for any compliance plan set up within the practice:

- *Written policies and procedures.* There should be written policies and procedures for patient care, billing and coding, documentation, and payer relationships.
- *Designation of a chief compliance officer.* The officer may be an office manager or a biller. The officer's duties include monitoring the plan, conducting audits periodically, and investigating reports or allegations of fraud.
- *Training and education programs.* Education is an essential component because the physician relies on staff members to follow procedures that reduce the practice's vulnerability to fraud. All employees should receive training on how to perform their jobs according to the standards and regulations of the practice. Employees should also understand through their training programs that compliance is a condition of their continued employment.

- *Effective line of communication.* The practice should create an environment where there is an open-door policy and employees feel encouraged to report mistakes promptly and to report any potential problems without fear of retribution.
- *Auditing and monitoring.* An audit should be conducted at least once a year by a designated staff member or an outside consultant. The audit includes checking for data entry errors and confirmation that all orders are written and signed by a physician.
- *Well-publicized disciplinary directives.* Every staff member should understand the penalties for noncompliance. Disciplinary guidelines should include the circumstances under which someone would receive any one of a range of penalties, from a verbal warning to dismissal to referral for criminal prosecution.
- *Prompt corrective action for detected offenses.* Corrective action should be taken within 60 days from the date on which the problem is identified. Problems must be investigated at once; a policy on overpayments must be clear and enforced.

■ The Administrative Medical Assistant's Role in Compliance

The potential for accusations of fraud is always present in the complex areas of patient care, billing and coding, and documentation. If fraud is detected and not reported or corrected, the reputation and legal standing of the practice is put at grave risk. The assistant has job responsibilities related to all of these areas and plays a central role in helping to ensure that the practice is in compliance.

The assistant who is working efficiently and effectively is key to the success of a compliance plan. In the following areas of responsibility, the assistant helps the practice stay in compliance:

- *Accurate data entry.* Accurate work speeds the correct payment of claims and lessens the chances of federal audit.
- *Accurate documentation.* Good documentation reduces the chances for mistakes and provides an excellent trail if proof of corrective action is required. In addition to protecting the practice, accurate documentation contributes to improved patient care.
- *Timely filing and storing of records.* Keeping records in good order and for an appropriate length of time can show the physician's good faith efforts to apply the principles of compliance.
- *Prompt reporting of errors or instances of fraudulent conduct.* The assistant has the ethical and professional responsibility to help the physician correct mistakes and investigate instances of unlawful behavior.

■ Safeguards Against Litigation

The assistant needs to be aware that liability for negligence is recognized by law to include not only the physician's actions but also the actions of the physician's employees. An assistant who is performing tasks within the job description and as a proper assignment is considered to be the agent of the physician. It is the physician's responsibility to define the assistant's job properly, to state and regulate office policies, to assist in teaching the policies, and to see that policies and procedures are implemented. It is the assistant's responsibility to understand thoroughly his or her job description and the office policies. The assistant, then, must act responsibly within the scope of his or her job and according to office policies.

It is easier to prevent a malpractice claim than to defend one. Assistants who maintain good interpersonal relationships with patients and other staff members help reduce the likelihood of litigation. In particular, the following guidelines are useful:

- Keep everything that you hear, see, and read about patients completely confidential.
- Never criticize a physician to a patient.
- Do not discuss a patient's condition, diagnosis, or treatment with the patient, with other patients, or with staff members. What the physician tells the assistant about a patient is to be kept confidential, even from the patient.
- Do not diagnose or prescribe, even though you feel sure you know what the physician would prescribe. There are often circumstances in the case of which you are unaware. Prescribing constitutes the practice of medicine and is unlawful unless you are licensed.
- Notify the physician if you learn that a patient is under treatment by another physician for the same condition.
- Inform the physician of all information given by the patient, as when the patient has questions, appears confused, or seems not to understand directions or instructions given.
- Also inform the physician about any unpleasant incident that may have occurred between the patient and any staff member. In this case, the assistant writes a notation to the physician, which does not become part of the patient's record.
- Notify the physician if the patient mentions that he or she has no intention of returning to the office or complying with the treatment plan.
- Be available to assist the patient and the physician.
- Obtain proper authorizations for release of information and consents. File these with the patient's records.
- Keep complete and accurate records, including notations about a patient's failure to keep an appointment, cancellation of an appointment, or failure to follow treatment instructions.

- Be selective in giving information over the telephone. Many practices accept requests for information only when they are written.
- Observe the confidentiality of computerized records by shielding computer screens from the view of patients or other staff members, protecting passwords, and following practice security guidelines when using e-mail for transmitting information.
- Keep prescription pads and medications in a secure place.
- Be safety conscious. See that all equipment is in safe working condition, and be alert to potential safety hazards.

▶ **GO TO PROJECT 2.4 BELOW** ▶

Chapter Projects

PROJECT 2.1 Internet Research: Bioethical Topics

Using the Internet, research the location of articles on two different bioethical issues of interest to you. Read two articles on each issue. Be prepared to contribute the results of your reading in class.

PROJECT 2.2 Physician's Obligations and Medical Law

WP 3 contains statements that refer to the obligations of the physician and/or medical law. Mark each statement with either "T" for *true* or "F" for *false.* Be prepared to give your answers in class.

PROJECT 2.3 Medical Liability and Communications

WP 4 contains statements that refer to medical liability and communications. Mark each statement with either "T" for *true* or "F" for *false.* Be prepared to share your answers in class.

PROJECT 2.4 Legal Terms

In WP 5, match each legal term in Column 2 with the correct definition in Column 1. Be prepared to give your answers in class.

CHAPTER SUMMARY

1. Ethics are the standards of conduct that grow out of one's understanding of right and wrong. Medical ethics require physicians to practice high standards of patient care; respect patients' rights; treat patients with compassion; and safeguard the privacy of patients' communications. Bioethics deals with the ethical issues involved with medical treatments, procedures, and technology. Etiquette involves following medical manners and customs, such as using proper forms of address for the physician and for patients, cheerfully greeting all visitors to the office, and using good telephone techniques.

2. Three functions of medical practice acts are to set out and explain the rules for licensing, state the duties imposed by the license, and define the nature of acts of misconduct.

3. The physician's legal responsibilities include following medical practice acts, having the same skill as similar professionals and using this skill to benefit the patient, and preserving confidentiality.

4. Patient information is released only to ensure proper patient care, effective treatment, and accurate billing. Usually, information may be shared with insurance companies, medical facilities, and other physicians. The assistant ensures the proper transfer of information by double-checking the source and validity of the request and by securing a written release of information from the patient.

5. A medical compliance plan has policies and procedures that prevent the submission of erroneous claims or unlawful conduct involving federal health care programs. The assistant can contribute to compliance within the practice by accurate data entry, accuracy of all documentation of patient care, and prompt reporting of errors or fraudulent conduct.

6. Safeguards against litigation that the medical assistant can practice are exercising complete confidentiality, avoiding the discussion of a patient's condition with the patient or other staff members, obtaining proper authorizations for the release of information, and keeping accurate and complete records, including notations about a patient's failure to keep an appointment or failure to follow the physician's instructions.

KEY TERMS

The following terms appear in **boldface** type in this chapter. Administrative medical assistants must know the meaning and the correct use of each of these terms. Can you recall what each term means? Refer to this chapter or to the glossary for any terms you need to review.

abandonment

arbitration

assault

authorization

battery

bioethics

compliance

contributory negligence

defensive medicine

deposition

ethics

etiquette

express consent

fraud

Good Samaritan Act

Health Insurance Portability and
    Accountability Act (HIPAA)

implied consent

informed consent

liability

licensure

litigation

malpractice

medical practice acts

registration

release of information

settlement

statute of limitations

subpoena

summons

THINKING IT THROUGH

These questions cover the most important points in this chapter. Using your critical thinking skills, play the role of an administrative medical assistant as you answer each question. Be prepared to present your responses in class.

1. What are the major standards, as set forth in the AMA code of ethics, which doctors are expected to adhere to in their practices? What qualities does the AAMA creed emphasize for administrative medical assistants?

2. You hear Mr. Washington enter the office. He has come to keep a 3 p.m. appointment with the doctor. You are busily trying to rearrange the afternoon appointments to accommodate an emergency that occurred in the morning. You do not feel that you can raise your eyes from the complicated list of appointments before you. You simply say, in response to Mr. Washington's greeting, "Please have a seat." Have you violated any principles of office etiquette? Please give reasons for your answer.

3. In what ways would patients be in danger if it were not for medical practice acts?

THINKING IT THROUGH (continued)

4. In a casual conversation, a patient boasts that he has made his stomach pains disappear without taking any of the medicine prescribed by the doctor. He also says that although he had these pains far longer than he admitted to the doctor, his home cure worked. He then informs you, quite seriously, that he does not expect to receive a bill for services from the physician. How do you respond to the patient? What is wrong with the way this patient thinks about the doctor-patient relationship?

5. On what basis would you decide whether or not an individual's request for access to a patient's record should be fulfilled?

6. A request for a patient's medical record is sent by fax to the office. The fax cover sheet contains the letterhead of a nearby medical facility. You do not recognize the name of the physician, fax number, or telephone number stated for the physician's office. How do you respond to the request?

7. Payment from an insurance company has just arrived at the office. In processing the paperwork, you notice that an error has been made in coding the procedure. The error has resulted in an overpayment to the practice. The error is only the latest mistake in a growing number of errors, all made by the same staff member. What are your responsibilities in this situation?

8. In a dispute between a patient and the doctor, both parties have agreed to an alternative to trial. What happens in an arbitration? What advantages may arbitration have over a court trial?

9. What are the aspects of an administrative medical assistant's behavior and attention to procedure that help the practice avoid litigation?

3

Computer Usage in the Medical Office

OBJECTIVES

After studying this chapter, you will be able to:

1. List five key areas in which computers are used in the medical office.
2. Compare the major categories of computers and describe four major computer components.
3. Describe four types of computer software.
4. Discuss issues of patient confidentiality and computer security.
5. Discuss several ways of keeping up with changing office technology.

INTRODUCTION

Computers are used in nearly all aspects of the health care field. In clinical work, computer technology supports tasks from research to microsurgery. In the medical office, computers help track patients' appointments and maintain medical records. Electronic communication, which depends on computer technology, is used to transmit insurance claims as well as to share information with insurance companies and other health care providers.

KEY TERMS

Study these important words, which are defined in this chapter, to build your professional vocabulary:

application software	hard drive	networking	ROM	wireless communication
CD-ROM drive	input	on-line	scanner	word processing program
CPU	Internet	operating system	spreadsheet programs	Zip drive
databases	keyboard	output	supercomputers	
diskettes	laptops	palm computer	template	
e-mail	mainframes	passwords	voice-recognition software	
file server	minicomputers	personal computers		
graphics application	modem	printer		
	monitor	RAM		

3.1 COMPUTER USAGE

Many of the tasks an administrative medical assistant regularly performs require the use of a computer. Following are five areas where computers are commonly used in the medical office:

- Scheduling
- Creation and maintenance of patients' medical records
- Communications
- Billing, collections, claims, and financial reporting
- Clinical work

■ Scheduling

Many medical offices use electronic scheduling systems to set up and maintain appointments. These systems have many features that are not available with paper logbooks. For example, with an electronic scheduling system, an administrative medical assistant can print a daily list of appointments for the physician. Having such schedules available in a quick and easy-to-read format is helpful for everyone in the medical office.

Another advantage is efficient rescheduling of appointments. With a paper logbook, first the assistant locates the appointment that needs to be changed. Once the appointment is found, it has to be crossed through and a new entry made. With electronic scheduling, the assistant enters the patient's name in a search box, and the computer locates the appointment in seconds. Old appointments can be deleted with a single keystroke, and new ones keyed in within seconds. It is also easy to move an appointment to a different time, day, or month.

Another advantage of electronic scheduling is electronic searching for available time slots in a provider's schedule. For example, suppose a patient needs to schedule three 15-minute appointments during the next three weeks but is only available on Tuesday and Thursday afternoons. The assistant enters a set of criteria in the scheduler, and the computer locates the first available slots that match the criteria. This saves the assistant the trouble of leafing through several weeks of appointments in a paper log.

Electronic scheduling can also be used to keep track of providers' time away from the office, such as for medical conferences, surgical procedures performed in the hospital, and days off. Reminder notices or telephone calls that need to be made to patients before appointments can also be automatically generated.

FIGURE 3.1

Computer programs like NDCmedisoft™ Office Hours are used in many medical offices. *In what ways do such programs make the administrative medical assistant more efficient?*

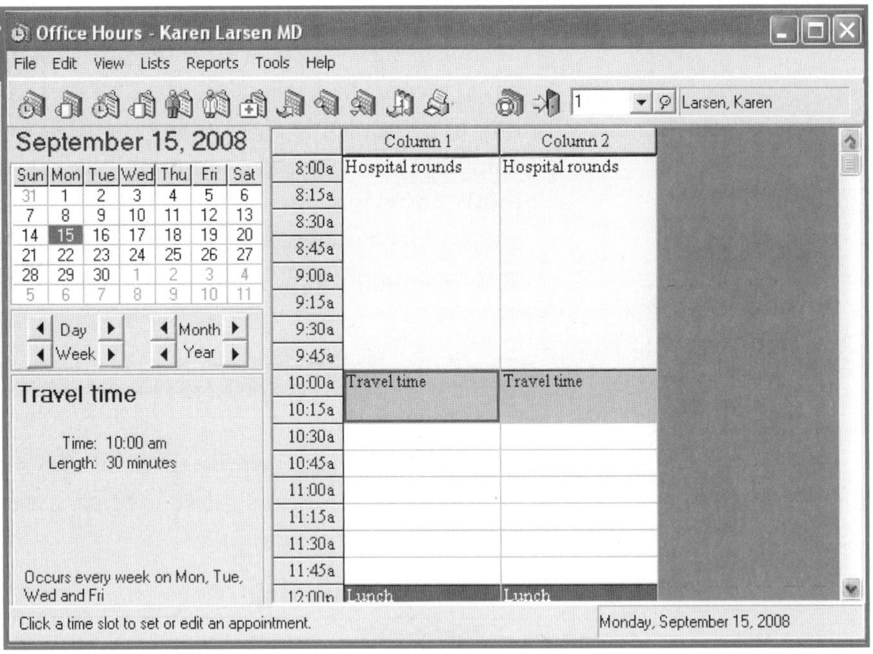

Creation and Maintenance of Patients' Medical Records

A medical record contains all the office's information about a patient, such as medical history, physician notes, medical reports, x-rays, charts, and correspondence. Most medical practices use computers to handle some part of patients' medical records. In some offices, the records are completely electronic. With electronic medical records, there are no actual paper records. All data about a patient, including x-ray images, lab test results, medical history, and so on, are created and stored on a computer.

The advantage of using electronic medical records is clear. For example, increasingly, clinical information is obtained electronically. Information such as the results of MRIs, x-rays, and blood tests can be transmitted in seconds to an electronic medical record. The time that would otherwise be required to output the results of tests, mail or fax them, and file them in a paper file is eliminated.

Perhaps one of the greatest advantages in using electronic medical records is that the data can be accessed instantly from any location. If a patient enters a hospital during an emergency, with the patient's permission, a physician can access the patient's medical record from the hospital in a matter of seconds to receive information on medical history, prior tests and lab work, medications prescribed, progress notes, and so on.

Electronic medical records also provide new opportunities for medical research. With access to large collections of patient information over a long period of time, medical researchers can look for patterns in similar cases, compare the results of treatments, and determine the best course of action.

Although the use of electronic medical records is growing, especially in large facilities such as hospitals, medical offices typically use some paper-based records because of the start-up costs and training involved in switching to a completely electronic system. There are also important issues of computer security and patient confidentiality to be resolved. Most experts think that in time, however, since so many of the items in a medical record are produced on a computer, the electronic patient record will be the most common method of capturing and storing all patient information.

■ Communications

Computers are used in the medical office to handle many communications tasks. An administrative medical assistant needs to be familiar with the use of the following:

- Word processing
- E-mail
- Computer networks
- The Internet
- Wireless communication

Word Processing. A **word processing program** is used to enter, edit, format, and print documents. A word processor can handle all the written correspondence an assistant usually creates: referral letters, consultation reports, routine letters about appointments or test reports, interoffice memorandums, as well as standard forms and reports used regularly in a medical office. In addition, the assistant may use a word processor in conjunction with a dictation machine to transcribe medical records, letters, reports, and articles.

FIGURE 3.2

This assistant is working with patients' medical records. *How can the assistant protect the confidentiality of data on a computer screen?*

A development in computer applications programs that directly affects word processing and medical dictation is the improvement of voice-recognition software. **Voice-recognition software** is used with word processors to transcribe spoken words into text without a keyboard. First, the user "trains" the software to recognize his or her particular speech patterns. Then, when the user speaks into a microphone attached to the computer, the words appear on the computer screen. No typing or transcription is necessary.

Although voice-recognition technology has existed for some time, only recently have refinements of the software resulted in its being widely recognized as a productivity tool in the health care industry. Earlier versions of the software required the dictator to pronounce words separately and distinctly for the computer to transcribe them correctly. Now, users can speak continuously and the computer recognizes the words. Other improvements include a full range of editing features and commands and a more extensive vocabulary—programs will recognize thousands of words and terms and specialized vocabularies. Voice-recognition software companies also provide a handheld remote device for dictation off-site. The device may later be plugged into a computer for automatic transcription into documents in almost any word processing program.

Since voice-recognition software is an excellent tool for medical dictation and transcription, it is expected to be used in many medical offices. In most cases, voice recognition will be used in place of dictation and initial transcription, and the skilled assistant will proofread and correctly format the material according to accepted standards for documentation and correspondence.

E-mail. A second widely used communications tool in the medical office is e-mail, or electronic mail. **E-mail** is a telecommunications system for exchanging written messages through a computer network. Both the sender and the receiver must have an e-mail address. E-mail messages can be sent to someone in the same office or as far away as another country. In either case, the process is the same.

The sender keys the message on his or her computer using an e-mail program. The e-mail program sends the message over telephone or cable lines to a central computer, where the message is stored. When the e-mail message reaches the central computer, the central computer alerts the recipient that there is a message waiting. At the recipient's convenience, the recipient retrieves the message from the central computer to his or her computer and reads it. The message can then be printed, saved, deleted, or forwarded to another e-mail address. Or, if desired, the recipient can key a response on the same page and return the e-mail to the sender.

E-mail is both inexpensive and efficient as a form of communication. In the medical office, an assistant might use e-mail to contact a person in a health insurance company to ask a question about billing. Or the assistant may e-mail another medical practice to supply a referral quickly. E-mail replaces correspondence that normally takes several days to process.

Medical office staff may use e-mail to communicate with each other. As with interoffice memos, e-mails can be sent to a number of people at the same time for various applications, such as to report news about an upcoming conference, to ascertain their views on a policy change, or to inform them of a schedule change. E-mail programs also have a courtesy copy feature (C:) for sending the same message to another person. Perhaps one of the most useful features of e-mail programs today is that users can attach files to an e-mail message. This means an e-mail program can be used to send almost any kind of computer document—word processing documents, graphics, video files, computer programs—to another computer across the world in seconds.

Computer Networks. A third type of communications tool used in a medical office is a computer network. A network links computers together so that software, hardware, and data files can be shared. **Networking** provides a means of communicating, exchanging information, and pooling resources among a group of computers. A user who goes **on-line** is connecting to a computer network. Networks provide:

- Simultaneous access to programs and files.
- A simple backup process.
- Sharing of computer devices.

In a network, a central computer, called a **file server** (or simply a "server"), stores the computer programs and data to be shared by all the computers in the network. Special network versions of software programs provide users simultaneous access to programs and data. Thus only one version of a program and its associated data are needed for everyone on the network. This arrangement saves storage space on computers and makes it much easier to keep track of information, since all information is stored in one place. In addition, computer data, such as patient billing information, can be used by more than one person at a time. If the computers are not linked together in a network, only one person can access a file at a time. In a large office that manages a high volume of data, this would be highly inefficient. Similarly, at the end of the day, an extra copy of all data for safekeeping (a backup copy) can be obtained by creating a duplicate of the data on the file server, rather than on many separate machines. This procedure saves time and introduces fewer errors, since one person, usually the file server manager, is in charge of all backups.

Computers in a network are also able to share external devices such as printers. Normally, every computer has its own external devices. If the computers are connected through a network, several computers can share the same equipment. This arrangement is less expensive for the office.

The Internet. An administrative medical assistant should also be familiar with the use of the Internet as a communications tool. The **Internet** is an enormous computer network that links computers and smaller computer networks worldwide. The Internet connects literally millions of computers around the world, making it possible to exchange information in seconds. The information that is shared can be text, graphics, sound, video, even whole computer programs.

Uses of the Internet in the medical office continue to expand. At present, an assistant should be familiar with using the Internet for the electronic transmission of health insurance claims (discussed in the next section and in Chapter 8) and to obtain general information such as travel fares or medical news releases. Many e-mail programs also rely on an Internet connection.

Some medical offices also use the Internet to order medical supplies and equipment. For example, after proper identification and verification, the physician's office can order some drugs through the Internet. Often, supplies and equipment cost less when ordered through the Internet since there is no distributor in the transaction. These discounts can save the practice money over time. The assistant should stay abreast of new ways of using the Internet as a communications tool.

Wireless Communication. All networks require some type of material to send data from one computer to another. In network communications these materials are referred to as "media." Types of media currently in use include twisted-pair wire, which is made of copper, and fiber-optic cable, made of a thin strand of glass that transmits pulsating beams of light. A new kind of communication system, referred to as **wireless communication,** or wireless connectivity, uses radio waves, rather than wires or cables, as the medium for transmitting data.

In a medical office, wireless communication may be used to transmit data between different areas of a network. Cell phones also use wireless communication. With a cell phone, a physician who is away from the office can connect (log on) to the office network from a laptop computer. Because wireless communication is more portable, it is very flexible and may become the most widely used medium.

■ Billing, Collections, Claims, and Financial Reporting

Computers are used in medical offices to manage financial records. Computers were originally invented as tools for working with numbers. This makes them well suited for managing financial accounts. Computers are often used in the medical office for:

- Billing and collections.
- Electronic transmission of insurance claims.
- Financial records relating to the operation of the office, such as employee records, payroll, accounts payable, and legal financial data.

Billing and Collections. Most medical offices now use a medical billing program, such as NDCmedisoft™, the program that is used with this text, to keep track of patients' accounts. It is important for any business to keep

FIGURE 3.3

Payment information from a patient's ledger is displayed by the NDCmedisoft™ program. *What kinds of numerical errors might using a computer program help eliminate?*

Karen Larsen, M.D.
Patient Account Ledger
As of September 15, 2008

Entry	Date	POS Description	Procedure	Document	Provider	Amount
ROBERSU0		Suzanne Roberts	(312)555-2267			
		Last Payment: -50.00	On: 7/25/2008			
138	7/25/2008		PATPAY	0307250000	1	-50.00
135	7/25/2008		88150	0307250000	1	33.00
134	7/25/2008		99395	0307250000	1	136.00
137	7/25/2008		81001	0307250000	1	24.00
136	7/25/2008		85018	0307250000	1	13.00
		Patient Totals				156.00
ROGERCL0		Clarence Rogers	(312)555-5297			
		Last Payment: -100.00	On: 10/3/2008			
139	7/25/2008		99203	0307250000	1	100.00
143	7/25/2008		81000	0307250000	1	10.00
141	7/25/2008		93000	0307250000	1	70.00
142	7/25/2008		71020	0307250000	1	70.00
		Patient Totals				250.00
SHERMFL0		Florence Sherman	(312)555-1217			
		Last Payment: -8.80	On: 10/8/2008			
154	6/3/2008		99213	0306030000	1	60.00
155	6/3/2008		71020	0306030000	1	70.00
156	6/3/2008		76091	0306030000	1	80.00
157	6/3/2008		84550	0306030000	1	20.00
158	6/3/2008		85022	0306030000	1	25.00
159	6/3/2008		93000	0306030000	1	70.00
160	9/15/2008	Medicare	INSPAY	0306030000	1	-48.00

track of its funds. Accurate financial records are required for tax reporting and are critical for the practice's success. Without them, the business's owners do not know whether they will meet their financial obligations each month and whether the business is working at a profit or loss.

It is the job of the administrative medical assistant to see that every patient who comes into the office is billed appropriately and that insurance claims are submitted for patients who have health insurance. It is also the responsibility of the assistant to see that payments received from patients and insurance carriers are properly recorded. A medical billing program is designed to keep track of the constant flow of bills and payments between patients, the medical practice, and insurance companies.

Although different medical offices use various types of software to keep track of patient accounts, all medical accounting systems require certain types of information. They are designed to use **databases,** which are collections of related data, such as:

- *Patient data.* The program's patient database contains information about each patient.
- *Transaction data.* The program's transaction database contains information about each patient's visits.

Electronic Transmission of Insurance Claims. One of the most important tasks of an administrative medical assistant is the creation of health insurance claims. When a patient with health insurance visits the office, a health insurance claim must be submitted to the patient's insurance company describing the date of the visit, the diagnosis, the procedures performed, the cost of each procedure, payments made by the patient, and so on. On the basis of this information, the insurance company determines how much, if anything, the insurer owes the practice and/or the patient. A medical billing program such as NDCmedisoft™ helps the assistant generate health insurance claims and can also be used to send the claims to insurance companies electronically. Filing claims electronically costs less than mailing printed forms, and payments from insurance companies are received faster.

Financial Records Relating to the Operation of the Office. In addition to keeping track of patients' accounts, computer programs can be used to keep track of office operations. Like any business, a medical office must keep employee records, take care of paying its employees (payroll) and suppliers, and maintain financial legal files. Computer programs are available to help in the creation and management of such records.

■ Clinical Work

Clinical usage of computers in the medical office is changing rapidly. Even simple procedures, such as recording a patient's pulse, blood pressure, or weight, or conducting a simple auditory test, which used to be performed by a doctor using simple handheld instruments, are now carried out with the help of computerized equipment. The variety of computers used in the field of radiology alone is staggering, from simple x-ray machines to specialized equipment designed to improve mammography (x-rays of the breast).

Medical labs, such as pathology labs and blood labs, also rely heavily on computers. Computers are required for administering tests, extracting results, and outputting test data. Indeed, the use of electronic medical records has been a natural outgrowth of the widespread clinical use of computers in the health industry.

Physician research today also takes advantage of computers. Physicians conduct research to help with patient care, to prepare papers for lectures, and to write articles for journals. In the past, physicians conducting research would turn to medical textbooks, journals, case studies, and other materials found in a medical library. Today, much of the same material can be accessed with the help of a computer.

▶ **GO TO PROJECT 3.1 ON PAGE 74** ▶

3.2 | COMPUTER HARDWARE AND SOFTWARE

Given the role of computers in health care administration and the widespread use of computers clinically, it is easy to understand how health care is quickly becoming an electronic industry. The work environment in medical practices is increasingly computerized. For this reason, the administrative medical assistant should be familiar with the major categories of computers, good design for people's use of the equipment, and the types of computer programs.

■ Computer Categories

Many of the specifications that have usually separated one type of computer from another are becoming harder to define. The smallest computers used today have processing powers that rival the processing powers of the largest computers made less than a decade ago. The terms used to describe the major categories of computers—*supercomputer, mainframe, minicomputer,* and *personal computer*—have remained the same, but the capabilities of each group have continued to change dramatically.

Supercomputers. **Supercomputers** are the most powerful computers available. Used by scientists, they are designed to process huge amounts of data. With a supercomputer, a scientist can test equations, carry out complex studies containing hundreds of thousands of variables, or simulate processes such as nuclear chain reactions, in which the computer keeps track of the millions of actions and reactions that take place among atoms in the smallest fraction of time. Supercomputers are extremely expensive, costing many millions of dollars.

Mainframe Computers. **Mainframes** are used in large businesses, hospitals, large clinics, and government organizations. They are designed to store massive databases that many users can access at the same time. Mainframes are most often used in conjunction with computer terminals. A computer terminal is a workstation that consists of a keyboard and screen. A computer terminal does not have its own processing unit or storage, since it uses the processing unit and storage of the mainframe to which it is connected, which may be feet or miles away.

In the past, mainframes occupied entire rooms. Today, they are much smaller and may look more like large file cabinets. Mainframes currently cost anywhere from $30,000 to many millions of dollars. Although they are not always kept in air-conditioned, isolated rooms or enclosed in glass as they were in the past, they still require a climate-controlled environment.

Minicomputers. **Minicomputers** have less power than mainframes. Some minicomputers are designed for single users, but many operate with tens or even hundreds of terminals. In size and shape, minicomputers resemble a large file cabinet. They cost between $20,000 and half a million dollars. Minicomputers are popular in all kinds of businesses because they have many of the features of a mainframe but are not as big or nearly as expensive.

FIGURE 3.4

Personal digital assistants (PDAs) are used by many professionals in the health care field. *What are the advantages of using these devices?*

Personal Computers. Most computer users are more familiar with the personal computer than with any other type of computer. **Personal computers**—PCs, or, less commonly, microcomputers—come in many sizes and shapes. Those that are designed to sit on a desk are desktop computers. To save space on the desktop, some models, called "tower models," are designed so that the system unit stands vertically on the floor. Portable models that are designed to fit into a briefcase are notebook computers, or **laptops.** These portable computers have the popular feature of being able to run on plug-in current or special batteries.

Personal computers cost between $600 and $8,000, depending on their design, storage capacity, and processing power. Personal computers come in many more designs and brand names than the other types of computers. The latest design in portable PCs is the **palm computer,** or palmtop, which is small enough to be held in the palm of a hand (usually about the size of a checkbook). The technical term for a palmtop is *personal digital assistant* (PDA). Although PDAs are much less powerful than other personal computers, most have built-in cell phone, fax, and e-mail capabilities and can be connected to larger computers to exchange data. They are used for specialized applications, such as keeping track of schedules and addresses.

■ Computer Hardware Components

Computer hardware means the permanent physical components of a computer, such as the processing unit, hard drive, and monitor. Computer peripherals are optional hardware devices, such as a modem, a scanner, or an external disk drive, that are attached to the basic components of a computer to perform special functions. For computer hardware to be useful, it must have software, the instructions that tell the hardware what to do. These instructions, or computer programs, are electronic in form and are designed for many different purposes, such as word processing or accounting.

A computer's hardware components can be grouped into four categories:

- Processor
- Memory
- Input and output devices
- Storage devices

The Processor. The processor—the central processing unit **(CPU)**—is the brain of the computer. It transforms raw data into organized information. Raw data are made up of letters, numbers, and, increasingly, sounds and images. Regardless of the type of data entered into a computer, the computer changes the data into numbers (1's and 0's) for the purpose of processing. Thus data on computers are referred to as *digital,* an indication that the data have been expressed as digits, or numbers.

The size of the central processing unit varies greatly depending on the type and amount of information the computer is designed to process. For example, computers that are used for computer animation require much larger processing units than computers designed for simple word processing. Overall, the processing unit is surprisingly small relative to the other components.

Memory. A computer uses random-access memory **(RAM)** to process data. RAM is sometimes described as the computer's electronic scratchpad. Generally, the more RAM a computer has, the more speed and power it has. The identifying characteristic of RAM is that it is temporary, as short-term memory is in people. Since RAM requires a constant supply of power, everything in RAM disappears when the computer is shut down, except for work that is saved in some form of storage.

In addition to RAM, another kind of memory is permanently built into a computer. This read-only memory **(ROM)** contains the instructions that the computer needs to start running when the power is first turned on.

Input and Output Devices. The processor and memory perform the magical functions of a computer, the work done behind the scenes. However, without instructions from a user, the processor and memory by themselves are of no use. For a computer and user to communicate with each other, input and output devices are required. Input and output devices are the means with which computers and users interact: **input**

devices receive instructions and data from a user, and **output** devices send processed data back to the user.

As computers have evolved, many types of input and output devices have been used. The most common input device is the **keyboard,** which consists of a set of keys with letters, numbers, and symbols, used for entering data and instructions into the computer. A mouse, another type of input device, is a handheld device (about the size and shape of a live mouse) that controls the movement of a pointer on the screen. When the mouse is dragged along a desktop, the ball inside it rolls and the pointer on the screen moves as well. A mouse is used to point to and select items, such as text, boxes, commands, or program names. In computer graphics programs, the mouse is used to draw on the screen. Another type of input device, the trackball, performs the same functions as a mouse. The trackball is a stationary ball, however, that is rolled with the tips of the fingers. It takes up less room than a mouse, and is often designed to be attached to the side of a portable PC.

A **scanner** is also an input device. A scanner takes a picture of a printed page and copies the picture into the computer's memory, enabling the user to bypass the time-consuming process of keying text on a keyboard manually. Scanners can also copy graphics into a computer's memory. Other examples of input devices include microphones and digital cameras.

The opposite of an input device, an output device returns processed data to the user. The two most common types of output devices are the display screen, also called a **monitor,** and a **printer.** The monitor displays the results of commands, instructions, and data input on the computer's screen. This display is adequate when a user needs only to see computer output. If a user wants to save a copy of the output on paper, the printer produces a paper copy, called a "hard copy."

FIGURE 3.5

The flat-screen monitor shown here is an output device. *What other output devices are used in the medical office?*

Some hardware components perform both input and output functions. An example is a modem. **A modem allows computers to communicate through telephone or cable lines.** Modems are usually built into the computer system. The acronym *modem* comes from the term *MOdulator DEModulator.* The modem accepts data in digital format from the computer and converts it into analog signals for phone or cable transmission. When, in the future, phone lines become digital, modems will no longer be needed.

Storage Devices and Media. Just as a filing cabinet is needed to store paper documents, computer storage is used to keep copies of computer work. Storage devices can be located inside the computer or outside it. The most commonly used type of storage is the hard disk, which is permanently installed in most personal computers. This round, flat disk spins on a turntable-type storage device, called a **hard drive,** while being read or written to. The hard drive and its accompanying disk serve as the computer's main filing cabinet.

In addition to having an internal hard drive, a computer can be equipped with one or more external storage devices. These allow different media used for storage to be inserted into the computer system and then removed and kept elsewhere. External storage devices make it possible to keep backup copies of work and to exchange information with computers outside the office network.

Diskettes, small disks encased in plastic, are used for external storage on many personal computers. The diskettes are inserted into a special external disk drive on the computer. Once the computer work has been saved on it, the diskette is removed and stored in an appropriate location. Diskettes hold considerably less data than hard disks; their capacity is 1.44 megabytes.

A similar storage device is the **Zip drive,** produced by Iomega. Diskettes used for the Zip drive are similar to regular diskettes, but they hold much more data—from 100 to 250 megabytes. This popular device is often used to store large files or to create archives of files for long-term storage.

Another storage medium is the CD (compact disk), which is inserted into its own drive. Since a regular CD can hold about 450 times as much data as a diskette, it is often used by manufacturers to store computer programs. A manufacturer's CD-ROM (compact disk—read-only memory), which can be read but not recorded on, is inserted into a **CD-ROM drive,** and the program is copied onto the computer's hard drive for use. A newer type of CD, which can be used for storage (written to), is the CD-RW (compact disk—read-write). A CD-RW also requires its own drive.

Another storage medium, a DVD (digital video disk), also now comes in read-only and read-write formats. DVDs can store huge video graphics files along with audio and data, such as the kinds of files required for feature films. Computers equipped with the appropriate DVD drives can store extremely large amounts of data.

Storage media may be classified by the technology they employ. Hard disks, diskettes, and Zip disks are magnetic media. Information is stored and read magnetically. CDs and DVDs are examples of optical storage media. A third medium is used with solid-state storage devices, which are found in many types of computers, including handheld machines. Removable hard drives and tape drives are other storage devices that are sometimes used.

■ Ergonomics

Ergonomics is the science of designing the work environment to meet the needs of the human body. Ergonomics theories are finding practical application in computerized offices because of the number of injuries associated with working long hours on computers. The physical ailments that can result from long hours at a computer are known as cumulative trauma disorders or repetitive stress injuries.

Two hardware components—the keyboard and the monitor—are especially problematic. A person who spends long periods at a computer performing repetitive movements should take frequent breaks. It is also a good idea to stretch the wrists and upper body at given intervals to avoid such problems as carpal tunnel syndrome and frozen shoulders. Following are a number of ergonomic tips to help avoid the stress and strain that often result from working on a computer:

- Position the monitor at or below eye level, between 2 and 2.5 feet away, to avoid unnecessary neck strain and eyestrain.
- Use a copyholder to hold up any papers you need to refer to, and place it at eye level, a comfortable distance from your eyes (about 1.5 feet away), to avoid neck strain and eyestrain. Do not place papers flat on the desk, which forces you to keep your neck bent for long periods of time.
- Lower the height of the keyboard, if necessary, so that your hands are at the same level as your wrists. The arms should be relaxed and the forearms parallel to the floor. This is the best way to avoid injuring the wrists.

FIGURE 3.6

An ergonomic keyboard is designed to be more comfortable for the user. *Why is it important for the administrative medical assistant to pay attention to ergonomics when working?*

FIGURE 3.7

Maintaining the correct position for keyboarding reduces strain. *How can incorrect keyboarding techniques affect a computer user?*

- Hand and wrist supports are highly recommended to avoid the fatigue and stress to the hands and wrists that result from repetitive motions at the keyboard or with a mouse.
- Adjust the height and tilt of the chair so that both feet are flat on the floor and the back is properly supported. Arm rests are recommended for office chairs.
- Focus the eyes on distant objects at regular intervals to avoid the eyestrain and headaches associated with focusing on a computer monitor for long periods. This is the best way to avoid injuring the eyes.

■ Computer Software

Computer hardware, no matter how powerful, is useless without computer software. *Computer software* refers to the instructions that tell the hardware what to do. Since there are many things a computer can do, there are thousands of types of software. Before the software performs any specialized function, however, such as word processing or mapmaking, the computer's **operating system** gets the computer running and keeps it working. **Application software,** which includes word processing, graphics, spreadsheet, and database management software, applies the computer's capabilities to specific applications.

Operating System. The operating system tells the computer how to use its own components. When the computer is first turned on, the operating system runs various self-tests to check what devices are attached to the computer and whether the computer memory is functioning properly. Next, the operating system is loaded into the memory to control the basic functions of the computer, telling the computer how to interact with the user and the various input and output devices. The operating system continues to run in the background until the computer is turned off. The administrative medical assistant who uses computers regularly should know what operating system the computer uses, in case there are problems with the computer and technical help is required. It is also important for the assistant to keep up to date with new versions of the operating system and learn how to take advantage of them.

Word Processing Programs. Most computer users are familiar with word processing programs. Microsoft Word and WordPerfect are two of the most popular examples. In addition to allowing the user to enter, edit, and format text quickly and easily, a word processor can be used to create templates. A **template** is a standard version of a document that is used over and over. It is altered slightly for each new document and saves the assistant the time required to key and format each document anew. Word processors also have features for checking spelling and grammar. Spell checkers are used to verify the spelling of words in a document before proofreading. The assistant can add words, such as uncommon medical terms for a given specialty that come up often in a physician's dictation, to a customized dictionary in the computer. The spell checker will include these words each time it checks a document for spelling errors.

Graphics Applications. A **graphics application** allows the user to manipulate images. Some graphics programs, called paint or draw programs, allow the user to create illustrations from scratch electronically. Others are designed to mix and match already created images, text, video, sound, and animation.

Another type of graphics application, which is more likely to be used in a medical office, is presentation software. It can be used to create professional-looking visual aids for presentation to an audience. These aids may include photographic transparencies; paper printouts such as cover sheets, colored graphs, and charts; or computer slide shows.

Spreadsheet Programs. Spreadsheet programs are designed to imitate paper bookkeeping ledgers. An electronic spreadsheet is a grid made up of rows and columns. Each box on the grid is a cell, and each cell has an address. For example, the address for the cell at the intersection of Column D and Row 3 is D3. By keying a combination of text labels, numerical data, and mathematical formulas into the cells, the user controls which calculations are to be carried out where in the spreadsheet. The result is that any number of calculations can be carried out at great speed. Anyone in charge of creating and maintaining a budget will find a spreadsheet program indispensable.

In a medical office, spreadsheets can be used for any activity involving numbers, for example, to keep track of supplies, to prepare budgets, or for financial planning. Personnel departments often use spreadsheets to track wages and salaries paid to employees.

Database Management Software. Database management software helps the user enter data into a database and then sort the data into useful subsets of information. There are a number of database management programs that are popular for personal computers, such as dBase, Paradox, and R:BASE. Often organizations that handle specialized data require custom-made database management programs to meet their needs. NDCmedisoft™, the medical billing software that is used with this text, is an example of customized database management software. It is designed to meet the unique accounting needs of a medical practice. These include scheduling appointments, recording patient information, recording diagnoses and procedures, billing patients and filing insurance claims, and reviewing and recording payments. NDCmedisoft™ helps accomplish all these tasks.

The four categories of application software discussed—word processing, graphics, spreadsheets, and database management—are perhaps the most widely used of all computer applications. Each type of software may be purchased separately, or an integrated software package—also called an "office suite"—may be bought. An integrated package combines several application programs.

Other categories of software generally include desktop publishing software, entertainment and education software, utilities software, and communications software. Utilities software helps with the upkeep and maintenance of the computer. Communications software includes the software that is used to set up a network, for example, or the software that connects a modem to an on-line service provider such as America Online.

 GO TO PROJECT 3.2 ON PAGE 74

3.3 COMPUTER SECURITY AND PATIENT CONFIDENTIALITY

Although everyone working in a medical office must maintain the strict confidentiality of patients' medical records, proper treatment and billing often require information from these records to be released to insurance companies and other medical facilities or to other physicians. Because much of the information used in health care is stored and accessed using computers, special care must be taken to preserve the confidentiality of computerized information about patients. Following are some steps a medical office can take to safeguard computerized information.

Screen Savers. Assistants and other office workers should not leave their desks and allow a computer screen showing information about a patient to remain visible. If a worker must be away from the desk for short periods of time regularly, a screen saver can be used to protect data from being seen by others. Screen savers, which were originally used to prevent an image from being "burned" into the computer screen, are programs that display moving images on the screen if no input is received for several minutes. As soon as input resumes, the moving images disappear. Although burning is no longer a problem because of improved monitor design, screen savers, with their full array of designs, are still popular for customizing a desktop and to protect the contents of a computer screen from being seen by casual viewers.

Inspection of Audit Trails. Another security measure that is used with computerized patient data is the periodic inspection of a data entry log. The inspection is usually done by the chief compliance officer or the practice manager. Whenever new information is entered or existing data in a database are changed, the computer records the time and date of the entry as well as the name of the computer operator. This computer record creates an audit trail that can be used to trace unauthorized actions to the responsible person.

Passwords for Limited Access. The use of electronic medical records and electronic insurance claims raises questions about who should have access to such files and how the information in them can be safeguarded so that it does not end up where it does not belong. Often, the information in an electronic medical record, for example, is highly confidential,

COMPLIANCE TIP

The medical practice's data entry log should be examined on a regular basis to check for any irregularities or suspicious activity. This procedure is particularly important if the computer used for data entry is part of a network, since people outside the medical office may be able to gain access to the information and alter it.

since it contains all the details of a case, including a patient's medical history, the patient's ledger, and insurance information.

One security measure for safeguarding computerized information is the use of passwords. **Passwords** are assigned to limit the number of individuals who have access to particular computer files. In a medical office, passwords may be limited to physicians and certain authorized personnel, such as the practice manager.

Standard Release-of-Information Forms.
Electronic medical records must be kept as confidential as any other type of medical record. Therefore, a signed and dated release-of-information form must be on file before an electronic record can be transmitted. As with paper-based records, the release of information should be limited to the purpose mentioned in the request so that only the portion of the medical records specifically requested is transmitted. Similarly, any conditions about when the permission expires, such as "permission expires in 60 days," must be carefully met.

Special Safeguards for Electronic Claims Transmission.
Some states issue special regulations for safeguarding electronic claims in addition to the regular rules for protecting the privacy of patients and the confidentiality of their records. For example, most on-line systems in medical practices are required to use a password to authenticate that a person trying to access patient information is authorized to do so. This technique is similar to one used by banks to protect on-line banking transactions. The computer systems in a medical practice are set up to meet these requirements.

On-line systems may also use some form of encryption to safeguard data that is being transmitted electronically. Encryption is a method of turning data into unintelligible gibberish during transmission.

Electronic signature systems may also be used to maintain the security of transmitted data in a medical practice. Electronic signature systems, which are regulated by state authorities, are used with electronic medical records and electronic prescriptions as well as for electronic claims transmission. Similar to a password system, an electronic signature system identifies the sender and the recipient of the data being sent. It locks the document so that the document can only be opened by the intended recipient, who has the unlocking key.

The use of the Internet for transmitting claims may be less safe than using other on-line systems because of the large potential for security violations. At the same time, transmission using the Internet has advantages. One way of protecting data transmitted over the Internet is to use a firewall. A firewall is a software program developed specifically to prevent outside parties from gaining access to particular areas of an organization's computer files. Other means of protecting files that are transmitted over the Internet include the use of some combination of passwords, encryption, and electronic signatures.

Full Disclosure Policy.
It is a good practice for the medical office to display a written policy about who has access to patients' medical records,

as well as what that level of access is. Informing patients of such a policy protects the medical practice from potential lawsuits.

■ Other Safeguards

Other safeguards for protecting confidential patient information include backing up the system regularly and using special software programs to root out possible computer viruses that can damage files or an entire hard disk.

Backing Up Data. There are many unpredictable ways computer files can be lost or destroyed. A hard disk failure, power surge, or destructive computer virus can wipe out days and weeks of work. Every computer system should have a regular procedure for backing up data to safeguard against lost or corrupted files. On a network, the person in charge of managing the file server takes charge of backing up files. On stand-alone (independently operated) computers, each individual user is responsible. On a personal computer, for instance, a full backup copy of all files should be made once or twice a month. Partial backups of files that have been worked on in the course of a day should be made at the end of every day. Although backing up files this often may seem extreme, it is important to consider the potential loss. The amount of time and work at stake are often high.

Virus Checkers. A computer virus is a program written as a prank—or as a malicious act—with the intention of damaging another user's data, software, or computer. Generally, the virus is buried within a legitimate program or hidden somewhere on a disk. By running the program or using the disk, the user unknowingly activates the virus. Viruses can be programmed to do many things, such as to destroy data or to erase an entire hard disk. One way of contracting viruses is by downloading unknown programs or files on the Internet.

A virus checker is a utilities program that periodically searches a computer system for viruses. Antivirus software is designed to root out a virus before it does damage. Antivirus programs check every file on a disk and can be set up to check periodically or continuously. If they find infected files or suspicious programs, they attempt to remove them. Because so many viruses are sent through the Internet as e-mail or attached files, it is best to set up the virus checker to receive updated virus-detection information from the manufacturer's Internet site at least every other week. The virus checker automatically downloads information on new viruses that have been identified and runs the check to detect their presence on the PC.

■ Keeping Up With Office Technology

Computer technology is constantly changing. Indeed, computer hardware and software are changing at a pace few users can keep up with. Because so many of the tasks performed in a medical office are dependent on computers, it is important for all staff to try to keep abreast of changes in office technology. One way of keeping up to date is to take advantage of continuing education programs in your area. Such programs offer introductory and advanced courses in the latest computer technology and computer applications as well as in new electronic media.

It is also helpful to develop the habit of referring to user documentation. The user manuals and CD-ROMs that are packaged with new computer products have become very user-friendly over the years. Often the "getting started" instructions are all that is needed for learning to use a new program or piece of equipment in a medical office.

Finally, most computer products offer technical support, either on-line or over the phone. Although users may have to wade through a complicated menu system or click their way through many Web pages, the results are usually worth the time spent. Web sites are particularly good in offering technical support since they lend themselves to various layers of information. New files can be easily downloaded through the Internet if required. Many software producers publish "e-newsletters," information in a traditional newsletter format sent to a list of e-mail subscribers.

In addition, in large offices, technical support is often available at a central help desk. Technical personnel are usually on call to solve problems that arise with network connections or other computer equipment.

▶ GO TO PROJECT 3.3 BELOW ▶

Chapter Projects

PROJECT 3.1   Internet Research: E-mail Features

Using the Internet, research the features of an e-mail service. For example, the service may offer Send To, Copy To, Blind Copy To, Address Book, and Attachments. Be prepared to discuss your findings in class.

PROJECT 3.2   Computer Terms

On WP 6, match each computer term in Column 2 with its proper definition in Column 1. Be prepared to discuss your decisions in class.

PROJECT 3.3   Computer Technology

WP 7 contains statements that refer to computer technology in the medical office. Mark each statement with either "T" for *true* or "F" for *false*. Be prepared to give your answers in class.

CHAPTER 3 REVIEW

CHAPTER SUMMARY

1. Computers are used in the medical office in scheduling appointments; in the management of patients' medical records; in communications—word processing, e-mail, computer networks, the Internet, and wireless communication; in billing and collections, claims, and financial records; and in clinical usage, such as radiology, lab work, and physician research.

2. The different categories of computers are supercomputers, mainframes, minicomputers, and personal computers. One of the newest designs in personal computers is the palmtop. The four major components of computer hardware are the processor, or central processing unit (CPU); memory; input and output devices (such as the keyboard and printer); and storage devices (such as hard disk drives).

3. Computer software refers to the instructions that tell the hardware what to do. There are two major types of computer software: system software, including the operating system, and applications software. Applications software is usually grouped into eight categories. The first four categories, word processing programs, graphics applications, spreadsheets, and database management software, are the most well known. Other categories include desktop publishing software, entertainment and education software, utilities software, and communications software.

4. Because much of the information used in health care is stored and accessed using computers, special care must be taken to preserve the confidentiality of computerized information about patients. A medical office should take steps to safeguard computerized information: screen savers should be used to protect data from being seen by others; a practice manager should inspect data entry logs regularly for any suspicious activity; the practice may issue a written statement about who has access to what databases for the clarification of all involved; and passwords can be used to limit access to particular files. As with paper-based records, to transmit an electronic medical record, the patient's signed and dated release-of-information authorization must be on file. For the transmission of electronic insurance forms, especially over the Internet, safeguards must be in place, such as the use of passwords, encryption, electronic signature systems, and firewalls. Other ways of protecting data are to make backup files regularly and to be sure that the system is using antivirus software.

5. Keeping up with office technology can involve continuing education courses in computers, user documentation, and on-line technical support.

KEY TERMS

The following terms appear in **boldface** type in this chapter. Administrative medical assistants must know the meaning and the correct use of each of these terms. Can you recall what each term means? Refer to this chapter or to the glossary for any terms you need to review.

application software	on-line
CD-ROM drive	operating system
CPU	output
databases	palm computer
diskettes	passwords
e-mail	personal computers
file server	printer
graphics application	RAM
hard drive	ROM
input	scanner
Internet	spreadsheet programs
keyboard	supercomputers
laptops	template
mainframes	voice-recognition software
minicomputers	wireless communication
modem	word processing program
monitor	Zip drive
networking	

THINKING IT THROUGH

These questions cover the most important points in this chapter. Using your critical thinking skills, play the role of an administrative medical assistant as you answer each question. Be prepared to present your responses in class.

1. Why should an administrative medical assistant be familiar with the use of e-mail and the Internet? What are some situations in which an assistant might find them useful?

2. How would you organize your computer workstation to be more ergonomically sound?

3. Why is it useful for an assistant to know the difference between system software and application software?

4. A coworker informs you about confidential patient information she has been working on by saying, "Did you know that Sally Benson is being tested for HIV?" How should you respond?

5. Your office has just received a new piece of equipment—a laser printer that also acts as a scanner, fax, and copier. You have been asked to learn how to use it. How might you proceed?

2 Administrative Responsibilities

CHAPTER 4
Telephone Procedures and Scheduling

CHAPTER 5
Records Management

CHAPTER 6
Written Communications

Part 2 discusses the important duties of the administrative medical assistant concerning oral and written communications. It also presents the tasks involved with scheduling the physician's appointments and handling mail.

CONSIDER THIS: Communication skills are at the heart of successful relations with the medical staff, patients, and others in the physician's practice.

What steps can you take to improve your effectiveness in speaking and in writing?

CHAPTER 4

Telephone Procedures and Scheduling

OBJECTIVES

After studying this chapter, you will be able to:

1. Describe the telephone skills that an administrative medical assistant should have to properly handle incoming calls.
2. Discuss the importance of planning outgoing calls and the procedure for making them.
3. Explain the various ways an administrative medical assistant follows through on calls.
4. Discuss the major methods for scheduling appointments and the guidelines for determining in what order patients should be seen by the physician.
5. Discuss the ways in which an administrative medical assistant can help keep the office on schedule.
6. Discuss the types of appointments that may be scheduled out of the office and the patient information required for each type.

INTRODUCTION

The main channel of communication between the patient and the physician is the telephone. Almost all patients make their first contact with the physician by telephone. Urgent and emergency cases are also reported by telephone. The administrative medical assistant must learn to recognize the situation in each type of call and handle it correctly. Often, the physician is engaged with another patient's problems, and the assistant must be able to reassure the caller without interrupting the physician.

Attitudes are contagious. Patients judge the care they receive by the attitude of office personnel (reflected by the speaker's voice, tone, and choice of words in telephone situations) as well as by the actual medical service provided by the physician. The caller should be paid the same attention given a person in a face-to-face conversation.

KEY TERMS

Study these important words, which are defined in this chapter, to build your professional vocabulary:

double-booking	fixed office hours	screening calls	triage
appointments	no show	telephone etiquette	wave scheduling

4.1 TELEPHONE SKILLS

Telephone calls may be incoming, outgoing, or interoffice. Since administrative medical assistants typically handle all incoming calls to medical offices, they should use each call as an opportunity to present a positive image for the physician and the practice. An assistant must:

- Follow proper **telephone etiquette** (conduct).
- Screen calls according to the office's policy.
- Take complete and accurate messages.

■ Telephone Etiquette

When answering the telephone, try to visualize the person with whom you are talking. Think about who the caller is, what the caller is asking, how the caller feels, and whether he or she is a patient. If you do this, your voice will sound alert, interested, and concerned during the conversation.

FIGURE 4.1

When answering the phone, the administrative medical assistant presents an image of the physician and the office. *How can the assistant present a positive image to callers?*

Use a pleasant tone that conveys self-assurance to the caller along with a genuine desire to be understanding and helpful. This is what is meant by the phrase *using a "voice with a smile."*

Use variations in pitch and phrasing to avoid sounding monotonous, and never indicate impatience or annoyance through the sound of your voice. When speaking into the telephone, hold the mouthpiece about an inch from your mouth to avoid distortion or faintness of voice. Speak clearly and distinctly; do not run words together or mumble. Even if you answer the phone with the same greeting many times a day, say the words slowly enough for the caller to understand. Always speak at a moderate pace throughout the conversation, giving the caller time to think about and understand what you have said.

When concluding a conversation, say "Good-bye" and use the caller's name. This will leave the caller with a pleasant impression. Finally, replace the receiver gently when you hang up.

Promptness. Courtesy begins with promptness in answering the call. The ideal time to answer a call is on the second ring. This allows the caller a moment of preparation time to begin the conversation (the caller will expect to hear at least one ring before there is an answer).

Greeting and Identifying. There are many ways to answer the phone, but the preferred method is to answer with the name of the physician or clinic followed by the assistant's name. Answering with "Good morning" or "Good afternoon" adds a personal touch but may be inefficient in a busy office. It may be more important to take the time to say the name of the office slowly and distinctly. If the physician has a common surname, the physician's full name may be used to avoid confusion.

EXAMPLE

Assistant: Dr. Karen Larsen's office. Linda speaking.

In large clinics, the person who is operating a switchboard may answer the call by identifying the name of the clinic and asking how the call should be directed. After a call has been transferred, employees in individual departments will then identify themselves.

EXAMPLE

Assistant: Northeast Clinic. How may I direct your call?

Patient: I'd like to make an appointment with Dr. Nasser.

Assistant: I will transfer you to Sharon at the appointment desk.

Second assistant: Appointment desk. This is Sharon. How may I help you?

Following are some other tips to remember as part of proper telephone etiquette:

- Identify the nature of the call, so that it can be properly handled. For example, calls may be categorized as routine versus emergency.
- Use courteous phrases such as *please* and *thank you.*
- Listen carefully.
- Use words appropriate to the situation, but avoid using technical words.
- Offer assistance as necessary.
- Avoid unnecessarily long conversations.
- Avoid using colloquial or slang expressions such as *you know, ain't,* and *uh-huh.*
- Conclude calls properly by saying "Good-bye" and using the caller's name. If necessary, repeat information at the close of the call.

■ Screening Calls

Most incoming calls concern matters that can be handled by an administrative medical assistant guided by the preferences of the physician. Some physicians may prefer to speak to patients no matter what the circumstances. However, this routine is likely to be inefficient because it can cause interruptions to the patients who are being seen at the time by the physician. Also, medical records are probably not available for the physician's reference at the time of the call. In some offices, a nurse is available to answer patients' questions. Other offices have a policy that nonemergency calls are returned by the physician during preset hours, such as after 4 p.m.

Screening calls, or evaluating calls to decide on the appropriate action, is often a difficult problem for the beginner, who may be afraid to assume the responsibility of making decisions. It is important to discuss this aspect of the job with the physician at the very beginning and to ascertain to what extent the administrative medical assistant will handle calls alone, what information should be given out, when messages should be taken, and when to tell the patient that the physician or nurse will return the call. A call screening sheet, such as the one shown in Figure 4.2 on page 82, can be used to assist you in screening and transferring calls.

The administrative medical assistant must be guided by the physician's wishes in deciding whether to handle a call or to transfer it to the physician. The first priority is to determine the nature of the call. You will then have a good idea of how to handle the call.

FIGURE 4.2

Call Screening Sheet

CALL SCREENING SHEET

Purpose of Incoming Call	Doctor	Nurse	Message	Other
MEDICAL				
Emergency: Dr. in				Come in
Emergency: Dr. out of office				Send to ER
Seriously ill		✔		
Test results from lab			✔	
Information; advice; test results			✔	
Rx renewal			✔	
Doctor	✔			
Hospital: ER, ICU			✔	
Other				
NONMEDICAL				
Appointment				Appt. desk
Medical records				Arlene
Insurance				Tina
Billing/charges				Tina
Personnel				Gary

Message-Taking Situations. Many calls can be handled by taking a message. Examples of such calls include the following:

Transfer Nurse → An ill new patient wants to talk with the physician about treatment.

Take a Message → A patient already under treatment wants to talk with the physician.

Not allowed information → A patient's relative requests information about the patient.

Take a message → A personal friend or relative of the physician calls for the physician.

Take a message → Attorneys, financial planners, hospital personnel, and so on call about business.

Transfer 2 Nurse → A patient calls with a satisfactory or unsatisfactory progress report (for example, a patient was told at the time of an appointment to call back with how a medication or treatment is working).

Message → Lab or x-ray results are called in.

Message → Prescription refills are requested.

The following calls are usually put through to the physician:

- Calls from other physicians.
- Emergency calls, for example, calls from the intensive care unit or the emergency room of the hospital.
- Calls from patients the physician has already identified (for example, out-of-town patients, the family of a seriously ill patient calling to check on the patient's condition, or a patient in labor).
- Calls from a patient with an acute illness, such as a severe reaction to a medication.

If there is a nurse in the office, many of these calls can be routed to the nurse, who will then decide whether to interrupt the physician in an examination room.

Some examples of various screening situations follow:

EXAMPLE: CALL TO SCHEDULE AN APPOINTMENT

Assistant: Dr. Karen Larsen's office. Linda speaking.

Caller: I would like to speak to Dr. Larsen.

Assistant: Dr. Larsen is with a patient. May I help you?

Caller: Well, I need to make an appointment for next week.

Assistant: Mary, at the appointment desk, will be able to help you. Would you like me to transfer your call to her?

or

I can schedule an appointment for you. Are you a patient of Dr. Larsen's?

The assistant can then proceed to schedule an appointment for the patient.

EXAMPLE: CALL TO DISCUSS A MEDICAL QUESTION

Assistant: Dr. Larsen's office. Linda speaking.

Caller: I need to talk to Dr. Larsen.

Assistant: Dr. Larsen is with a patient. May I help you?

Caller: I'm a patient of Dr. Larsen's, and I have some questions about my medications.

Assistant: May I ask who is calling?

Caller: This is Wendy Chen.

Assistant: I will transfer you to the nurse, Ms. Chen. She should be able to help you.

or

The nurse should be able to help you with those questions, but she will need to pull your medical records. Let me take a message and ask her to return your call.

Transferring Calls. Telephone systems are provided with buttons for transferring a call to another line within the office. When calls are transferred, the phone system automatically puts the outside caller on hold. This means that the two people within the office can speak privately if necessary before one of them returns to the outside caller. For example, the administrative medical assistant can ask a question and relay the answer to the caller without having the physician or nurse speak to the patient, or else the assistant can ask the physician or nurse to pick up the call and speak with the caller directly.

Emergency Calls. An emergency call may come at any time. The person who telephones will probably be upset, and people who are excited often forget to give the most important information. It is imperative that the assistant remain calm and handle the call efficiently, reassuring the caller that help will come as quickly as possible. The importance of obtaining the name, address, and telephone number of the patient cannot be emphasized too strongly. The more information you can obtain, the better.

A physician who is in the office when an emergency call comes through will speak with the patient. However, the person answering the phone should screen the call to determine if it is urgent. Great tact and excellent judgment are needed to do this. These qualities are developed through training by the physician in what is a real emergency as the practice defines it and how to handle the calls.

Nonmedical Screening Situations. One of the most difficult situations to handle over the telephone is the person who refuses to state the purpose of the call, saying that it is a "personal call" or a "personal matter." A personal friend does not hesitate to state that fact. Similarly, a legitimate caller will give a name and state the reason for the call. The administrative medical assistant may explain that the physician will not return the call unless the nature of the call is known, if the physician has given such instructions. If the caller absolutely refuses to give information, it is permissible to suggest that a letter be written and marked "Personal" so that the physician can become acquainted with the matter and give a response. A confident, pleasant voice will help you make the physician's position clear while avoiding needless disputes.

COMPLIANCE TIP

Correctly maintaining patients' medical records requires all communications from patients, including telephone calls, to be properly documented. Correct documentation is legible, signed, and dated.

■ Taking Messages

Because most calls cannot be taken immediately by a medical staff member, the assistant must take clear messages so that the telephone calls can be returned later.

Remember the following procedures for taking efficient, informative telephone messages:

- Always have pencil and paper on hand.
- Make notes as information is being given.

- Ask politely to have important information repeated.
- Verify information such as names, spellings, numbers, and dates for accuracy. You might ask "Would you spell that prescription's name, please?" or "Let me repeat that to be sure I have noted it correctly."
- Make inquiries tactfully. A tactful question might be "Will Gary know what this is about?" or "Could I tell Sue what this is about?" or "Is this a medical matter? If so, the physician will need your medical record."

The more information you include in the message, the better. Be brief, yet thorough.

When taking a phone message, do not say "I will have the physician call you." This makes a commitment on behalf of the physician. It is better to say "I will give the message to the physician" or "I will ask the physician to call you."

After taking a message regarding a patient's care, the assistant should obtain the patient's chart. The telephone message should be attached to the chart with a paper clip and placed in the message center for the nurse or the physician. The message slip, or a transcription of it, as well as the physician's or the nurse's actions, will be permanently documented in the patient's medical record.

Message Slips. Printed telephone message slips are available from stationers for writing down messages efficiently and fully. See Figure 4.3 for an example of such a slip. Telephone message slips have blanks for noting basic information about the phone call, such as the date, time, to and from information, and the subject of the call. In some offices, the computer system is used to enter and send messages to the physician.

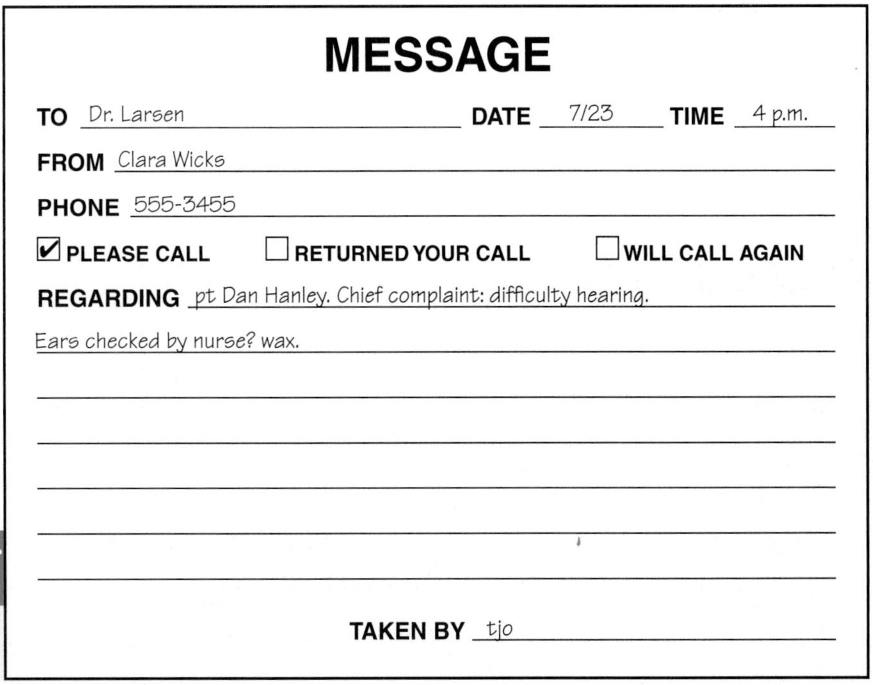

MESSAGE

TO Dr. Larsen   **DATE** 7/23   **TIME** 4 p.m.

FROM Clara Wicks

PHONE 555-3455

☑ **PLEASE CALL**   ☐ **RETURNED YOUR CALL**   ☐ **WILL CALL AGAIN**

REGARDING pt Dan Hanley. Chief complaint: difficulty hearing.

Ears checked by nurse? wax.

TAKEN BY tjo

FIGURE 4.3

Telephone Message Slip

Some physicians also design their own telephone message slips and have them printed. A message slip customized for a physician's office will list the standard symptoms related to a given physician's specialty or field of practice. When a patient calls, the administrative medical assistant can take a message by checking off symptoms on the list that pertain to the patient. Figure 4.4 shows an example of a telephone message slip customized for a physician's office.

Verifying Information. When you are taking messages, it is a good idea to repeat important details, such as the date and time of an appointment or a telephone number. Verifying information reassures both parties of the call. If you are not sure of the correct spelling of a name, say "I'm sorry. Will you spell your name again, please?" or "I want to get your name correctly. Will you please repeat that?"

Answering Services. Physicians' offices often use commercial answering services or answering machines for phone coverage when the office is closed. Commercial answering services can be hired by the physician's office to answer the office's calls from a remote location. All unanswered calls are forwarded to an operator during nonoffice hours. This operator takes messages for routine calls or contacts the physician if the call is an emergency. The physician or the administrative medical assistant checks in with the answering service for any messages after returning to the office. An answering machine connected to the office telephone line plays a prerecorded message to the caller. It tells the caller what to do when the call is urgent or routine. The message can be changed according to the circumstance. Remember that the answering machine needs to be turned off when the staff is in the office.

TELEPHONE MESSAGE

DATE	TIME	PHYSICIAN
10/8/--	1:30	Larsen

PATIENT	AGE	PHONE
Patricia Strand	18 months	555-7643
		Mother—Betty

__ Abdominal pain	__ Earache	__ Sore throat
__ Cough	__ Headache	__ Swollen glands
__ Cramps	__ Nasal congestion	✔ Temperature _100 R_
✔ Diarrhea	__ Rash	__ Urinary
__ Dizziness	__ Runny nose	✔ Vomiting

REGARDING: Patricia sick x 24 hours. Keeps some clear liquids down. Just finished 10 days of Septra DS.

tjo

FIGURE 4.4

Customized Telephone Message Slip

> **GO TO PROJECT 4.1 ON PAGE 105**

4.2 OUTGOING CALLS

In addition to answering calls, administrative medical assistants place calls for the medical practice to patients, hospitals, clinics, and laboratories, as well as to insurance companies, suppliers, banks, and other businesses.

■ Planning the Call

Plan the conversation before making a call by gathering important papers (such as the patient's medical record), obtaining necessary information, and outlining questions to ask. Know the specifics of the call before you dial. Ask yourself who, what, where, when, and why, and make appropriate notations. Be aware of the following:

- Whom to call and ask for once the phone is answered.
- What information to give or obtain.
- Questions to ask.
- When to call.
- Possible situations that might arise during the call (what-if situations).

EXAMPLE

Dr. Larsen: Linda, please call Dr. Martin and ask him to see Lucy Barlow.

To successfully complete the call requested in the example above, Linda will need to ask Dr. Larsen the following:

- What is Lucy's diagnosis (if applicable)?
- When should Lucy be seen by Dr. Martin?
- What are the contingency plans (what-ifs)? For example, what is the alternative if Lucy must be seen today but Dr. Martin is not in the office today?

Always obtain the necessary information and have it on hand before scheduling services (such as referrals, laboratory and x-ray procedures, surgery, and hospital admissions) for patients.

■ Using Resources

Numerous resources are available to the administrative medical assistant as aids in placing calls and in managing the flow of calls in a medical office.

Telephone Directories. An alphabetic directory, or white pages, lists telephone customers by name in alphabetic order. The white pages usually contain other information such as directory-assistance numbers, billing information, long-distance calling procedures, and area code maps. In large cities, information concerning government agencies, including phone numbers, is often listed in the blue pages section of the alphabetic directory.

A classified directory, or yellow pages, lists telephone subscribers under headings for types of businesses such as "Office Supplies or Laboratories—Medical." Classified directories also contain advertising for subscribing businesses and sometimes contain local street maps and ZIP Code listings.

There are also many directory services available on the Internet—for example, AOL NetFind, Switchboard.com, YellowPages.com, B2B (Business to Business) Yellow Pages, 555-1212, and many more. These directories use search engines to locate phone numbers, addresses, and e-mail addresses locally, in the United States, and in some cases, foreign countries.

A personal directory is used for phone numbers that are frequently called by the office staff. The personal directory should be kept near the phone for easy access and would probably include a list of the following phone numbers:

- Hospitals
- Insurance companies
- Laboratories
- Medical supply companies
- Pharmacies
- Hospital emergency room
- Specialists for referrals made to patients

Most phone systems are equipped with an automatic speed-dial feature that allows the user to store 20 or 30 numbers electronically. A frequently dialed number can be stored under one or two digits to save time in dialing. If speed-dial numbers are used, they can be listed in a separate column or table in the personal directory.

Other Automated Features. Desk phone systems today, such as the one shown in Figure 4.5, are designed to provide automated features such as call pickup, call forwarding, call transfer, automatic hold recall, and automatic call distribution. They can also be programmed to place a call at a set time or to notify the user when a previously dialed busy line is open. One day, automated phone systems may be used to carry out routine functions in a medical office, such as turning on the lights or the heating system at a preprogrammed time, or locking the door when the office is closed.

FIGURE 4.5

Telephone systems use computer technology to improve office efficiency. *What telephone system features are helpful in a medical office?*

■ Placing the Call

When you have the proper information and are prepared to place a call, use the following procedures:

- Identify yourself and the physician's office. If you are calling for the physician, identify the physician.
- State the reason for the call.
- Provide the necessary information.
- Ask tactfully for information.
- Listen carefully and make notes as needed.
- Verify information.
- If the person you are trying to reach is unavailable, leave a message for that person to call you back. Remember to follow the confidentiality guidelines of the office.

■ Using the Fax Machine

A facsimile (fax) machine may be used to send or receive information about patients immediately. The physician must develop and follow guidelines for faxing information about patients. A patient's confidentiality must be protected—the fax machine should be located where only authorized personnel have access to it. Federal and state laws must be followed for maintaining medical records. Generally, follow these guidelines:

- Contact the receiver before transmitting the information.
- Send a release of information with a facsimile cover letter (see the example shown in Figure 4.6 on page 90).
- File the original cover letter in the chart.
- Request a signed return receipt of the faxed information.
- Photocopy documents received on thermal fax paper before placing them in a patient's chart because thermal fax paper deteriorates over time.

FIGURE 4.6

Facsimile Cover Letter
With Return Receipt

KAREN LARSEN, MD

2235 South Ridgeway Avenue   312-555-6022

Chicago, IL 60623-2240   Fax: 312-555-0025

FACSIMILE COVER LETTER

DATE: _____ TIME: _____ a.m./p.m.

TO: _____
(name)

_____
(facility)

_____
(address)

FAX NUMBER: _____

RE: _____

FROM: _____
(name/department)

KAREN LARSEN, MD

Number of pages including cover letter: _____

NOTICE OF CONFIDENTIALITY: The faxed document or documents contain confidential information. The information is only for use by the above-named receiver. Use of the information in any form is strictly prohibited if you are not the intended receiver. Please notify our office immediately if you received this fax in error. Contact our office by telephone to arrange for the return of the original fax document.

RETURN RECEIPT: Please complete the following statement and return it to the above-stated fax number.

I, _____, verify that I have received ____ pages
Authorized Receiver

from _____.
Sending Facility

Faxing may be done using stand-alone equipment—not connected to any other machine—or through fax software on a computer. Some printers function both as printers and stand-alone fax machines. Whatever type of fax machine is used, a telephone line must be available. Most medical practices have dedicated fax lines, which means that the fax machine is connected to a separate phone line reserved only for sending and receiving faxes. With a dedicated fax line, the fax machine is available 24 hours to receive or send faxes.

■ Using Electronic Mail (E-mail)

Messages and files can be transmitted in digital form from computer to computer through an electronic mail system, commonly known as e-mail (see Chapter 3). Electronic mail saves time, conveys messages rapidly, and promotes flexibility. Users may access the system outside the office to send or receive e-mail messages and files from home or other locations. Electronic voice mail operates in the same manner, storing voice messages. It is critical to note that e-mail must be subject to the same strict privacy rules as other forms of communication. The medical office adopts guidelines to protect the confidentiality of patients' electronically transmitted medical data.

■ Following Through on Calls

Proper handling of telephone calls does not end after the phone is hung up. The administrative medical assistant must follow through on all requests made and instructions provided in the conversation. See Figures 4.7 through 4.9 (pages 91–92) for examples of follow-through methods.

FIGURE 4.7

Follow-Through Notation Made Directly on a Telephone Message Slip

MESSAGE

TO Nurse   **DATE** 10/6   **TIME** 10:20

                                     11:00 Told to come for cultures

FROM Laura Paulson   for all family members.

PHONE 555-7261   Sue, R.N.

☑ **PLEASE CALL**   ☐ **RETURNED YOUR CALL**   ☐ **WILL CALL AGAIN**

REGARDING Jason has strep. Andy + Eric now have sore throats. Should family come in for cultures?

                                TAKEN BY tjo

FIGURE 4.8

Follow-Through Memo Summarizing a Telephone Call

```
MEMO TO:   Karen Larsen, MD

FROM:      University Hospital

DATE:      September 25

SUBJECT:   Dr. Dean Ashcroft's seminars


The University Hospital telephoned at 4 p.m. today about
a series of four seminars titled "Educating Caregivers."

   1. Early Care: Prenatal
   2. Prevention of Accidents Involving Household Poisons
   3. Early Abusive Behaviors
   4. Addictive Caregivers

Dr. Ashcroft is the sponsor of the series. Please let
me know if you would like to register for any of these
seminars.

TJO
```

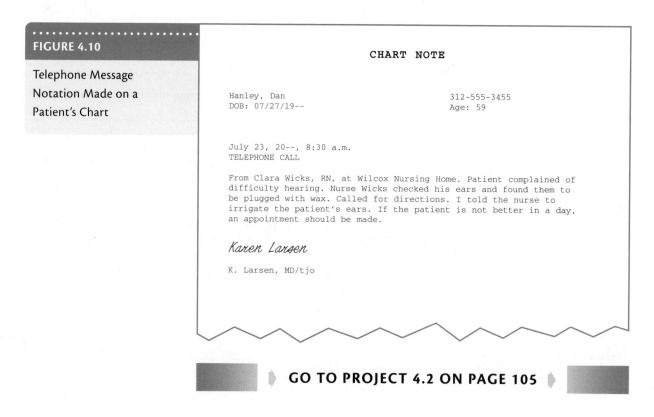

FIGURE 4.9

Follow-Through Notation on a To-Do List

TO-DO LIST

Date _____ 7/23 _____

RUSH	ITEMS TO DO	DONE
	~~Send records to Dr. Peters re: Jill Sommers.~~	7/26
	~~Reserve conference room 7/31 at 8 a.m.~~	7/26
	Remind Dr. Larsen to get slides for 7/31.	
*	Call Brent Ashwood 7/23 re: disability form at 555-7287.	

The physician may wish to have all telephone messages entered into the patient's medical record. In such cases, the message slip can be taped or filed inside the chart after it has been acted on. Some offices may have a page in the patient's record specifically for messages. In other cases, the physician may dictate a note to be entered into the patient's medical record instead of entering the actual message form (see Figure 4.10 for an example).

FIGURE 4.10

Telephone Message Notation Made on a Patient's Chart

CHART NOTE

Hanley, Dan   312-555-3455
DOB: 07/27/19--   Age: 59

July 23, 20--, 8:30 a.m.
TELEPHONE CALL

From Clara Wicks, RN, at Wilcox Nursing Home. Patient complained of
difficulty hearing. Nurse Wicks checked his ears and found them to
be plugged with wax. Called for directions. I told the nurse to
irrigate the patient's ears. If the patient is not better in a day,
an appointment should be made.

Karen Larsen

K. Larsen, MD/tjo

GO TO PROJECT 4.2 ON PAGE 105

4.3 APPOINTMENT SCHEDULES :)

Scheduling appointments is one of the principal duties of the administrative medical assistant. To be able to do so efficiently and intelligently is an important skill. Appointments must be entered into an appointment book or computer scheduling software. The assistant is responsible for collecting the necessary data for an appointment, such as the patient's name, phone number, and reason for making the appointment.

To help in juggling patients' appointment preferences with the policies of the physician and the availability of office personnel and equipment, a number of scheduling methods are used. Changes in scheduled appointments, such as cancellations, must be indicated and the time slot used for another patient whenever possible. The physician's outside appointments should be listed and, if necessary, the physician reminded of them in advance. Clear and accurate communication between the administrative medical assistant and the physician yields beneficial results for both the practice and the patients.

■ Following the Physician's Policy

The physician's policy for seeing and treating patients is the initial guideline in scheduling. Policy may be affected by the physician's office hours, specialty, how quickly the physician works, the treatment or procedure to be performed, the available office personnel and equipment, and the type of facility.

Office Hours. Before appointments can be made, the administrative medical assistant must know the basic schedule of the physician's office. The physician probably will have to make the rounds of patients at one or more hospitals on certain days and at certain hours. Office hours, therefore, may vary on different days. Some physicians have office hours in the evenings and on weekends. If there are several physicians in the practice, the hours of each physician may be different. The administrative medical assistant should be aware of each physician's hours as well as how and where each physician can be reached at other times. While office hours may differ depending on the requirements of the practice, a thorough understanding of specific policies within a practice contributes to greater efficiency.

COMPLIANCE TIP In most practices, changes that patients make to scheduled appointments, such as cancellations, are documented in the patient's medical record.

Length of Time Required for Appointments. The length of time required for different types of appointments is based on the procedure, the equipment used, and the amount of time usually spent with a patient. The assistant must be aware of the range of possibilities. A complete physical examination takes longer than a routine blood pressure checkup, for example. The physician may also specify to the assistant when certain types of procedures are best scheduled. For example, the physician may ask the assistant to schedule lengthy appointments such as complete physicals as the first appointment available in the morning or afternoon, or not to schedule them on certain days or at certain times of the day.

Other Policies, Preferences, and Obligations of the Physician. Most physicians treat patients only in their immediate field of practice. The assistant must be familiar with the types of patients the physician sees. For example, the physician might not see patients under age 16. Other preferences the physician has that affect the daily schedule may include a preferred lunch time, as well as times for meetings or appointments attended on a regular basis. A primary consideration in scheduling is allotting time for the physician's hospital rounds. Hospital visits at set hours should be noted.

Once the basic schedule of the office is set, specific guidelines are used to schedule appointments for patients.

■ Types of Scheduling

An efficient scheduling system reduces the waiting period for patients, makes the best use of the physician's time, and takes advantage of available personnel and facilities. A number of systems are commonly used.

Scheduled Appointments. Many physician's offices and clinics use a scheduling system in which each patient is given a set appointment time, that is, an approximate time the patient will be seen by the physician. This system decreases the waiting time for the patient and gives the office staff more control over the flow of patients in the office. Also, because the reason for each patient's visit is known in advance, the staff can make the best use of office facilities, equipment, and medical staff time.

Fixed Office Hours. Many clinics have **fixed office hours** during which the physician is in the office and available to see patients—from 10 a.m. to noon, for example. Patients sign in with the receptionist and are seen in the order in which they arrive. This system allows patients the freedom to come to the clinic when they wish, but it also has several drawbacks:

- The reason for the patient's visit is not known until the patient arrives at the office.

- It is difficult to control the flow of patients. Thus, many patients may arrive at the same time, causing crowding and long waits. At other times, there may be no patients, causing the physician's and the staff's time to be used inefficiently.
- Equipment and office facilities may be used inefficiently.

Wave Scheduling. One way to avoid these problems is to combine fixed office hours with scheduled appointments. This system is called **wave scheduling.** In an office using wave scheduling, the administrative medical assistant arranges for a certain number of patients (such as six) to come between 9 a.m. and 10 a.m., then arranges for the next six patients who call to arrive between 10 a.m. and 11 a.m., and so on throughout the day. Wave scheduling gives patients the flexibility of open office hours while allowing the assistant more control over the flow of patients. This method works well in practices such as dermatology and endocrinology, in which the physician often does not need laboratory and x-ray results in order to diagnose and treat the patient.

Another version of wave scheduling is to schedule a patient with a complex problem on the hour (for example, 10:00 a.m.) and to schedule short routine exams for the remainder of the hour.

Double-Booking. When the schedule is full and there are more patients who need to be seen, some offices use the method of **double-booking appointments.** The extra appointments are entered in a second column beside the regularly scheduled appointments. In some cases triple columns are used for triple-booking of appointments.

See Figure 4.11 on page 96 for examples of appointment books using these various scheduling methods.

Computer Scheduling. A variety of computer scheduling software programs are used in medical offices. Most scheduling software allows the user to search for the next available slot for the amount of time needed. For example, if the assistant must schedule a complete physical, the computer searches for the next available 1-hour appointment. After this slot has been located, the assistant can confirm that the date and time are acceptable to the patient and then enter the appropriate information to fill the slot.

In addition to a printout of the daily schedule, most scheduling software can generate reports of cancellations and no shows. A **no show** is a patient who, without notifying the physician's office, fails to show up for an appointment. Figure 4.12 on page 97 shows a screen from the scheduling program Office Hours from NDCmedisoft™ (the patient billing program used as an example in this text). Most scheduling programs can also be used to generate patient registration information as well as chart labels for patients' records.

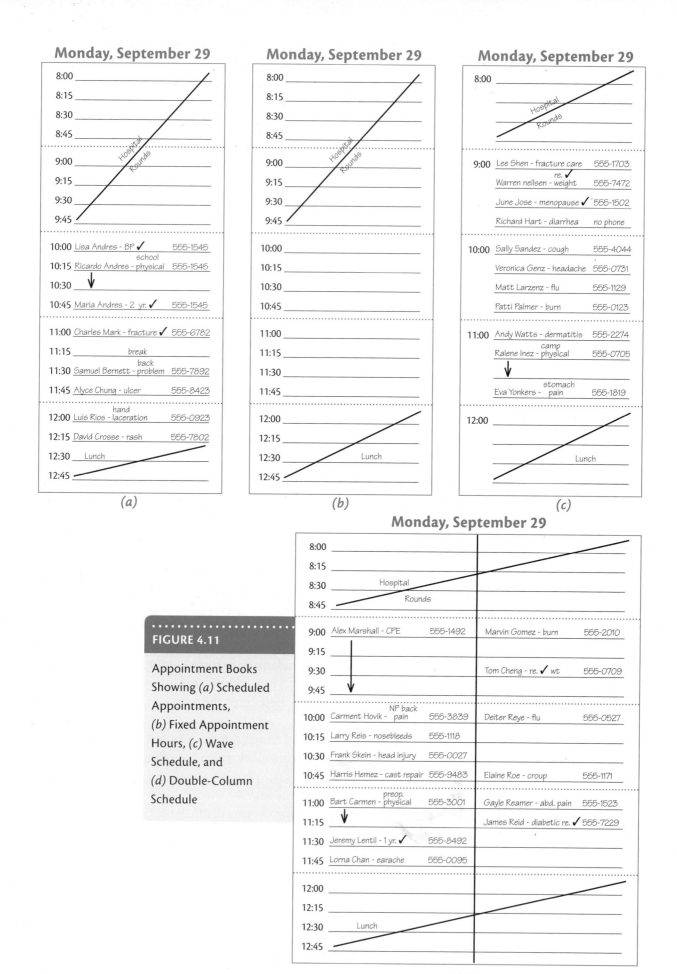

Monday, September 29 *(a)*

8:00	
8:15	
8:30	
8:45	
	Hospital Rounds
9:00	
9:15	
9:30	
9:45	
10:00	Lisa Andres - BP ✓ 555-1545
10:15	Ricardo Andres - physical *(school)* 555-1545
10:30	↓
10:45	Maria Andres - 2 yr. ✓ 555-1545
11:00	Charles Mark - fracture ✓ 555-6782
11:15	break
11:30	Samuel Bernett - *back* problem 555-7892
11:45	Alyce Chung - ulcer 555-8423
12:00	Luis Rios - *hand* laceration 555-0923
12:15	David Crosse - rash 555-7802
12:30	Lunch
12:45	

Monday, September 29 *(b)*

8:00	
8:15	
8:30	
8:45	
	Hospital Rounds
9:00	
9:15	
9:30	
9:45	
10:00	
10:15	
10:30	
10:45	
11:00	
11:15	
11:30	
11:45	
12:00	
12:15	
12:30	Lunch
12:45	

Monday, September 29 *(c)*

8:00	
	Hospital Rounds
9:00	Lee Shen - fracture care 555-1703
	re. ✓
	Warren neilsen - weight 555-7472
	June Jose - menopause ✓ 555-1502
	Richard Hart - diarrhea no phone
10:00	Sally Sandez - cough 555-4044
	Veronica Genz - headache 555-0731
	Matt Larzenz - flu 555-1129
	Patti Palmer - burn 555-0123
11:00	Andy Watts - dermatitis 555-2274
	Ralene Inez - *camp* physical 555-0705
	↓
	Eva Yonkers - *stomach* pain 555-1819
12:00	
	Lunch

FIGURE 4.11

Appointment Books Showing *(a)* Scheduled Appointments, *(b)* Fixed Appointment Hours, *(c)* Wave Schedule, and *(d)* Double-Column Schedule

Monday, September 29 *(d)*

8:00		
8:15		
8:30	Hospital	
8:45	Rounds	
9:00	Alex Marshall - CPE 555-1492	Marvin Gomez - burn 555-2010
9:15		
9:30	↓	Tom Cheng - re. ✓ wt 555-0709
9:45		
10:00	Carment Hovik - *NP back* pain 555-3839	Deiter Reye - flu 555-0527
10:15	Larry Reis - nosebleeds 555-1118	
10:30	Frank Skein - head injury 555-0027	
10:45	Harris Hemez - cast repair 555-9483	Elaine Roe - croup 555-1171
11:00	Bart Carmen - *preop.* physical 555-3001	Gayle Reamer - abd. pain 555-1523
11:15	↓	James Reid - diabetic re. ✓ 555-7229
11:30	Jeremy Lentil - 1 yr. ✓ 555-8492	
11:45	Lorna Chan - earache 555-0095	
12:00		
12:15		
12:30	Lunch	
12:45		

FIGURE 4.12

NDCmedisoft™ Office Hours
Appointment Scheduler

Office Hours - Karen Larsen MD

File   Edit   View   Lists   Reports   Tools   Help

September 15, 2008

Sun	Mon	Tue	Wed	Thu	Fri	Sat
31	1	2	3	4	5	6
7	8	9	10	11	12	13
14	15	16	17	18	19	20
21	22	23	24	25	26	27
28	29	30	1	2	3	4
5	6	7	8	9	10	11

◄ Day ►   ◄ Month ►
◄ Week ►   ◄ Year ►

Castro, Joseph

Phone: (312) 555-1020
Time: 11:15 am
Length: 15 minutes

Chart: CASTRJ00

	Column 1	Column 2
8:00a	Hospital rounds	Hospital rounds
8:15a		
8:30a		
8:45a		
9:00a		
9:15a		
9:30a		
9:45a		
10:00a	Travel time	Travel time
10:15a		
10:30a	Baab, Thomas	
10:45a		
11:00a	Casagranda, George	
11:15a	Castro, Joseph	
11:30a		
11:45a		
12:00p	Lunch	Lunch

Monday, September 15, 2008

■ Screening Patients' Illnesses

When scheduling an appointment, the administrative medical assistant must use good judgment to determine how soon a patient needs to be seen. This process is called screening, or **triage** (tree-ahj´). Some patients must come to the office *stat* (the term used in health care to mean "immediately"), some may be scheduled for later the same day or the following day, and others may be scheduled at a later time that is convenient for both the physician and the patient.

Figure 4.13 on page 98 lists the guidelines for scheduling appointments that are to be used throughout this text. Many offices have their own protocol for scheduling; thus, an administrative medical assistant on the job must adapt to that office's scheduling guidelines.

The difference between stat and today appointments depends on the severity of the condition, which is determined by the questions and answers received when talking with the caller. For example, a patient with a nosebleed that is bleeding profusely would be seen sooner than a patient who reports an occasional nosebleed. It is also always better to make an appointment sooner than to leave a critical condition until later. Patients with life-threatening conditions should be instructed to hang up and dial 911 or to go directly to an emergency room, according to office procedure.

FIGURE 4.13 Guidelines for Scheduling

The following guidelines for scheduling appointments are to be used throughout this text. Note, though, that to offer more convenient appointments to patients, many facilities have adopted SDA (same day appointments); therefore, the following breakdown is just a general guideline.

The difference between STAT and Today appointments is the severity of the condition, which is known from the questions and answers received when talking with the caller. For example, a nosebleed that is bleeding profusely would be seen sooner than an occasional nosebleed. It is also always better to make an appointment sooner than to leave a critical condition until later.

STAT and/or TODAY	TOMORROW	LATER
abdominal pain	blood in stools	elective procedures
blurry vision	cast repair	follow-ups
breathing difficulty	dermatitis symptoms	physicals
burn	flu, unless severe or in	rechecks
chest pain	a child	well checks
croup	hemorrhoids	
foreign bodies	hernia	
head injury	rash unless other symptoms	
laceration	vaginal discharge	
migraine/severe headache	vague complaints	
nausea and vomiting		
nosebleed		
pain when urinating		
possible fractures		
pregnancy with		
cramps/bleeding		

It is imperative to understand that a tomorrow appointment can change to an emergency situation with the addition of another symptom; e.g., cast repair would become a today appointment if the patient stated that there was swelling around the cast, change in the color of skin, and/or moisture drainage.

■ Considering Patients' Preferences

The trend is to offer more convenient appointments to patients. As a result, many facilities have adopted same-day appointments (SDA). Figure 4.13 provides a general guideline. Be aware that an appointment for tomorrow can change into an emergency situation with the addition of another symptom. For example, cast repair would become a today appointment if the patient stated that there was swelling around the cast, change in the color of skin, and/or moisture drainage.

Some patients prefer to be seen at a certain time or on a certain day of the week. Try to schedule appointments according to patients' preferences if the schedule allows, taking into consideration the urgency of the appointment situation. Some physicians have office hours on certain evenings, such as every other Thursday evening, or on Saturday mornings, to better accommodate their patients' work schedules.

■ Necessary Data

When patients' appointments are scheduled, all necessary data should be collected and recorded. In general, this includes some or all of the following information:

- Patient's first and last names }
- Telephone number
- Address   *stated by Patient*
- Date of birth (DOB)
- Reason for the appointment
- Patient status: new (NP), established (EP), or referred by another physician
- Referring physician
- Insurance provider
- Notations regarding any laboratory tests or x-rays required before the examination

Always verify the patient's name and its spelling and repeat telephone numbers. Confirm the appointment time by repeating it to the patient. For example, "Sara, your appointment with Dr. Larsen is for Wednesday, July 16, at 2:15." When the patient arrives in the office, the information taken when the appointment was scheduled should be verified. New patients complete patient information forms, and established patients are asked at least once a year whether any information previously given has changed.

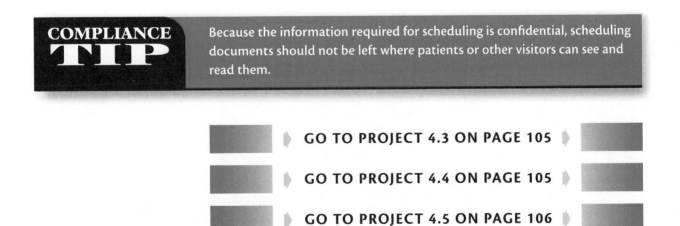

COMPLIANCE TIP Because the information required for scheduling is confidential, scheduling documents should not be left where patients or other visitors can see and read them.

GO TO PROJECT 4.3 ON PAGE 105

GO TO PROJECT 4.4 ON PAGE 105

GO TO PROJECT 4.5 ON PAGE 106

4.4   KEEPING TO THE SCHEDULE

Any number of situations arise in the course of a day that require the administrative medical assistant to cancel and reschedule appointments or to work an appointment into the existing schedule. In addition, the assistant must adjust the schedule for any emergencies that arise as well as set up next appointments for patients currently in the office who need a follow-up encounter with the physician.

■ Irregular Appointments

Occasionally a patient walks in without an appointment. If the physician is busy and it is judged that the walk-in patient should be seen at that time, you may explain that the physician will see the patient for a few minutes when the patient can be worked into the schedule.

A patient with a true emergency should be seen on arrival. The administrative medical assistant should notify the nurse or physician of the emergency and escort the patient to an available examination room. The assistant must tactfully explain the presence of walk-in and emergency patients to other waiting patients who have made appointments that will now be delayed. If a physician outside the office calls to request that a patient be seen that day by one of the physicians in your office, that patient must also be worked into or added to the day's schedule.

On days when the schedule is full, the office nurse may be used to help determine whether a patient is truly an emergency case and to ask the physician for further instructions. In some cases, the physician may request that emergency patients who telephone be referred to the emergency room. Do not refer the patient to another physician or clinic unless you are directed to do so by your physician or employer.

In addition to appointments for patients, physicians have hospital commitments, seminars, lectures, meetings, and personal appointments that may change at the last minute. All these changes must be logged into the appointment calendar to avoid schedule conflicts later on.

Late Patients. The entire schedule may be thrown out of balance because a patient is late. Patients who are late for appointments may have to be asked to wait until the physician has seen the next patient or until a treatment room is available. It is not the administrative medical assistant's place to criticize a patient for tardiness, but most physicians wish to be notified of a patient who is habitually late since it is an inconvenience to other patients. Sometimes, the patient who is late may have to be asked to reschedule.

Extended Appointments. Schedules also fall behind when either the physician or the patient loses track of the time during an examination, causing the appointment to go past the allotted period. The physician may have to be reminded if the visit runs over the scheduled time. The administrative medical assistant can use the intercom or knock on the examination room door and hand the physician a written reminder when the physician comes to the door. The physician can then decide whether or not to conclude the visit with the patient.

Out-of-Office Emergencies. The schedule may also be disrupted when the physician is called out of the office for an emergency. The administrative medical assistant should explain the situation to waiting patients and ask patients whether they wish to wait for the physician or to reschedule their appointments.

EXAMPLE

> **Assistant:** Dr. Larsen has been called out on an emergency. She is not likely to be back for at least an hour. Would you like to wait for her to return, or shall I reschedule your appointment?

As a courtesy, patients should also be informed if the physician is running late as a result of unforeseen interruptions. The administrative medical assistant might explain as follows: "Dr. Larsen is running behind schedule by about 30 minutes. Would you like to wait, or shall I reschedule your appointment?" Do not offer to reschedule if the schedule is behind by only a few minutes.

■ Registering Arrivals

Registering new patients on arrival at a physician's office or clinic is the duty of the administrative medical assistant. Patients are asked to register, or sign in, on arrival. The assistant should then verify the patient's name, address, and other information with the patient's record. If a computerized scheduling program is being used, it is all the more important to verify the spelling of each patient's name, since an exact spelling will help to locate the patient's appointment time and information quickly.

When an appointment is made for a new patient, many offices ask the patient to arrive a few minutes early to complete information forms. At this time, the practice's policy regarding payment is explained to the patient. Preparing new patient packets with information about the practice, insurance coverage accepted, payment policy, and similar items will save time in the schedule.

COMPLIANCE TIP It is important to ensure that patients' names on an office sign-in sheet remain confidential.

When the patient has signed in, the administrative medical assistant leaves the medical file for the nurse or physician's assistant, indicating that the patient is ready to be seen. If an appointment book is used, a check mark is entered to show that the patient has arrived. It is the assistant's responsibility to see that the patient's chart is in order and that all forms are completed before the patient is seen by the physician.

The registration record can be periodically checked against the appointment schedule to make sure that a patient who has arrived has not forgotten to sign in.

■ Canceling and Rescheduling Appointments

Almost every patient will cancel an appointment at one time or another; some patients make a habit of doing so. When a patient calls to cancel an appointment, a new appointment time should be suggested. A notation regarding the cancellation may also be entered into the patient's medical record (especially if the cancellation is made on the same day as, or the day before, the scheduled appointment).

If a manual schedule is kept, cancellations are noted by drawing a line through the appointment and entering a new one. In computer scheduling systems, the medical assistant must perform a number of specific steps to locate the appointment and reschedule it. As changes in the appointment book are made throughout the day, the assistant must remember also to make the changes on the workstation schedule used by the physician and nurse.

■ No Shows

The administrative medical assistant should also make a notation in the patient's medical record if the patient fails to keep an appointment and does not call to cancel. Figure 4.14 shows an example of a chart note recording a no-show appointment.

The physician will decide what action to take if a patient repeatedly makes appointments and does not keep them. Specialty practices sometimes charge patients for no-show appointments or canceled appointments when notification is not made 24 hours in advance.

FIGURE 4.14

Chart Notation for a No-Show Appointment

```
August 14, 20--
Patient failed to show for appointment. Called the
nursing home and left a message for the head nurse
to call our office.

tjo
```

■ Next Appointment

Before a patient leaves the examination room, the physician will tell the patient when to return. When the patient stops at the checkout area, the administrative medical assistant should inquire whether another appointment is needed. In many offices, the need for another appointment—often referred to as a "recall"—is noted on the encounter form or in the patient's medical record that is given to the assistant after the appointment by the physician.

In most cases, the physician will tell the patient when to return to the office for follow-up, with instructions such as "Return in 10 days" or "Return in three weeks." The assistant should schedule the patient's next appointment for a convenient time as close as possible to the suggested return date.

Never trust an appointment time to memory with the intention of entering it later, no matter how hectic the office is. Make it a habit to enter the information into the appointment book or computer immediately, and then write an appointment card, which will serve as a reminder for the patient of the next visit. See Figure 4.15 for an example of an appointment card.

Many offices use a system of follow-up telephone calls to remind a patient of an appointment for the next day. If the follow-up appointment is several months in the future, the patient may be asked to complete a postcard with the patient's address before leaving the office so the card can be sent as a reminder to the patient. If the office uses a computerized scheduling system, the computer can print reminders to be sent to patients scheduled for follow-up visits.

FIGURE 4.15

Appointment Card

Bill Fleming

YOUR APPOINTMENT IS:

July 1   AT 10:30

SPECIAL INSTRUCTIONS:

KAREN LARSEN, MD
2235 South Ridgeway Avenue
Chicago, IL 60623-2240
312-555-6022

PLEASE CALL IF YOU CANNOT KEEP THIS APPOINTMENT.

■ Open Slots for Catching Up

No matter how carefully appointments are scheduled, crowding is sometimes unavoidable and appointments fall behind schedule. Leaving a 15- or 20-minute interval free in the late morning and again in the middle of the afternoon each day will help you to straighten out a delayed schedule. If no delays occur, these open slots can be used to catch up with other work. Open slots also allow time for emergency patients and unscheduled patients.

▶ **GO TO PROJECT 4.6 ON PAGE 107** ▶

4.5 OUT-OF-OFFICE APPOINTMENTS

Appointments that may be scheduled outside the office include hospital admissions, surgery, and diagnostic or other special procedures. Follow basic scheduling procedures for such appointments, obtaining the necessary patient data required for each type of appointment.

Hospital Admissions. The following information is needed for hospital admissions:

- Complete name of patient.
- Patient's information: age, DOB, address, and telephone number.
- Diagnosis or problem.
- Preferred date of admission.
- Accommodations preferred.
- Previous admissions.

Surgical and Diagnostic Procedures. For surgery or for diagnostic or other special procedures, information to be noted should include:

- Surgery or other procedure to be performed.
- Length of time needed for surgery (if known).
- Approximate date and time desired.
- Specific surgical assistants required.
- Type of anesthesia to be used and person administering it.
- Special requirements, such as diagnostic testing that may be required before the patient undergoes the procedure.

Other considerations for scheduling include:

- Scheduling the appropriate time required by the physician in each situation.
- Giving patients clear and simple instructions for hospital admission.
- Informing patients about any preparations that are required before undergoing a surgical or diagnostic procedure (for example, informing them that they are to have nothing to eat or drink after midnight of the night prior to the procedure).
- Confirming that any special assistants and/or anesthesiologists that have been requested are available.

GO TO PROJECT 4.7 ON PAGE 107

Chapter Projects

PROJECT 4.1 Taking Messages

Today's date is October 13, and Dr. Larsen is not available for telephone calls. Using WP 8–15, take complete messages for the following situations:

- Andrew Kramer at 312-555-1913 calls at 9:30 a.m., stating that his 8-year-old son Jeffrey, a patient of Dr. Larsen's, has been complaining about a sore throat and an earache for two days. They are unable to come to the office for an appointment today. Jeffrey has no fever, is on no medications, and has no allergies. Is there any over-the-counter medication they can use until they can make an appointment?
- Sara Babcock, an established patient, calls at 9:45 a.m. Her telephone number is 312-555-5441. She would like to have her Ortho Tri-cyclen® birth control medication refilled at Consumer Pharmacy (312-555-1252). It was last filled one year ago.
- At 9:50 a.m., Wanda Norberg, MD, calls to set up an appointment with Dr. Larsen. Dr. Larsen has hired Dr. Norberg to work part-time starting in January. She can be reached after 5:30 p.m. at 312-555-1322.

Put the remaining message slips in your supplies folder.

PROJECT 4.2 Internet Research: ZIP Codes

Using your favorite search engine, search for the keyword *ZIP Code.* Visit the Web site and store the address as a reference under the Favorite option or Bookmark.

PROJECT 4.3 Scheduling Decision Making

Using WP 16, choose the appropriate answer for each situation. Be prepared to discuss your answers in class.

PROJECT 4.4 Setting Up Dr. Larsen's Practice

This icon precedes certain projects and simulations throughout this textbook. The icon indicates that all or part of a task can be done in NDCmedisoft™ using the Student Data Disk you received with this package. Make sure to read Appendix A (pages 303–329) before you begin using NDCmedisoft™. (Note: Remember, not every part of every project can be done in NDCmedisoft™. Follow the instructions below.)

Dr. Larsen's practice is already set up and stored on a backup file on the Student Data Disk. Appendix A provides instructions on restoring the backup file from the Student Data Disk to your computer. After the backup file is restored, click the Appointment Book option on the Activities menu to open Office Hours, and enter October 13, 2008, as the date. Then enter the following appointments using the Break Entry shortcut botton:

- October 16, 2008, from 5 to 6 p.m., University Meeting
- October 23, 2008, from 5 to 6 p.m., Dinner Meeting
- October 28, 2008, from 7 to 8 p.m., Lecture

Enter the appropriate information in the Name and Length boxes, and click the Save button. Print Dr. Larsen's scheule for all three days (October 16, 23, and 28).

This icon accompanies instructions for completing the project *without the use of NDCmedisoft*™.

Information about Dr. Larsen's appointment schedule is found on WP 17. WPs 18–33 are Dr. Larsen's appointment calendar pages.

You will use WPs 17–33 throughout most of the course, entering, canceling, and rescheduling patients' appointments, as well as Dr. Larsen's other appointments. Remove these pages, and secure them in your appointment calendar. Place WP 17 as the first page of the binder or folder you will use for your appointment calendar.

Today's date is October 10. Check the calendar for the week of October 13, noting that Dr. Larsen is attending an all-day seminar at the University on October 13. Some appointments have been preset on your calendar.

Enter Dr. Larsen's following commitments on the appropriate pages:

- October 16, University Hospital Accreditation Meeting from 4 to 6 p.m., Whitman Hall, Rosewood Room.
- October 23, 5 p.m., University Hospital Dining Room, dinner meeting with Wanda Norberg, MD.
- October 28, 7 p.m., lecture on resident requirements, Dr. Margo Matthews at University Hospital, Whitman Hall, Room 203.

PROJECT 4.5   **Scheduling Appointments**

Today's date is October 10, 2008. Using Office Hours, enter the appointments listed below on Dr. Larsen's schedule and then print out the schedule for each day (October 14–15 and 20–22). Appointments are 15 minutes long unless other noted. Complete the Chart and Length fields only. (Note: For new patients, leave the Chart field blank and fill in the Name and Phone fields.)

Today's date is October 10. On your appointment calendar, enter the appointments listed below. Dr. Larsen's policy is to enter the first and last name of the patient, the reason for the visit, and the telephone number. The amount of time needed for the appointment (15 minutes, unless otherwise noted) is blocked out with arrows.

Appointments:

- October 14, 10:30 a.m., David Kramer, new patient, kindergarten physical, 312-555-8153, mother Erin Mitchell.
- October 14, 10:45 a.m., Erin Mitchell, new patient, backache, 312-555-8153.
- October 14, 11:00 a.m., Gary Robertson, established patient, urinary problems, 312-555-9565.
- October 14, 11:15 a.m., Laura Lund, established patient, cramps, 312-555-4106.
- October 14, 11:45 a.m., Charles Jonathan III, established patient, knee pain, 312-555-3097.
- October 15, 10:30 a.m., Ardis Matthews, established patient, nausea, 312-555-3178.
- October 20, 10:30 a.m., Thomas Baab, established patient, CPE (1 hour), 312-555-3478.
- October 20, 11:45 a.m., Doris Casagranda, established patient, rash, 312-555-1200.
- October 21, 11:00 a.m., Sara Babcock, established patient, CPE (1 hour), 312-555-5441.
- October 22, 11:15 a.m., Ana Mendez, established patient, neck pain, 312-555-3606.

PROJECT 4.6   Rescheduling Appointments

Today's date is October 13. Reschedule each of the following patients according to the instructions given below.

Using Office Hours, cancel and reschedule the appointments listed below. Then print out the new schedules.

Dr. Larsen's policy is to draw a single line through canceled appointments. Reschedule the appointments listed below.

Appointments:

- Thomas Baab telephones to ask if he could cancel his appointment on October 20 at 10:30 a.m. and reschedule it for this week, same time, Wednesday. You inform him that 11:00 a.m. on Wednesday, the 15th, is available. He agrees to that time. Make the appropriate changes.
- Charles Jonathan III stops in to change his October 14 appointment. You reschedule him for October 21 at 10:45 a.m. Complete an appointment card using the form on WP 34. Make the appropriate changes. Place the unused appointment cards in your Supplies folder.

PROJECT 4.7   Out-of-Office Scheduling

Using WP 35, choose the appropriate answer for each situation. Be prepared to discuss your answers in class.

CHAPTER SUMMARY

1. An administrative medical assistant should take advantage of answering the practice's incoming calls to present a positive image for the physician and the practice. An assistant should follow proper telephone etiquette, screen calls according to the office's policy, and always take full and accurate messages.

2. The assistant should plan outgoing calls by noting who, what, where, when, and why before placing the call. A variety of telephone directories are available for locating telephone numbers for patients and businesses. At the end of a call, the medical assistant should always verify important information.

3. The administrative medical assistant can follow through on telephone calls by making a notation directly on the telephone message slip, on a to-do list, or on a medical work sheet or by summarizing the phone call in a memo. All requests made over the phone need to be attended to and the information received must be recorded, acted on, and then filed. Most physicians request that telephone messages be entered into the patient's medical record.

4. Every medical office has its own policy for scheduling appointments. A number of scheduling systems are used, including scheduled appointments, fixed office hours, wave scheduling, double-booking, and computer scheduling. Triage, or screening, is the process of determining how soon a patient needs to be seen by the physician. The assistant must obtain basic data when scheduling an appointment, such as the patient's name, phone, insurance, and reason for making the appointment.

5. Irregular appointments include walk-in patients, emergency patients, work-ins (patients sent by other doctors), and late patients. The administrative medical assistant must reschedule appointments as necessary and explain any delays to patients in a tactful way. Leaving open time slots in the schedule will help to straighten out a delayed schedule.

6. Appointments that are scheduled outside the office include hospital admissions, surgery, and diagnostic procedures. The administrative medical assistant should follow basic scheduling procedures, obtaining the patient data required for each type of appointment and explaining other information to the patient as necessary.

KEY TERMS

The following terms appear in **boldface** type in this chapter. Administrative medical assistants must know the meaning and the correct use of each of these terms. Can you recall what each term means? Refer to this chapter or to the glossary for any terms you need to review.

double-booking appointments   telephone etiquette
fixed office hours   triage
no show   wave scheduling
screening calls

THINKING IT THROUGH

These questions cover the most important points in this chapter. Using critical thinking skills, play the role of an administrative medical assistant as you answer each question. Be prepared to present responses in class.

1. What type of image should an assistant present for the physician and the practice while answering the practice's incoming calls? What are some examples of the proper telephone etiquette an assistant should demonstrate as part of this image?

2. The physician you work for has just asked you to call about the results of a patient's blood work. The blood work was sent to an outside lab, and the results should have arrived by now. What preparations should you make before placing the call? What situations might arise during the call that you need to plan for?

3. You receive a call from an assistant at Dr. Janis's office about a referral from your office. The referral is scheduled for today, but Dr. Janis cannot locate the referral letter sent by your office. How can e-mail help in this situation?

4. Raymond Slozak, a patient of Dr. Duffy, calls to make an appointment on the following Tuesday at 3:00 p.m. for his yearly physical. You check the schedule and find that the physician has a personal appointment at that time. What should you say to the patient?

5. A patient calls at 11:15 a.m. on a Tuesday morning to say that she has slipped on the ice while going out to get her mail and may have fractured her wrist. There is a good deal of pain and swelling. Her son is available to drive her to the office. You check today's schedule and find that it is full. What is the best way to respond to the patient?

6. A patient is being admitted to the hospital for tests. What information should be obtained for the hospital admission?

CHAPTER 5

Records Management

OBJECTIVES

After studying this chapter, you will be able to:

1. Discuss the importance of maintaining accurate medical records.
2. List the steps in filing a document.
3. Compare alphabetic, numeric, and subject filing systems.
4. Describe two advantages and two disadvantages of the alphabetic filing system.
5. List five suggestions for locating a missing file.
6. Discuss the purpose of a retention plan.

INTRODUCTION

Accurate and efficient records management is essential in medical offices. Accurate medical records comply with federal and state regulations and help protect physicians from potential lawsuits. Records, however, are useful only if they can be located when needed, so efficient filing of records is equally important.

KEY TERMS

Study these important words, which are defined in this chapter, to build your professional vocabulary:

accession book	cross-reference	inspecting	out guide	sorting
active files	sheet	documents	patient medical	storing
AHIMA	cuts	labels	record	subject filing
alphabetic filing	dead storage	lateral files	records	tabs
ARMA	folders	micrographics	management	tickler file
closed files	guides	mobile-aisle files	releasing	vertical files
coding	inactive files	numeric filing	retention	
color-coding	indexing	open-shelf files	rotary circular file	

ARMA International
13725 W. 109th Street
Suite 101
Lenexa, KS 66215
Phone: 913-341-3808 or
800-422-2762
Web site: www.arma.org
E-mail: hq@arma.org

Records management is the systematic control of records from their creation through maintenance to eventual storage or destruction. To handle these tasks, administrative medical assistants have a source of helpful information in the Association of Records Managers and Administrators **(ARMA).** This international organization's members include information managers, archivists (those who specialize in control of records storage), librarians, and educators. One of the major purposes of the organization is to set standards for filing and retention of records. Although ARMA standards are voluntary, rather than set by the government, following them makes it possible for medical offices to manage records more efficiently.

Recorded information in any form—whether in a computer file, in a paper document, or stored on disks or tapes—is considered a record. In medical offices, the three main types of records are (1) patient medical records, (2) correspondence related to health care, and (3) practice management records.

1. *Patient medical records:* The central responsibility of the physician's practice is patient care. For this reason, the proper handling of the **patient medical record** is critical. This record, also known as the patient "file" or "chart," contains chart notes, all medical and laboratory reports, and all correspondence about a patient.

2. *Correspondence related to health care:* General correspondence includes items about the operation of the office, such as orders for medical supplies. It also includes physicians' research reports; articles from medical journals related to new procedures or treatments; and correspondence, newsletters, and announcements from professional organizations.

3. *Practice management records:* Materials about the business and financial management of the practice must also be carefully kept. These documents include insurance policies, income and expense records, copies of tax returns for the practice, financial statements, and leases or contracts related to office space or the premises. Also kept are copies of managed care contracts and the office's compliance program and privacy policy. Personnel and payroll records are also part of practice management.

The two broad categories of files are centralized files and decentralized files. Centralized files—those kept in one place—must be used by many people in the medical office. Thus, ease of access is necessary. Information of use to only one staff member, such as a physician's correspondence, is stored in a decentralized file convenient to the user. The kinds of filing equipment and supplies that best suit a medical office depend on how records are used and who needs to use them.

■ Filing Equipment

Open-Shelf Files

Open-shelf files are bookcase-type shelves that hold files. These shelves may be adjustable or fixed and may extend from floor to ceiling. Folders are placed in the files sideways with identifying tabs protruding, as shown in Figure 5.1.

The need to conserve space in many offices has made open-shelf files popular. They take up less floor and aisle space and are also less expensive to purchase than most other kinds of filing equipment. Because staff members do not need to open drawers, these files also save time and labor. However, open shelves do mean that records are less secure than if they were held in closed steel drawers. The records are also more vulnerable to accidents, including fire and water damage.

FIGURE 5.1

The medical assistant must understand the ways in which the office files are used, the organization of the files, and the principles and procedures for accurate filing. *How can an assistant get help in learning the filing procedures of a specific medical office?*

Filing Cabinets

There are many kinds of filing cabinets available. The best choice for a particular office will be based on available space, cost, and the level of security that is desirable.

Rotary Circular File. Index cards containing the names, addresses, and phone numbers of patients, businesses, medical personnel, and other necessary information may be kept in a **rotary circular file.** The rotary circular file—a small desktop file that is designed to rotate and permits the use of both sides of each index card—is the simplest storage system (Figure 5.2). These space-saving files may be conveniently placed so that they are accessible when the user needs to telephone or address a letter or envelope. The most famous trade name of rotary circular files is Rolodex®.

Vertical Files. Drawer files, called **vertical files,** are contained in cabinets of various sizes. These letter-size cabinets, meant for documents that are 8½ by 11 inches, are usually metal. They vary in capacity from one to five drawers; files are arranged from front to back in each drawer. Vertical

FIGURE 5.4

Drawers open horizontally in lateral file cabinets to provide easy access to files. *How important is it for the medical assistant to have easy access to files?*

files, shown in Figure 5.3, are popular because they provide a large amount of filing space. Vertical files can be moved fairly easily compared to open-shelf files. However, because these cabinets have drawers that must be opened and closed, using vertical files takes more of an assistant's time in filing and retrieving records. The space required to open the drawers is also a consideration in planning efficient use of storage space and aisle space.

Lateral Files. In **lateral files** the drawers or shelves open horizontally and files are arranged sideways, from left to right, instead of from front to back. Lateral files, as shown in Figure 5.4, may have standard drawers. They may have, instead of drawers, doors that are rolled down from the top of the shelf and retract when the shelf is being used. Lateral files do not project as far into an aisle as vertical files. Thus, if space is a major consideration, lateral files may be a good choice.

Mobile-Aisle Files. The **mobile-aisle files** contain open-shelf files that are moved manually or, more often, by a motor. The platform upon which shelves are mounted may be specially constructed, or the tracks and mechanism may be on the floor. When these files are motorized, the person using the files may access a file quickly and easily. Mobile-aisle filing systems, shown in Figure 5.5 on page 115, also hold a large volume of records. Because this system holds so many records and because the system is mechanized, safety features and the amount of weight the files will safely hold are important factors in the decision to install this system.

■ Filing Supplies

Folders, labels, tabs, and guides are all designed to make the location of and access to files efficient. The important considerations in choosing filing supplies are durability of material and the uses of color and positioning within a file to make the user's task easier.

Folders. File **folders,** which may be open on one, two, or three sides, hold the items that are filed. Folders may be purchased in various colors, styles,

FIGURE 5.5

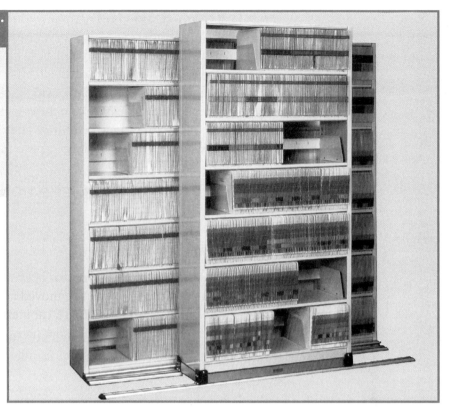

weights, and tab cuts. **Tabs** are the projections that extend beyond the rest of the folder so that the folder can be labeled and easily viewed. "Tab **cuts**" refers to the position of the tab. For example, the first cut creates a tab at the left; a center cut, at the center. Folders are filed in such a way that tab cuts with the accompanying labels are read in an orderly fashion from left to right.

Labels. Oblong pieces of paper, frequently self-adhesive, are called **labels.** Once the person establishing the file has keyed in a descriptive title or subject on the label, it is used to identify a file. (Handwritten labels are to be avoided, as they are hard to read.) Labels are available in perforated rolls or on self-adhesive strips. Many assistants now use a computer and printer to key in file titles and print out the required labels. Labels with a color band on top for ease of identification are also available.

Guides. **Guides** are rigid dividers placed at the end of a section of files to indicate where a new section or category of files begins. Because guides are made of rigid material, they support folders and are visual clues to the user of the file, showing exactly where in the file drawer new main subjects begin.

Out Guides. An **out guide** is a card placed as a substitute for a file folder that serves to indicate that a folder has been removed from the file. The front of the out guide has lines to record the name of the person who is taking the file, the date the file was removed, and the material contained in the file. When the file is returned, these annotations are crossed out and the out guide may be reused. Out guides are particularly useful when there are many users of a particular set of files. Everyone always knows where a particular file may be found.

Cross-Reference Sheets. Frequently, there are documents that can be coded and filed under more than one heading. For example, a letter from the physician's insurance company verifying coverage may be placed in the physician's correspondence file. It may also belong with insurance policies kept in a different file. In cases such as this, a **cross-reference sheet** is prepared to indicate where the original material is filed and where in the files other copies may be found. The cross-reference sheet may be in a different color from the file folders to make identification simpler.

▶ **GO TO PROJECT 5.1 ON PAGE 129** ▶

5.2 | STEPS IN FILING

Following logical, consistent, systematic steps in preparing materials for filing enables the assistant to file accurately, to find materials quickly, and to refile documents efficiently.

The steps in filing are:

- Inspecting documents
- Indexing
- Coding
- Sorting
- Storing

■ Inspecting Documents

The assistant is responsible for **inspecting documents** received for filing. Each document should be in good physical condition, and the information should be complete. For example, if an attachment is indicated, it should be present. If the document says that an action should be taken—for example, that a form letter should be sent to an insurance company—the item relating to the action should be present or there should be an indication, like a check mark, that the action was taken. The document must also bear a release mark. **Releasing** is the indication, by initial or by some other agreed-upon mark, that the document has been inspected and acted upon and is ready for filing. Note that a release mark is different from a time-date stamp.

■ Indexing

Once the document has been released, it is ready to be indexed. **Indexing** is the mental process of selecting the name, title, or classification under which an item will be filed and arranging the units of the title or name in the proper order. For example, information about a patient named *José Gomez* would be filed under *G* for *Gomez*. Selecting the proper classification for an item is critical to finding the document when it is needed.

■ Coding

Coding is the placing of a number, letter, or underscore beneath a word to indicate where the document should be filed. For example, in the correspondence of José Gomez, the name *Gomez* would be underscored or coded in some way. Or the code might be written on the document, usually in the upper right-hand corner.

If the document should be coded and filed under more than one title or heading, cross-referencing the document is required. Cross-referencing is the indication, made on a cross-reference sheet or card, of other files where a copy of the document may be found. The cross-reference sheet is filed under the cross-reference location. For example, a cross-reference sheet for *José Gomez* might be found under "José."

■ Sorting

The assistant working with a number of items prepares them for the file by **sorting** them, or arranging them in the order in which they will be filed. Before they can be sorted, documents must be indexed and coded. When the assistant is indexing the item, the code should also be chosen.

■ Storing

Storing, or filing, is the actual placement of an item in its correct place in the file. When the item is placed in the folder, the top of the item should be to the left. Documents are placed in the folder with the most current document on top. The folder is then placed in the file cabinet with the tab side to the rear of the file.

■ Follow-Up Procedures

Many items that have been stored may require some further action to be taken. For example, even though the correspondence relating to José Gomez has been filed, Mr. Gomez may require a reminder to return for his annual checkup.

The special file used for follow-up actions is called a **tickler file.** A useful tickler file needs to be consulted daily by the assistant. An arrangement of index cards by months of the year and, within each month, by days of the month is practical. Notations of actions to be taken are placed on cards behind specific dates of the month. At the end of the

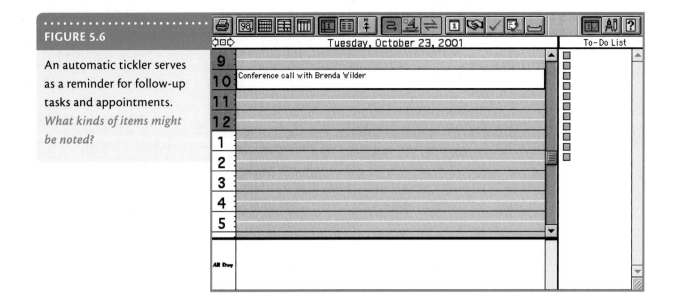

FIGURE 5.6

An automatic tickler serves as a reminder for follow-up tasks and appointments. *What kinds of items might be noted?*

current month, new cards are placed behind each date of the next month. There are also electronic monthly calendars available in most software application suites, as shown in Figure 5.6. If actions to be taken are entered on specific dates of the electronic calendar, the software will provide an automatic tickler—a message on the screen—on the appropriate date. The assistant may find this system more efficient and easier to use.

Another way to be reminded of a follow-up action is to use a colored index tab clipped to a patient's record. The colored tab indicates that some kind of action is required. Different colors may be assigned to stand for different kinds of actions.

▷ **GO TO PROJECT 5.2 ON PAGE 129** ▷

5.3 FILING SYSTEMS

Effective records management requires records to be filed in the way they will be accessed. Several filing systems are used. Most offices actually use more than one filing system to organize their different types of information. The major filing systems are alphabetic, numeric, and subject. Each system has features that are advantages, as well as certain disadvantages.

FIGURE 5.7

Alphabetized Patient List in
NDCmedisoft™

Karen Larsen, M.D.
Patient List
9/15/2008

Chart	Name	CityLine	Phone
ARMSTM00	Monica Armstrong	Chicago, IL 60644-5519	(312)555-4413
BAABTH00	Thomas Baab	Chicago, IL 60625-1220	(312)555-3478
BABCOSA0	Sara Babcock	Chicago, IL 60644-4455	(312)555-5441
BURTOPA0	Paul Burton	Chicago, IL 60641-6730	(312)555-7292
BURTOPA1	Randy Burton	Chicago, IL 60641-6730	(312)555-7292
CASAGHE0	George Casagranda	Chicago, IL 60632-1406	(312)555-1200
CASAGHE1	Doris Casagranda	Chicago, IL 60632-1406	(312)555-1200
CASTRJO0	Joseph Castro	Chicago, IL 60634-3727	(312)555-1020
DAYTOTH0	Theresa Dayton	Chicago, IL 60610-2816	(312)555-2231
GRANTTO0	Todd Grant	Chicago, IL 60660-3299	(312)555-9825
JONATCH0	Charles Jonathan III	Chicago, IL 60638-3391	(312)555-3097
KRAMEAN0	Andrew Kramer	Chicago, IL 60640-5607	(312)555-1913
KRAMEAN1	Jeffrey Kramer	Chicago, IL 60640-5607	(312)555-1913
LUNDLAW0	Lawrence Lund	Chicago, IL 60633-2010	(321)555-4106
LUNDLAW1	Laura Lund	Chicago, IL 60633-2010	(321)555-4106
MATTHEA0	Earl Matthews	Chicago, IL 60624-8966	(312)551-2349
MATTHEA1	Ardis Matthews	Chicago, IL 60624-8966	(312)551-2349
MENDEAN0	Ana Mendez	Chicago, IL 60629-4270	(312)555-3606
MITCHAL0	Alan Mitchell	Chicago, IL 60651-2248	(312)555-8153
MITCHAL3	Donald Mitchell	Chicago, IL 60651-2248	(312)555-8153
MORTOES0	Esther Morton	Chicago, IL 60621-2314	(312)555-2324
MORTOES1	Sarah Morton	Chicago, IL 60621-2314	(312)555-2324
MURRARA0	Raymond Murray	Chicago, IL 60634-3276	(312)555-6343
PHANTAM0	Tam Phan	Chicago, IL 60620-8129	(312)555-3344

■ Alphabetic Filing

The most popular filing system is **alphabetic filing,** the arrangement of
names, titles, or classifications in alphabetic order. This system is popular because it is based on the familiar letters of the alphabet. It provides
a direct reference—if the name is known, the record can be located. An
alphabetic system enables a user to find a misfiled paper document easily and has low setup and maintenance costs. It is commonly used by word
processing software to organize lists of files. Most programs include a sort
feature that automatically alphabetizes a list of entries (Figure 5.7).

There are, however, several disadvantages to alphabetic filing. Because
the system is so simple and so easily recognizable, there is much less confidentiality. File labels may be easily seen and read; computer files can be
quickly searched. It is also possible that similar names will be confused
or that a letter will be transposed and the document misfiled. A typing
error can cause a patient's information to be filed incorrectly. An alphabetic system for paper records offers limited filing space and makes
expanding the system difficult when folders labeled alphabetically are full.

The assistant must thoroughly understand the basic rules for alpha-
betizing and indexing in order to accurately manage records. ARMA's general rules for alphabetic filing, which are the standard for medical offices,
are described here.

General Filing Rules

a. Each filing segment is considered a unit.
b. Alphabetize units by comparing letter-by-letter within that unit.
c. Ignore all punctuation marks.
d. File "nothing before something." In a letter-by-letter comparison of two terms, if one term has nothing and the other item has an "a," the term with nothing is put first.
e. Arabic and roman numerals are filed sequentially before alphabetic files, with Arabic numerals coming before roman numerals.

Rule 1. Index individual names in the following order: surname (last name), given name (first name), and then middle name or initial.

Names	Indexing Order		
	1	2	3
Wade R. Benje	Benje	Wade	R
Wayne Benje	Benje	Wayne	
Wayne M. Benje	Benje	Wayne	M

Rule 2. Prefixes are considered part of the surname, not separate units. Some prefixes include *Aba, Abd, a la, D', Da, De, Del, De la, Den, Des, Di, Dos, Du, El, Fitz, ibn, La, Las, Le, Lo, Los, M, Mac, Mc, O', Saint, San, Santa, Santo, St., Te, Ten, Ter, Van, Van de, Van der, Von,* and *Von der.*

Names	Indexing Order		
	1	2	3
Lorne Fitzgerald	Fitzgerald	Lorne	
Esther Ann O'Reilly	Oreilly	Esther	Ann
David R. Van de Wan	Vandewan	David	R

Rule 3. Index hyphenated names as one unit.

Names	Indexing Order	
	1	2
Karen Ames-Battle	Amesbattle	Karen
Ann-Marie Lesa	Lesa	Annmarie

Rule 4. Abbreviated and shortened forms of personal names are not spelled out. Use the abbreviation or shortened form. Make sure the patient states his or her legal name.

Names	Indexing Order		
	1	2	3
Bill J. Wicks	Wicks	Bill	J
Geo. Lester Wilson	Wilson	Geo	Lester

Rule 5. Professional or personal titles *(Dr., Mr., Mrs., Ms., Prof.)*, professional suffixes *(MD, DDS, Ph.D., CPA)*, and seniority designations are the last indexing unit. When a name has both a title and a suffix, the title is the last unit. If you have only a title and one name, index the name as it is written. In seniority terms, the sequence is numbers *(2nd, 3rd)*, roman numerals *(I, II)*, and then junior *(Jr.)* and senior *(Sr.)*.

Names	Indexing Order		
	1	**2**	**3**
Alan Berg MD	Berg	Alan	MD
Matthew Blue 2nd	Blue	Matthew	2
Charles Jonathan III	Jonathan	Charles	III
Charles Jonathan Jr.	Jonathan	Charles	Jr
Sister Mary-Margaret	Sister	Marymargaret	

Rule 6. When names are identical, index the names by city, state (spelled in full), street name, quadrant *(NE, NW, SE, SW)*, and house or building number in numeric order (lowest number first).

Names

Emily Beck
1055 Maple Lane
Chicago, IL 60623-9623

Emily Beck
8275 Maple Lane
Chicago, IL 60623-9627

Indexing Order

1	2	3	4	5	6	7
Beck	Emily	Chicago	Illinois	Maple	Lane	1055
Beck	Emily	Chicago	Illinois	Maple	Lane	8275

Rule 7. Index business and organizational names as written. When *The, A,* or *An* is the first word of the name, it is indexed as the last unit. Prepositions *(of, in, on, over)* are separate units. Compound expressions are treated as written—if there is a space between terms, the terms are separate units. Single letters are indexed as written—if they are separated by a space, then they are separate units. Spell out symbols *(&, #)*. Acronyms and call letters (for TV and radio) are single units.

Names	Indexing Order			
	1	**2**	**3**	**4**
A B C Clinic	A	B	C	Clinic
A&D Surgical Supplies	AandD	Surgical	Supplies	
A-B-C Clinic	ABC	Clinic		
Clinic On Main	Clinic	On	Main	
The Free Clinic	Free	Clinic	The	
John St. Claire Clinic	John	Stclaire	Clinic	
South West Clinic	South	West	Clinic	
Southwest Clinic	Southwest	Clinic		
Kare TV Station	Kare	TV	Station	

Rule 8. Arabic numerals and roman numerals are considered a single unit and are filed in numeric order before alphabetic characters (Arabic comes before roman). Ignore ordinal endings *(st, d, th)*.

Names	Indexing Order		
	1	**2**	**3**
1-A Physical Therapy	1A	Physical	Therapy
5th Avenue Clinic	5	Avenue	Clinic
50+ Retirement Group	50plus	Retirement	Group
Sixty-Third Street Pharmacy	Sixtythird	Street	Pharmacy

Rule 9. Committees, hospitals, universities, hotels, motels, and churches are indexed as written. Cross-reference items to ensure finding them.

Names	Indexing Order			
	1	**2**	**3**	**4**
Alexander Hotel	Alexander	Hotel		
Committee for Academic Affairs	Committee	for	Academic	Affairs

(Could be cross-referenced under *Academic Affairs Committee for*)

St. Paul's Medical Center	Stpauls	Medical	Center	
University of Illinois Hospital	University	of	Illinois	Hospital

Rule 10. Government names are indexed first by the governmental unit (country, state, county, or city). Next, index the name of the department, bureau, office, or board. Words such as *Office of* or *Department of* are separate indexing units and are transposed.

Federal Government

The first three units of all federal government names are *United States Government*.

Names	Indexing Order				
	1	**2**	**3**	**4**	**5**
U.S. Department of Health and Human Services	United	States	Government	Health	and
	6	**7**	**8**	**9**	
	Human	Services	Department	of	

State and Local Governments

Names	Indexing Order				
	1	**2**	**3**	**4**	**5**
City of Anoka Health Department	Anoka	City	Health	Department	of
Anoka County Health Department	Anoka	County	Health	Department	
Illinois Bureau of Health	Illinois	Health	Bureau	of	

Foreign Governments

Names	Indexing Order				
	1	2	3	4	5
Republic of Sweden Health Department	Sweden	Republic	Health	Department	of

GO TO PROJECT 5.3 ON PAGE 129

■ Numeric Filing

Offices with a large volume of patient records may use a **numeric filing** system, that is, one in which each patient is assigned a number. The patient number is assigned from an **accession book,** which is a book of consecutive numbers indicating the next available number to be assigned. A cross-index is then prepared to match the number with the name.

There are several ways to assign numeric values. Two of the most frequently used ways are straight-numeric filing and terminal-digit filing.

1. *Straight-numeric filing:* The straight-numeric system uses ascending numbers in consecutive order. For example, File 125203 would be filed after File 125202 and before File 125204.
2. *Terminal-digit filing:* The terminal-digit system uses the terminal (last) digit, or set of digits, as the indexing unit. The file numbered 33-52-12 would be filed in Section 12 (the last digit) behind 52 (the guide number) and would be the 33d item in sequence.

There is a filing method that is a combination of alphabetical and numerical filing. This alphanumeric system is used in software available for use in physicians' practices. NDCmedisoft™ uses both the alphabet and numbers to assign patient codes (Figure 5.8.)

Numeric filing is a very accurate method of filing. It is more difficult to misfile or to lose files. Therefore, there is speedier storage and retrieval. It is a method that helps to maintain confidentiality of files. In a numeric

FIGURE 5.8

NDCmedisoft™ Screen Showing Patient Account Numbers

Chart Nu...	Name	Date of Birth
ARMSTM00	Armstrong, Monica	8/12/1958
BAABTH00	Baab, Thomas	10/6/1954
BABCOSA0	Babcock, Sara	12/20/1986
BURTOPA0	Burton, Paul	10/22/1979
BURTOPA1	Burton, Randy	1/16/2006
CASAGHE0	Casagranda, George	11/22/1971
CASAGHE1	Casagranda, Doris	9/1/1992
CASTRJ00	Castro, Joseph	11/2/1989
DAYTOTH0	Dayton, Theresa	3/13/1986
GRANTT00	Grant, Todd	5/18/1976

List of cases for: Armstrong, Monica

Number	Case Description
3	Menopausal bleeding
47	Annual exam

filing system, expansion is unlimited, depending only on the next unassigned number in the sequence.

Although numbers provide accuracy, there is still an opportunity to transpose numbers, especially if the sequence is a long one. More guides are required, and there is a need to consult and maintain an alphabetic cross-index. Using the system efficiently also requires a thorough training program for staff members.

■ Subject Filing

Subject filing is the placement of related material alphabetically by subject categories. It is a useful method for keeping nonpatient correspondence, research articles, practice management files, and other material of a general nature. A computer database is also organized by subject. For example, in the NDCmedisoft™ program, databases are set up for patients, insurance companies, physicians, and guarantors. (A guarantor is the person who is responsible for payment to the physician.) In each database, the entries are listed alphabetically.

Subject categories depend on the specific needs of the physician and on the amount of material to be filed under each heading. Manuscripts are filed alphabetically under the title of the article or book. Reviews of, and references to, the physician's own writing are also filed under the title of the article or book. Abstracts of research articles, excerpts, and other reviews may be clippings from magazines or newspapers. Whether these are filed by the author's name or by the subject depends on how the physician plans to use the items. Figure 5.9 illustrates a relative subject index with a sample of headings that might be used in subject filing.

When all items pertaining to the same subject may be found in one location, as they are with subject filing, valuable time is saved. Statistics and other types of information are easily accessible. The relative subject index is easy to expand. However, when there is a great amount of material, subject categories may overlap or extensive cross-referencing may be required for complex topics. It can become time-consuming, even for those who are experienced in filing, to file and to retrieve materials.

■ Color-coding

Color-coding is used in many medical offices. In a color-coded system, color folders are used for patients' files to help identify categories visually. Different colors stand for various letters of the alphabet or for numbers. For example, to organize the file of patient medical records, red folders may be used to file the letters A through D; yellow to file E through H; green to file I through N; blue for O, P, and Q; and purple for the letters R through Z.

FIGURE 5.9 Relative Subject Index

Advertisements
Drugs
Medical
Office

Automobile
Insurance
Maintenance

Clinic Property
Building
Inventory
Maintenance
Medical Equipment
Office Equipment

Collections
Accounts Receivable
Agency Contracts
Form Letters

Education
Doctor's Continuing
Employee
Patient

Entertainment

Financial Information
Annual Financial
Banking
Monthly Financial

Forms
Applications
Consent
Release From Work
Release of Information

Hospital
Policy
Reports
Staff Meetings

Insurance
Clinic
Fire
Liability—Doctor's

Patients
Index Control File
Patient Billing List

Personnel
Applications—Inactive
Benefits and Policies
Current Employees
Doctor's Personal File—Diplomas,
    Licenses, Publications

Referral Information

Society Information
American Medical Association
Seminars
State Medical Society

Subscriptions and Publications
Drug Companies
Lobby Magazines
Medical Magazines
Newspapers
Professional Library

Supplies
Inventory
Medical
Office
Order Forms

Taxes
Payroll
Personal (Doctor's)
Property

Travel
Expenses
Pending

Utilities
Electricity
Gas
Telephone
Water

■ Locating Missing Files

Even in a well-organized office, paper documents will occasionally be lost or misfiled. Here are a number of suggestions for locating a missing file:

- Look directly behind and in front of where the item should be filed.
- Look between other files in the area.
- Look in the bottom of the file drawer and under the file folders if they are suspended.
- Check for the transposition of first and last names, for example, *Wheng, Hart* instead of *Hart, Wheng*.
- Check alternate spellings of the name, for example, *Thomasen* and *Thomason*.

- In a numeric filing system, check for transposed numbers, for example, *19-63-01* instead of *19-01-63*.
- In a subject filing system, check related subject files or the Miscellaneous file.
- With the permission of those who have used the file recently, search the desk or work area of previous users of the file.
- Check with other office personnel.

▶ GO TO PROJECT 5.4 ON PAGE 130 ▶

5.4 RETENTION OF RECORDS

Every medical practice has files from previous years and all types of information. For example, patient medical records include files for patients who are currently being treated by the physician, those who have not seen the physician for some time, and those who are no longer patients for one reason or another.

For management purposes, these files are classified as:

- **Active files,** pertaining to current patients.
- **Inactive files,** related to patients who have not seen the physician for six months or longer.
- **Closed files,** containing the files of those patients who have died, moved away, or terminated their relationship with the physician.

Each office sets the criteria and time frames for placing files in one of the categories. This policy is part of a larger policy for record **retention**— the length of time records must be retained and the proper disposition of them when they should no longer be stored. Record retention policies protect physicians from exposure to risk and legal problems.

■ Legal Requirements

Federal law does not regulate retention time frames for patients' medical records. Many states, however, have specific requirements for the length of time such records must be kept. Existing state laws and regulations must always be observed. Health care providers who receive payment under the federal Medicare program must also comply with Medicare's conditions for record retention.

In January 1997 the American Health Information Management Association **(AHIMA)** proposed this guideline in one of its practice briefs:

> Each health care provider should develop a retention schedule for patient health information that meets the demands of its patients, physicians, researchers, and other legitimate users while complying with all legal, regulatory, and accreditation requirements. Providers should also create guidelines that specify what information should be kept, the time period for which it will be kept, and the type of storage medium in which it shall be kept (paper, microfilm, optical disk, magnetic tape, or other).

■ Retention Time Frames

The following time frames have been recommended by AHIMA as retention schedules, subject to local laws and regulations:

- *Patient health records (adults):* Ten years after patient's most recent encounter.
- *Patient health records (minors):* Age of majority plus statute of limitations on malpractice.
- *Diagnostic images (such as x-rays):* Five years.
- *Master patient index, register of births, register of deaths, register of surgical procedures:* Permanently.

The office policy should include a variety of other records related to the physician's practice management:

- *Insurance policies:* Current policies are kept in safe storage in an accessible file. Professional liability policies are kept permanently.
- *Tax records:* Tax records for the three latest years are kept in a readily accessible file. The remaining records may be kept in a less accessible storage area.
- *Receipts for equipment:* Receipts for both medical and office equipment are kept until the various pieces of equipment are fully depreciated, that is, until the value of the equipment has completely diminished.
- *Personal records and licenses:* Professional licenses and certificates are kept permanently in safe storage. Banking records such as statements and deposit slips are kept in the file for three years. They may then be moved to a storage area. Other personal records, such as noncurrent partnership agreements, property records, or other business agreements, are also kept permanently in a storage area.

■ Paper Versus Electronic Records

To save space, paper records can be stored through a process called **micrographics** in which miniaturized images of the records are created. These images are usually in a microfiche (sheet of film holding 90 images) or ultrafiche (compacted film holding up to 1,000 images) format and are viewed on readers that enlarge the images. Micrographic records may be stored in card files or binders. With the increased use of the large memory capacity afforded by computers, paper records may also be scanned and stored in a space-saving way on a hard disk, CD, or DVD. All electronically stored records must be kept according to the same retention schedule as paper records.

■ Disposition of Records

Records that have been closed or those that must be kept permanently—patient records, personal records, and business records—may be transferred and are said to be in **dead storage,** a storage area separate from the area where active files are kept. Dead storage need not be easily accessible and can be in a location other than the office.

There are financial and storage considerations for every practice. All records cannot be kept indefinitely. Some states have laws related to the destruction of records and even specify the method of destruction. General guidelines provided by AHIMA include the following:

- Appropriate ways to destroy records include burning, shredding, and pulping. Records must be destroyed so that there is no possibility of reconstructing them.
- When destroying computerized data, overwriting data or reformatting the disk should be done. Other methods delete file names but do not really destroy data. Microfilm, microfiche, and laser disks may be destroyed by pulverizing.

 GO TO PROJECT 5.5 ON PAGE 130

Chapter Projects

Internet Research: ARMA

Visit the ARMA Web site (www.arma.org) and research current headlines. What resources are listed as available to members?

PROJECT 5.2 **Cross-Referencing**

[handwritten: # Sheet of Paper]

Indicate the file and cross-reference entries for the following:
- ▶ Randolph Car Service (formerly Carl's Car Service)
- ▶ James Henry University
- ▶ File folders bought from Oliver Systems and Viking Office Supplies

PROJECT 5.3 **Preparing Patients' Files**

Dr. Larsen maintains a file folder for each patient. You will find the patient information forms on the CD-ROM that accompanies this text-workbook. Print out each form and begin an alphabetic file for each patient. Note that each patient should have an individual chart or file. Material that pertains to each patient should be filed chronologically within that patient's folder. Prepare a chart note and new folder whenever a new patient arrives for an appointment.

Prepare the chart note in this way: Center the words *CHART NOTE* on the first line. Triple space; then key information about the patient as shown below. Save the document on your disk by the patient's last name, followed by the first initial: *Armstrong, M.*

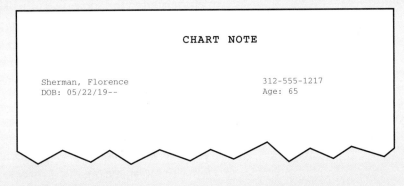

```
                        CHART NOTE



Sherman, Florence                        312-555-1217
DOB: 05/22/19--                          Age: 65
```

Update information on the patient information form as necessary. You may update the form on the CD-ROM and print a new form if a patient changes a home address, for example. Place the alphabetized patient folders in your expandable portfolio.

Print a list of all patients. Check this list against the patient information forms you printed from the CD-ROM. (*Hint:* The Patient List report is available on the Reports menu, under the Custom Report List option.)

PROJECT 5.4 — Using Subject Filing

On a plain sheet of paper, write the subject heading for each of the following items. Use Figure 5.9 as a guideline for your choices. Be prepared to discuss your answers in class.

▶ A copy of an article that Dr. Larsen had published in the *Journal of the American Medical Association (JAMA)*.

▶ A new contract for employees' health insurance.

▶ A bulletin about next month's continuing education seminar for the nursing staff.

▶ The minutes from the hospital staff's last meeting.

▶ A December itinerary for a symposium related to family practice physicians that Dr. Larsen will attend.

PROJECT 5.5 — Internet Research: Using AHIMA as a Resource

AHIMA exists to serve health information management professionals. The organization offers credentials such as Registered Health Information Administrator. Like many professional groups, this organization also keeps those responsible for managing information current with the latest legislation and news and serves consumers of health care with topics of interest to them. Visit the AHIMA Web site at www.ahima.org. Follow the link from the home page to the page that allows you to search by keyword. Key in the term *patient record* and read one of the articles related to this topic. Two other keywords that will be of interest are *information security* and *patient confidentiality*. Read at least one article on each of these topics. Be prepared to share the results of your reading with the class. Contact information for AHIMA is shown below.

American Health Information Management Association
233 North Michigan Avenue, Suite 2150
Chicago, IL 60601
Phone: 312-233-1100
Web site: www.ahima.org
E-mail: info@ahima.org

CHAPTER SUMMARY

1. Efficiently maintaining medical records is important because the correct filing of documents ensures that they are also easy to retrieve. In this way, time is saved. Proper records management procedures also contribute to the compliance of the practice and help protect it from legal problems.

2. The systematic steps in filing a document are inspecting documents, indexing, coding, sorting, and storing.

3. In alphabetic filing, names, titles, or classifications are arranged in alphabetical order. The assistant must consider each word segment a unit and must alphabetize unit by unit, comparing letter by letter within the unit. All punctuation marks are to be ignored and the rule of filing "nothing before something" is followed.

   Numeric filing is a system in which each patient is assigned a number and the numeric value is cross-indexed to match the number with the name. Numeric filing may be either straight number, using ascending numbers in systematic order, or terminal-digit, using the last digit, or last set of digits, as the indexing unit.

   Subject filing is the placement of related material alphabetically by subject categories.

4. Two advantages of alphabetic filing are that (a) because it is based on symbols with which most people are familiar, a training program is not necessary and (b) a misfiled document is easily found. Two disadvantages of alphabetic filing are that (a) it does not protect confidentiality because its symbols are so easy to read and (b) it offers limited filing space and makes expanding the system difficult.

5. To locate a missing file, look directly behind and in front of where the item should be filed; look in the bottom of the file drawer and under the file folders if they are suspended; check for the transposition of first and last names; check alternate spellings of the name; and check with other office personnel. You can also look between other files in the area; check for the transposition of numbers; check the Miscellaneous folder; and search (with permission) the area where the file was last used.

6. Retention of records within the legal time lines is important because patients, physicians, and researchers rely on the information. Sound record retention protects the practice from legal problems and risks.

KEY TERMS

The following terms appear in **boldface** type in this chapter. Administrative medical assistants must know the meaning and the correct use of each of these terms. Can you recall what each term means? Refer to this chapter or to the glossary for any terms you need to review.

accession book	lateral files
active files	micrographics
AHIMA	mobile-aisle files
alphabetic filing	numeric filing
ARMA	open-shelf files
closed files	out guide
coding	patient medical record
color-coding	records management
cross-reference sheet	releasing
cuts	retention
dead storage	rotary circular file
folders	sorting
guides	storing
inactive files	subject filing
indexing	tabs
inspecting documents	tickler file
labels	vertical files

THINKING IT THROUGH

These questions cover the most important points in this chapter. Using your critical thinking skills, play the role of an administrative medical assistant as you answer each question. Be prepared to present your responses in class.

1. What are two important tasks you need to do to maintain office records efficiently?

2. What might be some likely results of not following one or more systematic steps in filing?

3. Of the three filing systems—alphabetic, numeric, subject—which one do you believe offers the greatest advantages? Why?

4. You have noticed several times that patient records are misfiled. How do you handle this situation?

5. How would you go about locating a missing file?

6. How would you respond to a patient who visits the office after a 5-year period and asks to see a copy of the patient statement from the last visit?

6 Written Communications

After studying this chapter, you will be able to:

1. State the importance of good written communication skills to the administrative medical assistant.
2. Compose written communications, applying correct letter formatting and letter styles.
3. Prepare a professional report.
4. Describe techniques for proofreading and editing.
5. List the procedures for opening and sorting mail.
6. Describe mail classifications.

INTRODUCTION

In the health care profession, an important part of the administrative medical assistant's job is interacting with patients, building relationships with coworkers, and representing the physician and the quality of the practice. These are all good reasons to develop outstanding communication skills. It is not only in interpersonal relationships but also in letters, memos, reports, and e-mail that the assistant represents the practice. Success as an assistant is due as much to written and oral communication skills as to technical skills.

KEY TERMS

Study these important words, which are defined in this chapter, to build your professional vocabulary.

annotate	endnotes	modified-block-style letter	restricted delivery
bibliography	Express Mail	open punctuation	return receipt
block-style letter	first draft	Priority Mail	simplified-style letter
certified mail	footnotes	proofreading	standard punctuation
editing	insured mail	registered mail	title page
electronic mail service	Media Mail		

6.1   COMPOSING CORRESPONDENCE

Writing and speaking effectively have these points in common:

- The communication has an appropriate tone—a way of phrasing ideas, announcements, directions, and requests that is pleasant, positive, and reassuring.
- The communication has a clear purpose, aim, or goal.
- The message is directed to a person or "listener" who is to receive it.
- Correct English is used—including acceptable grammar, spelling, and punctuation.
- Complete information is given in a direct and courteous way.

This chapter focuses on preparing written communications and the office procedures that deal with receiving and sending correspondence. However, the qualities of positive tone, clear purpose, a sense of the intended audience, use of good English, and a direct and courteous delivery of complete information are necessary whether you are writing or speaking.

■ Reasons for Written Rather Than Oral Communication

Because there are so many issues of law, ethics, and confidentiality in medical offices, written communication may often be preferable to a conversation or phone call. Written communication may be required for many reasons, including the following:

- *Giving complex directions or instructions:* Patients who are anxious or distracted may need to read information at a time when they are calm. Repeating the physician's instructions or other information in writing may be more effective than oral communication.
- *Being efficient:* Writing a brief message may not require the time and effort of a phone call or face-to-face conversation.
- *Documenting an event or fact:* The written documentation of aspects of patient care and practice management helps protect the practice from legal problems.
- *Providing for confidentiality:* It may be difficult or improper to use the telephone for certain communications with a patient.

■ Formatting

Before dealing with the content of correspondence, it is necessary to consider the appearance of the letter on the page. When a letter from your office is received, it should be pleasing to the eye and should invite the reader's attention.

COMPLIANCE TIP

Test results, arrangements for a surgical procedure, or messages about a patient's condition may be better protected in written messages. These messages should always be placed in envelopes marked "Confidential" or "Private."

The format, or arrangement, of the letter on the page may be one that your employer has selected and is shown in the office procedures manual. If this is not the case, you will need to choose one of the accepted formats for correspondence. There are three frequently used letter formats that give the letter a well-balanced and attractive appearance:

Block Style. The major rules for a **block-style letter,** shown in Figure 6.1 *(a)*, are:

- Begin all lines, including those that start new paragraphs, at the left margin.
- Allow at least three blank lines beneath the date.
- Single-space the body of the letter. Double-space between paragraphs.
- Center a one-page letter vertically, from top to bottom, on the page.

LETTERHEAD	**KAREN LARSEN, MD** 2235 South Ridgeway Avenue 312-555-6022 Chicago, IL 60623-2240 Fax: 312-555-0025
DATE	September 15, 20--
	↓ 4
INSIDE ADDRESS	Ethan Hershey, MD 4366 Maple Avenue Baltimore, MD 21227-3643
	↓ 2
SALUTATION	Dear Dr. Hershey:
	↓ 2
SUBJECT LINE	SUBJECT: JASON WHITEMORE DOB: 4/2/--
	↓ 2
BODY OF LETTER	Enclosed is the laboratory report that was inadvertently omitted from Jason Whitemore's referral letter of September 10, 20--.
	↓ 2
	I hope this has not inconvenienced you. Please send us your evaluation as soon as you have examined Jason.
	↓ 2
COMPLIMENTARY CLOSE	Sincerely,
	↓ 4
TYPED SIGNATURE	Theresa J. Olssen Medical Assistant
	↓ 2
ENCLOSURE NOTATION	Enclosure

FIGURE 6.1 *(a)*

Block-Style Letter With Standard Punctuation

Modified-Block Style. The major rules for a **modified-block-style letter,** shown in Figure 6.1 *(b)*, are:

- Position the date line, complimentary closing, and signature line beginning at the center point of the page.
- Begin all other lines at the left margin or, if you wish, indent new paragraphs 0.5 inch.
- Single-space the body of the letter. Double-space between paragraphs.
- Center a one-page letter vertically.

Simplified Style. The rules for a **simplified-style letter** are:

- Begin all lines at the left margin.
- Substitute a subject line, all in capital letters, for the salutation.

FIGURE 6.1 *(b)*

Modified-Block-Style Letter
With Open Punctuation

- Omit the complimentary closing.
- Key the writer's name, all in capital letters, on one line.
- Open punctuation, explained below, is always used.

■ Punctuation

There are two styles of punctuation used in business letters:

- **Standard punctuation.** Place a colon after the salutation and a comma after the complimentary closing.
- **Open punctuation.** Do not use *any* punctuation outside the body of the letter unless the line ends with an abbreviation.

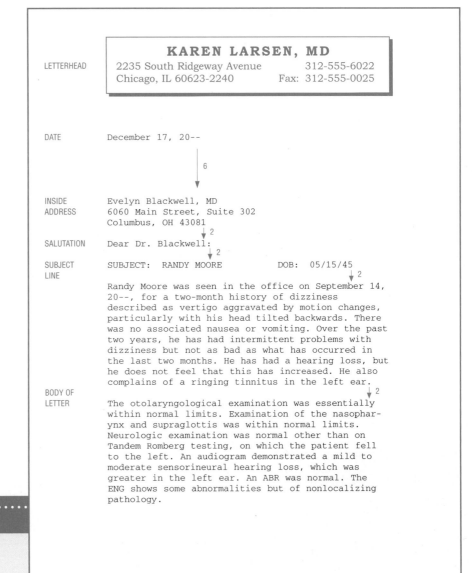

LETTERHEAD

KAREN LARSEN, MD
2235 South Ridgeway Avenue   312-555-6022
Chicago, IL 60623-2240   Fax: 312-555-0025

DATE
December 17, 20--

6

INSIDE
ADDRESS
Evelyn Blackwell, MD
6060 Main Street, Suite 302
Columbus, OH 43081

2

SALUTATION
Dear Dr. Blackwell:

2

SUBJECT
LINE
SUBJECT: RANDY MOORE   DOB: 05/15/45

2

Randy Moore was seen in the office on September 14, 20--, for a two-month history of dizziness described as vertigo aggravated by motion changes, particularly with his head tilted backwards. There was no associated nausea or vomiting. Over the past two years, he has had intermittent problems with dizziness but not as bad as what has occurred in the last two months. He has had a hearing loss, but he does not feel that this has increased. He also complains of a ringing tinnitus in the left ear.

2

BODY OF
LETTER
The otolaryngological examination was essentially within normal limits. Examination of the nasopharynx and supraglottis was within normal limits. Neurologic examination was normal other than on Tandem Romberg testing, on which the patient fell to the left. An audiogram demonstrated a mild to moderate sensorineural hearing loss, which was greater in the left ear. An ABR was normal. The ENG shows some abnormalities but of nonlocalizing pathology.

FIGURE 6.1 *(c)*

First Page of a
Two-Page Letter

■ Continuation Pages

When a letter has more than one page, always use blank stationery of the same quality as that of the first page. Do not use stationery with a letterhead even when the first page has a letterhead. Use a top margin of 1 inch on pages after the first page, and add an appropriate heading. See the example of a letter with more than one page in Figure 6.1 *(c)* on page 137 and *(d)*.

Valuable resources are a good dictionary and a copy of a comprehensive reference manual, such as *The Gregg Reference Manual,* Ninth Edition, by William A. Sabin (Glencoe/McGraw-Hill, Columbus, Ohio, 2001).

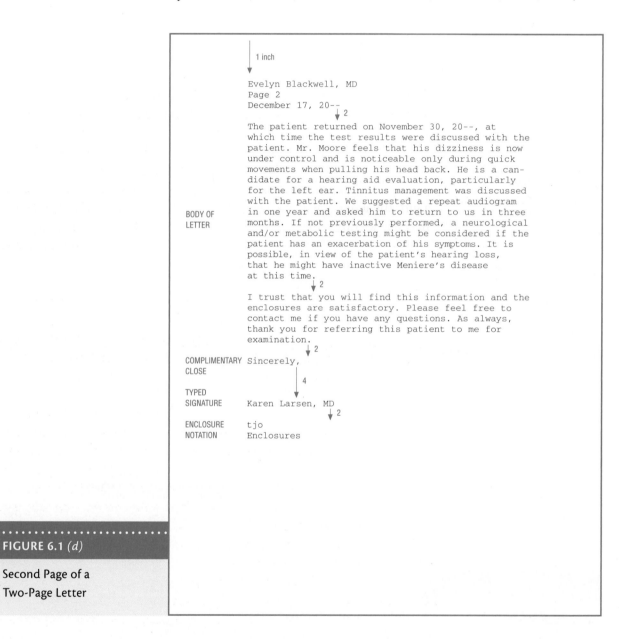

1 inch

Evelyn Blackwell, MD
Page 2
December 17, 20--
↓ 2

BODY OF LETTER

The patient returned on November 30, 20--, at which time the test results were discussed with the patient. Mr. Moore feels that his dizziness is now under control and is noticeable only during quick movements when pulling his head back. He is a candidate for a hearing aid evaluation, particularly for the left ear. Tinnitus management was discussed with the patient. We suggested a repeat audiogram in one year and asked him to return to us in three months. If not previously performed, a neurological and/or metabolic testing might be considered if the patient has an exacerbation of his symptoms. It is possible, in view of the patient's hearing loss, that he might have inactive Meniere's disease at this time.
↓ 2

I trust that you will find this information and the enclosures are satisfactory. Please feel free to contact me if you have any questions. As always, thank you for referring this patient to me for examination.
↓ 2

COMPLIMENTARY CLOSE

Sincerely,
↓ 4

TYPED SIGNATURE

Karen Larsen, MD
↓ 2

ENCLOSURE NOTATION

tjo
Enclosures

FIGURE 6.1 *(d)*

Second Page of a
Two-Page Letter

■ Types of Correspondence

The assistant is responsible for composing letters about many different kinds of office matters. The kinds of letters frequently initiated by the assistant, or written at the request of the physician, include:

- Letters of acknowledgment
- Letters of information
- Referral and consultation letters
- Follow-up letters
- Interoffice memorandums

Letters of Acknowledgment. The receipt of certain letters, materials, gifts, or requests for information requires a letter of acknowledgment. Such a letter may be written and signed by the assistant, or written by the assistant for the physician to sign. The letter of acknowledgment should include the date on which the item or request was received and some description of what was received. If the letter is a request for some response or decision, the assistant should acknowledge the inquiry but make no promises in the name of the physician about the exact date or nature of the response.

The main purpose of a letter of acknowledgment is to let the sender know as soon as possible that a request is being handled. In the case of a gift, the letter states that the gift has been received and is appreciated. Because writing letters of acknowledgment is a frequent task, a form letter may be used. Such form letters are easy to create with the templates found in word processing programs.

Letters of Information. Letters of information must have clear and complete information. Concise statement of the information is also appreciated by the recipient. If the information contains instructions related to treatment, the letter usually has the physician's signature although the physician may ask the assistant to compose the letter.

Referral and Consultation Letters. Referral letters are used when a physician transfers part or all of the patient's care to another physician. For example, a general practitioner may refer a patient with a heart condition to a cardiologist for an extended period of treatment. Requests for a consultation happen when the physician asks another physician to examine a patient and report back findings on a specific question. For example, a general practitioner may ask a gastroenterologist to perform a colonoscopy and report the results of that examination as part of a patient's comprehensive physical examination.

Some practices send a brief letter thanking the physician who sent the patient when a patient is referred. The note is usually sent once the patient has been seen so that a brief medical report can be included. Figure 6.2 on page 140 is an example of this type of letter and may be used as a guide in drafting a referral letter. If a referred patient does not make or keep an appointment, a letter should be sent to the referring physician explaining that the patient did not appear, after a reasonable period of time has passed.

FIGURE 6.2

Letter Thanking a Physician
for the Referral of a Patient

KAREN LARSEN, MD
2235 South Ridgeway Avenue   312-555-6022
Chicago, IL 60623-2240   Fax: 312-555-0025

August 14, 20--

Hugh Arnold, MD
Suite 440
2785 South Ridgeway Avenue
Chicago, IL 60647-2700

Dear Dr. Arnold:

RE: FRANZ GUEHN   DOB: 08/05/--

Thank you for referring Franz Guehn to me.
I have just completed his examination. Mr. Guehn
was first examined by me on June 4. His diagnosis
at that time was otitis externa, bilaterally;
defective hearing, mixed type, bilaterally. The
results of the audiogram are enclosed.

In July, Mr. Guehn had another audiogram (results
are also enclosed). At that time, a considerable
loss of high tones indicated a beginning degeneration of the auditory nerve, associated with severe
tinnitus.

Thank you for referring this patient to me.

Sincerely,

Karen Larsen, MD

tjo
Enclosures

Many medical insurance plans require patients to see a general practitioner before they can see a specialist. In these plans, the patient receives a referral letter or form from the general practitioner and takes it to the specialist's office. The referral contains an authorization number, which the assistant records as part of the patient's information. This type of referral may be handled differently by the medical office and generally does not require a thank-you note. The administrative medical assistant must learn the policies of the office for these situations.

To make a referral or ask for a consultation, the physician who is sending the patient usually writes or telephones the other physician giving the reason for the request and a summary of the results of the pertinent tests or treatments the patient has had. If the referral is discussed on the phone, a letter confirming the conversation is sent. The other physician then knows that a patient is expected and has a brief history of the patient's problem. The referring office may sometimes also schedule an appointment

COMPLIANCE TIP

Remember that if medical records are attached to correspondence, the patient must first sign a release form.

for the patient with the other physician. Figure 6.3 is an example of this type of letter and may be used as a guide in drafting a referral letter.

 GO TO PROJECT 6.1 ON PAGE 155

Follow-Up Letters. Sometimes it is necessary to follow up on a request or on a letter that has not received a response. In writing such a letter, be courteous, give the recipient the details of the original request, and be clear about what action you wish the recipient to take.

Interoffice Memorandums. Informal messages exchanged within an organization may be written as interoffice memorandums, usually referred to as "memos." Memos are written on stationery that may have a preprinted heading, such as *Interoffice Memorandum* or the name and logo of the practice.

KAREN LARSEN, MD
2235 South Ridgeway Avenue   312-555-6022
Chicago, IL 60623-2240   Fax: 312-555-0025

September 16, 20--

Lynn Corbett, MD
Professional Building, Suite 300
8672 South Ridgeway Avenue
Chicago, IL 60623-2240

Dear Dr. Corbett:

RE: JANET SCHMIDT   DOB: 09/30/--

Janet Schmidt, a four-year-old female, has had
a heart murmur since birth and recently has had
extreme pressure on her chest. I am referring Janet
to you for examination.

Enclosed is Janet's complete medical history, along
with the results of the latest tests.

Janet's mother is to call you for an appointment
within the next two weeks.

I would appreciate receiving your evaluation.

Sincerely,

Karen Larsen, MD

tjo
Enclosures

FIGURE 6.3

Letter Informing a Physician
of the Referral of a Patient

FIGURE 6.4

Interoffice Memorandum

```
                        INTEROFFICE MEMORANDUM


        MEMO TO:    Gary Libinksi, Laboratory Manager

        FROM:       Karen Larsen, MD

        DATE:       September 15, 20--

        SUBJECT:    Outside Laboratory Usage


        After careful study, I have decided that Penway
        Laboratory will be our outside resource laboratory
        for the next three months. They have contracted to
        provide us with fast, reliable service. They are
        certified by Medicare to provide all necessary lab
        test results.

        Our contact person at Penway will be Gina
        McPherson. She will bill us directly for any out-
        side services we use with Penway. Also, she will
        send us monthly reports on our usage of their
        facility. Gary, I also want you to keep an accurate
        report of turnaround results and other problems
        encountered with the lab tests we send to Penway.

        During the week of December 20, we will have a
        meeting to discuss our usage of Penway. You and
        Gina will meet with me to discuss the continued
        usage of Penway Laboratory.

        tjo
```

There may be preprinted guide words near the top of the page, such as *TO:*, *FROM:*, *DATE:*, and *SUBJECT:*. If you require more guide words, such as *DEPARTMENT:* or *EXTENSION:*, you may use two columns so that the memo heading does not take too much space.

If the memo is being sent to a number of people, after the guide word *TO:*, you may wish to key the words *See Distribution*. On the second line below the writer's initials at the end of the memo, key the word *Distribution* followed by a colon. Leave one line blank, and then type the names of those to whom the memo is to be sent, arranging the names either by title or alphabetically.

Memos do not usually contain an inside address or complimentary closing as a letter does. When memos are announcements to a number of people, there is no salutation. However, if the memo concerns only one individual, a salutation followed by a colon may be used, such as *Dear Tom:* or the name *Tom:* alone.

A signature may or may not appear above the name of the sender, depending on the procedures followed in your office. The writer's name or initials may be keyed two lines below the end of the message. The keyboarder's initials should appear two lines below the writer's name or initials or two lines below the body of the message. An example of an interoffice memo is shown in Figure 6.4.

GO TO PROJECT 6.2 ON PAGE 155

6.2 PREPARING PROFESSIONAL REPORTS

Many physicians are involved in writing articles, books, or reports on the results of research. They may also need to prepare speeches or presentations. Helping to prepare reports is often a duty of the administrative medical assistant.

■ Preparing Draft Manuscript

The manuscript that will eventually be submitted to a publisher starts out as a draft. Some writers begin with an outline, jotting down headings and subheadings. The rough draft may then be filled in with notes keyed to the outline. Other writers make many notes, ask the assistant to key the notes, and write from these.

The **first draft** is the first complete keying of the manuscript. All text should be double-spaced or triple-spaced to allow ample room for corrections and additions. The manuscript may go through many drafts before it is final. Each draft should be identified by number—*Draft 1, Draft 2,* and so on. Before saving a draft to the computer file, be sure that you have labeled it with its correct draft number or used the word processor's automatic draft-numbering feature.

After each round of corrections, additions, and deletions, the physician will ask you to key the changes and to proofread and edit the draft. Suggestions for proofreading and editing are given later in this chapter.

■ Preparing Final Manuscript

The purpose of the writing determines the final format selected. The purpose of some reports is to share information; these reports may be meant for distribution only within the organization. Such reports may have an informal format and may even be prepared as a letter or memo. There are several templates for formats provided in word processing applications. If the procedures manual in your office does not dictate a format, you may want to choose one of these templates. An example of the first page of an informal report is shown in Figure 6.5 *(a)* on page 144.

Formal reports, usually more complex and longer than informal reports, are often written for readers outside the organization. Documents meant as professional reports or manuscripts for publication often have special features, such as a table of contents, list of illustrations, summary, and list of sources consulted by the writer. The publisher of a journal article can give rules for format and style to help the assistant prepare the manuscript. For other kinds of formal reports, the specifications given here can be followed.

FIGURE 6.5 *(a)*

First Page of an Informal
Professional Report

CHICKENPOX (VARICELLA)

By Karen Larsen, MD
University Hospital

January 25, 20--

DEFINITION

Chickenpox is a highly contagious, acute infection causing
pruritic rash, slight fever, malaise, and anorexia.

ETIOLOGY

Herpesvirus varicella-zoster causes chickenpox. It is transmitted by direct contact (respiratory secretions more prominent-
ly than skin lesions) and by indirect contact (air waves). The
highest communicable period is the early stages of skin lesion
eruption. Incubation period ranges from 13 to 17 days.

CLINICAL SYMPTOMS

The prodrome of chickenpox generally begins with slight
fever, malaise, and anorexia. The pruritic rash begins within
24 hours as erythematous macules, then progresses to papules,
and then to clear vesicles. The vesicles turn cloudy and break.
Scabs then form. The rash begins on the trunk or scalp. After
the vesicles become cloudy and break, the rash spreads to the
face but rarely spreads to the extremities.

TREATMENT

The patient should remain in isolation for at least one week
after the onset of the rash. Local or systemic antipruritics,
calamine lotion, cool soda baths, and antihistamines should be
used for relief of symptoms. If a bacterial infection develops,
an antibiotic should be prescribed. Varicella-zoster immune
globulin (passive immunity) can be given to susceptible patients
within 72 hours of exposure to varicella.

- *Title page:* On the first manuscript page, called the **title page,** key the title of the report in all-capital letters. Key the subtitle, if there is one, in capital and small letters, double-spaced below the title. Boldface should be used for the title and subtitle. Key *Prepared by* 12 lines below the subtitle. Then double-space to key the writer's name and credentials; writer's title, if appropriate; and writer's affiliation on separate lines. Key the date of the report 12 lines below the affiliation. Center all the text horizontally and vertically on the page. Figure 6.5 *(b)* shows the title page of a formal report.
- *Text:* The text of the report should be double-spaced, with the first line of each paragraph indented 0.5 inch. There should be 1-inch margins on all sides.

CHICKENPOX (VARICELLA)

Prepared by

Karen Larsen, MD
University Hospital

January 25, 20--

- *Numbering:* The title page should not be numbered; all other pages should be numbered in the upper right-hand corner. Pages are numbered consecutively, starting with the number 1, from the beginning to the end of the manuscript.
- *Headings:* Section headings, such as *SUMMARY, INTRODUCTION,* and *CHAPTER 1,* should be keyed in all-capital letters in boldface type. Each section should start on a new page, with a 2-inch top margin, and there should be two blank lines below the section heading. Main text headings, which alert readers to new subjects within a section, should be keyed in all-capital letters and placed flush with the left margin on a separate line. Text subheadings should be keyed in capital and small letters, indented 0.5 inch, and followed by a period; text should follow right after the subheading

on the same line. Boldface should be used for text headings, and there should be one blank line above headings.

- *Italics and underscoring:* Words within the text that are to be emphasized may be underscored or italicized. Although foreign words should also be italicized or underscored, medical terms that are foreign words but are in common use should not be either italicized or underscored.
- *Quotations:* If quotations are brief, they may be set in quotation marks and may appear as part of the text. Longer quotations should be single-spaced and indented 0.5 inch from the left and right margins.
- *Notes:* Writers use notes in a report to (1) add parenthetical comments or (2) provide the sources for information or quotations. A raised number appears in the text at the point of reference for the note; the note itself is also numbered. Notes that are positioned at the bottom of the page on which the reference appears are called **footnotes.** Notes that are grouped together at the end of the report are called **endnotes.** Most word processing programs have a notes feature that enables the keyboarder to create footnotes or endnotes.
- *Illustrations:* If a manuscript that is to be sent to a publisher or printer contains photographs, tables, charts, or graphs, these illustrations may be submitted as digital computer files or as reproduction copy. If digital files are needed, a scanner can be used to create a computer file of the illustration. The file name should describe the illustration. If reproduction copy is to be submitted, each illustration should be mounted on a separate sheet of blank, letter-size paper and identified by a title, caption, or brief description written on the sheet of paper. The manuscript page number containing the reference to the illustration should also be noted on the paper. Every photograph submitted should be a glossy print. Care should be taken not to write on either the front or the back of the photograph.
- *Bibliography:* All the works consulted by the writer, including items given in notes, are listed, alphabetically by author, in a **bibliography** at the end of the report. The publisher or an appropriate reference manual should be consulted for the format and style required. The University of Chicago's *Chicago Manual of Style,* the *Publication Manual of the American Psychological Association,* the American Medical Association's *Manual of Style,* and *Scientific Style and Format: The CBE Manual for Authors, Editors, and Publishers,* published by the Council of Biology Editors, are manuals that the writer may wish to consult for detailed descriptions of how to style and format notes and bibliographies.

▶ **GO TO PROJECT 6.3 ON PAGE 155** ▶

6.3 PROOFREADING AND EDITING

High quality in written communications is necessary because both internal and external correspondence represents your employer and the practice. The professional image of the practice depends in part on the impressions others form through the correspondence they receive. Incorrect, careless, or unclear communications may be damaging.

Two processes used to ensure accuracy and clarity are proofreading and editing. **Proofreading** is the careful reading and examination of a document for the sole purpose of finding and correcting errors. **Editing** is the assessment of a document to determine its clarity, consistency, and overall effectiveness. The good proofreader asks, Is this document entirely correct? The good editor asks, Does this document say exactly what the writer intended in the best way possible?

■ Proofreading Methods

Frequently, only one person reads a document for accuracy, comparing it to the original document. A single proofreader is all that is required for most routine correspondence and reports. For complex documents or highly technical materials, two proofreaders may work as partners. One person reads the original document aloud, including all punctuation and significant style and format elements; the other person examines the new copy carefully and makes the required corrections.

If you are the writer of the original document, proofreading is more difficult because there is no document against which to check for accuracy. For this task, an excellent working knowledge of English grammar, usage, punctuation rules, and spelling is required. In cases where someone else has written the document, both the proofreader and the author should proofread the document.

Proofreading on the Computer Screen. Proofreading documents on the computer screen is an essential skill. You may want to use a piece of paper held against the screen to show only one line so that you concentrate line by line on the text. Once you have examined the document line by line for errors and have corrected these, proofread your corrections carefully. Now you are ready to print and send a correct document.

Using Spell Checkers. It is all too easy when you are proofreading on the screen to believe that the spell-check and grammar features in the word processing program have found all the errors for you. However helpful these features are, they simply cannot find many types of errors.

Spell checkers have a dictionary of a certain number of words. Specialized words that are used frequently can be added to the spell checker's dictionary. The software will always highlight or underscore a word it does not recognize. You will then need to decide whether the word is correct. The spell checker does not usually alert you to a word that is spelled correctly but may be misused. In some word processing programs, ordinary mistakes of this kind are underscored. For example, using *their* where *there* should be used will be underscored by the software. However, certain other words that are frequently misused are not underscored. In the following examples the mistakes will not be underscored by the software: "There are *too* of them (using *too* instead of *two*)"; "He did not *except* the gift (using *except* instead of *accept*)." The spell-check and grammar features are not adequate substitutes for a knowledgeable, alert reader.

■ Proofreading Symbols

There are standard symbols that proofreaders and editors use to indicate specific corrections to documents. If the document is to be published, the symbols will guide those who print the document. When corrections are made on the computer, these symbols on the paper copy guide the person keying the corrections. These proofreaders' marks, shown in Figure 6.6, should always be used when making corrections.

FIGURE 6.6

Proofreaders' Marks

Mark	Meaning	Example		Mark	Meaning	Example
∧	Insert word or letter	add it (*so*)		∧#	Insert a space	addso it
↵	Omit word	and so it		{	Insert a space	andso it
····	No, don't omit	and so it		⊂	Omit the space	10 a. m.
＼	Omit stroke	and soo it		—us	Underscore this	It may be
/	Make letter lowercase	And so it		↻	Move as shown	it is not
≡	Make a capital	if he is		⌣	Join to word	the port (*re*)
≣	Make all capitals	I hope so		word	Change word	and if he (*So*)
⌐⌐	Move as indicated	and so ⌐⌐		∘	Make into period	to him
=	Line up horizontally	TO: John		⬯	Don't abbreviate	Dr. Judd
‖	Line up vertically	‖ If he is		○	Spell it out	1 or 2 if
ss[	Use single spacing	and so it		¶	New paragraph	¶ If he is
⌣	Transpose	raed it so		∨	Raise above line	Hale1 says
ds[	Use double spacing	and so it		↗#	More space here	It may be
=/	Insert a hyphen	white hot		↑#	Less space here	If she is
s⌐	Indent — spaces	s⌐ If he is		2#	2 line spaces here	It may be
∼	Bold	He is not		—	Italicize	It may be

■ Proofreading Techniques

It is always necessary to read every document several times. There are many elements in any written document. Therefore, there are many opportunities for error. Each time you read a document, you are concentrating on a different element of the document:

1. Read for content. Does the document agree *exactly* with the original? Have any words been omitted? Have any words been repeated, especially at the ends of lines?
2. Read for correct grammar, spelling, usage (both words and numbers), and keyboarding errors.
3. Check the format. Has everything been keyed with correct spacing, margins, headings, centering, and page numbers? Is the format consistent throughout the document?
4. When you are reading for consistency, check that the writer always uses the same style for phone numbers and dates. For example,
   Either *(212) 555-7952* or *212-555-7952*
   Either *10/19/2003* or *10-19-2003*
5. When proofreading for clarity, be sure that the simplest words are used to communicate the idea. For example, do not use *exhibit* or *demonstrate* for *show,* or *utilize* for *use.*
6. In a separate step, proofread all numbers once again. Be sure that the number of digits in items such as addresses or ZIP Codes is correct. Be sure there are no transposed numbers.
7. Carefully check and confirm important data, such as the correct spelling of names, addresses, all numbers, and the use of titles such as *Dr.* or *Rev.*
8. Read the document again after you have made all the corrections. Be sure that in making required corrections, you have not introduced any new errors.
9. Use the spell-check and grammar features available in word processing, but keep a good dictionary and English reference manual close at hand.

■ Common Errors

The following is a list of common errors that you may find when you proofread documents:

- Keyboarding mistakes such as the omission or repetition of words and other typographical errors; misstrokes of keys, for example, keying *slepp* instead of *sleep.*
- Errors of transposition in both letters and numbers, for example, keying *flies* instead of *files* or *appointment on October 13* instead of *appointment on October 31.*
- Spacing errors, including not spacing correctly between words, such as keying *patientdoes* instead of *patient does;* incorrect spacing within a word, such as keying *the re* instead of *there;* too much spacing between lines.

■ Editing Techniques

If you are the person who originates the document, you may find it difficult to assess your own work. However, you do have a thorough understanding of your purpose. When you are editing a document created by someone else, you need to be careful that you understand the writer and the situation well enough that you do not make inappropriate changes.

When you edit a document, you are judging clarity, organization, and consistency of format and style. In editing, you also use your proofreading skill. You have the overall objective of making the document as effective as possible. To assess the document:

1. Read the whole document first to get a sense of its organization and purpose.
2. Look at sentence structure to determine that it is correct. Look at sentences to be sure that they are not awkwardly constructed.
3. Assess the correctness of spelling, grammar, punctuation, and English usage.
4. Look for problems in the tone of the letter. Is the tone appropriate for the intent of the letter?
5. Determine that the content is complete and clear. If you have any questions, be sure to get clarification from the writer.

▶ **GO TO PROJECT 6.4 ON PAGE 156** ▶

6.4 PROCESSING INCOMING MAIL AND PREPARING OUTGOING MAIL

In addition to writing correspondence and preparing articles and reports, the administrative medical assistant spends a significant part of each day processing mail. Every physician receives an enormous amount of mail every day, so the efficient handling of correspondence is vital.

As an assistant, you must learn to distinguish quickly between the types of mail most often received. You must use sound judgment to sort mail according to its importance. The mail generally falls into these categories:

- Important items, such as those sent by Express or Priority Mail, or mail that is registered or certified (or sent via overnight services such as Federal Express).
- Regular first-class mail.
- The physician's personal mail.
- Periodicals and newspapers.
- Advertising materials.
- Samples.

■ Processing Guidelines for Incoming Mail

Use the following guidelines to process incoming mail. Sort the items by category, depending on their importance:

1. Open all letters except those marked "Personal," unless you are authorized to open all mail.
2. Check the contents of each envelope carefully.
3. Stamp the date on each item to show when it was received.
4. Attach enclosures to each item.
5. Carefully put aside checks from patients to be recorded and deposited later.
6. Check to be sure the envelope is empty and is not needed before discarding it.
7. Write a reminder on the calendar or in the follow-up (tickler) file about material that is being sent separately.
8. Attach the patient's chart to correspondence regarding the patient. Place such correspondence in a high-priority area on the physician's desk.
9. If a business letter responds to a request, pull the relevant file and attach the letter to it.
10. Set aside correspondence that can be answered without the physician's seeing it, such as payments needing receipts, insurance forms or questions, and bills, and other routine business matters.

In some offices, the assistant is required to **annotate** communications. That is, the assistant skims an item and writes necessary or helpful notes in the margin or on an attached self-stick note.

It may save time if those items that require the physician's attention are placed on the desk in the order of importance. Medical journals are placed on the physician's desk with other mail. Medical samples should be unpacked and placed in the physician's supply cabinet if they can be used. If they cannot be used, follow the office policy, which may include saving them for a charity. Samples should not be thrown in the trash.

■ Preparation of Outgoing Mail

Outgoing mail consists of professional, business, and personal correspondence. Professional correspondence concerns patients, clinical matters, and research. Business correspondence relates to the management of the office and may concern insurance companies, lawyers, supply houses, and bills to patients. Personal correspondence pertains to the physician's personal rather than professional life, such as notes to friends or letters about the physician's personal business interests.

Mail Classifications. For mail to be handled in the most efficient and cost-effective way, the assistant must know the various classifications of mail and services offered. The United States Postal Service (USPS) provides excellent information in easy-to-use formats.

The USPS Web site (www.usps.gov) has a complete listing and description of services and rates. The site is an easy reference for ZIP Codes and correct state abbreviations as well as for all domestic rates and fees; it has postal rate calculators and information on new rates and mailing rules. The local post office will also supply leaflets describing USPS services. The assistant must always be aware of current postal rates, requirements, and available services.

The following are mail classifications specified by the USPS:

- *First-class Mail:* First-class mail includes all correspondence, whether handwritten or typewritten; all bills and statements of accounts; all materials sealed against postal inspection and weighing 13 ounces or less.
- *Priority Mail:* **Priority Mail** offers two-day service to most domestic destinations. Items must weigh less than 70 pounds. This is the fastest way to send heavier items. Rates will vary depending on weight and distance. Pickup service is available for a charge. For all materials that can be sent in a flat-rate envelope (provided by the USPS), there is one low charge.
- *Express Mail.* The fastest service, **Express Mail** offers next-day delivery to most destinations. Express Mail deliveries are made 365 days a year. All items must weigh less than 70 pounds. The charge depends on weight. There is pickup service. For all materials that can be sent in a flat-rate envelope (provided by the USPS), there is one low charge.
- *Parcel Post:* Parcel Post is used for mailing certain items—books, catalogs, other printed matter, or merchandise—not weighing more than 70 pounds. The charge depends on weight.
- *Media Mail (book rate):* **Media Mail** is generally used for books, film, loose-leaf binders containing medical information, or loose-leaf pages. The rates are low and depend upon weight. There is a category called Bound Printed Matter for any material bound by permanent fastenings such as staples or glue. These items may not be stationery, such as blank pads or printed forms. The rate is low and is determined by weight and destination.

Mail Services. The following services are available through the USPS:

- *Certified mail:* **Certified mail** provides the sender with a mailing receipt. The USPS keeps a record of delivery. This service is available with first-class or Priority Mail.

- *Insured mail:* **Insured mail** is covered for loss or damage. Coverage is available for up to $5,000. First-class mail, Parcel Post, and Media Mail may all be insured for rates determined by the amount of coverage desired.
- *Registered mail:* The greatest security for valuables is provided by **registered mail.** The sender gets a receipt at the time of mailing, and a delivery record is kept by the USPS. The mailing post office also maintains a record of mailing. Only first-class and Priority Mail may be registered. Postal insurance is provided for articles with a declared value up to $25,000. The charge is determined according to the declared value of the item.

There are special services that may also be of use:

- *Return receipt:* A **return receipt** provides the sender with evidence of delivery. It is available for most kinds of mail classifications when mail is insured for $50 or more.
- *Certificate of mailing:* This certificate provides only proof of an item's having been mailed. It does not provide proof of delivery. It must be purchased at the time of mailing.
- *Signature confirmation:* A signature confirmation provides the date and time of delivery or attempted delivery. This service may be purchased only at the time of mailing.
- *Restricted delivery:* **Restricted delivery** permits a sender to authorize delivery only to the addressee or the addressee's authorized agent. The addressee must be specified in the address by name.

Electronic Mail Services. The USPS offers **electronic mail service.** One service, the Post Electronic Courier Service (PosteCS), allows secure transmission of documents over the Internet. The system provides encryption and password protection to ensure security. It is a system advertised as tamperproof. Documents are sent with a digital authentication seal, and stamped with an official date and time.

For people who need to track or confirm certain mailings, the USPS also offers a track-and-confirm feature available to those who have an electronic link to the Postal Service. Electronic bill-paying and stamp-purchasing features are also offered.

■ Other Types of Shippers

In addition to the USPS, there are other shippers who may provide useful services, depending on the situation. The company that used to be known as United Parcel, and is now called UPS, is the largest delivery company. UPS delivers about three billion documents and packages a year.

The company has many levels of service, ranging from SonicAir BestFlight, which fills same-day and urgent needs, through Next Day Air, 2nd Day Air, 3 Day Select, and UPS Ground services. SonicAir BestFlight service is domestic and international, operating 24 hours a day, 365 days a year. There are no size or weight restrictions. However, depending on the method of shipment chosen, there are additional charges: for packages weighing more than 25 pounds; for the use of two separate airlines, if required; for delivery farther than 20 miles from the airport. This premium service, like other services, is priced by exact destination. The UPS Web site (www.ups.com) contains a calculator for determining the exact cost of any planned shipment.

UPS Next Day Air guarantees delivery by 8 a.m. in major cities in the 48 contiguous states. This service offers Saturday pickup and delivery and confirmation of deliveries. The second- and third-day air services deliver to all 50 states and guarantee delivery by 10:30 a.m., noon, or the end of the business day on the scheduled delivery date, and by 1:30 p.m. on Saturday.

UPS Ground service provides, as does UPS for its other services, definite-day delivery. The day is provided to the customer at the time of making arrangements for delivery.

Federal Express, well-known to most people as FedEx, offers comparable air delivery services—overnight and second-day air—as well as comparable ground delivery services. FedEx promotes its services as especially useful to small businesses, and it specializes in document and small-package delivery to home addresses. Like UPS, it maintains a calculator on its Web site (www.fedex.com) to make the shipping process easy for customers.

DHL Worldwide Express (www.dhl.com) offers services similar to those of the other two companies. It also specializes in transporting perishable goods and maintains a patented form of packing for such materials.

Premium services providing same-day or next-day delivery using air transport are very expensive. Their use should be restricted to situations where such quick delivery is necessary. Second-day, third-day, and ground services—considering pickup, money-back guarantees available in many cases, and tracking services—are still more expensive than most comparable USPS services, but they may be a viable choice, depending on circumstances.

These three major companies maintain helpful Web sites, enabling the customer to select a method of shipment, arrange for pickup, track the progress of the package sent, and receive confirmation of receipt.

There are also companies that are much smaller and that maintain a presence locally within cities. These messenger and courier services may be reputable and trustworthy for sending documents and packages locally.

▶ **GO TO PROJECT 6.5 ON PAGE 156** ▶

Chapter Projects

PROJECT 6.1   Composing a Referral Letter

WP 36 contains a list of Dr. Larsen's outside services. Keep this list in your Supplies folder to refer to when necessary. Add any new contact in the space provided.

Dr. Larsen has asked you to compose a referral letter for her signature. The purpose of the letter is to refer Florence Sherman to an ophthalmologist, Richard Diangelis, MD. Summarize the key points from the October 8 chart note, found in WP 37. This referral letter confirms a conversation between the two physicians on October 8. Date the letter you write October 13. Address an envelope. File the referral letter and Florence's chart note (WP 37) in Ms. Sherman's patient file.

PROJECT 6.2   Composing an Interoffice Memo

Dr. Larsen has asked you to prepare a memo from her to be sent throughout the medical center informing the staff of the following information.

Wanda Norberg, MD, will start working part-time in January while Dr. Larsen takes a two-month sabbatical to update the University Hospital Resident Program Guidelines (publication date is April 1). Dr. Norberg currently has an office at 2901 West Fifth Avenue, Suite 425, Chicago, Illinois 60612-9002. Her current phone number is 312-555-4525. Her hours will be 9 a.m. to 12 noon, Monday through Thursday, and Tuesday and Thursday evenings from 6 p.m. to 9 p.m. Employees are needed who will be able to work during these hours. If interested, contact Linda at extension 6022.

Date the memo October 13. Remember to add Dr. Norberg's information to the Outside Services list. File the memo in your Miscellaneous folder.

PROJECT 6.3   Internet Research: Journal Citations

Using your favorite Web browser, locate the American Medical Association's Web site. Visit the *Journal of the American Medical Association (JAMA)* and research author instructions. What are some of the criteria for acceptance of manuscripts? Can manuscripts be submitted by e-mail? Be prepared to discuss your findings in class.

Chapter Projects

PROJECT 6.4   Editing and Proofreading Reports

Dr. Larsen has asked you to edit and proofread two reports that she will use for her classroom teaching. The reports are on the CD-ROM, labeled **project6.4a** and **project6.4b**. The physician has marked the changes to be made on WP 38 and 39. The reports also contain unmarked errors. First save the reports on your own disk as Project 6.4 reports. Then edit and proofread the reports. Remember to save your work.

PROJECT 6.5   Communications Terms

On WP 40, match the communications term in Column 2 with its definition in Column 1.

CHAPTER SUMMARY

1. The administrative medical assistant represents the physician and the practice through the use of good written communication skills. Often, the assistant's opportunities for career advancement depend in part on the quality of these skills.

2. The three commonly used letter formats are block style, modified-block style, and simplified style. Punctuation may be either standard or open. Assistants may compose letters of acknowledgment, information, referral or consultation, and follow-up, as well as interoffice memorandums.

3. Professional report preparation usually involves using word processing to create a draft and then a final manuscript. Reports follow specific layout guidelines.

4. Proofreading involves finding and correcting errors in a document. Editing involves assessing the clarity, consistency, and overall effectiveness of a communication.

5. Sort mail according to its importance: (1) items sent by Express or Priority Mail, or registered or certified mail; (2) regular first-class mail; (3) the physician's personal mail; (4) periodicals and newspapers; (5) advertising materials; and (6) samples. The procedures for opening mail are (1) open all letters except those marked "Personal" unless you are authorized to open all mail; (2) check the contents of each envelope carefully; (3) stamp the date on each item to show when it was received; (4) attach enclosures to each item; (5) carefully put aside checks from patients to be recorded and deposited later; (6) check to see that the envelope is empty and not needed before discarding it; (7) write a reminder on the calendar or in the tickler file about material being sent separately; (8) attach the patient's chart to correspondence regarding the patient and place it in a high-priority area on the physician's desk; (9) if a business letter responds to a request, pull the relevant file and attach the letter to it; and (10) set aside correspondence that can be answered without the physician's seeing it.

6. Mail classifications include first-class mail, Priority Mail, Express Mail, Parcel Post, and Media Mail.

KEY TERMS

The following key terms appear in **boldface** type in this chapter. Administrative medical assistants must know the meaning and correct use of each of these terms. Can you recall what each term means? Refer to this chapter or to the glossary for any terms you need to review.

annotate	Media Mail
bibliography	modified-block-style letter
block-style letter	open punctuation
certified mail	Priority Mail
editing	proofreading
electronic mail service	registered mail
endnotes	restricted delivery
Express Mail	return receipt
first draft	simplified-style letter
footnotes	standard punctuation
insured mail	title page

THINKING IT THROUGH

These questions cover the most important points in this chapter. Using your critical thinking skills, play the role of an administrative medical assistant as you answer each question. Be prepared to present your responses in class.

1. In a job interview, you are asked to describe the quality of your written communication skills and to state why these skills are important. How do you respond?

2. Mrs. Court, who has a history of missed appointments, has just missed her latest one. The doctor asks that you contact her about the missed appointment, to mention politely that this has happened before, and to ask her to reschedule as soon as possible. Why would you choose to write a letter rather than to call the patient?

3. Prepare a draft of the body of the letter to Mrs. Court. Keep in mind the doctor's directions about the content and tone.

4. A colleague sends you this e-mail: "Please help! I need to prepare final manuscript for an article Dr. Trelando is submitting." You decide to e-mail the directions for preparing the title page and text pages for final manuscript. What does your e-mail say?

5. State four important procedures in opening and sorting the mail.

6. What steps would you take to investigate the lowest-cost shipping method for a small package that must be delivered overnight?

YOUR ROLE

Welcome to the practice of Dr. Karen Larsen! Today, you begin to apply the skills you have learned in this text as you assume the role of Linda Schwartz, Dr. Larsen's administrative medical assistant.

Simulation 1 is the first of three simulations in the text. These simulations provide practical experience in working in a physician's office. You will discover how various tasks relate to each other.

The daily events in the office are narrated on the Simulation Recordings that accompany the text. As you listen to the recordings, you will handle various assignments as the assistant. Your simulation work will include making and canceling appointments, preparing messages, creating communications, preparing various medical forms, and following through on daily tasks.

BEFORE YOU START

The following suggestions apply to all the simulations:

1. Review the content of the previous chapters to ensure familiarity with procedures.

2. Prepare three file folders:
   a. Label as *Day 1 and your name.*
   b. Label as *Day 2 and your name.*
   c. Label as *Day 3 and your name.*

3. Assemble and organize necessary materials as listed under *Materials* on the next page.

4. Set priorities each day by organizing your work in order of importance and completing the work in that sequence. Any work left over from Day 1 should be carried over into Day 2, and so forth. The work left over from any previous day should be taken into account in setting the priorities for that day. It is also possible that you may have work left over from the final day. It is important to remember to complete major tasks each day.

5. Be prepared for interruptions. These occur frequently as they would in a physician's office. Do not let interruptions upset you—learn to rearrange priorities.

6. Develop shortcuts, easier procedures, and better ways of doing tasks.

PROCEDURES

Day 1, Tuesday, October 14

1. Check today's appointments. Pull chart folders for today's appointments. Keep them together.

2. Organize any other materials you will need. Arrange your desk in an orderly fashion, leaving room for you to work.

3. Use your *To-Do List* (WP 45), checking off tasks as you complete them.

4. Use the *Telephone Log* form (WP 44) to list the answering service and all incoming calls. Make only brief notations on this form, checking off items as you follow through on them.

5. The simulation begins with the call to the answering service. You will hear conversations between the assistant and the answering service, the patients, and other callers. (Remember, you are assuming the role of Linda Schwartz, administrative medical assistant for Karen Larsen, MD.) You will hear Dr. Larsen giving you directions and dictation. You will **not** hear the voices of all patients—only those who ask you to do something.

6. Dr. Larsen may give new directions. There may be additional telephone calls. Listen to the conversations continuously, stopping to obtain information, to have information repeated, and to obtain the appointment calendar, message blanks, and other items. Make appropriate notes as you listen.

7. As you complete tasks, place them in your *Day 1* folder, organizing them as directed by your instructor. Place any incomplete work in your *Day 2* folder.

Day 2, Wednesday, October 15

1. Follow the same procedures as in Day 1. Remember that some of Day 2's new items may be more important than work left over from Day 1. Again, listen to conversations continuously, stopping as necessary.

2. At the end of Day 2, put all your completed work in the Day 2 folder, following your instructor's directions. Follow your instructor's advice with what to do with incomplete work.

MATERIALS

You will need the following materials to complete Simulation 1. If these materials are not already in the proper folders, obtain them from the sources indicated.

Materials .... Source ....

Appointment calendar

Supplies folder:

Appointment cards	WP 34
Letterhead	CD-ROM
Notepad	You provide.
Plain paper	You provide.
Patient information forms	WP 41 & 42
Records release form	WP 43
Telephone log	WP 44
Telephone message blanks	WP 8–15
To-do list	WP 45

To-Do Items ....

Note: If you have completed all the projects and do not have the following listed items, discuss the missing items with your instructor.

Day 1 folder:
Place patients' charts for October 14.

Day 2 folder:
Place patients' charts for October 15.

Miscellaneous folder:
Wanda Norberg, MD—message (Project 4.1) and interoffice memo (Project 6.2)

Patients' folders:

The following patients' folders (charts) should contain the chart note, patient information form, and any other items listed.

Armstrong, Monica

Baab, Thomas

Babcock, Sara—message   (Project 4.1)

Burton, Randy

Casagranda, Doris

Castro, Joseph

Dayton, Theresa

Grant, Todd

Jonathan, Charles III

Kramer, Jeffrey—message   (Project 4.1)

Matthews, Ardis

Mendez, Ana

Morton, Sarah

Murrary, Raymond

Phan, Marc

Richards, Warren

Roberts, Suzanne

Robertson, Gary

Sherman, Florence—referral letter,   (Project 6.1)
   chart note, and envelope

Sinclair, Gene

Sun, Cheng

Villano, Stephen

EVALUATION

You will be evaluated as follows:

1. Good judgment in establishing priorities—did you use good judgment? Did you accomplish the most important tasks?
2. Work of good quality—are tasks accurate and neat?
3. Quantity—did you complete a reasonable amount of work? Would a physician be satisfied with your rate of accomplishment?

NDCmedisoft™ INSTRUCTIONS

If your instructor has assigned the use of NDCmedisoft™, you will complete certain parts of Simulation 1 using the software program.

To complete this simulation in NDCmedisoft™, you must be able to:

- Schedule appointments
- Print physician's schedule
- Enter new patients
- Update patient information

Specific instructions are in Appendix A.

Enter the new appointments in Office Hours. Then print Dr. Larsen's schedule for October 14 and 15. Remember that Office Hours uses the Windows System Date as the default date, so you will need to change the date that appears in the Office Hours calendar.

Enter the two new patients. Information about new patients is entered in the Patient/Guarantor dialog box and the Case dialog box. In the Patient/Guarantor dialog box, complete the following boxes:

Name, Address Tab

Chart Number
Last Name
First Name
Middle Initial
Street
City
State
Zip Code
Home Phone
Birthdate
Sex
Social Security Number

Other Information Tab

Type
Assigned Provider
Signature on File
Emergency Contact: Name, Home Phone

In the Case dialog box, data should be entered in the following boxes:

Personal Tab

Description
Guarantor
Marital Status

Account Tab

Assigned Provider

Policy 1

Insurance 1
Policy Holder 1
Relationship to Insured
Policy Number
Group Number
Assignment of Benefits/Accept Assignment (yes)
Insurance Coverage Percents:
  Box A: 80
  Boxes B–H: 0

Edit the record for the patient whose phone number has changed. Edit the record for the patient whose phone number and address have changed.

Patient Records

CHAPTER 7
Patient Medical
Records

CHAPTER 8
Insurance and Coding

CHAPTER 9
Billing,
Reimbursement,
and Collections

Part 3 discusses the important duties of the administrative medical assistant concerning patients' medical records. It also presents the tasks involved with insurance, medical coding, billing, and collections.

CONSIDER THIS: Attention to detail and accurate work are essential attributes of the successful administrative medical assistant. *When processing data concerning patients' medical records and bills, what steps can you take to ensure accuracy?*

CHAPTER

7

Patient Medical Records

OBJECTIVES

After studying this chapter, you will be able to:

1. List the components that make up medical records and discuss their importance to the practice, including their role as legal documents.
2. Describe the components of the SOAP format—the most common format used for recording medical information about patients.
3. Identify the three parts of the problem-oriented medical record (POMR) format.
4. Transcribe medical data dictated by a physician, while applying guidelines for punctuation, capitalization, and the use of standard medical abbreviations, numbers, and symbols.
5. Discuss the preservation of medical records.
6. Explain who actually owns a patient's medical record.
7. List standards to be used for quality assurance in maintaining medical records.

INTRODUCTION

There are three main categories of records found in medical facilities: (1) medical records of the patient's state of health, (2) correspondence pertaining to the field of health care, and (3) documents related to the business and financial management of the practice. The first category, the patient's medical record, is the topic of this chapter.

KEY TERMS

Study these important words, which are defined in this chapter, to build your professional vocabulary:

assessment	objective	review of systems (ROS)
chief complaint (CC)	past medical history (PMH)	rule out (R/O)
diagnosis (Dx)	physical exam (PE)	SOAP
family history (FH)	plan	social history (SH)
history of present illness (HPI)	problem-oriented medical record (POMR)	subjective
impression		

The patient medical record, also referred to as the patient's "chart" or "file," is the source of information about all aspects of a patient's health care. Accurate and up-to-date medical records are vital to a medical practice. Current records are necessary for enabling a continuum of care for patients, for financial and legal success, and for research purposes. It is not surprising, therefore, that one of the most important skills an administrative medical assistant can demonstrate is the ability to maintain accurate and complete medical records. In working with medical records, the assistant should be familiar with:

- Why medical records are regarded as legal documents.
- The types of reports and information typically found in a medical record.
- The importance of well-maintained medical records for the practice.
- The method for making corrections to a medical record.

Medical Records as Legal Documents

A patient's medical record constitutes the legal record of the medical practice. On occasion, patients' records may have to be produced in court, either to uphold the rights of the physician if the physician is involved in litigation or to substantiate the claim of the patient if the physician is called as a witness. In malpractice cases, the content and quality of a medical record can be pivotal, leaving a greater impression on a jury, it is said, than even the physician's credentials, personality, or reputation. If the data in a medical record are incomplete, illegible, or poorly maintained, a plaintiff's attorney may be able to make even the best patient care appear negligent. Therefore, it is important for the administrative medical assistant to help the physician maintain medical records as carefully as possible. The assistant should bear in mind that any record could become a vehicle for defending a clinical course of action down the road.

What Is in a Medical Record?

A patient's medical record holds all data about that patient. Medical records generally include the following items.

- *Chart notes:* A chronological record of ongoing patient care and progress, chart notes are entries made by the physician, nurse, or other health care professional regarding pertinent points of a given visit or communication with the patient. The chart notes for a new patient may be extensive, often containing the details of a medical history and physical. Thereafter, chart notes may simply describe changes in the patient's condition or medication. Figure 7.1 is an example of a simple chart note entered by a registered nurse regarding a telephone call received from a patient.

- *History and physical (H&P): History* refers to the patient's complete medical history (usually obtained by the physician during an interview with the patient on his or her first visit); *physical* refers to the initial results of a physical examination by the physician.
- *Referral and consultation letters:* Copies of letters sent to other physicians, referring the patient for specific examinations, tests, and so on, are part of the medical record.
- *Medical reports:* Lab reports, x-ray reports, and reports from special procedures such as electrocardiograms are kept in the medical record. The type and number of medical reports in the file depend on the patient's condition and the specialty of the attending physician.
- *Correspondence:* Copies of all correspondence with the patient, including letters, faxes, and notes of telephone conversations and e-mail messages are part of the medical record.
- *Clinical forms:* Forms such as immunization records and pediatric growth and development records are included.
- *Medication list:* A listing of all medications prescribed, including dosage, dispensing instructions, and so on, as well as a list of the patient's known allergies to medications, if any, are in the medical record.

In addition to medical data, the patient's record contains administrative data such as the patient's personal information—including insurance and billing records—and the release of information and assignment of benefits.

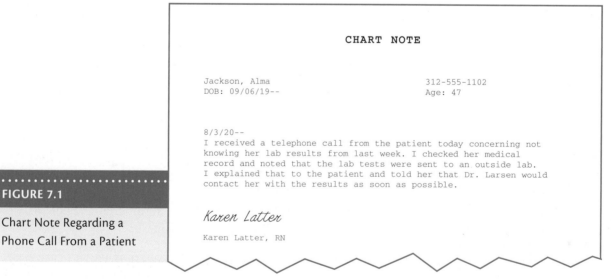

FIGURE 7.1

Chart Note Regarding a Phone Call From a Patient

```
                          CHART NOTE


    Jackson, Alma                        312-555-1102
    DOB: 09/06/19--                      Age: 47


    8/3/20--
    I received a telephone call from the patient today concerning not
    knowing her lab results from last week. I checked her medical
    record and noted that the lab tests were sent to an outside lab.
    I explained that to the patient and told her that Dr. Larsen would
    contact her with the results as soon as possible.

    Karen Latter

    Karen Latter, RN
```

■ Reasons for Maintaining Medical Records

Medical records provide the practice with complete information regarding the patient. Thus, they are used by the practice in the following ways:

- As the main source of information for coordinating and carrying out patient care among all providers involved with the patient.
- As evidence of the course of an illness and a record of the treatment being used.
- As a record of the quality of care provided to patients.
- As a tool for ensuring communication and continuity of care from one medical facility to another.
- As the legal record for the practice.
- As the main record to ensure appropriate reimbursement.
- As a source of data for research purposes, for example, as background material for preparing a lecture, an article, or a book.

Because the medical record is the basis for so many activities in a practice, every effort should be made to maintain it well. The following procedures should be used. Each time the patient is seen by a provider—such as for a blood pressure check or a special procedure, or on a return visit for a medication, whether in the office or at another location—an entry or notation must be made in the patient's medical record. Entries must be keyed or handwritten in ink. As the sample chart note in Figure 7.1 illustrates, every entry should contain: (1) patient identifying information—name, phone number, date of birth, and age; (2) the date of the patient's visit or communication; and (3) the signature and title of the responsible provider or other health care professional. If an entry is transcribed, it is signed with the name of the dictator, followed by the initials of the transcriptionist. Two blank lines should be left on the record for the dictator's handwritten signature.

EXAMPLE

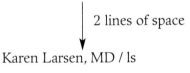

2 lines of space

Karen Larsen, MD / ls

COMPLIANCE TIP

Remember that no part of a record should be altered, removed, deleted, or destroyed. Only proper correction procedures may be used. Great care must be taken when entering data to ensure that they are inserted in the correct chart. If an error or discrepancy is discovered in the medical record at a much later date, the physician may dictate an addendum to the record to correct the discrepancy.

Entries should be made in a compact way, without leaving large gaps between notes. This eliminates the possibility of someone's tampering with the record later on and also ensures that the entries will be sequential. It is also important to make entries in a medical record promptly. Frequent delays in making entries will reflect poorly on the provider. Finally, the items in the record should be grouped according to type and placed within each section in a consistent chronological order, either ascending or descending.

■ Making Corrections

Because medical records are legal documents, it is not permissible to use an eraser or correction fluid to correct them. If you make an error while recording an entry in a medical record, use the following method to correct it:

- Use the strike-through feature in the word processing program or draw a single line through the incorrect statements in the medical record (making sure the inaccurate material is still legible).
- Enter the word *error* next to the deleted statement.
- Write your initials and the date next to the correction.
- Enter the correct information into the medical record.

▶ **GO TO PROJECT 7.1 ON PAGE 185** ▶

7.2 THE SOAP METHOD OF RECORD KEEPING AND THE POMR FORMAT

The **SOAP** method is the most common system for outlining and structuring chart notes for a medical record. It facilitates the creation of uniform and complete notes in a simple format that is easy to read. The acronym *SOAP* stands for the following headings that are used to structure the chart note: *SUBJECTIVE, OBJECTIVE, ASSESSMENT,* and *PLAN.* Each of these headings contains a specific type of information as follows.

■ The SOAP Method

S O A P
Subjective Findings

Subjective Findings. Subjective findings are the patient's description of the problem or complaint, including symptoms troubling the patient, when the symptoms began, external or associated factors, remedies tried, and past medical treatment. The subjective information in a SOAP record may include any or all of the subheadings that follow.

- **Chief complaint (CC):** The reason for the visit or why the patient is seeking the physician's advice.

- **History of present illness (HPI):** Information about the symptoms troubling the patient—when they began, what affects them (for example, pain upon exertion), any opinion the patient may have as to their cause, what remedies the patient has tried, and any medical treatment the patient may have been given.
- **Past medical history (PMH):** A listing of any illnesses the patient has had in the past along with the treatments administered or operations performed. This history also includes a description of any accidents, injuries, congenital problems, or allergies to medicines or other substances the patient may have.
- **Family history (FH):** Facts about the health of the patient's parents, siblings, and other blood relatives that might be significant to the patient's condition. For example, family history is especially important in treating hereditary diseases.
- **Social history (SH):** The patient's social history and marital history, especially if they are pertinent to the patient's treatment. Information regarding the patient's eating, drinking, or smoking habits, the patient's occupation, and the patient's interests may also be included in this section.
- **Review of systems (ROS):** The physician's review of each body system with the patient (for example, the respiratory system and the genitourinary system). The physician asks specific questions about the functioning of each system and reviews information in the patient's record.

FIGURE 7.2

During the first visit of a new patient, the physician usually takes note of the patient's complete medical history. *Why is it important for patients' medical histories to be placed in their charts promptly?*

In some chart notes, the three subheadings *PMH, FH,* and *SH* (for *past medical history, family history,* and *social history*) may be combined into one subheading, *PFSH.*

S O A P
Objective Findings

Objective Findings. The **objective** findings in a SOAP record are the physician's examination of the patient. Results of the examination may be dictated under the heading **physical exam (PE).** The exam may be a complete physical examination, in which the findings for each of the major areas of the body are included, or it may cover only the pertinent body systems for that visit. The following subheadings give body systems that may be included in a physical exam:

VITAL SIGNS (VS): The patient's temperature, pulse, and respirations (TPR); blood pressure (BP); and height and weight are included in this category.

GENERAL: A general description of the patient might be, for example, "This is a well-developed, well-nourished, 27-year-old Caucasian female."

HEENT: This abbreviation stands for *head, eyes, ears, nose,* and *throat.*

NECK

HEART

CHEST

LUNGS

ABDOMEN

PELVIC

RECTAL

EXTREMITIES

NEUROLOGICAL

FIGURE 7.3

Findings from the physician's examination must be recorded accurately in the patient's chart. *How can the administrative medical assistant ensure that the transcription is accurate?*

The results of lab tests, x-rays, and other diagnostic procedures are also part of the objective findings. These results may be included in the corresponding body system review, or they may be listed as separate entries or under a separate heading, such as *LAB,* usually after the list of body systems.

SOAP
Assessment

Assessment. The **assessment** in a SOAP record is the physician's interpretation of the subjective and objective findings. The term *assessment* is used interchangeably with the terms **diagnosis (Dx)** and **impression** and gives a name to the condition from which the patient is suffering. Sometimes the assessment is tentative, pending further developments. Occasionally, the physician uses the phrase **rule out (R/O)** before a diagnosis, meaning that the diagnosis, while possible, is not likely and that further tests will be performed for confirmation.

SOAP
Plan

Plan. The **plan,** or treatment, section lists the following information regarding the physician's treatment of the illness:

- Prescribed medications and their exact dosages
- Instructions given to the patient
- Recommendations for hospitalization or surgery
- Any special tests that need to be performed

Figures 7.4 and 7.5 on pages 172–173 contain examples of chart notes that incorporate the SOAP format. In Figure 7.4, although not all the SOAP headings are spelled out, the entries clearly follow the SOAP format described above. The subjective findings begin with *CC* (chief complaint) and continue up to *PHYSICAL EXAM,* which contains the objective findings. The assessment and plan follow with their own headings.

In Figure 7.5, the SOAP format is more apparent, with the addition of a *LAB* heading after the objective findings. Notice that the level of detail contained in the entries in Figure 7.4 is much greater than that in Figure 7.5. This is because the patient described in Figure 7.4 is a new patient, and therefore a complete history and physical have been performed. The patient described in Figure 7.5 is a returning patient who is visiting for help with a specific illness.

As can be seen from an examination of Figures 7.4 and 7.5, the SOAP format can accommodate many variations. The value in using the SOAP outline, or a variation of it, is that by following the simple formula of the acronym, the person writing or dictating the note is more likely to cover all the important issues. In addition, the logic of the format lends itself well to displaying the provider's thought processes in deciding on a course of treatment. Having such a record improves communication for all those involved in the care of the patient. It also minimizes the provider's exposure to legal risk.

```
                    HISTORY AND PHYSICAL REPORT

Paulson, Laura                                          312-555-7261
DOB: 03/01/19--                                         Age: 44

3/6/20--
CC: Annual female exam for this 44-year-old black patient.

PMH: Tonsillectomy at age 3; wisdom teeth pulled at age 29.

ALLERGIES: SULFA.

CURRENT MEDICATIONS: None.

FH: Father died at age 70 of multiple problems including carcinoma of larynx,
stroke, and pneumonia. Mother, age 66, is in good health. No siblings.

SH: Laura completed high school, plus one to two years of college. Patient works
at a dry cleaner, pressing machine and front desk. Does not smoke nor use alcohol.
She was never on birth control pills or any other major medication.

MARITAL HISTORY: Husband, age 46, is in good health. They have been married 24 years
and have three children in good health.

ROS:
SKIN: Negative.
HEENT: Patient wears glasses with last eye exam 3 months ago. She has occasional
sinusitis.
CHEST: No chest pain or palpitation.
RESPIRATORY: Negative.
ABDOMEN: Negative.
PELVIC: LMP 3 weeks ago. Gravida 3, para 3. Patient uses OTC birth control products.
MUSCULOSKELETAL: Occasional stiffness of elbow.
NEUROLOGICAL: Negative

PHYSICAL EXAM:
GENERAL: Alert black female in no acute distress. BP, 116/82. Pulse, 86.
Respirations, 24. Height, 64 inches; weight, 128 pounds.
HEENT: Normocephalic. Ears, TMs normal. Eyes, PERLA; EOMs, intact. Nose, patent.
Throat, within normal limits.
NECK: Supple. Thyroid, not enlarged. Carotids, equal without bruits.
BREASTS: Fine lumps bilaterally; nothing suspicious.
HEART: Regular sinus rhythm without murmurs.
LUNGS: Clear to A&P.
ABDOMEN: Soft; without masses, tenderness, or scars.
PELVIC: Cervix, clean. Uterus, anteverted and smooth. Adnexa and vagina, WNL.
Rectovaginal confirms.
EXTREMITIES: Within normal limits with fine varicosities bilaterally.
NEUROLOGICAL: Cranial nerves II-XII, intact.

ASSESSMENT: Generally healthy female.

PLAN:   1. Schedule mammogram.
        2. Routine screen labs.
        3. UA.
        4. Hemoccults x 3.

Karen Larsen

Karen Larsen, MD/ls
```

Problem-Oriented Medical Records (POMR)

Another form of record keeping revolves around a list of the patient's problems. A record organized in this way is referred to as a **problem-oriented medical record (POMR).** In a problem-oriented medical record, there are three essential components.

Database. The database consists of the complete history of the patient, including the problem, history of present illness, past medical history, family history, social history, and review of systems, followed by information derived from a complete examination and routine diagnostic tests.

FIGURE 7.5

Chart Note in the SOAP Format

CHART NOTE

Benson, Harriett   312-555-9823
DOB: 07/29/19--   Age: 23

March 6, 20--
SUBJECTIVE: Patient presents with mild urinary urgency and frequency.
Patient has also had frequent lower abdominal pain, but no abnormal
vaginal symptoms.

OBJECTIVE: Temperature, 98.6°. Pulse, 76 and regular. Respirations,
20. Abdominal exam reveals mild suprapubic tenderness; otherwise,
exam is unremarkable.

LAB: Urinalysis is negative; urine culture is pending.

ASSESSMENT: Suspect urethritis.

PLAN: Patient placed on 7-day course of ciprofloxacin 500 mg b.i.d.
She was reminded to drink at least 8 glasses of water daily. RTC if
not improving.

Karen Larsen

Karen Larsen, MD/ls

Initial Plan. Based on the database and the initial problems of the patient, the physician begins a course of treatment detailed in this section.

Problem List. The problem list is a running account of the patient's problems. It is referred to and updated at each clinic visit. This procedure helps assure that all problems are considered during a visit. Using the list, the physician can, at a glance, learn what problems the patient has had, how often they have appeared, and the treatment prescribed. This list saves time in that the physician does not have to study the patient's entire chart before obtaining relevant information.

FIGURE 7.6

Chart Note for a Problem-
Oriented Medical Record
(POMR)

CHART NOTE

Pander, Ian   312-555-9256
DOB: 08/02/19--   Age: 22

March 7, 20--
PROBLEM 1: Tonsillitis.

CHIEF COMPLAINT: Sore throat times two days.

S: Sore throat, difficulty swallowing.

O: Temperature 101°. Pharyngitis with exudative tonsillitis.

PLAN: 1. Throat culture.
        2. 1.2 units CR Bicillin.
        3. Recheck in 10 days.

Karen Larsen

Karen Larsen, MD/ls

March 14, 20--
PROBLEM 1:

S: Recheck. Patient feels better.

O: Temperature, normal. No problem with swallowing.

A: Problem 1 resolved.

P: Gargle with warm salt water if necessary. Pharyngitis with exudative
   tonsillitis resolved.

Karen Larsen

Karen Larsen, MD/ls

June 11, 20--
PROBLEM 2: Chip fracture lunate, left.

S: Pain in instep and tarsal bones.

O: Swelling and ecchymosis, left foot.

A: X-ray shows questionable undisplaced chip fracture of lunate.

P: 1. Continue supportive shoes.
        2. Referred to orthopedics for further evaluation.

Karen Larsen

Karen Larsen, MD/ls

Generally, the SOAP format is used for organizing entries within the problem list. The SOAP format may also be used to outline the history and physical for the database section. Figure 7.6 is an example of a problem-oriented medical record. Notice how each entry begins with the date of the patient visit, followed by a reference to the problem being treated—*PROBLEM 1, PROBLEM 2,* and so on. This type of record-keeping format is one of the most commonly used in medical practices.

GO TO PROJECT 7.2 ON PAGE 185

7.3   TRANSCRIPTION GUIDELINES

Part of an administrative medical assistant's role is to transcribe physicians' chart notes and other medical documents. Using dictation equipment, physicians may dictate notes for a medical record and then give or transmit the recording to an assistant for transcription during the course of the day or week.

■ Listening Techniques

Dictation equipment comes in various formats. Either digital media, such as a CD, or analog media, such as a cassette tape, store the recording. The principles of transcription are the same regardless of the equipment. Tone, volume, and rate of speed can be regulated for the assistant's own comfort and rate of transcription. A foot pedal is used for starting the machine and for reversing it. Headphones are provided to keep the recorded information confidential and to avoid disturbing other people in the office. Another helpful item is a counter, which makes it possible to locate a specific reference speedily and to judge the length of a document.

Since using a transcribing machine is something of a balancing act for the ear, foot, and keyboard, a good technique is to listen to three or four words at a time, key those words, and then listen to the next three or four words. Generally, headings and subheadings are easy to determine from the dictation, especially once you become familiar with a standard format.

■ Office Policy

Because every office uses its own format for transcribing chart notes, assistants need to become familiar with the policy of the office where they work. In transcribing material, you should listen carefully to what the dictator says, including any instructions or corrections he or she may have included. Above all, you should not add anything that is not there, such as headings or changes to the sentence structure. If there is anything in the dictation that is not clear, it is important to flag the problem. Then, at a time that is convenient for the physician, you should ask for clarification.

■ Basic Medical Transcription Guidelines

Skill in spelling, knowledge of punctuation and capitalization, and familiarity with medical terminology help make the assistant efficient in transcribing a physician's dictation. Also important is knowing the basic guidelines for capitalization and the use of standard medical abbreviations, numbers, and symbols. Study and refer to the following list of guidelines for transcribing medical documents.

1. Use commas in the following situations:

   a. Set off nonessential words and phrases.
   Dr. Jones, a first-year resident, is on call.
   Janice, who was hired last month, will attend next week's conference.

   b. Set off introductory clauses or phrases.
   After the cast was applied, the x-ray showed the fracture to be in good alignment.
   If so, the physician will have to leave an hour before closing.

   c. Separate the year in a complete date. Do *not* use commas when only the month and year are presented. *(Note:* Do *not* use numerals for dates in text material; for example, "The surgery is scheduled for 11/01/03.")
   The surgery is scheduled for Wednesday, May 1, 2002.
   The patient was last seen in May 2000 for an ultrasound.

   d. Separate degrees, titles, and so on after names.
   The patient was referred to Phil Stevens, PhD, for psychological testing.

   e. Separate items in a series.
   The sponge, needle, and instrument counts were correct.

   f. Separate independent sentences connected with a conjunction.
   Mrs. Tina Roe called in the last hour, and she still insists on seeing the physician today.

   g. Set off direct address in a sentence.
   Set the chart on the desk, Janis, and take the new dictation tape with you.

   h. Separate equal adjectives (modifiers).
   The patient is a well-nourished, well-developed female.
   The 15-year-old Caucasian male has brain cancer. (The adjective 15-year-old" modifies both *Caucasian* and *male;* therefore, no comma separates them.)

   i. Place commas and periods inside quotation marks.
   The patient states he feels "fuzzy in the head," and he needs medication for this symptom.

j. Use a comma to indicate missing words.
Chest x-ray, normal. (Note: Chest x-ray was normal.)

k. Use a comma to separate parts of an inverted diagnosis.
Ankle sprain, left.

2. Use semicolons in the following situations:

a. Separate related independent clauses (sentences) without a conjunction.
The surgery was scheduled for 4 p.m.; it lasted 4 hours.

b. Set off independent clauses that already contain one or more commas and have a conjunction, if a misreading might result.
If, following the call, the appointment has been made, Janet can leave at 9:30 p.m.; but if the appointment has not been made, she needs to leave right away.

c. Separate a transitional word or phrase that begins an independent sentence, such as *therefore, however, in fact, namely,* and *thus* from another independent sentence.
The physician will be 2 hours late; however, there are no patients scheduled until this afternoon.

d. Separate items in a series when the items have commas.
The physician has lectures scheduled in St. Paul, Minnesota; Fargo, North Dakota; and Des Moines, Iowa.

e. Place semicolons outside of quotation marks.
The patient said, "I will obtain my medical records"; she did not bring them to the office.

3. Use a colon in the following situations:

a. Introduce a list, series, or enumeration.
The patient complains of the following symptoms: dizziness, lightheadedness, and palpitations.
The patient was instructed to do the following:
1. Follow a low-fat, low-cholesterol diet.
2. Exercise 3 times a week.
3. Retest cholesterol in 3 months.

b. Separate hours and minutes.
The surgery is scheduled to begin at 12:30 p.m.

c. Introduce an example, a rule, or a principle.
We have only one choice: immediate surgery.

4. Use capital letters in the following situations:

   a. Emphasize allergies in full capital letters. *(Note:* An alternative method is to use boldface.)
      The patient was ALLERGIC TO PENICILLIN.
      ALLERGIES: Penicillin.

   b. Do *not* capitalize common nouns designating rooms, such as *operating room* or *emergency room.* Capitalize the official names of designated rooms.
      The patient was seen in the intensive care unit. (Note: The patient was seen in the ICU.)
      The patient is scheduled for the operating room in an hour.
      The patient was sent to Recovery Room C at 9 a.m.
      The meeting will take place in the Viking Room.

   c. Do *not* capitalize medical specialties or variations of specialties.
      The patient was referred to cardiology.
      The cardiologist sent the patient back to the family practice physician.

   d. Capitalize trade and brand names but do not capitalize generic names; for example, Tylenol #3, pHisoHex, and Cardizem, but alcohol, catgut, and aspirin.

   e. Capitalize races, peoples, religions, and languages but generally not color designations such as *black* or *white* when they refer to race *(Caucasian, African American, Jewish, Hispanic, Mexican American, English,* and so on).
      The patient is a well-developed, well-nourished Puerto Rican male.
      The patient is a well-developed, well-nourished white female.
      The 31-year-old black patient was discharged yesterday.

   f. Use all-capital letters for headings and subheadings in the medical document.
      GENITOURINARY: Exam will be completed next month.

5. Use a hyphen in the following situations:

   a. Connect the elements of compound adjectives that appear before nouns.
      She had a low-grade temperature. (Note: Her temperature was low grade.)
      This was a well-developed Asian American male.
      There was a 5-cm lesion on the left side.

   b. Form *self*-compounds.
      The patient was self-employed.

c. Look up compound nouns in a current dictionary to determine if they are hyphenated or closed-up. Use two separate, non-hyphenated words for two-word verbs.

The patient is scheduled for a follow-up visit.
The patient's checkup was delayed.
The patient will follow up with hematology.

d. Join a single letter to a word to form a coined compound word.

The patient had a T-cell abnormality. (Note: We will measure the patient's T cells.)
The x-ray results will be sent to the office.

e. Insert a hyphen between a prefix and a capitalized word, as in *non-Hodgkin* or *mid-March*.

6. Use abbreviations as follows:

a. Use published abbreviations.

The mole is 1.25 cm in circumference with irregular borders.

b. Use proper abbreviations for transcribing medication administration times.

The patient was placed on Augmentin 125 mg t.i.d. x 5 days.
A prescription for tetracycline 500 mg q.i.d. was given to the patient.
(Note: Always keep units of measurement on the same line.)

c. Do not abbreviate the diagnosis, conclusion, or procedural/operative title in medical documents. Nondisease-related words in the diagnostic or procedural titles may be abbreviated.

DIAGNOSIS: End stage renal disease. (Note: not ESRD)
OPERATION: Excise 0.5-cm polyp from right naris.

d. Spell out a word if the abbreviation could be misunderstood.

The patient has no history of a cancer problem. (Note: The abbreviation CA could mean calcium, cancer, or coronary artery.)

e. Do *not* abbreviate beats per minute.

Pulse was 72 beats per minute.

f. Use lowercase letters with periods for *a.m.* and *p.m.* (preferred style). Spell out even times when *a.m., p.m.,* or *o'clock* is not used.

The next available appointment is for 10 a.m.
The patient will be seen at three.

7. Use numbers as follows:

a. Spell out numbers at the beginning of a sentence, or recast the sentence.

Ten milligrams was given to the patient.
Then 10 mg was given to the patient.

b. Use Arabic numbers with technical measurements.

A #14 Foley catheter was inserted.
A No. 4 Foley catheter was inserted.
The surgeon suggested 5- to 6-inch elastic stays.
The patient was given 10 tablets.
The patient was prescribed Paxil 20 mg q.d., #60.

c. Express ages in figures when used as significant statistics or as technical measurements.

This 5-year-old boy has had cold symptoms for the past 2 weeks.
The 5½-month-old child was not left unattended.

d. Spell out ordinal numbers and simple fractions (preferred style).

The patient was discharged on the fifth postoperative day.
Next, one-third of the abdomen was prepped.

e. Use roman numerals for cranial nerves, ECG leads, EEG leads, clotting factors, and noncounting listings (preferred style).

The exam found the cranial nerves II-XII were intact.
The patient had stage II carcinoma.
The patient had type II diabetes mellitus.

f. Use Arabic numbers with grades.

The patient had a grade 2 systolic ejection murmur.

g. Insert a zero in front of the decimal point when a decimal is less than a whole number.

The patient's prescription was changed to 0.125 mg.

h. Enumerate listings as much as possible.

DIAGNOSES: 1. Right otitis media.
*   2. Laryngitis.*
*   3. Pharyngitis.*
The diagnoses were (1) right otitis media, (2) laryngitis, and (3) pharyngitis.

i. Do *not* repeat units of measure in a series.

The patient was given 5, 10, and 20 cc.

8. Use symbols when transcribing numbers or abbreviations. Some common examples are shown below.

Heard	Keyboarded
used two oh chromic catgut	*used 2-0 chromic catgut*
two by point five millimeter	*2.0 x 0.5 mm*
number two oh silk	*#2-0 silk* or *2-0 silk*
one point two percent	*1.2%*
pulses are two plus	*pulses are 2+*
blood pressure one hundred twenty over eighty	*Blood pressure: 120/80*
fifty-five milligrams percent	*55 mg%*
diluted one to one hundred	*diluted 1:100*
ninety-nine degrees Fahrenheit	*99°F*
the plane was raised ten degrees	*The plane was raised 10 degrees. (Note: Spell out degrees in expressing angles.)*
at a minus two station	*at a − 2 station*
medication times three days	*medication × 3 days*
one hundred milligrams per hour	*100 mg/h*
normal es one and es two	*normal S_1 and S_2 or normal S1 and S2 or normal S-1 and S-2*
one hundred milligrams per teaspoon	*100 mg/teaspoon*
ten to fifteen wbcs	*10-15 wbc's or 10-15 WBCs*
two to four plus	*2 to 4+*

9. Follow proper guidelines for letters and memorandums. Use a reference manual.

10. Consult a reference manual about questionable punctuation, capitalization, or grammar.

11. Use an acceptable or approved format for each medical document.

FIGURE 7.7 Abbreviations Commonly Used in Medical Records

a.c.	before meals	HPI	history of present illness	q.2h.	every two hours
AP	anteroposterio	HS	hour of sleep	q.d.	every day
b.i.d.	twice a day	I&D	incision and drainage	q.h.	every hour
BP	blood pressure	ICU	intensive care unit	q.i.d.	four times a day
BUN	blood urea nitrogen	IM	intramuscular	q.o.d.	every other day
C&S	culture and sensitivity	IV	intravenous	R/O	rule out
CBC	complete blood count	kg	kilogram	ROS	review of systems
CC	chief complaint	L	liter	RTC	return to clinic
cc	cubic centimeter	LLQ	left lower quadrant	RLQ	right lower quadrant
cm	centimeter	LMP	last menstrual period	RUQ	right upper quadrant
CNS	central nervous system	LUQ	left upper quadrant	Rx	prescription
CPE	complete physical exam	m	meter	SDA	same day appointment
D&C	dilation and curettage	mcg	microgram	SH	social history
DS	double strength	mEq	milliequivalent	S/P	status post
DTR	deep tendon reflexes	mg	milligram	stat or STAT	immediately
Dx	diagnosis	mL	milliliter	STD	sexually transmitted diseases
ECG	electrocardiogram	mm	millimeter		
EEG	electroencephalogram	n.p.o.	nothing by mouth	subq/subcu	subcutaneous
EENT	eyes, ears, nose, throat	OB	obstetrics	T&A	tonsillectomy and adenoidectomy
ENT	ears, nose, throat	OTC	over-the-counter (as in medications)		
EOM	extraocular movements			t.i.d.	three times a day
ER	emergency room	P&A	percussion and auscultation	TM	tympanic membrane
FH	family history	p.c.	after meals	TPR	temperature, pulse, respirations
F/U	follow-up	p.o.	per os (by mouth)		
FUO	fever unknown origin	p.r.n.	as desired or as needed	UA	urinalysis
Fx	fracture	PE	physical exam	UC	urine culture
g or gm	gram	PERLA	pupils equal, reactive to light and accommodation	URI	upper respiratory infection
GI	gastrointestinal				
gr	grain	PERRLA	pupils equal, round, reactive to light and accommodation	UTI	urinary tract infection
GU	genitourinary			VD	venereal disease
GYN	gynecology			VS	vital signs
h	hour	PMH	past medical history	wbc	white blood cells
H&P	history and physical	PSA	prostate specific antigen	WBC	white blood count
HEENT	head, eyes, ears, nose, throat	q.	every	WNL	within normal limits

■ Abbreviations

In the transcription of medical documents, care must be taken with the use of abbreviations. It is important to use only standard, approved abbreviations. Figure 7.7 contains a list of abbreviations commonly used in medical records. The list includes the following types of abbreviations, grouped together and arranged in alphabetical order for ease of use:

- Weights and measures (mainly medication dosages and lab values); for example, *mL* ("milliliter").
- Designations of times and methods; for example, *b.i.d.* ("twice a day").
- Terms typically found in chart notes; for example, *TPR* ("temperature, pulse, respirations").

Although it is standard practice to abbreviate all measurements and pharmaceutical language, do not use abbreviations for other terms unless instructed to do so. Many physicians require the assistant to spell out the terms even though the dictator used abbreviations when dictating. If you are unsure about the abbreviation and you cannot find it in references, it may be acceptable to transcribe the abbreviation as dictated.

▶ **GO TO PROJECT 7.3 ON PAGE 185** ▶

7.4 RECORD RETENTION, OWNERSHIP, AND QUALITY ASSURANCE

As discussed in Chapter 5, every medical practice has a variety of files that need to be preserved. Patient medical records, in particular, require special attention because of their importance to the practice and their value as legal documents. All medical records should be kept until the possibility of a malpractice suit has passed. This time period is determined by the state's statute of limitations. Although most medical records are, in fact, kept permanently, they are generally removed from an active file (pertaining to current patients) to an inactive file or to closed storage (for patients who have died, moved away, or terminated their relationship with the physician).

Every provider should have guidelines for transferring patient medical records from one classification to another. These guidelines should specify the information that is to be kept and, if possible, the type of storage medium to be used. It is important for an administrative medical assistant to be familiar with these guidelines since their application will help to protect the physician and the practice from potential legal complications.

■ Ownership

The ownership of medical records is addressed by the American Medical Association Council on Ethical and Judicial Affairs. According to the council, medical notes made by a physician—the actual chart notes, reports, and other materials—are the physician's property. The notes are for the physician's use in the treatment of the patient.

However, the physician cannot use or withhold the information in the record according to his or her own wishes. For example, the physician is ethically obligated to furnish copies of office notes to any physician who is assuming responsibility for care of the patient (with a record-release form signed and dated by the patient). It is understood that even though the notes made by the physician are the physician's property, the information in the record—the nature of the patient's diagnosis and so on—belongs to the patient. For this reason, patients have the right to control the amount and type of information that is released from their medical record. Furthermore, patients alone hold the authority to release information to anyone not directly involved in their care. A fee may be charged for furnishing copies of complex medical reports; however, information should not be withheld because of an unpaid fee.

■ Quality Assurance

The medical record probably is the best measure of the quality of care given a patient. The medical assistant helps the physician maintain high standards of care by paying attention to the data that are entered in the medical record.

If the assistant is unsure about a word dictated (for example, it may be unclear whether the physician said *"15"* or *"50"* milligrams) or has a question regarding the correctness of what the assistant heard when transcribing, the item should be flagged for the physician's attention. The assistant should not interrupt the physician if he or she is attending to other tasks at that time.

The assistant should make sure that each record contains the following:

- Dated notations describing the service received by the patient.
- Notations regarding every procedure performed.
- Accurate notations. An addendum by the physician should be made if a discrepancy occurs (for example, a previous notation about a condition may have stated "left side," while the latest notation states "right side").
- Justification for hospitalization.
- If necessary, a discharge summary regarding hospitalization before the patient arrives for a follow-up visit.

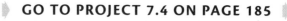

▶ **GO TO PROJECT 7.4 ON PAGE 185** ▶

Chapter Projects

PROJECT 7.1 Internet Research: Medical Records Institute

The Medical Records Institute promotes the development and acceptance of electronic health records systems nationally and internationally. The organization offers resources on electronic health records. It also is a network for exchanging knowledge, experiences, and solutions among health care professionals who are using or are interested in using electronic medical records systems.

Visit the Web site at www.medrecinst.com, and check the current survey results regarding barriers to electronic records, possible solutions, and facilities that use electronic records.

PROJECT 7.2 Chart Entries

Dr. Larsen instructs you to make the following chart notations for her signature. Both should be dated October 13.

- Sara Babcock: Patient called for refill of Ortho Tri-Cyclen®. She has a physical scheduled for October 21, and we will deal with the prescription renewal at that time.
- Jeffrey Kramer: Father called for OTC help for Jeffrey for sore throat and earache. I advised the father to make an appointment as soon as possible. Patient to gargle with warm salt water q.3-4h. and be given children's Tylenol® for pain relief p.r.n.

PROJECT 7.3 Chart Transcription

Dr. Larsen has dictated her findings on the patients from October 14 and 15. Obtain the transcription source from your instructor. Use the formats presented in Figures 7.4 and 7.5 to transcribe the dictation onto each patient's medical record.

PROJECT 7.4 Lab Message Entries

The following lab results were received by telephone message. Dr. Larsen instructed you to make notations in the charts for her signature.

- October 16: Gary Robertson's urine culture results from October 14 show Enterobacter greater than 100,000 colonies, sensitive to sulfa. Left message for patient with results. Patient to continue Septra and follow up in two weeks, sooner p.r.n.
- October 16: Erin Mitchell's urine culture results from October 14 revealed bacterial count greater than 100,000/mL. Talked with patient today. Patient to continue ciprofloxacin as directed. RTC if symptoms do not clear.

CHAPTER SUMMARY

1. The patient medical record is the source of information about all aspects of a patient's health care. It is also the legal business record of the medical practice and could potentially be produced in a court of law if the physician is involved in litigation or is called as a witness. Medical records generally include the following clinical items: chart notes, history and physical, referral or consultation letters, medical reports, correspondence, clinical forms, and a list of medications taken by the patient. Medical records may contain the following administrative items as well: the patient registration form and the release of information and assignment of benefits form. Because medical records are used as the basis for so many activities in a medical practice—from ensuring adequate reimbursement to coordinating and carrying out all aspects of patient care—every effort should be made to maintain them well. The administrative medical assistant should always help the physician to maintain high standards of care by paying attention to the data that are entered in the medical record and by carefully following the prescribed procedure for making corrections to a medical record.

2. The SOAP method is the most common system for outlining and structuring chart notes in a medical record. The acronym *SOAP* stands for the following headings that are used to structure the chart note: *SUBJECTIVE, OBJECTIVE, ASSESSMENT,* and *PLAN.* The subjective findings include the patient's chief complaint (CC), history of present illness (HPI), past medical history (PMH), family history (FH), social history (SH), and review of systems (ROS). The objective findings are the results of the physician's physical examination (PE) of the patient as well as the results of lab tests, x-rays, and other diagnostic procedures. The assessment is the physician's interpretation of the subjective and objective findings, and the plan is the physician's plan for treating the patient.

3. A problem-oriented medical record (POMR) revolves around a list of the patient's problems. It has three essential components: (1) a database consisting of the complete medical history of the patient together with the results of a complete physical exam and routine diagnostic tests; (2) the physician's initial plan for treatment; and (3) a problem list, which is a running account of the patient's problems and suggested treatments and results. The problem list is consulted and updated at each clinic visit. The POMR is one of the most common forms of medical records in use.

4. The administrative medical assistant should become proficient in transcribing chart notes and other medical documents dictated by a

physician. In transcription, a good technique is to listen to three or four words at a time, key them, and then listen to the next three or four words. The assistant should become familiar with the format for transcribing chart notes that is used in the office. Basic transcription guidelines regarding punctuation, capitalization, and the use of standard medical abbreviations should be followed.

5. Patient medical records should be kept until the possibility of a malpractice suit has passed. This time period is determined by the state's statute of limitations. Although most medical records are, in fact, kept permanently, they are transferred over a period of time from an active file to an inactive file or to closed storage. The administrative medical assistant should follow the provider's guidelines for transferring records from one classification to another.

6. Medical notes made by a physician—the actual chart notes, reports, and so on—are the physician's property. However, the information in the record—the nature of the patient's diagnosis and so on—belongs to the patient. For this reason, even though physicians may own the notes and reports in the record, it is only the patient who has the right to control the amount and type of information that is released from the record.

7. An administrative medical assistant should always help a physician to maintain a high standard of care for his or her patients. For this reason, the assistant should make sure that every medical record is as complete, accurate, and up-to-date as possible.

KEY TERMS

The following key terms appear in **boldface** type in this chapter. Administrative medical assistants must know the meaning and the correct use of each of these terms. Can you recall what each term means? Refer to this chapter or to the glossary for any terms you need to review.

assessment
chief complaint (CC)
diagnosis (Dx)
family history (FH)
history of present illness (HPI)
impression
objective
past medical history (PMH)
physical exam (PE)

plan
problem-oriented medical
  record (POMR)
review of systems (ROS)
rule out (R/O)
SOAP
social history (SH)
subjective

MEDICAL VOCABULARY USED
IN THIS CHAPTER

Be sure that you are familiar with the following terms.

adnexa   accessory parts to the main structure

amoxicillin   an antibiotic

anginal   relating to constricting chest pain

bronchitis   inflammation in the bronchi

bruit   murmur

colonoscopy   visualization of the colon with a scope

costochondritis   inflammation of the cartilage between the ribs

dysmenorrhea   menstrual cramps

dysuria   painful or difficult urination

ecchymosis   black and blue or purple skin discoloration; bruise

exudative   relating to tissue material deposited as a result of infection

gallop   an abnormal heart sound

hepatosplenomegaly   liver and spleen enlargement

injection   congestion or increase in fluid

lymphadenopathy   enlargement of lymph nodes

malaise   feeling of uneasiness

normocephalic   relating to a normal-size head

ophthalmic   relating to the eye

otitis media   inflammation of the ear

PE tubes   polyethylene tubes

pharyngitis   inflammation of the throat

rhonchi   musical pitch heard on chest auscultation

sclera   the white of the eye

Sitz bath   a type of bath that consists of soaking the area from the
tailbone to the lower abdomen in a tub of warm water

supple   easily moveable

tinea cruris   a fungal infection in the male perineal or groin area

tonsillitis   inflammation of the tonsils

THINKING IT THROUGH

These questions cover the most important points in this chapter. Using your critical thinking skills, play the role of an administrative medical assistant as you answer each question. Be prepared to present your responses in class.

1. You are going through a patient's medical record to find information on a specific lab report, and you notice that several chart notes are not dated. What should you do?

2. How does the use of the SOAP format for record keeping minimize a provider's exposure to legal risk?

3. You retrieve a patient's medical record and notice the abbreviation *WDWNWF* is used several times in the chart notes. You know that this is not an approved abbreviation, though you eventually figure out that it stands for "well-developed, well-nourished white female." What do you do with this information?

4. You are asked to retrieve information regarding a patient's family history of intestinal cancer. The physician generally uses the POMR format. Where in the file should you look?

5. A former patient calls, hoping to locate x-rays taken more than five years ago. What should you say?

6. A patient calls and is moving out of town. She is concerned about her medical record. What would you suggest?

7. You are transcribing the physician's dictation and cannot understand several words in a chart note. What do you do?

CHAPTER

8

Insurance and Coding

OBJECTIVES

After studying this chapter, you will be able to:

1. Define medical insurance and coding terms.
2. Describe the differences between indemnity and managed care plans and discuss managed care options.
3. List the different types of insurance carriers, both in the private sector and government-sponsored plans.
4. Discuss the difference between a participating and nonparticipating provider and the methods used by insurance companies to determine how much a provider is paid.
5. Explain the process of diagnostic and procedural coding and discuss coding compliance.

INTRODUCTION

Medical insurance, also known as "health insurance," refers to insurance protection against medical care expenses. Administrative medical assistants must understand insurance in order to answer patients' questions about their health insurance policies and to process insurance claim forms properly so that the physician receives compensation for services.

KEY TERMS

Study these important words, which are defined in this chapter, to build your professional vocabulary:

accepting
  assignment
allowed charge
assignment of
  benefits
balance billing
birthday rule
Blue Cross and
  Blue Shield
  Association
  (BCBS)
capitation
carrier

Centers for
  Medicare
  and Medicaid
  Services (CMS)
CHAMPVA
code linkage
coinsurance
coordination of
  benefits (COB)
copayment (copay)
CPT
customary fee
deductible

diagnostic-related
  groups (DRGs)
fee-for-service
HCPCS
HMO (health
  maintenance
  organization)
ICD-9-CM
indemnity plan
insured
managed care
Medicaid
Medicare

participating
  (PAR) provider
patient encounter
  form
PPO (preferred
  provider
  organization)
preauthorization
premium
primary care
  provider (PCP)
provider
reasonable fee

referral
relative value
  scale (RVS)
resource-based
  relative value
  scale (RBRVS)
third-party payer
TRICARE
usual fee
workers'
  compensation

The administrative medical assistant must be familiar with basic insurance terminology in order to be helpful to patients and to process insurance claims.

■ The Medical Insurance Contract

Medical insurance is a policy, or certificate of coverage, between a person, called the "policyholder," and an insurance company, or **carrier.** The policyholder pays a certain amount of money to the insurance company in return for benefits. The benefits are in the form of payments from the insurance company for the medical services received.

In the medical insurance contract, the insurance company agrees to carry the risk of paying for services that may be required by the policyholder. The patient agrees to make regular payments to the insurance company to keep the policy intact. As with other types of insurance companies, medical insurance companies manage the risk that some individuals they ensure will require very expensive services by spreading that risk among many policyholders.

Insured. The person who takes out the insurance policy is referred to as the **insured.** Since a medical insurance policy often covers the insured and the insured's dependents, in the strict sense of the term, *policyholder* refers to the person in whose name the policy is written (the person who is responsible for making payments) and the term *insured* refers to anyone, such as the policyholder or a spouse, covered by the medical policy.

Premium. The rate charged to the policyholder for the insurance policy is the **premium.** Premiums are usually paid by the policyholder on a regular basis, for example, monthly or quarterly.

Third-Party Payer. According to contract law, when a physician agrees to treat a patient who is seeking medical services, there is an unwritten contract between the two. The physician or other health-care professional—the **provider** (the "first party")—agrees to treat the patient, and the patient (the "second party") assumes the legal responsibility of paying for the services received. If the patient has a policy with an insurance company, in which the insurance company agrees to carry the risk of paying for those services, the insurance company is referred to as the "third party" and is therefore called a **third-party payer.**

A patient who does not have insurance is referred to as a "self-pay." A self-pay patient is responsible for paying the physician directly for all services received.

Coordination of Benefits. The clause relating to **coordination of benefits (COB)** in an insurance policy provides that a patient who has two insurance policies can have only a maximum benefit of 100 percent of the health costs. If the insurance companies do not communicate with each other, there is the possibility that the patient can be reimbursed for more than she or he spent on services.

Under the terms of the coordination-of-benefits clause, one insurance carrier is named the primary carrier. The clause explains how the policy will pay—whether as a primary or secondary carrier—if more than one insurance policy applies to the claim. For example, the primary carrier may pay up to 80 percent and the secondary, 20 percent, not to exceed a maximum benefit to the insured of 100 percent.

The Birthday Rule. The **birthday rule** is used as a guideline for determining which of two parents with medical coverage has the primary insurance for a child. The rule states that the policy of the insured with the earlier birthday in the calendar year is the primary policy. The policy of the other parent, the secondary policy, may cover costs that were not covered by the primary policy. This ensures that the maximum benefit the insured may receive is only 100 percent.

■ Types of Medical Insurance Coverage

Medical insurance coverage can be purchased in a variety of forms for different levels of coverage. The greater the coverage, the more expensive the plan. It can also be purchased for a group or for an individual.

Under group insurance, one master policy is issued to an organization or employer and it covers the eligible members or employees and their dependents. Thus, all the members or employees have the same health care coverage. Group insurance provides better benefits with lower premiums than does individual insurance.

Individual insurance is usually purchased by people who are not eligible for group insurance, such as by those who are self-employed. Because it is not obtained at a group rate, the cost is higher than for group insurance.

Examples of the types of health insurance coverage that are available include:

- *Basic:* A basic insurance plan generally includes coverage of hospitalization, lab tests, surgery, and x-rays.
- *Medical:* Medical insurance covers benefits for outpatient medical care. An outpatient is a person who receives medical care at a hospital or other medical facility but is generally admitted for less

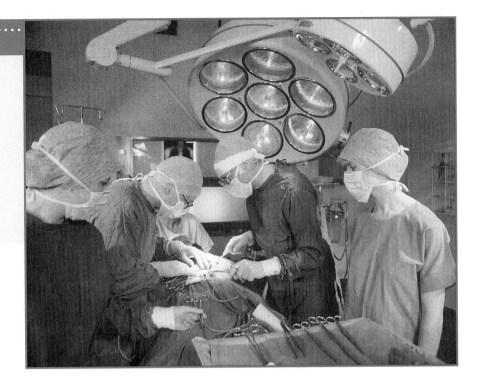

FIGURE 8.1

Medical insurance helps people pay for medical, surgical, and hospital costs. *Why is it important to both the patient and the provider for the administrative medical assistant to file insurance claims accurately and promptly?*

than 23 hours. The term *medical* refers to the physician's costs for nonsurgical services, whether in the office or a hospital. Special provisions are made for pathology, x-ray, and diagnostic lab fees.

- *Hospital:* Hospital insurance provides protection against the costs of hospital care. It generally provides a room allowance (a stated amount per day for a semiprivate room) with a maximum number of days per year. Special provisions are made for operating room charges, x-rays, laboratory work, drugs, and other medically necessary items while the insured person is an inpatient. An inpatient is a person who is admitted to the hospital for more than 23 hours.
- *Surgical:* Surgical insurance provides protection for the cost of a physician's fee for surgery, whether it is performed in a hospital, in a physician's office, or elsewhere (such as in a surgical center). Charges for anesthesia generally are covered by surgical insurance.
- *Major medical:* Major medical insurance offers protection from large medical expenses, such as extensive injuries from a car accident or those associated with a prolonged illness, that go above and beyond the maximum established by a regular health insurance policy.
- *Disability:* Disability insurance provides reimbursement for income lost because of the insured person's inability to work as the result of an illness or injury, which may be work-related or not.
- *Dental insurance:* Dental insurance can be obtained, often under a separate policy, to cover all or part of the costs of dental care.

GO TO PROJECT 8.1 ON PAGE 217

There are many medical insurance plans from which people can choose, and many different insurance companies that offer them. Most insurance plans use one of two payment methods: fee-for-service or capitation.

Fee-for-service. The first type of payment, **fee-for-service,** is made by the insurance carrier *after* the patient has received medical services. The insured pays for the medical services at the time of receiving them, and the insurance carrier reimburses the insured after receiving an insurance claim. Alternatively, the insured may instruct the carrier to pay the physician directly.

In a fee-for-service plan, fees are usually set by the physician. An insurance carrier and a physician may negotiate a *discounted fee-for-service* payment schedule. Under this schedule, a physician agrees to provide services for less than the usual charge. The physician makes up the difference in payment, at least in theory, by seeing more patients who have that insurance plan.

Capitation. Under the second type of payment, **capitation,** a payment is made in advance. Capitation is the *pre*payment by the insurance carrier of a fixed (per capita, or per head) amount to a physician to cover the health care services for each member of one of its plans for a specified period of time, such as for a month. The physician must provide all the care needed according to a predetermined set of services to each patient for which a capitation payment is made. In a capitated plan, the physician shares the risk with the insurance company for the cost and frequency of the services provided. For example, a physician may receive $30 per month for each assigned patient, regardless of the number of times the patient visits the physician during the month, or even if the patient receives no care during that month.

■ Types of Plans

Most medical insurance plans fall into one of two categories depending on their payment arrangements. Plans that use a fee-for-service payment arrangement are mostly indemnity plans. Those that use capitation as their payment arrangement are generally managed care plans.

Indemnity plans. Under most **indemnity plans,** the insurance company reimburses medical costs on a fee-for-service basis. This type of plan pays for a percentage of the cost, and the patient is responsible for the remaining portion. Patients receive medical services from the providers they choose, who usually file the required claims for payment on behalf of patients.

For each claim, three conditions must be met before reimbursement is made:

1. The policy's premium payment must be up to date.
2. A deductible has been paid. A **deductible** is a certain amount of medical expense the insured must incur before the insurance carrier will begin paying benefits. Deductibles usually range from $200 to $500 annually.
3. Any coinsurance has been taken into account. **Coinsurance** is the percentage of each claim that the insured must pay, according to the terms of the insurance policy. The coinsurance rate is expressed in terms of percentages, with the percentage the insurance company is to pay listed first. For example, a coinsurance rate of 80-20 means that the insurance company will pay 80 percent of the physician's fee and the insured must pay the remaining 20 percent.

Managed care plans. Managed care plans generally use capitation as the basis for making payments to physicians. These plans are the predominant type of medical insurance in the United States. There are two main types of managed care plans—HMOs and PPOs.

HMOs. HMOs were the earliest form of managed care. An **HMO (health maintenance organization)** is a medical center or a designated group of physicians that provides medical services to insured persons for a monthly or an annual premium. The insured is able to obtain health care on a regular basis with unlimited medical attention and minimal coinsurance payments. Thus, HMOs encourage insured persons to take advantage of preventive health care services in an attempt to make health care coverage more cost-efficient.

HMOs attempt to control costs by using a number of methods.

- *Restricting patients' choice of providers:* After enrolling in an HMO, members must receive services from the network of physicians, hospitals, and other health care providers connected with that HMO. The insurance will not cover visits to out-of-network providers, except for emergency care or in urgent situations when the member is away from home.
- *Requiring cost sharing:* Every time HMO members visit their physician, they pay a set charge called a **copayment (copay),** currently about $10 to $20. Higher copayments (about $50) are required when patients go to an emergency room or visit the office of a specialist.
- *Requiring preauthorization for services:* Often HMOs require **pre-authorization** before the physician will deliver certain types of service. This enables the HMO, ahead of time, to verify that the service is medically necessary and is covered under the patient's policy. The HMO may also require a second opinion, from a different physician, about whether a planned procedure is necessary before granting authorization. Figure 8.2 shows an example of a preauthorization form.

FIGURE 8.2

Preauthorization Form

Hospital admission: _____   Outpatient procedure: _____
Patient:

    Name: _____

    Address: _____

Insurance carrier: _____   Phone #: _____

Patient ID#: _____   Group #: _____

Provider ID#: _____   Name: _____

Phone #: _____   Fax: _____

Attending physician: _____

Diagnosis: _____

Symptoms: _____

Treatment plan: _____

Procedure date: _____   Planned discharge date: _____

Notes: _____

_____

Admit date: _____   Surgery date: _____

days pre-op: _____   # days post-op: _____

If second opinion, from: _____

AUTHORIZED: _____   Yes _____   No _____   Number _____

If not authorized, reason for denial: _____

Authorized by: _____

    Name: _____

    Title: _____

    Date: _____

Completed by: _____
Date: _____

Source: Bayes, Nenna L., et al., *Glencoe Medical Insurance*, NY: Glencoe/McGraw-Hill, 2001, p.15.

- *Controlling access to services:* In most HMOs, patients are required to select a **primary care provider (PCP)** from the HMO's list of general or family practitioners, internists, and pediatricians. The PCP's role is to act as a gatekeeper, coordinating patients' overall care and ensuring that all services provided are, in the PCP's judgment, necessary. For example, HMOs require members to obtain a medical **referral** from the PCP before seeing a specialist or for hospital admission. The referral document names the provider the patient is to use and specifies the exact services the patient can receive. If a member visits a provider without a referral, the member is directly responsible for the full cost of the service.

Preferred provider organizations. Another type of managed care plan, more popular now than HMOs, are PPOs. The **PPO (preferred provider organization)** contracts to perform services for PPO members at specified rates. These rates, or fees, are generally lower than the fees charged to regular patients. The PPO gives the insured a list of PPO providers from which to receive health care at PPO rates. If a patient chooses to receive treatment from a provider who is not in the PPO network, the patient has to pay more—usually a higher copayment or deductible, or by making up any difference between the PPO's rate and the outside provider's rate.

PPOs, like HMOs, are managed care systems. This means PPOs use many of the same types of practices as HMOs to control the cost of health care. For example, they encourage members to use providers in their own PPO network, they usually require preauthorization for some procedures, and they require members to share in the cost of care by making copayments each time they have an encounter with a provider.

Unlike HMOs, PPOs do not generally require patients to choose a primary care physician to oversee their care. Nor are referrals to specialists required. As a result, however, premiums and copayments tend to be higher than those for HMO members.

■ Medical Insurance Payers

Medical insurance plans, whether indemnity plans or managed care plans, are available through commercial insurance companies in the private sector, such as Aetna or Cigna Health Care, or, for eligible individuals, through government-sponsored programs such as Medicare and Medicaid.

Private-Sector Payers. The private-sector market is made up chiefly of a few very large national firms that offer all the leading types of insurance plans. Although most of these payers are for-profit, some are nonprofit, such as Kaiser Permanente, which is the largest nonprofit HMO.

The **Blue Cross and Blue Shield Association (BCBS),** one of the largest private-sector payers in the United States, has both for-profit and nonprofit components. As with many of the private-sector payers, BCBS offers both indemnity and managed care plans, with many individual policy variations in each category. Its HMO network, HMO Blue USA, is the largest managed care network in the country, providing coverage to more than 14 million members in 47 states and the District of Columbia. BCBS member plans offer many types of managed care programs, including an HMO, a PPO, and others. There are also BCBS plans that make it easy for patients to receive treatment outside their local service area (the BlueCard program); nationwide BCBS plans for corporations with offices in more than one state; and a BCBS Federal Employee Health Benefits (FEHB) plan that employees of the federal government may select as their health insurance plan.

Medicare. **Medicare** is a federal health plan that provides insurance to citizens and permanent residents aged 65 and older; people with disabilities, including kidney failure; and spouses of entitled individuals. Medicare is divided into two parts—Part A, hospitalization insurance; and Part B, medical insurance.

Medicare Part A covers hospital, nursing facility, home health, hospice, and inpatient care. Those who are eligible for Social Security benefits are automatically enrolled in Medicare Part A. Medicare Part B covers outpatient services, services by physicians, durable medical equipment, and other services and supplies. Medicare Part B coverage is optional. Everyone eligible for Part A can choose to enroll in Part B by paying monthly premiums.

There are deductibles in Parts A and B that must be met before payment benefits begin, such as the first $100 for covered services in Part B. In a traditional fee-for-service program (Part B), called "the Original Medicare Plan," after the deductible has been met, Medicare pays 80 percent of approved charges and the patient is responsible for the remaining 20 percent. In a Medicare managed care program, the terms are different: most managed care plans charge a monthly premium and a small copayment for each office visit, but do not charge a deductible. Medicare+Choice is a group of insurance plans under Medicare Part B that offer beneficiaries a wider selection of coverage plans, including a variety of managed care plans and variations of fee-for-service plans.

Medicaid. **Medicaid** is a health benefit program, jointly funded by federal and state governments, that is designed for people with low incomes who cannot afford medical care. Each state formulates its own Medicaid program under broad federal guidelines. As a result, programs vary in coverage and benefits from state to state. In some states, the program is known by a different name. For example, in California, Medicaid is called MediCal.

TRICARE. **TRICARE** (formerly *CHAMPUS*) is the Department of Defense's health insurance plan for military personnel and their families. Those eligible include active or retired members of the following uniformed services and their families: the Army, Navy, Marines, Air Force, Coast Guard, Public Health Service, and National Oceanic and Atmospheric Administration. Coverage also applies to dependents of military personnel who were killed while on active duty.

All military treatment facilities, including hospitals and clinics, are part of the TRICARE system, which also contracts with civilian facilities and physicians to provide more extensive services to beneficiaries. TRICARE offers three different health care plans: TRICARE Standard, TRICARE Prime, and TRICARE Extra. TRICARE Standard, a fee-for-service program, is the most expensive of the plans. TRICARE Prime is a managed care plan, similar to an HMO, and TRICARE Extra is an alternative managed care plan for individuals who want to receive services primarily from civilian facilities and physicians rather than from military facilities. To be certain a patient is eligible, the administrative medical assistant checks the individual's military ID card and ensures that coverage is still valid by examining the expiration date.

CHAMPVA. **CHAMPVA,** which stands for "Civilian Health and Medical Program of the Veterans Administration," is a government health insurance program that covers the expenses of the families of veterans with total, permanent, service-connected disabilities. It also covers surviving spouses and dependent children of veterans who died in the line of duty. Each eligible beneficiary possesses a CHAMPVA Authorization Card, known as an "A-Card." Most CHAMPVA enrollees pay an annual deductible and a portion of their health care charges.

Workers' Compensation. Each state has its own **workers' compensation** laws to guarantee that an employee who is injured or who becomes ill in the course of employment will have adequate medical care and an adequate means of support while unable to work. The employer must obtain insurance against workers' compensation liability and is liable whether or not the employee is at fault for an accident or injury. Workers' compensation insurance operates under the jurisdiction of the state department of labor or under that of a special industrial commission.

The administrative medical assistant must verify with the employer that a patient who claims workers' compensation was indeed injured or became ill in the course of employment. The physician must submit a report, usually within 48 hours, to the workers' compensation insurance carrier, which notifies the Workers' Compensation Board. (The time period during which the physician must file the report varies by state and ranges from 24 hours to 10 days.) The report must include the patient's case history, symptoms, complete medical findings, tentative diagnosis,

COMPLIANCE TIP

Clinical notes of work-related illness or injury should be separate from other medical services and labeled "Workers' Compensation." A separate file should be kept for each workers' compensation case, even if the individual is an established patient. One reason it is very important not to mix a patient's regular medical records with workers' compensation records is that workers' compensation claim information is not subject to the same confidentiality rules as private medical records. Most states allow insurance personnel and employers unrestricted access to the workers' compensation files. Copies of workers' compensation reports may be kept in the patient's regular medical record for future reference. Copies may be necessary to document the treatment provided by the physician if the dispute comes before an arbitration board or court.

prescribed treatment, and length and extent of disability or injury. Work-related injuries are grouped into five categories, which are defined by the state and administered by its department of labor:

- Injury without disability
- Injury with temporary disability
- Injury with permanent disability
- Injury requiring vocational rehabilitation
- Injury resulting in death

Progress reports on the case must be filed regularly until the physician releases the patient from care. The final report must be designated as such, indicating that the patient has recovered fully from the work-related disability.

> **GO TO PROJECT 8.2 ON PAGE 218**

8.3 PARTICIPATION AND PAYMENT METHODS

Physicians must decide which insurance plans they want to participate in. They judge which plans to join based on the types of patients they serve and the financial arrangements the plans offer them. Because more people are members of managed care plans than any other type of plan today, most physicians have contracts with a number of managed care plans in their area. Often, to avoid confusion, a medical practice displays a list of plans it participates in so that patients know what to expect given the insurance they have. Figure 8.3 is an example of such a list.

■ Plan Participation

A physician who joins an insurance plan is a **participating (PAR) provider** in that plan. As a participating provider, the physician agrees to provide medical services to the insurance plan members according to the plan's rules and payment schedules. The insurance carrier offers various incentives, such as faster payment, to participating providers.

A nonparticipating provider, or nonPAR, chooses not to join a particular insurance plan. A nonPAR physician who treats members of a plan does not have to obey the rules or follow the payment schedule of that plan. At the same time, a nonPAR physician will not receive any of the benefits of participation.

FIGURE 8.3

Example of an Insurance
Plan Participation List

Welcome to our practice.

In order to make your visit as pleasant as possible, we have compiled a list of the most commonly asked questions regarding insurance and billing in this office.

With which insurance plans does the physician participate?

Aetna/US Healthcare Plans	Medicaid
CIGNA	MedSpan
Blue Choice PPO: POS, PPO, Prestige, Select	MD Health Plan
Focus Workers Compensation PPO	Oxford Health Plan
Health Care Value Management, Inc.	Physician Health Services
Health Choice	Prudential Healthcare
Health Direct	POS Plan
Kaiser Permanente	Wellcare
Medicare	

What can I expect if the physician participates with my insurance?

We will file a claim with your insurance company for any charges. Your insurance may require you to pay a copay at the time of services. You are responsible for any deductibles and non-covered services. You may need to obtain a referral from your primary care physician. Failure to obtain a referral may result in rescheduling of your appointment until you can obtain one.

What can I expect if the physician does not participate with my insurance?

Payment is expected at the time of service. You will receive a statement within two weeks. Use it to file a claim. As a courtesy, we will submit any surgery claims to your insurance carrier, but you are responsible for payment.

■ Fee Schedules

In a private managed care plan, contracts that set fees are often negotiated between the insurance company and the physician. In Medicare, the **Centers for Medicare and Medicaid Services (CMS)** is responsible for setting up the terms of the plan. This agency was called the Health Care Financing Administration, commonly known as "HCFA" (pronounced "hic-fuh"), before 2001. An agency of the Department of Health and Human Services (HHS), CMS administers the Medicare and Medicaid programs to millions of Americans. Part of its role is to review managed care plans that want to become Medicare coverage providers.

■ Payment Concepts

Every health insurance plan has its own payment methods, rules, and regulations. An administrative medical assistant must keep up with the different options available in each plan in order to be sure a patient has coverage for a given service and to process insurance claims for patients properly. Following is a list of the basic concepts used in insurance contracts regarding methods of making payments to providers.

Allowed Charge. When insurance companies set up the payment terms for an insurance contract, many set an **allowed charge** for each procedure or service a provider performs. This amount is the most the insurance company will pay any provider for that work.

Balance Billing. When the amount the physician charges is more than the insurance company's allowed charge, the difference in cost must be absorbed either by the patient or the physician. If the physician decides the patient should absorb the cost, the physician bills the patient for the unclaimed amount, a practice referred to as **balance billing.**

Many insurance plans specify that a participating provider may *not* bill patients for balances. This means a PAR provider must accept the payment from the insurance company as payment in full for the procedure and not collect ("write off") the difference between the physician's usual fee and the allowed charge. In other words, the physician subtracts the unpaid amount from the patient's bill.

Accepting Assignment. A PAR provider who agrees to accept the allowed charge set forth by the insurance company as payment in full for a service and not bill the patient for the balance is **accepting assignment.** PAR providers must always accept assignment.

A nonPAR provider, on the other hand, decides whether to accept assignment on a claim-by-claim basis. A nonPAR provider who decides to accept assignment on a given claim does not bill the patient for the balance. Conversely, if the nonPAR provider decides not to accept assignment, the patient is billed for the unclaimed amount.

Assignment of Benefits. A physician who accepts an **assignment of benefits** agrees to receive payment directly from the patient's insurance carrier. In this case, the patient signs an assignment of benefits statement on the insurance claim form. This statement authorizes the insurance company to make a payment directly to the physician.

When a nonPAR physician does not accept assignment on a claim, the patient is usually asked to pay for the service in full at the time of the visit so that the medical office can avoid having to collect payment later. Some practices ask the patient to assign benefits for the claim at the time of the visit, and then bill the patient later for any amount the insurance company does not pay.

COMPLIANCE TIP

In a private plan, a nonparticipating provider can usually bill the patient for any unpaid balance after the insurance company has paid its responsibility. In the case of government-sponsored programs, however, other rules protect the patient. In a Medicare plan, for example, nonPAR providers are subject to a limiting charge for each procedure. The limiting charge is a way of preventing Medicare patients from having to pay the unclaimed portion of a bill.

Examples of PAR and NonPAR Provider Fees for a Medicare Patient. Suppose a patient whose primary insurance carrier is Medicare visits a physician for a procedure. Normally, the physician charges $120 for the procedure; the Medicare allowed charge for the procedure, however, is only $60. How much can the physician charge for the procedure, and how much will Medicare reimburse? Depending on whether the physician participates in the Medicare program (physicians decide each year whether to participate), the amount the physician can charge will vary. PAR providers are reimbursed more than nonPAR providers. As part of its standard policy, Medicare sets the fees for nonPAR providers 5 percent less than those for PAR providers for the same services.

Furthermore, depending on whether a nonparticipating physician decides to accept assignment or not, and the limiting charge imposed on a nonPAR provider who does not accept assignment, the amount Medicare pays varies. If a nonPAR provider decides not to accept the Medicare assigned amount as payment in full, and decides rather to bill the patient for the balance, Medicare subjects the assigned amount to a 115 percent limiting charge, thus limiting the amount of unpaid balance the physician can bill the patient for. In effect, the limiting charge prevents the physician from balance billing the patient for the full unclaimed amount.

The following three fee structures illustrate the three possible scenarios:

Participating Provider

Physician's standard fee	$120.00
Medicare fee	60.00
Medicare pays 80% ($60.00 × 80%)	48.00
Patient or supplemental plan pays 20% ($60.00 × 20%)	12.00
Provider adjustment ($120.00 − $60.00)	60.00

Nonparticipating Provider Who Accepts Assignment

Physician's standard fee	$120.00
Medicare nonPAR fee	57.00
Medicare pays 80% ($57.00 × 80%)	45.60
Patient or supplemental plan pays 20% ($57.00 × 20%)	11.40
Provider adjustment ($120.00 − $57.00)	63.00

Nonparticipating Provider Who Does Not Accept Assignment

Physician's standard fee	$120.00
Medicare nonPAR fee	57.00
Limiting charge ($57.00 × 115%)	65.55
Patient billed	65.55
Medicare pays patient ($57.00 × 80%)	45.60
Total provider can collect	65.55
Patient pays balance ($65.55 − $45.60)	19.95

These examples can also be used to illustrate the different options for assigning benefits on Medicare claims. In the first and second scenarios, since the physician has agreed to accept the assigned Medicare amounts ($60 and $57, respectively) as reimbursement in full for the procedure, the physician would also accept an assignment of benefits, authorizing Medicare to pay the physician directly.

In the third scenario, since the provider has decided not to accept the Medicare assigned amount of $57 as payment in full for the procedure, the provider will also not accept an assignment of benefits for the claim. Instead, Medicare will send the payment directly to the patient, and the patient will be responsible for paying the bill in full, including the balance.

■ Setting Fees

Third-party payers use different formulas and systems for setting up fee schedules for the procedures and services they will reimburse. The most common types of payment systems are:

- A list of usual, customary, and reasonable (UCR) fees.
- A relative value scale (RVS).
- A resource-based relative value scale (RBRVS).
- Diagnosis-related groups (DRGs).

UCR Fees. To set fees for their services, providers establish a list of their usual fees for the procedures and services they frequently perform. In every geographic area, there is a normal range of fees for each procedure. Different practices set their fees at some point along this range. Third-party payers, to set the rates they pay providers, analyze providers' usual fees and establish a schedule of UCR (for usual, customary, and reasonable) fees for each procedure.

- A **usual fee** is an individual provider's average charge for a certain procedure.
- A **customary fee** is determined by what physicians with similar training and experience in a certain geographic location typically charge for a procedure.
- A **reasonable fee** is one that meets the two previous criteria, or a fee allowed or approved by the insurance carrier for a difficult or complicated service.

Relative Value Scale (RVS). Another payment system is the **relative value scale (RVS).** A relative value scale sets fees for medical services based on an analysis of the skill and time required to provide them.

Resource-Based Relative Value Scale (RBRVS). The payment system used by Medicare is the **resource-based relative value scale (RBRVS).** The RBRVS, like the RVS, on which it is based, is a scale that establishes relative prices for services.

Also, many private insurance companies use resource-based fee structures to establish what to pay for each procedure when company managers believe a resource-based fee structure more fairly reflects the real costs involved in providing medical services than the historical fees.

Diagnostic-Related Groups (DRGs). Another payment system, used by Medicare for establishing payment for hospital stays, is **diagnostic-related groups (DRGs).** Diagnostic groupings are based on the resources that physicians and hospitals used nationally for patients with similar conditions, taking into account factors such as age, gender, and medical complications.

GO TO PROJECT 8.3 ON PAGE 218

8.4   CODING AND COMPLIANCE

To keep track of the many thousands of possible diagnoses and of procedures and services rendered by physicians, and to simplify the process of verifying the medical necessity of each procedure, two coding systems are used.

- *Diagnostic coding:* Codes for reporting what is wrong with the patient, or what brought the patient to see the physician.
- *Procedural coding:* Codes for reporting each procedure the physician performed in treating the patient.

These systems are used to convert the physician's medical terminology into numerical (or alphanumerical) codes. In some medical practices, the physicians assign these codes; in others, a medical coder or a medical insurance specialist handles this task. In either case, an administrative medical assistant must be familiar with both coding systems to work effectively with encounter forms and insurance claims. A **patient encounter form** is the form used in the medical office to record the procedures performed during a patient's visit.

■ Diagnostic Coding

Accurate diagnostic coding gives insurance carriers clearly defined diagnoses to help them process claims efficiently. An error in coding conveys to an insurance carrier the wrong reason a patient received medical services. This causes confusion, a delay in processing, and possibly a reduced payment or denial of a claim. An incorrect code may also raise the question of fraudulent billing if the insurance company decides that, based on the diagnosis, the services provided were not medically necessary. Active diagnostic code databases can also provide statistics for medical researchers, physicians, and third-party payers about costs, trends, and future health care needs.

The *ICD-9-CM*. The diagnosis codes are found in the **_ICD-9-CM_**, the *International Classification of Diseases*. The *ICD* lists codes according to a system assigned by the World Health Organization of the United Nations. *ICD* codes are used by government health care programs, professional standards review organizations, medical researchers, hospitals, physicians, and other health care providers. Private and public medical insurance carriers also use the codes.

The *ICD* has been revised a number of times. In the title, *ICD-9-CM,* the initials *CM* indicate that the edition is a clinical modification. For example, the *ICD-9-CM* is the clinical modification of the ninth revision of the *ICD*. Codes in this modification describe various conditions and illnesses with more precision than did earlier codes. Since 1988, *ICD-9-CM* coding has been required on all Medicare claims. Most insurance carriers now also require *ICD-9-CM* codes on insurance claims. Updates of the *ICD-9-CM* are published every year. Medical offices should have a copy of the most recent publication.

The *ICD-9-CM* uses three-digit codes for broad categories of diseases, injuries, and symptoms. Fourth- and fifth-level codes are created by the addition of a decimal point followed by a one- or two-digit subclassification suffix (for example, *380.01* represents a fifth-level diagnostic code). Such subclassification permits the specification of a diagnosis as exactly as possible.

In addition to the categories for diseases, there are two sections of *ICD-9-CM* codes that begin with the letters *V* and *E*. These letters are followed by up to four digits. The codes that begin with a *V* are used for visits for reasons other than illness or injury. In these situations, patients often do not have a complaint or active diagnosis. For example, a routine annual physical examination is a reason for an office visit without a complaint. Visits for treatments for already diagnosed conditions, such as for chemotherapy for cancer, also receive codes beginning with a *V.* Codes beginning with an *E* indicate the external cause of an injury or poisoning. For example, a patient's harmful reaction to the proper dosage of a drug is assigned an E code. V codes and E codes are described in more detail later in this section.

COMPLIANCE TIP

Using fourth- and fifth-level *ICD* codes is not optional. When coding, always use the highest code digit available. Use a three-digit code only if there are no four-digit codes within the category. Likewise, use a four-digit code only if there is no five-digit code for that subcategory. Use the five-digit subclassification code wherever possible. Most *ICD-9-CM* books use a symbol such as ⑤ next to a subcategory to indicate that a five-digit code is required.

An insurance claim for a patient must show the diagnosis that represents the patient's major health problem for *that particular encounter's* claim. This condition is known as the "primary diagnosis." The primary diagnosis must provide the reason for medical services listed on that claim. At times, there is more than one diagnosis because many patients are treated by a health care provider for more than one illness. The primary diagnosis—the underlying condition—is listed first on the insurance claim. After that, as many as three other coexisting conditions may be listed. Coexisting conditions occur at the same time as the primary diagnosis and affect the treatment or recovery from the condition shown as the primary diagnosis.

The information for identifying a patient's diagnosis and any coexisting conditions is found in the patient's medical record. Notes about the patient's chief complaint may be entered in the patient's medical record by an administrative medical assistant, nurse, or physician. However, *only* the physician determines the diagnosis.

When the diagnosis is reported on the patient encounter form after the patient's visit, the physician or coder converts the physician's written diagnosis statement to the correct code. In many medical offices, the encounter form lists the most frequently used diagnoses together with their codes for that particular medical practice. The physician can then simply check off the appropriate diagnosis from the list on the form, without having to look up the code in the *ICD*.

When a diagnosis code is not provided by the physician, the coder must know how to use the *ICD-9-CM* to look up and correctly code the physician's written statement about the diagnosis. Similarly, an administrative medical assistant may need to use the *ICD-9-CM* to verify a diagnosis code or to ensure that the codes listed on the office's current encounter form are consistent with the annual updates of the *ICD-9-CM*.

Using the *ICD*. Whether the *ICD* is bound as a single book or a set of two or three books, three sections are available:

> Volume 1—Diseases: Tabular List
> Volume 2—Diseases: Alphabetic Index
> Volume 3—Procedures: Tabular List and Alphabetic Index

Notice that the *ICD* covers two major areas—diseases and procedures. The procedures (Volume 3) are used only for hospital tests and treatments. An administrative medical assistant in a medical office would generally need to refer only to the diagnosis codes (Volumes 1 and 2).

In the *ICD,* diagnoses are listed two ways, as illustrated in Figures 8.4 and 8.5 on pages 208–209. One is the Alphabetic Index, which lists diagnoses in alphabetic order with their corresponding diagnosis codes. The other is the Tabular List, which provides diagnosis codes in numerical order with additional instructions.

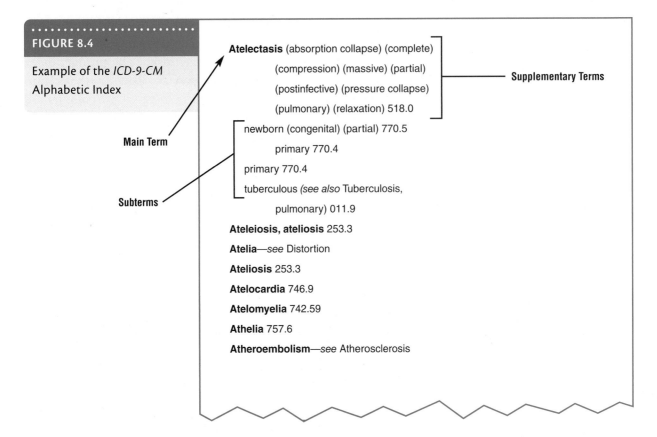

FIGURE 8.4

Example of the *ICD-9-CM* Alphabetic Index

Atelectasis (absorption collapse) (complete) (compression) (massive) (partial) (postinfective) (pressure collapse) (pulmonary) (relaxation) 518.0 — Supplementary Terms

Main Term

Subterms

    newborn (congenital) (partial) 770.5
        primary 770.4
    primary 770.4
    tuberculous (*see also* Tuberculosis, pulmonary) 011.9

Ateleiosis, ateliosis 253.3

Atelia—*see* Distortion

Ateliosis 253.3

Atelocardia 746.9

Atelomyelia 742.59

Athelia 757.6

Atheroembolism—*see* Atherosclerosis

Both the Alphabetic Index and the Tabular List are used to find the right code. The Alphabetic Index is never used alone, because it does not contain all the necessary information. After a code is located in the Alphabetic Index, it is looked up in the Tabular List. Notes in this list may suggest or require the use of additional codes. Alternatively, notes may indicate that conditions should be coded differently because of exclusion from a category.

The Alphabetic Index is organized by main terms in boldface type according to condition, as shown in Figure 8.4. A main term may be followed by a series of terms in parentheses called "supplementary terms." These supplementary terms help define the main term but have no effect on the selection of the code. Because of this fact, they are referred to as "nonessential" supplementary terms. Another type of term, a "subterm," is indented underneath the main term in regular type. Subterms do affect the selection of appropriate diagnosis codes. They describe essential differences in body sites, etiology (the cause of disease), or clinical type.

In contrast to the Alphabetic Index, the Tabular List in the *ICD* presents diagnosis codes in numerical order. It also organizes the codes according to body system, site, or type of procedure, rather than according to medical condition, as in the Alphabetic Index.

V codes and E codes are found in numerical order following the Tabular List. V codes classify factors that influence health status or give reasons why a patient may seek medical services when there is no clear diagnosis or disease process. Examples of V codes include routine care during pregnancy and immunizations or vaccinations.

⑤ **362 Other retinal disorders**

> **Excludes** *chorioretinal scars (363.30–363.35)*
>
> *chorioretinitis (363.0–363.2)*

⑤ **362.0 Diabetic retinopathy**

Code first diabetes (250.5)

362.01 Background diabetic retinopathy

Diabetic macular edema

Diabetic retinal edema

Diabetic retinal microaneurysms

Diabetic retinopathy NOS

362.02 Proliferative diabetic retinopathy

⑤ **362.1 Other background retinopathy and retinal vascular changes**

362.10 Background retinopathy, unspecified

362.11 Hypertensive retinopathy

362.12 Exudative retinopathy

Destructive deposits inflaming the posterior eye.

Coats' syndrome

362.13 Changes in vascular appearance

Vascular sheathing of retina

Use additional code for any associated atherosclerosis (440.8)

Some insurance companies accept V codes for primary diagnoses. In these cases, the V code is listed first, followed by the code for the condition that requires medication or treatment. Other insurance companies require that the condition being treated be listed first, followed by a V code. Medical insurance specialists verify the requirement of each plan.

It is appropriate to use V codes:

- When a patient is not sick but receives a service for a purpose, such as an ultrasound during pregnancy.
- When a patient with a current or recurring condition receives treatments, such as physical therapy.
- When a patient has a past condition that affects current health status or has a family history of disease.

E codes are diagnosis codes for external causes of poisonings and injuries. E codes are used *in addition to* the main code that describes the injury or poisoning itself; they are never used as primary codes. For example, if a person had a concussion from the impact sustained in a car accident, an E code would be used to indicate the external cause of the diagnosis. E codes are primarily required for workers' compensation and liability insurance, since they are used to define what happened and where it happened.

Basic Steps in Diagnostic Coding. Diagnostic coding follows a five-step process.

Step 1 *Locate the statement of the diagnosis in the patient's medical record.* If necessary, decide which is the main term or condition of the diagnosis. For example, in the diagnosis *peptic ulcer,* the main condition is *ulcer,* and peptic describes what type of ulcer it is.

Step 2 *Find the diagnosis in the* ICD*'s Alphabetic Index.* Look for the condition first. Then find descriptive words that make the condition more specific. Read all cross-references to check all the possibilities for a term and its synonyms. Examine all subterms under the main term in the Alphabetic Index to be sure the correct term is found. Do not stop at the first one that "sounds right." When you find the correct term, make a note of the code that follows it.

Step 3 *Locate the code from the Alphabetic Index in the* ICD*'s Tabular List.* The Tabular List gives codes in numerical order. Look for the number in boldface type.

Step 4 *Read all information and subclassifications to get the code that corresponds to the patient's specific disease or condition. Note fourth- or fifth-digit code requirements and exclusions.* Observe all notes for help in locating the exact code. For example, the *ICD* may indicate "fifth code required." This note means that the correct code for the diagnosis must have five digits. The *ICD* may also use the boxed and italicized word *Excludes* under a main term to indicate that a certain entry is not to be included as part of the preceding code. The note may also give the correct location of the excluded condition.

Fourth- and fifth-digit code requirements and exclusions are generally used in the *ICD* to accommodate the changes in diagnoses that occur over time. Where, in the past, a single code was used for a condition, now multiple codes might be used to specify the various types and complications of the condition. This requires adding more digits to a code or grouping related codes differently.

Step 5 *Record the diagnosis code on the insurance claim, and proofread the numbers.* As part of the proofreading process, a coder should always ask: Have all the numbers been entered in the right order? Are the codes complete? Has the highest code level been used?

Coding becomes easier with practice, but do not be tempted to take shortcuts. Every case is different, and additional terms or digits may be necessary to make a diagnosis code as specific as possible. If a step is skipped, important information may be missed. If more than one diagnosis is listed in a patient's medical record, work on only one diagnosis at a time to avoid coding errors.

■ Procedural Coding

The procedural coding system classifies services rendered by physicians. Each procedure code represents a medical, surgical, or diagnostic service performed by a provider. A coding specialist in an insurance company compares the procedure codes with the stated diagnoses on every insurance claim to determine whether the procedures were medically necessary. An administrative medical assistant should be very meticulous in working with codes on encounter forms and insurance claims, since accurate procedural coding is the only way to ensure that providers receive the maximum reimbursement for services.

CPT-4. The most commonly used system of procedure codes is found in the *Current Procedural Terminology,* Fourth Edition, a book published by the American Medical Association and known as the **CPT.** An updated edition of the *CPT* is published every year to reflect changes in medical practice. Newly developed procedures are added, and old ones that have become obsolete are deleted. These changes are also available in a computer file, because some medical offices use a computer-based version of the *CPT*.

CPT codes are five-digit numbers, organized into six sections as follows:

Section	Range of Codes
Evaluation and Management	99201–99499
Anesthesiology	00100–01999, 99100–99140
Surgery	10040–69990
Radiology	70010–79999
Pathology and Laboratory	80049–89399
Medicine (except Anesthesiology)	90281–99199

With the exception of the first two sections, the *CPT* is arranged in numerical order. Codes for evaluation and management are listed first, out of numerical order, because they are used most often. Each section opens with important guidelines that apply to its procedures. This material should be checked carefully before a procedure code is chosen.

Procedure codes are located by referring to the *CPT*'s index, an alphabetic list of procedures, organs, and conditions in the back of the book. Boldface main terms may be followed by descriptions and groups of indented terms. The coder selects the correct code by reviewing each description and indented term under the main term.

COMPLIANCE TIP

Medical offices should have the current year's *CPT* available for reference. Previous years' books should also be kept in case there is a question about already submitted insurance claims.

CPT Organization

The six primary sections of the *CPT* are divided into categories. These in turn are further divided into headings according to the type of test, service, or body system. Code number ranges included on a particular page are found in the upper-right corner. This helps the coder to locate a code quickly after using the index.

In the *CPT* sections, four symbols are used to highlight changes or special points. A bullet, which looks like a black circle (●), indicates a new procedure code. A triangle (▲) indicates a change in the code's description. Facing triangles (▶ ◀) enclose other new or revised information. A plus sign (+) is used for add-on codes, indicating procedures that are usually carried out in addition to another procedure. For example, Code 90471 covers one immunization administration, and Code +90472 covers administering an additional shot. Add-on codes are never reported alone. They are used together with the primary code.

The *CPT* uses a special format to show codes and their descriptions. The "parent code" description begins with a capital letter and may be followed by indented descriptive codes. The indented codes include the description of the parent code up to the semicolon, plus the indented information. See Figure 8.6 for an example of *CPT-4* code listings.

Notes and Modifiers

CPT listings may also contain notes, which are explanations for categories and individual codes. Notes often appear in parentheses after a code. Many times notes suggest other codes that should be considered before a final code is selected.

One or more two-digit modifiers may need to be assigned to the five-digit main number. Modifiers are written with a hyphen before the two-digit number. Modifiers show that some special circumstance applies to the service or procedure the physician performed. Appendix A of the *CPT* explains the proper use of each modifier.

Some services or procedures occur so infrequently that they are not listed in the *CPT*. Others are too new to be included. Unlisted procedures codes are provided for these situations. When a code for an unlisted procedure is used, a special report must be attached to the insurance claim. It describes the procedure, its extent, and the reason it was performed.

Coding Evaluation and Management Services. To diagnose conditions and plan treatments, physicians use different amounts of time and effort, and different kinds of skill, depending on the patient and the circumstance. In the guidelines to the Evaluation and Management (E/M) section, the *CPT* explains how to code different levels of these services. Three key factors documented in the patient's medical record help determine the level of service:

- The extent of the patient history taken
- The extent of the examination conducted
- The complexity of the medical decision making

FIGURE 8.6

Example of the *CPT-4*
Code Listings

Digestive System

Lips

(For procedures on skin of lips, see 10040 et seq)

Excision

40490	Biopsy of lip
40500	Vermilionectomy (lip shave), with mucosal advancement
40510	Excision of lip; transverse wedge excision with primary closure
40520	V-excision with primary direct linear closure
	(For excision of mucous lesions, see 40810-40816)
40525	full thickness, reconstruction with local flap (eg, Estlander or fan)
40527	full thickness, reconstruction with cross lip flap (Abbe-Estlander)
40530	Resection of lip, more than one-fourth, without reconstruction
	(For reconstruction, see 13131 et seq)

Common Descriptor

Semicolon

Indented Terms

In addition to level of service, insurance carriers want to know whether the physician treated a *new patient* or an *established patient*. Physicians often spend more time during new patients' visits than during visits from established patients, so the E/M codes for the two types of patients are separate. For reporting purposes, the *CPT* considers a patient "new" if that person has not received professional services from the physician within the past three years. Medical offices commonly use the abbreviation *NP* for a new patient. An established patient is one who has seen the physician within the past three years. (Note that the current visit need not be for a problem treated previously.) Medical offices commonly use the abbreviation *EP* for an established patient. Emergency patients are not classified as either new or established patients.

The *CPT* has a range of five codes each for new-patient or established-patient encounters. The lowest-level code is often called a Level I code; the codes go up to a Level V code. Annual physical examinations are located under the heading *Preventive Medicine Services* in the E/M section and are coded based on the age of new or established patients. For example, the procedure code 99395, in the "established patient" category, covers the routine examination, with tests and counseling, of a patient between the ages of 18 and 39.

Location of the service is also important, because different E/M codes apply to services performed in a physician's office, a hospital inpatient room, a hospital emergency room, a nursing facility, an extended-care facility, or a patient's home.

Coders should also be familiar with the difference between a referral and a consultation, since codes connected with these services are different. Sometimes one physician sends a patient to another physician for examination and treatment. This transferring of the responsibility for the patient's care for that condition is called a "referral." Standard E/M codes are used by the physician who assumes the responsibility. In contrast, a consultation occurs when an attending physician requests advice from another physician, but retains responsibility for the care of the patient. The *CPT* E/M section lists several codes for consultations, depending on the level and location of the service.

Coding Surgical Procedures. In the Surgery section, an asterisk (*) is a starred procedure indicating that the service as listed includes only that service, not associated pre- and postoperative services. In contrast to these procedures, most codes listed in the Surgery section include all routine elements. Services combined under one code are called "surgical packages."

Coding Laboratory Procedures. Organ or disease-oriented panels listed in the Pathology and Laboratory section of the *CPT* include tests frequently ordered together. An arthritis panel, for example, includes tests for rheumatoid factor, uric acid, sedimentation rate, and fluorescent non-infectious agent screening. Each element of the panel has its own procedure code. However, when the tests are performed together, the coder must use the code for the panel, rather than list each test separately.

Coding Immunizations. Injections and infusions of immune globulins, vaccines, toxoids, and other substances require two codes—one for giving the injection and one for the particular vaccine or toxoid that is given. For example, for an influenza shot, the administration code 90471 is used for the injection, along with one of the codes for the specific vaccine, such as 90657, 90658, or 90659. An E/M code is not used along with the codes for immunization unless a significant evaluation and management service is also done.

COMPLIANCE TIP

If each test in a panel or procedure in a surgical package is listed separately, it will "unbundle" the panel or package. The review performed by the insurance carrier's claims department will rebundle the services under the appropriate code, which could delay payment. Note that when unbundling is done intentionally to receive more payment than is correct, the claim is likely to be considered fraudulent.

HCPCS Codes. The Health Care Financing Administration's Common Procedure Coding System, commonly referred to as **HCPCS,** was developed by the CMS for use in coding services for Medicare patients. The HCPCS (pronounced "hic-picks") coding system uses both all the codes in the *CPT* and additional codes that cover many supplies, such as sterile trays, drugs, and DME ("durable medical equipment"). The additional codes have five characters—either numbers, letters, or both—and a different set of modifiers. Examples of these codes follow.

Code Number	Description
G0104	Colorectal cancer screening; flexible sigmoidoscopy
V5299	Hearing service, miscellaneous

In medical offices where the HCPCS system is used, regulations issued by the CMS are reviewed to determine the correct code and modifier for claims.

Basic Steps in Procedural Coding. Five steps are used for finding procedure codes in the *CPT*, as follows.

Step 1   *Become familiar with the* CPT. Read the introduction and main section guidelines and notes. For example, look at the guidelines for the Evaluation and Management section. They include definitions of key terms, such as *new patient, established patient, chief complaint, concurrent care,* and *counseling.* They also explain the way E/M codes should be selected.

Step 2   *Find the services that were provided.* The next step is to check the patient's encounter form to see which services were performed. For E/M procedures, look for clues as to the extent of history, examination, and decision making that were involved, and the amount of time the physician spent with the patient.

Step 3   *Look up the procedure code.* First, pick out a specific procedure or service, organ, or condition. Find the procedure code in the *CPT*'s index. For example, to find the code for "burns, dressing," first look alphabetically in the index for the procedure. Then, turn to the procedure code in the body of the *CPT* to be sure the code accurately reflects the service performed. Although it may seem tempting to record the procedure code directly from the index, resist the shortcut. Explanations and notes in the guidelines and main sections more accurately lead to finding main numbers and modifiers that reflect the services performed. That is the only way to ensure reimbursement at the highest allowed level.

Step 4 *Determine appropriate modifiers.* Check section guidelines and Appendix A to find modifiers that elaborate on details of the procedure being coded. For example, a bilateral breast reconstruction requires the modifier *–50*. Find the code for "breast reconstruction with free flap": 19364. To show the insurance carrier that the procedure was performed on both breasts, attach –50: 19364–50.

Step 5 *Record the procedure code.* After the procedure code is verified, it is posted to the insurance claim form (see Chapter 9). If the patient has more than one diagnosis for a single claim, the primary diagnosis is listed first. Likewise, the corresponding primary procedure is listed first. The *primary procedure* is the main service performed for the condition listed as the primary diagnosis.

The physician may perform additional procedures at the same time or in the same session as the primary procedure. If additional procedures are performed, match up each procedure with its corresponding diagnosis. If this is not done, the procedures will not be considered medically necessary, and the claim will be denied.

For example, Ms. Silvers, who saw Dr. House for chest pain and shortness of breath, also has asthma. While the patient was in the office, Dr. House renewed her prescription for asthma medication along with performing the ECG. If the ECG is mistakenly shown as a procedure for asthma, the claim will be denied, because that procedure is not medically necessary for that diagnosis.

Coding procedures become easier as the coder becomes more familiar with *CPT* codes. In fact, most medical offices use only a limited number of procedure codes.

■ Coding Compliance

On correct claims, each reported service is connected to a diagnosis that supports the procedure as necessary to investigate or treat the patient's condition. Insurance company representatives analyze this connection between the diagnostic and the procedural information, called **code linkage,** to evaluate the medical necessity of the reported charges. Correct claims also comply with many other regulations from government agencies and private payers.

Claims are denied because of lack of medical necessity when the reported services are not consistent with the symptoms or the diagnosis, or are not in keeping with generally accepted professional medical standards. Correctly linked codes that support medical necessity meet these conditions:

- The *CPT-4* procedure codes match the *ICD-9-CM* diagnosis codes.
- The procedures are not elective, experimental, or nonessential.
- The procedures are furnished at an appropriate level.

Medical necessity rules are established by each third-party payer. For example, each Medicare carrier has its own guidelines for particular procedures and the diagnoses that must be linked for payment. Private payers may impose a different set of rules, and contradictions are not uncommon.

Common Coding Errors. There are many factors that contribute to coding errors. Some of the more common coding errors include:

- Reporting diagnosis codes that are not at the highest level of specificity available.
- Using out-of-date codes.
- Altering documentation after the services are reported.
- Coding without proper documentation to back up the codes selected.
- Reporting services provided by unlicensed or unqualified clinical personnel.
- Reporting services that are not covered or that have limited coverage.
- Using modifiers incorrectly, or not at all.
- Upcoding—using a procedure code that provides a higher reimbursement rate than the code that actually reflects the service provided.
- Unbundling—billing the parts of a bundled procedure as separate procedures.

Most medical practices have a system, formal or informal, for evaluating coding errors in an effort to achieve better coding compliance. Some examples of efforts that can be made include the appointment of a compliance officer and committee, regular training plans, and ongoing monitoring and auditing of claim preparation.

GO TO PROJECT 8.4 ON PAGE 218

Chapter Projects

PROJECT 8.1 Insurance Terminology

GO TO... Working Papers

On WP 46, match each insurance term in Column 2 with its definition in Column 1. Be prepared to discuss your answers in class.

Chapter Projects

PROJECT 8.2   Internet Research: The Medicare Web Site

The official U.S. government site for Medicare information on the Internet provides information about Medicare basics, Medicare plan choices, publications, nursing homes, a participating physician directory for your area, the top 20 questions from the Medicare helpline, and more. Visit the Web site at www.medicare.gov and look up information about the different Medicare plan choices available nationally, as well as what plans are available in your area. Be prepared to share the results of your reading with the class.

PROJECT 8.3   Insurance Plans, Payers, and Payment Methods

WP 47 contains statements about various types of insurance plans, payers, and payment methods. Mark each statement with either "T" for *true* or "F" for *false*. Be prepared to discuss your answers in class.

PROJECT 8.4   Identifying Diagnostic and Procedure Codes

Refer to WP 48 *(ICD-9-CM* Diagnostic Codes) and WP 49 (patient encounter form for Janet Provost's annual exam) to answer the following questions regarding diagnostic and procedure codes.

1. What is the *ICD-9-CM* diagnostic code for each of the following conditions?
   a. Migraine headache   _____
   b. Chest pain   _____
   c. Lightheadedness   _____
   d. Annual physical exam, age 39   _____
   e. Family history of heart disease _____
   f. Test for pregnancy   _____
   g. Osteoarthritis   _____

2. Review Janet Provost's patient encounter form.
   a. What is the diagnostic code for Janet Provost's visit? _____
   b. What is the description given in the *ICD-9-CM* for this code? _____
   c. What procedures did Dr. Larsen perform? List the *CPT-4* procedure codes for each: _____
   _____
   d. How much did Dr. Larsen charge for the complete blood count (CBC)? _____

3. Do you think the *CPT-4* procedure codes marked off on the encounter form are in compliance with the *ICD-9-CM* diagnosis code given? _____

CHAPTER SUMMARY

1. Administrative medical assistants should be familiar with basic terms and concepts and the types of insurance.

2. Indemnity plans are usually fee-for-service plans that pay after services are provided. They offer benefits in exchange for regular payment of a fixed premium. Members must also pay deductibles and coinsurance. Managed care plans, in contrast, often use capitation, which is a fixed prospective payment made for services to be provided during a specified period of time. Managed care organizations contract with both patients and providers.

   In an HMO, patients agree to receive services from providers who have contracts with the HMO; usually a primary care physician coordinates the patient's care and makes referrals. In a PPO, patients are offered lower fees in exchange for receiving services from plan providers, but are usually not required to choose a primary care physician.

3. Insurance plans are available through commercial insurance companies in the private sector, or, for eligible individuals, through government-sponsored programs. The latter include Medicare, Medicaid, TRICARE, CHAMPVA, and workers' compensation.

4. A PAR provider agrees to provide medical services to plan members according to the plan's rules and payment schedules. A nonPAR provider does not have to abide by the rules or the payment schedule when treating members but does not receive any of the benefits of participation.

   The most common types of payment systems used by third-party payers for reimbursing physicians are based on *(a)* usual, customary, and reasonable (UCR) fees, *(b)* a relative value scale (RVS), *(c)* a resource-based relative value scale (RBRVS), or *(d)* diagnostic-related groups (DRGs).

5. The *ICD-9-CM* is used to report patients' conditions on insurance claims. Codes are made up of three, four, or five numbers and a description. The Alphabetic Index is used first to approximate the correct code for a diagnosis. Then the Tabular List is used to verify and refine the final selection of the code.

   CPT-4, a publication of the American Medical Association, contains the most widely used system of codes for physicians' medical, diagnostic, and procedural services. *CPT-4* codes are required for reporting physician practice services on insurance claims and encounter forms. The codes have five digits and a description. *CPT-4* contains six sections of codes—Evaluation and Management, Anesthesia,

Surgery, Radiology, Pathology and Laboratory, and Medicine—followed by six appendixes and an index. The index is used first in the process of selecting a code; then the body of the text is used to verify the code.

Diagnoses and procedures must be correctly linked when services are reported for reimbursement, because third-party payers analyze this connection to determine the medical necessity of the charges.

KEY TERMS

The following key terms appear in **boldface** type in this chapter. Administrative medical assistants must know the meaning and the correct use of each of these terms. Can you recall what each term means? Refer to this chapter or to the glossary for any terms you need to review.

accepting assignment
allowed charge
assignment of benefits
balance billing
birthday rule
Blue Cross and Blue Shield Association (BCBS)
capitation
carrier
Centers for Medicare and Medicaid Services (CMS)
CHAMPVA
code linkage
coinsurance
coordination of benefits (COB)
copayment (copay)
CPT
customary fee
deductible
diagnostic-related groups (DRGs)
fee-for-service
HCPCS
HMO (health maintenance organization)

ICD-9-CM
indemnity plan
insured
managed care
Medicaid
Medicare
participating (PAR) provider
patient encounter form
PPO (preferred provider organization)
preauthorization
premium
primary care provider (PCP)
provider
reasonable fee
referral
relative value scale (RVS)
resource-based relative value scale (RBRVS)
third-party payer
TRICARE
usual fee
workers' compensation

THINKING IT THROUGH

These questions cover the most important points in this chapter. Using your critical thinking skills, play the role of an administrative medical assistant as you answer each question. Be prepared to present your responses in class.

1. How would you explain to a patient who is unfamiliar with insurance terminology what is meant by the term *third-party payer*? How was the term derived?

2. Ellen Gold, a Medicare patient, does not understand her last month's medical statement. She already paid her deductible, yet the bill states that she owes $20 on a total bill of $100. How would you explain the bill to her?

3. Joe Cantinori inquires about his unpaid bill and asks whether the physician received payment from his insurance company. When you check his record, you find that your office submitted the insurance form on his behalf. However, the physician did not accept assignment on the claim since he is not a PAR provider in that program. This means that the insurance company will send the payment directly to Joe. How would you explain this to Joe?

4. A patient complained of symptoms usually associated with arthritis. The following tests were ordered by the physician: rheumatoid factor, uric acid, sedimentation rate, and fluorescent noninfectious agent screening. The insurance claim submitted contained procedure codes for each test. You have not received any response from the insurance carrier, even though payments for other claims sent to the same carrier on that day have been received. What do you think accounts for the delay?

CHAPTER 9

Billing, Reimbursement, and Collections

OBJECTIVES

After studying this chapter, you will be able to:

1. Compute charges for medical services and create patient statements based on the patient encounter form and the physician's fee schedule.
2. Explain the process of completing and transmitting insurance claims.
3. Discuss the advantages of using electronic claims.
4. Describe the different types of billing options used by medical practices for billing patients.
5. Discuss the procedures and options available for collecting delinquent accounts.

INTRODUCTION

Administrative medical assistants help maintain physicians' financial records. This includes billing patients, filing insurance claims, and collecting the appropriate fees. Billing, reimbursement, and collections are extremely important because the office depends on the cash flow generated by these functions. All the expenses of running the office, such as supplies, payroll, and liability insurance, depend on the revenue from patients' and insurance companies' payments. General rules for billing, filing, and collecting procedures are discussed in this chapter.

KEY TERMS

Study these important words, which are defined in this chapter, to build your professional vocabulary:

clearinghouse	cycle billing	fee adjustment	patient statement
CMS-1500 claim form	dependent	fee schedule	terminated account
collection agency	electronic claims	guarantor	third-party liability
collection at the time of service	EOB	monthly billing	write-off
	ERA	patient information form	

9.1 RECORDING TRANSACTIONS

Administrative medical assistants keep track of the services rendered and any payments made during a visit to the physician. After the patient completes the office visit, the administrative medical assistant updates the patient ledger to show the financial information for the encounter.

■ Patient Encounter Form

To facilitate the process of billing patients for physicians' services, medical offices use a patient encounter form. A blank patient encounter form is attached to the patient's medical record for completion. It is used to record the details of patients' encounters for billing and insurance purposes. In particular, it is designed to record each procedure the physician performs, the fee charged for each, as well as the diagnosis connected with the treatment.

Most encounter forms contain sections for recording the following information (see Figure 9.1 on page 224 for an example):

- The patient's name, address, and phone information and type of insurance.
- The date.
- The diagnosis for the current visit.
- Procedure information—a checklist of the most commonly administered examinations, lab tests, injections, and other procedures in that office, and the physician's fee for each.
- Financial information—the total fees for the day, payments made, and amount due for that visit.

The procedures listed on a patient encounter form are customized to represent the most commonly administered examinations, lab tests, injections, and other procedures for that particular practice. On some encounter forms, the fee for each procedure is printed beside the procedure code. In most cases, however, because the physician's fees may change from year to year, and because they are sometimes adjusted or discounted for different patients and insurance plans, a space is provided before each code (as in Figure 9.1) for the administrative medical assistant to enter the appropriate fee at the time of the visit.

The procedure for using the patient encounter form is:

1. A blank form is attached to the patient's file when the patient registers for the visit.

FIGURE 9.1

Completed Patient
Encounter Form

No.	Date	Description	Charge	Credit		Current Balance
				Payment	Adjustment	
	05/15/2008	Annual exam, HGB, UA	173.00	34.60	-------	138.40

Patient Information

Patient _____ Becker, Alison

7911 Riverview Lane N.
Address

Date: 05/15/2008   Chart # 1324

Chicago, IL 60632-1979
City, State, Zip

Karen Larsen, MD
2235 S. Ridgeway Avenue
Chicago, IL 60623-2240

Diagnoses:

312-555-6685   312-555-3385
Home phone   Work phone

1. __V70.0__

312-555-6022

2. _____

Alison Becker   self
Responsible Person   Relationship

3. _____

Fax: 312-555-0025

Real Insurance   470-55-8533
Insurance   Contract numbers

4. _____

OFFICE VISITS

New Patient	Established Patient

Preventive Medicine

New Patient			Established Patient	
	____ 99381	under 1 year	____ 99391	
____ 99201	____ 99382	1–4	____ 99392	____ 99211
____ 99202	____ 99383	5–11	____ 99393	____ 99212
____ 99203	____ 99384	12–17	____ 99394	____ 99213
____ 99204	____ 99385	18–39	136.00 99395	____ 99214
____ 99205	____ 99386	40–64	____ 99396	____ 99215
	____ 99387	65+	____ 99397	

Hospital Visits
Initial:
____ 99221
____ 99222
____ 99223
Subsequent:
____ 99231
____ 99232
____ 99233
Nursing Facility
Subsequent:
____ 99311
____ 99312
____ 99313
Other
_____
_____

Lab:
____ 80048 Basic metabolic panel (SMA-8)
____ 87110 Chlamydia culture
____ 85651 ESR; nonautomated
____ 83001 FSH
____ 82947 Glucose, blood
____ 85022 Hemogram (CBC) with differential
____ 80076 Hepatic function panel
13.00 85018 HGB
____ 86701 HIV-1
____ 83002 LH
____ 80061 Lipid panel
____ 86617 Lyme antibody

____ 86308 Monospot test
____ 88150 Pap
____ 85610 Prothrombin time
____ 84152 PSA
____ 86430 Rheumatoid factor
____ 82270 Stool hemoccult x 3
____ 87430 Strep screen
____ 84478 Triglycerides
____ 84443 TSH
24.00 81001 UA with microscopy
____ 87088 UC
____ 84550 Uric acid, blood
____ 81025 Urine pregnancy test

Injections:
____ 90471 admin 1 vac
____ 90472 each add'l vac
____ 90716 Chickenpox
____ 90702 DT
____ 90701 DTP
____ 90657 Influenza 6-35 months
____ 90658 Influenza 3 years +
____ 90665 Lyme disease
____ 90707 MMR
____ 90704 Mumps
____ 90713 Polio vac inactivated (IPV)
____ 90703 Tetanus Tox
ECG: ____ 93000 ECG

Other
_____
_____

2. As the physician performs various procedures during the visit, check marks are made in the appropriate boxes on the encounter form (or else the appropriate items on the form are circled). The diagnoses and corresponding codes are also recorded on the form.

3. At the end of the visit, the form is taken to the checkout area for the administrative medical assistant to record, or post, the necessary transactions in the office's billing system.

■ Fee Schedule

Each physician or medical practice has a **fee schedule** that lists the usual procedures the office performs and the corresponding charges. The administrative medical assistant should always refer to the practice's fee schedule in determining the total cost for each patient's visit.

Sometimes medical practices have more than one fee schedule. For example, if a physician is a participating provider in a PPO (preferred provider organization), the procedures may be discounted for PPO members according to an agreed-upon amount between the physician and the plan.

While dealing with the office's fee schedule, the assistant should also be familiar with the policy of the office regarding financial arrangements: the charges when a reduction of the fee is possible, the acceptable minimal payment, and any other facts needed to deal efficiently with problems concerning patients' payments.

Patients who call to make a first appointment may inquire about the charges. Patients should be told that it is difficult to discuss exact charges prior to a visit because the charges will depend on the extent of the examination, the tests, and the type of treatment provided. Ideally, the patient should be told the approximate cost of the procedures before treatment begins. Providing this information in advance will help avoid misunderstandings and will make collection of payments easier.

It may be necessary to explain the fee by calling attention to the time involved; the cost of medications or supplies; and the skill, knowledge, and experience of the physician. Either the physician or the administrative medical assistant can discuss the fee with patients. If the physician discusses the fee with a patient, the assistant needs to know what has been discussed.

It is a fair assumption that a patient who inquires about charges before a visit is concerned about the price and should be shown every consideration. If a definite amount is quoted and this amount seems to worry the patient, the administrative medical assistant can reassure the patient by saying that arrangements can be made to ease payment.

■ Patient Statements

The administrative medical assistant records all transactions—that is, charges incurred by the patient for office visits, x-rays, laboratory tests, and so on, and payments made by the patient or the patient's insurance company—in the patient ledger. The patient's copy of the information stored in the patient ledger is referred to as the **patient statement,** or patient bill.

The patient statement shows the professional services rendered to the patient, the charge for each service, payments made, and the balance owed. Figure 9.2 on page 226 shows an example of a patient statement. Notice that the statement contains transactions for two people—Alison and Mike Becker—since both are members of the same family and are under the same account.

Listing, or itemizing, the procedures on the statement reminds patients when they visited the physician and what services were performed. To save space on the statement, some common procedures are listed using procedural codes only, with no descriptions.

FIGURE 9.2

Patient Statement

STATEMENT

Statement Date: 03/11/20--

Account Number: 1324

Any change or payments made after the statement date will appear on the next statement.

Amount Enclosed _____

Please remit all payments to:

Karen Larsen, MD
2235 South Ridgeway Avenue
Chicago, IL 60623-2240
312-555-6022   Fax: 312-555-0025

Responsible Person's Name

Alison C. Becker
7911 Riverview Lane N.
Chicago, IL 60632-1979

Service Date	Patient's Name	Procedure Code	Diagnosis Code	Service Description	Charge	Insurance Paid	Adj.	Patient Paid	Amount Due
03-11-06	Alison	99201	786.2	NP problem focused	54.00	-0-	-0-	54.00	-0-
03-15-08	MIke	99202	729.1	NP expanded visit	73.00	-0-	-0-	-0-	73.00
04-01-08								73.00	-0-
05-15-08	Alison	99395	V70.0	Annual exam	136.00			34.60	101.40
		85018		HGB	13.00				114.40
		81001		UA	24.00				138.40
05-31-08				Real Insurance		138.40			-0-

ANY AMOUNT NOT PAID BY INSURANCE IS NOW THE PATIENT'S RESPONSIBILITY

ACCOUNT NUMBER	SSN	CURRENT	OVER 30 DAYS	OVER 60 DAYS	OVER 90 DAYS	OVER 120 DAYS	INSURANCE PENDING	AMOUNT DUE
1324	470-55-8533	-0-	-0-	-0-	-0-	-0-	-0-	-0-

Abbreviations:

CBC (complete blood count)
ECG (electrocardiogram)
EP (established patient)

HV (hospital visit)
LAB (laboratory work)
NP (new patient)

UA (urinalysis)
UC (urine culture)

The statement is generally sent to the patient who received treatment, although in some cases another person may be designated as the one responsible for receiving and paying the bill. In general, parents are responsible for the medical bills of minor children living in their home.

■ Computerized Billing

Most medical practices use a computerized billing program to generate patient statements. Many software programs, such as NDCmedisoft™, are available to handle patients' billing. Figure 9.3 shows an example of a NDCmedisoft™

patient statement. In addition to generating itemized patient statements, a computerized billing system is usually used to produce the following reports for accounting purposes:

- A daily report, called a "day sheet," listing all charges, payments, and adjustments entered during that day.
- Monthly reports summarizing the operation of the practice.
- Aging reports, which list the outstanding balances owed to the practice by insurance companies or patients.
- Lists of the amounts of money generated by various departments such as laboratory, x-ray, and physical therapy.
- Lists of the amounts generated by individual physicians in the practice.
- Reports on the frequency of procedure codes reported by each physician in the practice.

A patient billing program can also be used to print out blank patient encounter forms each day for patients who have appointments on that day. Medical billing programs are a valuable accounting tool for the physician, and the administrative medical assistant should be familiar with their use.

▶ **GO TO PROJECT 9.1 ON PAGE 246** ▶

FIGURE 9.3

Computerized Patient Statement from the NDCmedisoft™ Program

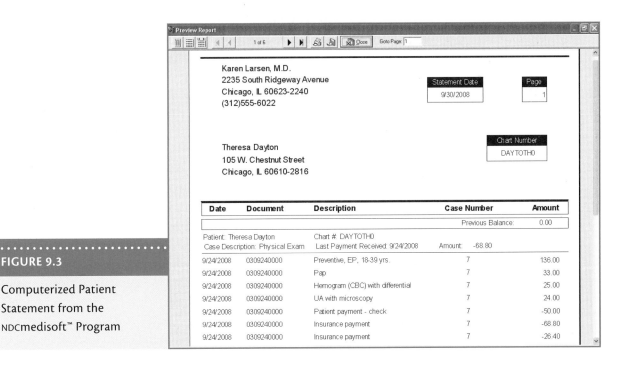

9.2 | INSURANCE CLAIMS

■ Overview of the Process

When patients receive services from a medical practice, they either pay for services themselves or the charges are submitted to their insurance company or government agency for payment. Most medical practices complete an insurance claim form on behalf of the patient. The insurance claim form contains both clinical and financial information and is transmitted to the patient's insurance carrier for partial or full reimbursement of the services rendered.

Using the CMS-1500 Paper Claim Form. The most commonly used paper claim form is the **CMS-1500 claim form** (formerly known as the HCFA-1500 claim form). See Figure 9.4 for an example. Accepted by private as well as government-sponsored programs, it is also called the "universal claim form." Two medical office forms are used to complete the CMS-1500 claim form: the **patient information form,** which is filled out or updated by the patient, and the patient encounter form. The patient information form may also include release-of-information and assignment-of-benefits statements. If a provider submits claims for a patient, a release-of-information statement must be signed, dated, and filed in the patient's medical record. Similarly, if the patient decides to authorize the provider to receive payments for medical services directly from third-party payers, an assignment-of-benefits statement must be signed by the patient and filed in the patient's medical record. For convenience, some medical practices include these statements on the patient information form. Other practices prefer to use separate forms for each of them.

Submitting Paper or Electronic Claims. Increasingly, medical offices are using computerized insurance claim forms, known as **electronic claims,** in place of paper claims. Electronic claims are prepared on a computer in the medical office and then transmitted to a computer at the insurance company using a modem. They are never actually printed on paper. The HIPAA claim is the standard format for electronic claims. Advantages of using electronic claims include immediate transmission, faster payment, and easier tracking of claim status.

Processing by a Third-Party Payer. When the claim form arrives at the office of the insurance carrier, either on paper or as a computer file, the insurance carrier processes the claim. This entails reviewing the information for accuracy and completeness, evaluating the treatment received, and deciding what benefits are due to the insured. The insurance company

FIGURE 9.4

Blank CMS-1500 Form

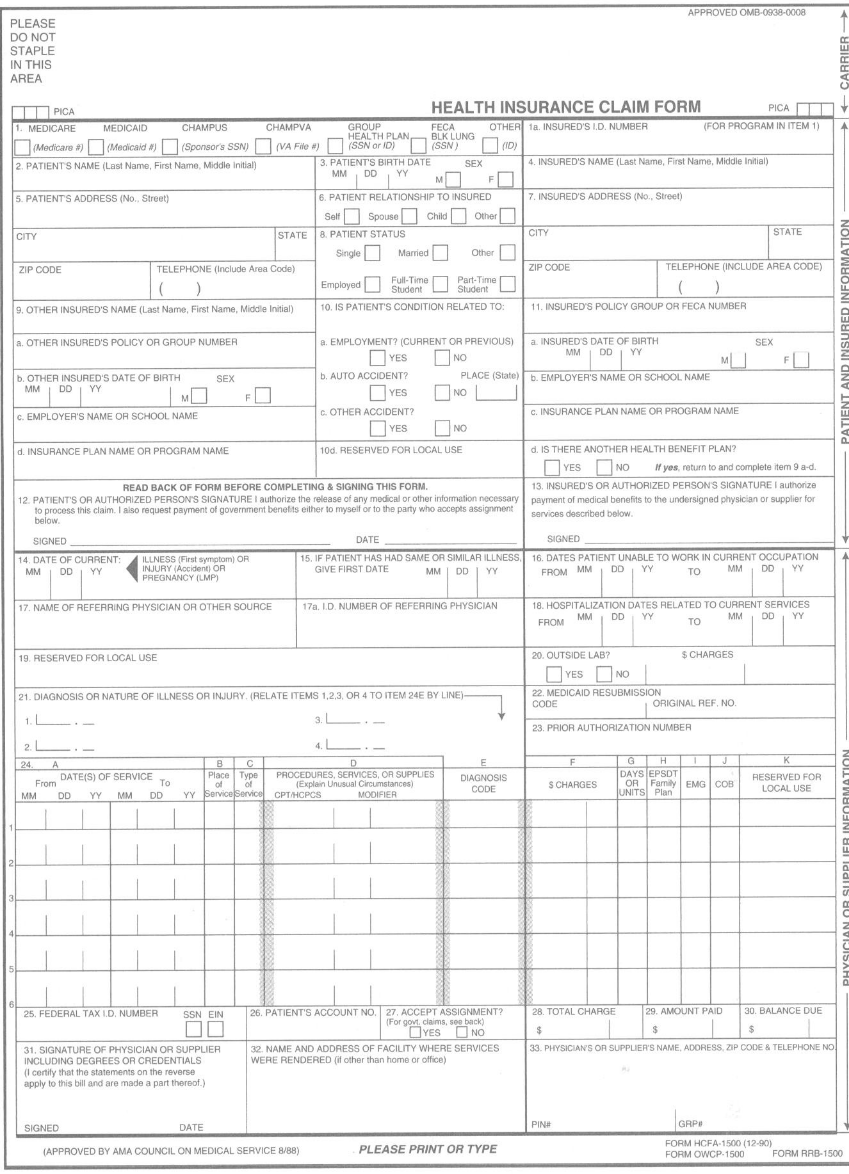
APPROVED OMB-0938-0008

PLEASE DO NOT STAPLE IN THIS AREA

CARRIER

PICA — HEALTH INSURANCE CLAIM FORM — PICA

1. MEDICARE (Medicare #) MEDICAID (Medicaid #) CHAMPUS (Sponsor's SSN) CHAMPVA (VA File #) GROUP HEALTH PLAN (SSN or ID) FECA BLK LUNG (SSN) OTHER (ID)

1a. INSURED'S I.D. NUMBER (FOR PROGRAM IN ITEM 1)

2. PATIENT'S NAME (Last Name, First Name, Middle Initial)

3. PATIENT'S BIRTH DATE MM DD YY SEX M F

4. INSURED'S NAME (Last Name, First Name, Middle Initial)

5. PATIENT'S ADDRESS (No., Street)

6. PATIENT RELATIONSHIP TO INSURED Self Spouse Child Other

7. INSURED'S ADDRESS (No., Street)

CITY STATE

8. PATIENT STATUS Single Married Other

CITY STATE

ZIP CODE TELEPHONE (Include Area Code) ( )

Employed Full-Time Student Part-Time Student

ZIP CODE TELEPHONE (INCLUDE AREA CODE) ( )

9. OTHER INSURED'S NAME (Last Name, First Name, Middle Initial)

10. IS PATIENT'S CONDITION RELATED TO:

11. INSURED'S POLICY GROUP OR FECA NUMBER

a. OTHER INSURED'S POLICY OR GROUP NUMBER

a. EMPLOYMENT? (CURRENT OR PREVIOUS) YES NO

a. INSURED'S DATE OF BIRTH MM DD YY SEX M F

b. OTHER INSURED'S DATE OF BIRTH MM DD YY SEX M F

b. AUTO ACCIDENT? PLACE (State) YES NO

b. EMPLOYER'S NAME OR SCHOOL NAME

c. EMPLOYER'S NAME OR SCHOOL NAME

c. OTHER ACCIDENT? YES NO

c. INSURANCE PLAN NAME OR PROGRAM NAME

d. INSURANCE PLAN NAME OR PROGRAM NAME

10d. RESERVED FOR LOCAL USE

d. IS THERE ANOTHER HEALTH BENEFIT PLAN? YES NO *If yes,* return to and complete item 9 a-d.

READ BACK OF FORM BEFORE COMPLETING & SIGNING THIS FORM.

12. PATIENT'S OR AUTHORIZED PERSON'S SIGNATURE I authorize the release of any medical or other information necessary to process this claim. I also request payment of government benefits either to myself or to the party who accepts assignment below.

SIGNED DATE

13. INSURED'S OR AUTHORIZED PERSON'S SIGNATURE I authorize payment of medical benefits to the undersigned physician or supplier for services described below.

SIGNED

PATIENT AND INSURED INFORMATION

14. DATE OF CURRENT: MM DD YY ILLNESS (First symptom) OR INJURY (Accident) OR PREGNANCY (LMP)

15. IF PATIENT HAS HAD SAME OR SIMILAR ILLNESS, GIVE FIRST DATE MM DD YY

16. DATES PATIENT UNABLE TO WORK IN CURRENT OCCUPATION FROM MM DD YY TO MM DD YY

17. NAME OF REFERRING PHYSICIAN OR OTHER SOURCE

17a. I.D. NUMBER OF REFERRING PHYSICIAN

18. HOSPITALIZATION DATES RELATED TO CURRENT SERVICES FROM MM DD YY TO MM DD YY

19. RESERVED FOR LOCAL USE

20. OUTSIDE LAB? YES NO $ CHARGES

21. DIAGNOSIS OR NATURE OF ILLNESS OR INJURY. (RELATE ITEMS 1,2,3, OR 4 TO ITEM 24E BY LINE)

1. ___ . __ 3. ___ . __

2. ___ . __ 4. ___ . __

22. MEDICAID RESUBMISSION CODE ORIGINAL REF. NO.

23. PRIOR AUTHORIZATION NUMBER

24. A DATE(S) OF SERVICE From MM DD YY To MM DD YY	B Place of Service	C Type of Service	D PROCEDURES, SERVICES, OR SUPPLIES (Explain Unusual Circumstances) CPT/HCPCS MODIFIER	E DIAGNOSIS CODE	F $ CHARGES	G DAYS OR UNITS	H EPSDT Family Plan	I EMG	J COB	K RESERVED FOR LOCAL USE

25. FEDERAL TAX I.D. NUMBER SSN EIN

26. PATIENT'S ACCOUNT NO.

27. ACCEPT ASSIGNMENT? (For govt. claims, see back) YES NO

28. TOTAL CHARGE $

29. AMOUNT PAID $

30. BALANCE DUE $

31. SIGNATURE OF PHYSICIAN OR SUPPLIER INCLUDING DEGREES OR CREDENTIALS (I certify that the statements on the reverse apply to this bill and are made a part thereof.)

SIGNED DATE

32. NAME AND ADDRESS OF FACILITY WHERE SERVICES WERE RENDERED (if other than home or office)

33. PHYSICIAN'S OR SUPPLIER'S NAME, ADDRESS, ZIP CODE & TELEPHONE NO.

PIN# GRP#

PHYSICIAN OR SUPPLIER INFORMATION

(APPROVED BY AMA COUNCIL ON MEDICAL SERVICE 8/88) PLEASE PRINT OR TYPE FORM HCFA-1500 (12-90) FORM OWCP-1500 FORM RRB-1500

may determine to pay the fee, deny the claim, or pay less for some or all of the procedures.

Receiving an EOB or ERA. After the insurance carrier reviews the claim and makes a final reimbursement determination, it sends a remittance report to the patient and the provider with an explanation of its decision. The remittance report also takes into account any deductibles or coinsurance the insured may owe. If the insurance company determines that there are benefits to be paid, a check for the appropriate amount is attached to the provider's report. In cases in which the benefits have not been assigned to the provider, the remittance is sent directly to the patient.

In the case of paper claims, the remittance report sent by the insurance company in response to the claim is transmitted through the mail and is referred to as an **EOB** (explanation of benefits). In the case of electronic claims, the report is transferred from one computer to another and is therefore referred to as an **ERA** (electronic remittance advice). As with an electronic claim, an ERA is never actually printed. Although the formats used for the EOB and the ERA differ, the information conveyed in both types of reports is the same—both explain the amount of benefits to be paid to, or on behalf of, the insured and how that amount was determined.

Checking the Reimbursement Details. After the medical office receives the remittance report (the EOB or ERA), the administrative medical assistant reviews it and checks it against the original claim. If all is in order, the assistant files the report with the patient's financial records. If a check from the insurance company is attached to the EOB, the administrative medical assistant posts the payment received to the appropriate patient's account and marks the check for deposit in the practice's bank account. Generally, if a claim is processed electronically, the method of payment is also electronic. In such cases, the payment attached to the ERA is deposited into the practice's bank account through an electronic funds transfer, rather than mailed in the form of a check to the medical practice.

Billing the Patient. If the patient still owes money to the medical practice after the EOB or ERA has been received—usually for charges that were not fully reimbursed by the insurance company—the assistant bills the patient for the amount due. If the patient is confused or has any questions about payments, the assistant can try to help by going over the terms of the insurance plan with the patient. The assistant may also need to call the insurance carrier and act as a go-between for patients. The assistant can build goodwill for the physician's office by using problem-solving and communication skills to fulfill this role. Patients understandably get upset when they receive unexpectedly large bills or an incorrect payment. The assistant is the patient's advocate with the insurance carrier. Sometimes explaining the solution again to the patient in different terms after speaking with the insurance carrier will help clear up the problem.

Patients may also accuse the medical office of billing incorrectly when they are unhappy with the benefits received. The assistant should remember to use respect and care in solving any miscommunications or misunderstandings in such circumstances.

Once the patient understands the terms of the payment due, the assistant follows up with the patient to see that the amount due is collected in a timely manner. When the patient pays the balance due, the account is listed as a zero balance and the insurance claim process is complete.

Appealing Claims. If the physician thinks that the reimbursement decision is incorrect or unfair, the medical office may initiate an appeal. The office makes an appeal for a claim by sending a written request to the carrier to review reimbursement. Each insurance company has its own appeal process. A representative from the insurance company can instruct the assistant on the appeal process the insurer uses, if necessary. This information may also be available on the Internet by initiating a search from the insurance carrier's Web site.

■ Completing and Transmitting the Claim Form

Completing and transmitting the claim form accurately for a patient is one of the most important steps in successful claim reimbursement. Therefore, the administrative medical assistant should be familiar with the details of the process.

Verifying Insurance Information. The first step in processing a claim is to verify the patient's insurance information. With new patients, most practices routinely check insurance coverage before the patient's first appointment. Basic information about the patient and the patient's insurance is obtained over the phone when the first appointment is scheduled. The assistant then contacts the insurer by telephone, fax, or the Internet to verify that the patient is currently enrolled in the plan as specified and has paid all required premiums or other charges.

Checking the Accuracy of Essential Claim Information. Claim forms must be completed accurately. The basic information that is required on most claim forms includes the following items:

- Contract numbers—that is, the group number and the insured's identification number from the insured's current insurance card.
- The patient's complete name, date of birth, sex, and relationship to insured.
- The insured's complete name, address, date of birth, and employer.
- Information on a secondary carrier—subscriber's name, date of birth, and employer.
- Information about whether the condition is job-related or accident-related and whether it is an illness or injury.
- The patient's account number (if your facility assigns numbers to patients).
- Complete *ICD-9-CM* diagnostic codes for the submitted claim.
- Information about the provider—name, address, identifying codes, and signatures.
- A statement of services rendered, which should include dates, procedural codes, charges, and total charges.

Completing the CMS-1500 Claim Form. Although not all insurance carriers use the CMS-1500 for processing claims, the information required on most insurance claims is the same. If the administrative medical assistant is familiar with the various fields on the CMS form, the same knowledge can be applied to other claim forms for successful completion.

Figure 9.5 shows a completed CMS-1500 claim form. Note that the form is divided horizontally into two parts: The top half contains patient and insured information (Items 1–13), while the bottom half contains physician or supplier information (Items 14–33). Figure 9.6 presents the information that should be entered in each numbered blank (called a "form locator").

After a claim has been completed and sent to the insurance company, make a notation in the patient ledger by entering the date and the phrase "Submitted to insurance" after the last entry. An updated patient statement is then sent to the patient for billing purposes on the next billing date. The patient or other designated person is still responsible for the complete charge, even if insurance is involved.

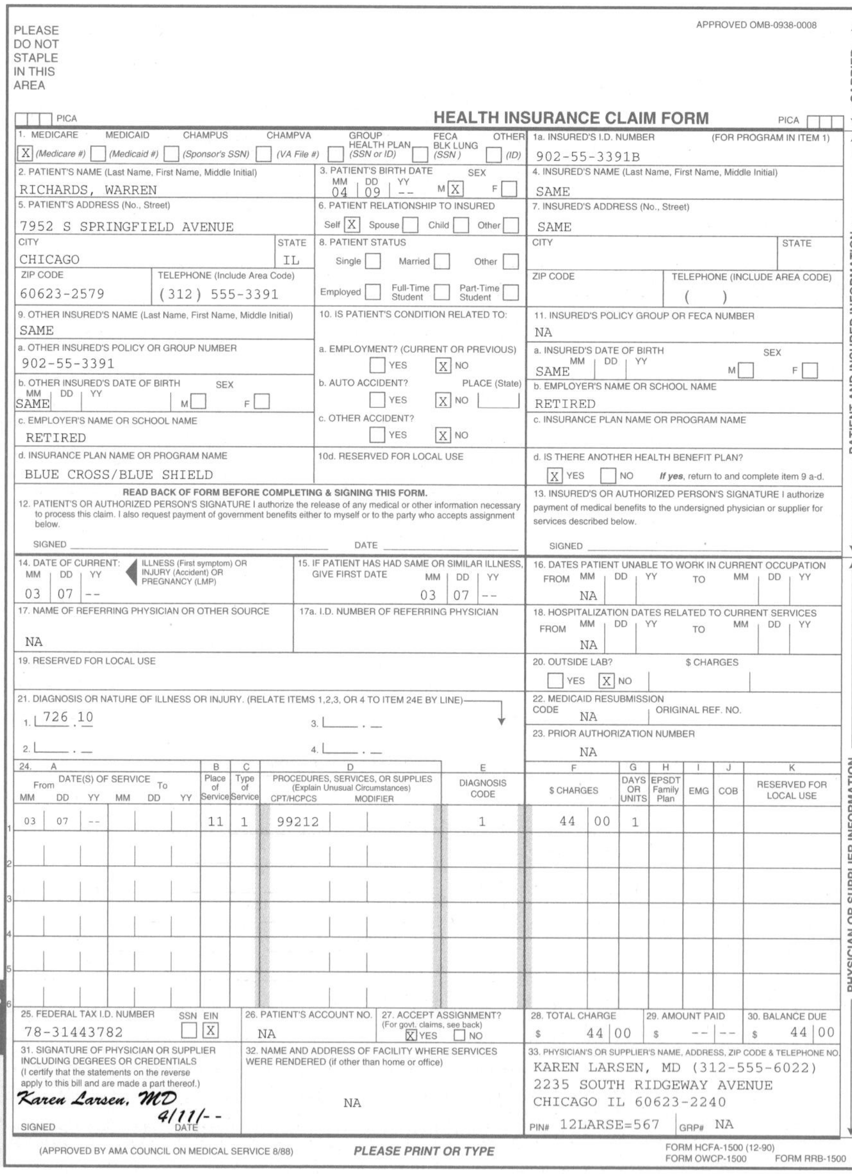

PLEASE DO NOT STAPLE IN THIS AREA

APPROVED OMB-0938-0008

CARRIER

PICA

HEALTH INSURANCE CLAIM FORM

PICA

1. MEDICARE [X] (Medicare #) MEDICAID [ ] (Medicaid #) CHAMPUS [ ] (Sponsor's SSN) CHAMPVA [ ] (VA File #) GROUP HEALTH PLAN [ ] (SSN or ID) FECA BLK LUNG [ ] (SSN) OTHER [ ] (ID)

1a. INSURED'S I.D. NUMBER (FOR PROGRAM IN ITEM 1): 902-55-3391B

2. PATIENT'S NAME (Last Name, First Name, Middle Initial): RICHARDS, WARREN

3. PATIENT'S BIRTH DATE MM DD YY: 04 09 -- SEX M [X] F [ ]

4. INSURED'S NAME (Last Name, First Name, Middle Initial): SAME

5. PATIENT'S ADDRESS (No., Street): 7952 S SPRINGFIELD AVENUE

6. PATIENT RELATIONSHIP TO INSURED: Self [X] Spouse [ ] Child [ ] Other [ ]

7. INSURED'S ADDRESS (No., Street): SAME

CITY: CHICAGO STATE: IL

8. PATIENT STATUS: Single [ ] Married [ ] Other [ ]; Employed [ ] Full-Time Student [ ] Part-Time Student [ ]

CITY STATE

ZIP CODE: 60623-2579 TELEPHONE (Include Area Code): (312) 555-3391

ZIP CODE TELEPHONE (INCLUDE AREA CODE) ( )

9. OTHER INSURED'S NAME (Last Name, First Name, Middle Initial): SAME

10. IS PATIENT'S CONDITION RELATED TO:

11. INSURED'S POLICY GROUP OR FECA NUMBER: NA

a. OTHER INSURED'S POLICY OR GROUP NUMBER: 902-55-3391

a. EMPLOYMENT? (CURRENT OR PREVIOUS) [ ] YES [X] NO

a. INSURED'S DATE OF BIRTH MM DD YY: SAME SEX M [ ] F [ ]

b. OTHER INSURED'S DATE OF BIRTH MM DD YY: SAME SEX M [ ] F [ ]

b. AUTO ACCIDENT? [ ] YES [X] NO PLACE (State)

b. EMPLOYER'S NAME OR SCHOOL NAME: RETIRED

c. EMPLOYER'S NAME OR SCHOOL NAME: RETIRED

c. OTHER ACCIDENT? [ ] YES [X] NO

c. INSURANCE PLAN NAME OR PROGRAM NAME

d. INSURANCE PLAN NAME OR PROGRAM NAME: BLUE CROSS/BLUE SHIELD

10d. RESERVED FOR LOCAL USE

d. IS THERE ANOTHER HEALTH BENEFIT PLAN? [X] YES [ ] NO *If yes*, return to and complete item 9 a-d.

READ BACK OF FORM BEFORE COMPLETING & SIGNING THIS FORM.

12. PATIENT'S OR AUTHORIZED PERSON'S SIGNATURE I authorize the release of any medical or other information necessary to process this claim. I also request payment of government benefits either to myself or to the party who accepts assignment below.

SIGNED ______ DATE ______

13. INSURED'S OR AUTHORIZED PERSON'S SIGNATURE I authorize payment of medical benefits to the undersigned physician or supplier for services described below.

SIGNED ______

PATIENT AND INSURED INFORMATION

14. DATE OF CURRENT: ILLNESS (First symptom) OR INJURY (Accident) OR PREGNANCY (LMP) MM DD YY: 03 07 --

15. IF PATIENT HAS HAD SAME OR SIMILAR ILLNESS, GIVE FIRST DATE MM DD YY: 03 07 --

16. DATES PATIENT UNABLE TO WORK IN CURRENT OCCUPATION FROM MM DD YY TO MM DD YY: NA

17. NAME OF REFERRING PHYSICIAN OR OTHER SOURCE: NA

17a. I.D. NUMBER OF REFERRING PHYSICIAN

18. HOSPITALIZATION DATES RELATED TO CURRENT SERVICES FROM MM DD YY TO MM DD YY: NA

19. RESERVED FOR LOCAL USE

20. OUTSIDE LAB? [ ] YES [X] NO $ CHARGES

21. DIAGNOSIS OR NATURE OF ILLNESS OR INJURY. (RELATE ITEMS 1,2,3, OR 4 TO ITEM 24E BY LINE)

1. 726 . 10
2. ___ . ___
3. ___ . ___
4. ___ . ___

22. MEDICAID RESUBMISSION CODE: NA ORIGINAL REF. NO.

23. PRIOR AUTHORIZATION NUMBER: NA

24.	A DATE(S) OF SERVICE From MM DD YY	To MM DD YY	B Place of Service	C Type of Service	D PROCEDURES, SERVICES, OR SUPPLIES (Explain Unusual Circumstances) CPT/HCPCS MODIFIER	E DIAGNOSIS CODE	F $ CHARGES	G DAYS OR UNITS	H EPSDT Family Plan	I EMG	J COB	K RESERVED FOR LOCAL USE
1	03 07 --		11	1	99212	1	44 00	1				
2												
3												
4												
5												
6												

25. FEDERAL TAX I.D. NUMBER: 78-31443782 SSN [ ] EIN [X]

26. PATIENT'S ACCOUNT NO.: NA

27. ACCEPT ASSIGNMENT? (For govt. claims, see back) [X] YES [ ] NO

28. TOTAL CHARGE: $ 44 00

29. AMOUNT PAID: $ -- --

30. BALANCE DUE: $ 44 00

31. SIGNATURE OF PHYSICIAN OR SUPPLIER INCLUDING DEGREES OR CREDENTIALS (I certify that the statements on the reverse apply to this bill and are made a part thereof.)

Karen Larsen, MD 4/11/- -

SIGNED DATE

32. NAME AND ADDRESS OF FACILITY WHERE SERVICES WERE RENDERED (if other than home or office): NA

33. PHYSICIAN'S OR SUPPLIER'S NAME, ADDRESS, ZIP CODE & TELEPHONE NO.: KAREN LARSEN, MD (312-555-6022) 2235 SOUTH RIDGEWAY AVENUE CHICAGO IL 60623-2240

PIN# 12LARSE=567 GRP# NA

PHYSICIAN OR SUPPLIER INFORMATION

(APPROVED BY AMA COUNCIL ON MEDICAL SERVICE 8/88)

PLEASE PRINT OR TYPE

FORM HCFA-1500 (12-90) FORM OWCP-1500 FORM RRB-1500

FIGURE 9.5

Completed CMS-1500 Form

FIGURE 9.6 CMS-1500 Guidelines Chart

CMS-1500 FORM GUIDELINES

ITEM NO.	DESCRIPTION	RESOURCE
1, 1a	Type of insurance and insured's ID number	ID card
2, 3, 5, 6	Patient's name, DOB, address, telephone number, and relationship to insured	Chart, patient's registration form
4, 7	Insured's name and address (Same)	Chart
8	Patient's status	Chart
9, 9a–d	Other insured's name and information—policies that supplement the primary carrier	Chart
10a–c	Patient's condition related to	Chart
11, 11a–d	Primary carrier information	Chart
12	Release of information may have signature on *Authorization for Release of Medical Information Statement*—"patient's signature on file"	Patient's and/or insured's signature
13	Authorization of payment of benefits to provider ("patient's signature on file" if have signed authorization on file)	Patient's and/or insured's signature
14	Date of current illness (first-symptom date), injury (accident date), or pregnancy (LMP)	Chart
15	First date of same or similar illness	Chart
16	Dates patient unable to work	Chart
17, 17a	Referring physician and ID number (PIN–provider individual number)	Chart, insurance manual
18	Hospitalization dates	Chart
19	Reserved for local carriers' specified information	Insurance manual
20	Usage of outside lab	Ledger/chart
21	*ICD-9-CM* diagnostic codes	Chart and code books
22	Only used on Medicaid claims	Medicaid procedures
23	Prior authorization number	Contact carrier
24A–G	Services rendered—one procedure per line, maximum of six lines on one claim	Chart, patient encounter form, ledger, coding books
24A	Dates of procedures	
24B	Place of service code: 11 Office 12 Patient's home 21 Inpatient hospital 22 Outpatient hospital 23 Hospital emergency room 24 Ambulatory surgical center 25 Birthing center 26 Military treatment center 31 Skilled nursing facility 32 Nursing facility 33 Custodial care facility 34 Hospice 42 Air or water ambulance 51 Inpatient psychiatric facility 52 Federally qualified health center 53 Community mental-health center 54 Intermediate care facility/mentally retarded 55 Residential substance abuse treatment 56 Psychiatric residential treatment center 61 Comprehensive inpatient rehabilitation 62 Comprehensive outpatient rehabilitation 65 End-stage renal disease treatment	
24C	Type of service codes: 1 Medical care 2 Surgery 3 Consultation 4 Diagnostic x-ray 5 Diagnostic laboratory 6 Radiation therapy 7 Anesthesia 8 Surgical assistance 9 Other medical services A Durable medical equipment B Drugs C Ambulatory surgery D Hospice E Second opinion on elective surgery F Maternity G Dental H Mental heath care I Ambulance J Program for people with disabilities L Renal supplies/home M Alternate payment for maintenance N Kidney donor V Pneumococcal vaccine Z Third opinion on elective surgery	
24D	*CPT* and/or HCPCS codes	
24E	Diagnosis code—relate the procedure codes to the appropriate diagnosis (i.e., 1, 2, 3)	
24F	Charges for each service	
24G	Number of times the procedure was given	
24H	Medicaid EPSDT Family Plan	
24I	Check if hospital medical emergency existed	
24J	Leave blank	
24K	Reserved for local use	
25	Employer's federal tax ID number (EIN)	Doctor's information
26	Patient's account number—if patient known as a number	Chart/ledger
27	Accept assignment	Doctor's information
28, 29, 30	Total, amount paid, balance due	Ledger
31	Signature of physician and date	
32	Name and address of outside facility used other than home or office	Chart/ledger
33	Provider's billing name, complete address, and telephone number—include PIN and GRP numbers (group number assigned by carrier)	

Using Computer Billing Programs. Generating claim forms (whether paper or electronic) on the computer is one of the major uses of computer technology in the medical office today. The computer automatically processes the information required to create a completed claim by transferring the patient's and the insured's information, the charges, the procedural and diagnostic codes, and so forth from the various databases set up in the computer onto the insurance claim form.

The computer stores facts about the medical practice in the practice database; information about the carriers that most patients use in the insurance carrier database; information about payments made by patients, as well as benefits received from insurance companies, in the transaction database; and information about each patient—personal as well as clinical data—in the patient database.

When all new data and transaction information has been entered and checked regarding a patient's visit to the physician, the administrative medical assistant issues the command to the software program to create the claim. The format for the claim—either the CMS-1500 or a specialized claim form—is also designated. The software program then organizes the necessary databases and selects the data from each one as needed to produce a completed claim form. A command can then be given to print the claim or transmit it electronically.

Electronic Claims Versus Paper Claims. The main difference between electronic claims and paper claims is the means by which they are transmitted to the insurance carrier. The use of electronic claims not only speeds up transmission and payments, it also ensures a greater degree of accuracy and is less expensive.

Paper claims, whether printed from a computer billing program or typed, are usually transmitted to insurance carriers through the mail. When they reach the insurance carrier, the information on the form must be keyed into the insurance company's computer by data-entry personnel. Alternatively, the information may be scanned using an optical scanning machine. In either case, a certain percentage of error is introduced. If a claim form is to be scanned, it is a good idea for the administrative medical assistant to use all-capital letters and avoid the use of symbols or punctuation in filling out the form. This will lead to fewer errors while scanning.

Electronic claims, on the other hand, are transmitted from one computer to another over a telephone or cable line using a modem. Because claim information is entered once, not twice, chances of error or omission are greatly reduced. It also costs less to file claims electronically; fewer personnel are involved, and neither paper forms, envelopes, nor postage is required.

An advantage to transmitting claims electronically is that the medical office receives immediate feedback whenever claims are transmitted. Medical offices generally transmit claims in batches, grouped by insurer.

Each office has is own schedule for sending claims. The usual practice is to transmit claims every day or every other day. When claims are transmitted electronically, the medical office receives a file acknowledgment—immediate feedback that tells the medical office the file has arrived at the insurance carrier's claims department. If the file is missing details (for example, if a required field is left blank) or if the claim form contains incorrect information, such as an invalid patient identification number, the computer will immediately notify the sender that the file has been rejected. The medical office that sent the claim can then fix the error and resubmit the claim.

Using Clearinghouses. A **clearinghouse** is a service bureau that collects electronic claims from many different medical practices and forwards the claims to the appropriate insurance carriers. Some insurance carriers who receive insurance claims electronically require information to be formatted in a particular way. Part of the service a clearinghouse provides is to translate claim data to fit the setup of each carrier's claims processing department. Because of this factor, many medical practices choose to use a clearinghouse instead of transmitting claims directly to insurance carriers themselves. With or without the use of a clearinghouse, electronic claims reach the insurance carrier almost immediately compared with paper claims.

■ Following Up on Claims

When the EOB or ERA from the third-party payer arrives, the assistant checks that:

- All the procedures listed on the claim also appear on the EOB/ERA.
- Any unpaid charges are explained.
- The codes on the EOB/ERA match those on the claim.
- The payment listed for each procedure is correct.

The assistant must routinely follow up on all submitted claims. Many medical offices use the Internet to contact carriers to check claim status. The time line for the follow-up varies according to the insurance carrier and insurance program. Most medical offices follow up on claim status 7 to 14 days after the claims are submitted. Experience with insurance will enable you to know when follow-up on a claim is necessary.

Some physicians automatically rebill in 30 days if they have not heard from an insurance company. Most medical offices, however, send a tracer as the first contact about overdue claims. A tracer, whether sent in print or by e-mail, contains the basic billing information and asks the carrier about its status.

In addition to regular claim follow-up, the administrative medical assistant will need to follow up claims that have been denied for unclear reasons, or are late because of special situations. Examples include the following:

- An unclear denial of payment or an incorrect payment is received on an EOB or ERA; follow-up should be done to determine the cause of the problem and to rectify it.
- The carrier asks for more information to process the claim, namely, a report on a new procedure for which there is no *CPT* code; the assistant should follow up with a report from the physician describing the procedure and the situation in which it was used.
- The carrier notifies the medical office that a claim is being investigated with regard to preexisting conditions; after a period of 30 days from receiving such a notice, if nothing further has been received, follow-up should be done.

In some situations, the administrative medical assistant will need to resubmit a claim. Examples include the following:

- A mistake has been made in billing: the physician forgot to check off a procedure on the patient encounter form.
- A claim was overlooked by the physician's office: a patient had a series of visits for allergy injections, and one of the visits was not included.

Similarly, there are situations in which the insurance carrier rejects a claim and asks for resubmission. For example:

- The wrong diagnosis codes or procedure codes are submitted.
- Information is incomplete or missing (for example, no accident date is given).
- The charges, units, and costs do not total properly.

In short, the administrative medical assistant should study the ERA/EOB carefully to understand any uncovered benefits, deductibles, copayment responsibilities, and other reasons for any noncoverage in the claim. If any of the explanations on a claim seem unfair or unclear, the insurance carrier should be contacted for help. Most insurance carriers have staff members whose primary job is to answer questions about claims. If necessary, an appeal should be initiated by the medical office. It is the responsibility of the assistant to take the time and care necessary to process and complete insurance claims accurately, and to follow up in whatever way is required, so that prompt and precise compensation is received.

GO TO PROJECT 9.2 ON PAGE 247

9.3 PAYMENTS FROM PATIENTS

Just as it is important for the medical office's cash flow to have claims approved and paid promptly by insurance carriers, it is also important to help ensure prompt payments from patients. The administrative medical assistant can facilitate the prompt receipt of payments from patients by keeping all transactions in each patient's account current and by being alert to the status of each account.

The method of payment is arranged at the time of the patient's first visit. In most offices, a combination of methods is used and may include the following:

- Patients pay at the time of the visit by cash or check (some offices may accept credit cards). This type of collection is referred to as **collection at the time of service.** Copayments, as required by HMOs and other managed care plans, are always collected at the time of service.
- Bills are mailed to patients monthly or at the end of a procedure or hospital stay.
- Patients pay a fixed amount weekly or monthly until the bill is paid in full.
- Bills are sent to health insurance carriers.
- Some physicians work on a cash-only basis.
- A patient with a poor credit rating may be on a cash-only basis.

■ Cash Payments

The assistant must be careful to enter each cash payment in the patient's ledger and in the daily summary record. The patient's name, the services rendered, the charges, the payment received on the account, and any balances should be included.

Payments should be given to the administrative medical assistant, not the physician. A receipt must be given to the patient who pays cash. An example of a receipt is shown in Figure 9.7 on page 238. Copies of receipts are kept as permanent records. The patient should be advised to keep the receipt and a copy of the patient encounter form for income tax purposes in claiming medical deductions. If the patient pays by check, the canceled check is the receipt.

Certain rules must be observed to safeguard money received. Cash, checks, and money orders should be kept in a secure location such as a locked drawer. Currency should be separated by denominations. Checks should be immediately stamped on the back with a restrictive endorsement, which specifies "Pay to the order of . . ." or "For deposit only." To minimize the danger of theft, money should be deposited in the bank daily.

FIGURE 9.7

Completed Receipt

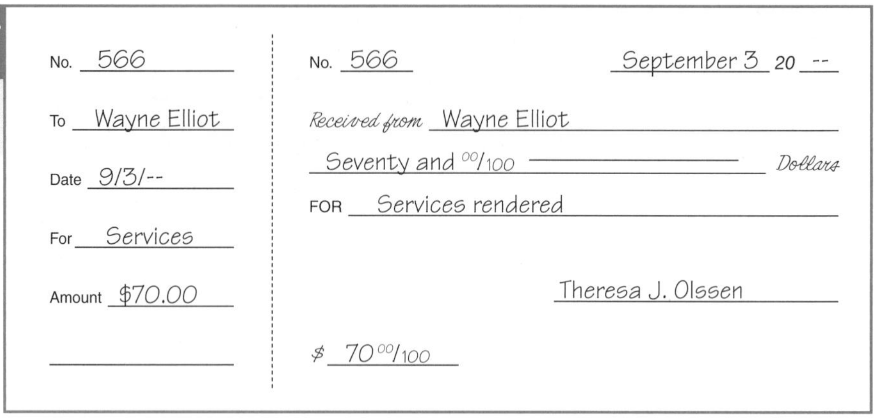

No. __566__

To __Wayne Elliot__

Date __9/3/--__

For __Services__

Amount __$70.00__

No. __566__   __September 3__ 20 __--__

Received from __Wayne Elliot__ _____

___Seventy and__ ^{00}/$_{100}$ _____ *Dollars*

FOR ___Services rendered__ _____

Theresa J. Olssen

$ __70__ ^{00}/$_{100}$ _____

Sending Statements

Although most bills are sent out once a month, a statement may be sent at the end of a procedure or upon discharge from the hospital. Practices decide to do either monthly billing or cycle billing. With **monthly billing,** bills are sent out once a month and are timed to reach the patient no later than the last day of the month, but preferably by the 25th of each month. Such a billing schedule enables patients to pay physicians' bills along with other monthly bills.

Traditionally, medical offices have used monthly billing. However, another system of billing, called **cycle billing,** is becoming more popular with medical offices. Cycle billing is designed to avoid once-a-month peak workloads and to stabilize the cash flow. It has been used by department stores, oil companies, and other large businesses for some time. With cycle billing, all accounts are divided into fairly equal groups, the number of groups depending on how many times you wish to do billing during a month. If you decide to do billing four times a month (once a week), for example, you would divide the accounts into four groups, usually alphabetically, with each group billed on a different date. If cycle billing is used, the patient should be informed on the first visit approximately when the bill will be mailed.

The advantage of using cycle billing is that the workload is apportioned throughout the entire month. Billing is a major task for the administrative medical assistant. If bills are prepared once a month, entire days are usually sacrificed from other routine duties during that period in order to get statements in the mail. Cycle billing allows the assistant to factor in billing as part of a daily or weekly routine. An additional benefit is that the possibility of error is reduced, because more time and consideration can be given to each account.

■ Payment Plans

For the patient who is unable to pay a medical bill in one lump sum, a schedule of payments, or contract, can be agreed upon by the patient and the assistant. The agreement should be in writing, and a copy of the plan should be given to the patient as a reminder of the commitment to pay the physician. The amount to be paid weekly or monthly is stated in the agreement, and the agreement is used as a reference when corresponding with the patient about unpaid bills.

■ Fee Adjustment

Should the need arise, the physician can adjust the cost of any procedure; the physician will then inform the administrative medical assistant of the **fee adjustment.** Fees should not be reduced as a way to receive payment quickly and avoid collection procedures.

One type of fee adjustment a medical office makes regularly with certain health plans is called a **write-off.** As explained in Chapter 8, according to the rules of many insurance plans—for example, with most HMOs—when the physician's fee for a given service is higher than the insurance company's allowed fee for that service, a participating provider is not permitted to bill the patient for the unclaimed portion of the fee. Instead, the physician must write off this amount by subtracting it from the patient's bill, and accept the payment from the insurance company as payment in full for the procedure. Write-offs are entered into the patient ledger as fee adjustments.

If a physician chooses to reduce or cancel a fee, the decision must be in writing for the protection of the physician since it is possible for such a reduction or canceling of a fee to be misinterpreted and even lead to a malpractice suit. For the same reasons, in computerized billing programs, it is important not to delete any transactions. Rather, corrections, changes, and write-offs are made with adjustments to the existing transactions. Most billing programs contain a column in the patient ledger that displays such entries. The adjusting entries give both the medical office and the patient a history of events in case there is a billing inquiry or an audit.

In cases that involve a considerable sum, the patient may not be able to pay the fee and may have to seek financial assistance. The assistant should be acquainted with the local agencies to which a patient can be referred when financial assistance is needed.

■ Health Insurance

Many patients carry health insurance that provides payment for a portion of their medical expenses. Depending on whether or not the physician accepts the health insurance the patient has, the payment arrangement varies. Essentially, there are two options: patients are billed at the time of service or after the insurance claim has been processed.

After an office visit, the new charges are entered into the patient's account. If the physician has not accepted assignment and is not going to file a claim for a patient, patients are usually required to pay at the end of the visit. The administrative assistant gives the patient a receipt for the payment. In some cases, patients in this situation arrange to be billed later for payments due, depending on the office's policy.

In contrast, when the physician accepts assignment and is going to file a claim, the patient usually pays only the required copayment at the time of service. The amount of the copayment is entered and subtracted from the balance due. Then the insurance claim for the service is created and transmitted to the insurance carrier. When insurance payment is received, it is entered in the patient's account. Ideally, the total paid by the patient and all carriers should equal the charges for the service provided.

If there are procedures for which the insurance company did not pay or paid less for than expected, the administrative medical assistant must sort out the various charges and benefits. The assistant determines which charges the patient should be billed for, if any are to be written off by the medical office, and which, if any, should be resubmitted, or even appealed, by studying the EOB or ERA. The patient's account is then updated accordingly, and a patient statement is sent on the appropriate billing date.

■ Third-Party Liability

Sometimes a person other than the patient assumes liability, or responsibility, for the charges. Such responsibility is called **third-party liability.** The assistant must contact this third party for verification of financial obligation. Relatives, particularly children of aged parents, may say they will be responsible for payment of the bill, but this promise must be in writing. Oral promises are not legally binding. A third party is not obligated by law unless he or she has signed an agreement to pay the charges. Therefore, a signed promise obtained prior to treatment will greatly reduce the credit risk.

By contrast, a **guarantor** is an individual who is a policyholder for a patient of a medical practice. For example, a parent who is a policyholder may be the guarantor for his or her **dependent** children—usually children under the age of 18 (or children under 21 who are full-time students).

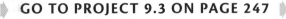

▶ **GO TO PROJECT 9.3 ON PAGE 247** ▶

9.4 DELINQUENT ACCOUNTS

A medical practice, like any business, has outstanding accounts. It is regrettable that patients are often slow and even delinquent in paying physicians. There are various reasons a patient might not pay a bill. For example, the patient may unintentionally or intentionally ignore the bill, the patient may not have the money to pay the bill, or the patient may be unwilling to pay the bill for a reason such as disagreeing with the amount of the bill. Other reasons for nonpayment of medical bills include a patient's excessive debt, unemployment, illness, disability, family problems, or marital problems. The administrative medical assistant must know how to handle patients' accounts properly to reduce the physician's losses from unpaid bills.

■ Communicating With Patients

In a sense, the collection process actually begins with effective communications with patients about their responsibility to pay for services. When patients understand the charges and agree to pay them in advance, collecting the payments is not usually a problem. Most patients pay their bills on time. However, every practice has some patients who do not pay their bills when they receive their monthly statements.

One way to minimize problems with payments is to notify patients in advance of the probable cost of procedures that are not going to be covered by their plan. For example, many private plans, as well as Medicare, do not pay for most routine services, such as annual physical examinations. Many patients, however, consider preventive services a good idea and are willing to pay for them. For these noncovered services, patients should be asked to agree to pay in writing. A letter of agreement signed by the patient should also specify why the service will not be covered and the cost of the procedure. For Medicare patients, this letter is called an Advance Notice for Noncovered Services, a form that providers should have patients sign. It explains the service, the reason it will not be covered by Medicare, and the estimated charge.

A patient should also be informed about fees before a complicated set of procedures begins. Or a physician—in particular, a nonPAR physician—may need to make clear payment arrangements with a patient before services are performed.

■ Guidelines for Payment

Management or the accounting department in every office must determine the collection ratio (total collections divided by net charges of the practice). The percentage will show the effectiveness of the collections (the higher the percentage, the more effective the collections). Management would then set the guidelines for payments—how much is to be collected daily, how much should be collected on each account, and so forth. As a general rule, at least one-third of the outstanding accounts should be collected each day.

■ The Office Collection Policy

It is often the duty of the administrative medical assistant to collect payments on overdue accounts. Each month delinquent accounts (any unpaid accounts with a balance that is 30 days past due) should be "aged" to show their status in the collection process (that is, 30, 60, or 90 days past due). If a computerized billing program is used, a patient aging report is generated to show which patients' payments are due or overdue. For this reason, payments must always be entered promptly so that at billing time there is no question about any balance due.

■ Laws Governing Collections

Collections from payers are considered business collections. Collections from patients, however, are consumer collections and are regulated by federal and state law. The Fair Debt Collection Practices Act of 1977 and the Telephone Consumer Protection Act of 1991 regulate debt collections, forbidding unfair practices, such as making threats, and using any form of deception or violence to collect a debt.

■ Course of Action

Every office needs to establish a course of action to be taken on overdue accounts. The physician will need to establish the office policy regarding collection procedures, including when to send statements, reminders, and letters and when to take final action.

Usually, an automatic reminder notice and a second statement are mailed when a bill has not been paid 30 days after it was issued. Some medical offices phone a patient with a 30-day overdue account. If the bill is not then paid, a series of collection letters is generated at intervals, each more stringent in its tone and more direct in its approach. Some medical offices use an outside collection agency to pursue large unpaid bills.

Federal laws regulate credit and collections for businesses. Also, individual states may have laws that guide the collection process. The material in this chapter discusses only basic collection procedures.

Collection by Telephone. A common method of collection is to telephone the patient personally. A telephone call can be effective in reminding a person who has unintentionally forgotten to pay. Tact and experience are necessary in order to be effective in telephone collections.

Techniques of telephone collection include the following:

- Identify yourself.
- Be sure you are talking to the person who is responsible for payment of the account.
- Make the collection call in the evening, especially if the person who is responsible for payment of the accounts is out during the day, but no later than 9 p.m.
- Never call a patient at a place of employment to inquire about an unpaid bill.
- Always use a pleasant manner to reflect your confidence that the problem can be resolved.
- Ask to discuss the bill to determine whether the patient has any questions. This query should elicit some response, which is your cue to continue the rest of the conversation.
- Listen carefully.
- Do not show irritation in your voice or appear to be scolding the patient.
- Inform the person that you need to know why the bill has not been paid or why inquiries about the unpaid bill have not been answered.
- If the patient promises to pay, ask when you can expect a payment and for what amount. Then make a note about the conversation, saying, for example, "I am making a note in your account file that you promised to pay $100 on September 10. Is that correct?"

When collecting by telephone, always keep complete, accurate records of who said what, who promised to pay, how much was promised, and when the payment was promised. Note any unusual circumstances. Ask the person responsible for the bill to write down the arrangement.

Collection by Letter. The longer a bill remains unpaid, the less likelihood there is of collecting it. A bill should be followed up most vigorously after being overdue for three months. An effective method of collection at this point is to write a letter to the patient. Writing collection letters that bring results is a skill. Collection letters should be personal letters, not form letters. The letter should show that you are sincerely interested in the patient's problem and want to work out a solution. Collection letters should be brief, with short sentences. The letters should appeal to the patient's sense of pride and fair play, and to the desire for a good credit rating. The amount that is due should be stated clearly in each collection letter, and the patient should be asked to telephone the assistant to discuss the situation. Figure 9.8 on page 244 shows an example of an effective collection letter.

FIGURE 9.8

Collection Letter

KAREN LARSEN, MD
2235 South Ridgeway Avenue   312-555-6022
Chicago, IL 60623-2240   Fax: 312-555-0025

July 1, 20--

Ms. Clair Munson
3492 Green Avenue South
Chicago, IL 60624-3422

Dear Ms. Munson:

In reviewing our accounts, I find that you have an
overdue balance of $162.

As you are aware, all bills are due within 30 days
of service. Is there some reason we have not heard
from you?

Please send us your check for $162 this week to clear
your account or contact our office immediately.

Sincerely,

Theresa J. Olssen

Theresa J. Olssen
Medical Administrative Assistant

Terminated Accounts. A physician who finds it impossible to extract payment from a patient may decide to terminate the physician-patient relationship. The account is then referred to as a **terminated account.**

If a patient comes to the office requesting medical care after an account has been terminated, the physician should be consulted and may decide to see the patient on a cash-only basis.

Collection by Agency. If the patient has not paid the bill after a reasonable time and routine collection procedures have failed, the physician has two ways of attempting collection. The physician can sue the patient and go to court, which is a time-consuming and costly procedure. The other method is to turn the account over to a **collection agency.** Once an account has been turned over for collection, the office will have no further contact with the patient concerning billing.

The use of a collection agency is not a very desirable option for collecting unpaid bills, as most agencies work on a contingency basis.

Approximately 40 to 50 percent of the amount due is lost when the account is turned over to an agency, and the longer the bill goes unpaid, the less money the physician will receive when the account is finally settled.

There are various types of collection agencies, and a physician will want to investigate an agency thoroughly to determine its reputation.

■ Statute of Limitations

If the physician fails to collect a fee within a certain period of time, the collection becomes illegal under the statute of limitations and no further claim on the debt is possible. Each state sets its own time limitation, which varies from 3 to 8 years. The physician should obtain legal counsel for advice concerning these statutes.

■ Credit Arrangements and the Truth in Lending Act

For large bills or special situations, some practices may elect to extend credit to patients. When credit agreements are made, patients and the practice agree to divide the bill over a period of months. Patients agree to make monthly payments. If no finance charges are applied to unpaid balances, this type of arrangement is between the practice and the patient, and no legal regulations apply.

If, however, the practice adds finance charges and the number of payments is more than four installments, the arrangement is governed by the federal Truth in Lending Act, which became law on July 1, 1960, and is part of the Consumer Credit Card Protection Act. Regulation Z requires that a disclosure form be complete and signed. The disclosure form notifies the patient in writing about the total amount, the finance charges (stated as a percentage), when each payment is due and the amounts, and the date the last payment is due. The disclosure form must be signed by both the practice manager and the patient.

■ Writing Off Uncollectible Accounts

If no payment has been made after the collection process, the administrative medical assistant follows the office policy on bills it does not expect to collect. Usually, if all collection attempts have been exhausted and it would cost more to continue than the amount to be collected, the process is ended. In this case, the amount is called an uncollectible account or bad debt and is written off from the expected revenues. Future services for patients who are responsible for uncollectible accounts are usually on a cash-only basis.

GO TO PROJECT 9.4 ON PAGE 247

Chapter Projects

Dr. Larsen asks you to update the billing. Access the patients' ledgers in the Transaction Entry window in NDCmedisoft™, and enter the charge transactions shown below for October 14 and 15. For the two new patients, David Kramer and Erin Mitchell, you will need to enter the diagnostic code listed below in the Diagnosis tab of the Case dialog box before you enter their charge transactions. The diagnostic codes for the remaining patients have already been entered.

If a patient has more than one case—in this instance, Robertson, Lund, Baab, and Matthews—be sure to apply the transaction(s) to the correct case. (*Hint:* In the Transaction Entry window, click the triangle button inside the Case box to display a list of cases for the selected patient.) After entering the charge transactions, print patient statements for patients who have transactions on October 14 and 15.

Dr. Larsen asks you to update the billing. The established patients' statements are stored as files on the CD-ROM, labeled according to the patients' last names. Save the statements onto your own disk. These are the billing statements that you will work from. Use Dr. Larsen's fee schedule (WP 50) and the following information to update the patients' statements. After updating the statements, print all of them for your file.

October 14, 20--:

David Kramer	NP preventive checkup, age 5; UA(81001); HGB	Diagnostic code: V70.3
Erin Mitchell	99201; UA(81001); UC	Diagnostic code: 599.0
Gary Robertson	99212; UA(81001); UC	Diagnostic code: 595.0
Laura Lund	99213; Pap smear	Diagnostic code: 625.3
Jeffrey Kramer	99212	Diagnostic code: 382.9
Joseph Castro	99212	Diagnostic code: 930.8

October 15, 20--:

Todd Grant	99212; ECG	Diagnostic code: 733.6
Thomas Baab	EP preventive, age 54; UA(81001); CBC; SMA-8; PSA; fasting lipid panel	Diagnostic code: V70.0
Ardis Matthews	99212	Diagnostic code: 008.8
Marc Phan	99212	Diagnostic code 466.0

Chapter Projects

PROJECT 9.2   Internet Research: Comparing Appeal Processes

Every third-party payer has its own appeal process. Using your favorite search engine, visit the Web site of your health plan, a friend's plan, or a major plan you know about, and research the plan's appeal process. Then go to the Medicare Web site at www.medicare.gov and read about how to appeal a Medicare claim. How does the process compare? Which one is more complicated? Why do you think this is the case?

PROJECT 9.3   Posting Payments

The following patients stop in the office on October 15 with checks to update their accounts.

- ▶ Florence Sherman   Pays $35.20
- ▶ Theresa Dayton   Pays $33.60
- ▶ Thomas Baab   Pays $82.20

Enter and apply the patients' payments in NDCmedisoft™ using the Transaction Entry feature. If a patient has more than one open case, be sure to enter and apply the payment to the correct case. Print a walkout receipt for each patient who has made a payment.

Post the payments to their statements. Reprint these statements.

PROJECT 9.4   Preparing an Effective Collection Letter

After updating the statements, you notice that Suzanne Roberts has not made a payment for three months. There are collection notations on her statement: September 30, reminder sent; and October 10, a follow-up telephone call. Compose a letter for your signature to Ms. Roberts requesting payment. Date the letter October 20. File a copy of the letter in Suzanne Roberts' record.

CHAPTER SUMMARY

1. The administrative medical assistant handles patient transactions, including entering charges for medical services rendered and payments received from patients and third-party payers, in the patient ledger. The assistant enters the transactions in the appropriate patients' account by referring to the information on the patient encounter form for the visit and the physician's fee schedule. The patient's account is then updated, and a patient statement, or bill, is created.

2. To receive payment from third-party payers, most medical practices must complete insurance claim forms—either paper or electronic—on behalf of their patients. The most commonly used paper insurance claim form is the CMS-1500 claim form. After verifying the patient's insurance information, the administrative medical assistant fills in the form and transmits it to the insurance carrier for review. The claim is then processed by the insurance company, which decides to pay the fee, deny the claim, or pay a certain portion of it. Finally, any payments received from the insurance company are posted to the patient's account in the patient ledger, and the patient is billed for any outstanding amount. Once the patient pays the remaining balance, the claim process is complete.

3. Electronic claims result in fewer errors and faster payments than paper claims forms.

4. As with third-party payers, the administrative medical assistant is responsible for receiving prompt payments from patients. The method of payment is arranged during the patient's first visit and may include a combination of the following: *(a)* patients pay at the time of the visit by cash, check, or credit card (copayments are always collected at this time); *(b)* bills are mailed to patients monthly or at the end of a procedure or hospital stay, using either monthly or cycle billing; *(c)* if necessary, patients may pay according to an agreed-upon payment plan; *(d)* bills are sent to health insurance carriers, and after payment is received, depending on the terms of the plan, the patient is billed for any balance due; *(e)* some physicians may work on a cash-only basis. Should the need arise, the physician can adjust the cost of any procedure. However, the decision must be in writing to protect against a malpractice suit if the adjustment is ever misinterpreted. For the same reasons, transactions in computerized billing programs should never be deleted. Rather, corrections are made with adjustments to the existing transactions.

5. Each office determines its own guidelines for payment—how much is to be collected daily, how much should be collected on each account, and so forth. Communicating with patients from the start about what is expected from them in terms of payment is the beginning of the collection process, including notifying them in advance of the probable cost of procedures not covered by their plan. Each office also determines how to handle overdue accounts. Usually, if it would cost more to continue collection attempts than the amount to be collected, the process is ended and the amount is written off as a bad debt. After a certain period of time—from 3 to 8 years, depending on state laws—the collection becomes illegal under the statute of limitations.

KEY TERMS

The following terms key terms appear in **boldface** type in this chapter. Administrative medical assistants must know the meaning and the correct use of each of these terms. Can you recall what each term means? Refer to this chapter or to the glossary for any terms you need to review.

clearinghouse	fee adjustment
CMS-1500 claim form	fee schedule
collection agency	guarantor
collection at the time of service	monthly billing
cycle billing	patient information form
dependent	patient statement
electronic claims	terminated account
EOB	third-party liability
ERA	write-off

THINKING IT THROUGH

These questions cover the most important points in this chapter. Using your critical thinking skills, play the role of an administrative medical assistant as you answer each question. Be prepared to present your responses in class.

1. Wayne Elliot asks you why he was charged for two office visits when his daughters, Emily and Rose, were seen at the same time in the same room for the same problem—an earache. Explain the reasoning behind the charges.

THINKING IT THROUGH (continued)

2. You receive an EOB for a patient who is covered by an HMO. The HMO did not pay for services received on May 5, which is when the patient visited Dr. Larsen for her annual Pap smear. You check your records and find that the same insurance carrier paid for previous Pap smears with the same patient in past years. What should you do?

3. You receive an ERA from Blue Cross/Blue Shield for a Medicare patient. The amount received for the claim is $60, which is $20 less than the usual fee of $80. Since the doctor you work for accepts assignment for Medicare patients, the medical practice will need to write off this amount. You decide to delete the initial fee of $80 in the computerized patient ledger and key in $60 so that the account balances. Why is this a mistake?

4. You notice that an elder patient is scheduled for a minor surgical procedure that will remove dark patches of skin that are unsightly, a procedure that is considered cosmetic by most insurance companies. Why is it a good idea to point this out to the patient before undergoing the procedure?

SIMULATION 2

Today you will begin a second simulation in Dr. Larsen's office. The simulation dates are Monday, October 20; Tuesday, October 21; and Wednesday, October 22.

PROCEDURES

Review the section "Before You Start" in Simulation 1. Note that these procedures also apply to this simulation. Also review the "Procedures," because they apply to this simulation. Pull the patients' charts following the appointment calendar, and put them in the appropriate day folder.

MATERIALS

You will need the following materials to complete Simulation 2. If these materials are not already in the proper folder, obtain them from the sources indicated.

Materials	Source
Appointment calendar	
Diagnostic codes	WP 48
Fee schedule	WP 50
Supplies folder	

To-Do Items

Day 1 folder:

Place patients' charts for October 20.

Telephone log	WP 51
To-do list	WP 52
Letter from Dr. Tai	WP 53
Receipts	WP 54
Patient encounter forms	WP 55–59

Day 2 folder:

Place patients' charts for October 21.

Patient encounter forms	WP 60–62

Day 3 folder:

Place patients' charts for October 22.

Patient encounter forms	WP 63–68

Patients' folders:

The following items have been added to the patients' folders since Simulation 1.

Babb, Thomas	Project 7.3
Babcock, Sarah	Project 7.2
Castro, Joseph	Project 7.3
Grant, Todd	Project 7.3
Kramer, David	Project 7.3
Kramer, Jeffrey	Project 7.2, 7.3
Lund, Laura	Project 7.3
Matthews, Ardis	Project 7.3
Mitchell, Erin	Project 7.3, 7.4
Phan, Marc	Project 7.3
Roberts, Suzanne	Project 9.4
Robertson, Gary	Project 7.3, 7.4
Patient statements for all current patients	Project 9.1, 9.3

MEDICAL VOCABULARY

Before working through this simulation's assignments, review the following terms to be familiar with their spelling and meaning.

Ace wrap

bacitracin—anti-infective agent

chronicity—long duration of time

clindamycin—anti-infective agent

COPD—chronic obstructive pulmonary disease

DTP—diphtheria, tetanus, and pertussis vaccine

effusion—escape of fluid from blood vessels or lymphatics into tissues or a cavity

FSH—follicle-stimulating hormone

gravida—pregnant woman

HDL—high-density lipoprotein

hematuria—urine containing blood

hemoccult—test for hidden (occult) blood within stool

hidradenitis—inflammation of sweat glands

incontinence—inability to prevent discharge of excretions, such as urine or feces

IPV—inactivated polio vaccine

IVP—intravenous pyelogram

LDL—low-density liproprotein

lymphadenitis—inflammation of lymph node or nodes

mediocondylar—middle rounded prominence on a bone

MMR—measles-mumps-rubella vaccine

OTC—over-the-counter

proximal—nearest

purulent—containing pus

pustular—marked by pustules (small skin elevations containing pus)

pyelonephritis—inflammation of renal pelvis and kidney

Robaxin—skeletal muscle relaxant

suppurative—producing pus

tendonitis/tendinitis—inflammation of tendon

valgus—bent or twisted outward from midline or body

varus—bent or twisted inward toward the midline or body

Vicodin—analgesics

Z-pack—analgesics

NDCmedisoft™ INSTRUCTIONS

If your instructor has assigned the use of NDCmedisoft™, you will complete certain parts of Simulation 2 using the software program. Follow these instructions:

To complete this simulation in NDCmedisoft™, you must be able to:

- Schedule appointments
- Print physician's schedule
- Enter charges
- Enter payments
- Print walkout receipts
- Print patient statements

Enter the new appointments in Office Hours. Then print Dr. Larsen's schedule for October 20, 21, and 22.

Enter all charge and payment transactions. Print walkout receipts for patients who made a payment.

Print patient statements for all patients who had transactions on October 20, 21, and 22.

4 Practice Finances and Management

CHAPTER 10
Practice Finances

CHAPTER 11
Office Management

Part 4 discusses the important duties of the administrative medical assistant in handling billing and other accounting tasks. It also presents the tasks involved with office management, such as travel arrangements and meeting preparations.

CONSIDER THIS: Financial duties are very important to a successful practice, and computers are often used to help handle this job. *How can you improve your computer-related skills?*

CHAPTER 10

Practice Finances

OBJECTIVES

After studying this chapter, you will be able to:

1. Define five accounting terms related to the responsibilities of the administrative medical assistant.
2. Demonstrate an understanding of accounting principles by explaining the procedures for maintaining two of the essential financial records.
3. List three banking duties of the assistant.
4. List the duties of the assistant related to the payroll process.
5. Explain how an employee's net salary is determined.

INTRODUCTION

The physician's time and medical expertise are perhaps the most valuable assets in a medical practice. Because the practice is a business as well as a service, it is required to produce a profit. The administrative medical assistant protects and enhances the assets of the practice by handling many financial responsibilities on the business side.

KEY TERMS

Study these important words, which are defined in this chapter, to build your professional vocabulary:

absolute accuracy	bank reconciliation	direct earnings	interest	practice analysis
accounting	blank endorsement	EFT	monthly summary	report
accounts payable	bookkeeping	employer identifica-	patient ledger cards	procedure day
accounts receivable	cash basis	tion number (EIN)	payroll	sheet
accrual method	charge/receipt slips	e-signature	pegboard	restrictive
aging reports	check	FICA	accounting	endorsement
annual summary	daily journal	full endorsement	petty cash fund	
audit	deductions	FUTA	posting	
balance sheet	deposits	indirect earnings		

10.1 ESSENTIAL FINANCIAL RECORDS

Administrative medical assistants help with the **accounting**—the methodical recording, classifying, and summarizing of business transactions—in the medical office. The physician must have a record of all transactions and must be able to prepare tax records. Either an accountant employed by the practice or the Internal Revenue Service (IRS) may wish to perform an **audit,** or review of all financial data in order to ensure the accuracy and completeness of the data. The assistant also makes all records available to the IRS and keeps all source documents for tax purposes. These tasks require a working knowledge of tax regulations and of the accounting process. The part of the process that is the accurate recording of transactions is called **bookkeeping.**

Accounting for the practice may be done in one of two ways: on a cash basis or on an accrual basis. If the practice operates on a **cash basis,** charges for services are not recorded as income to the practice until payment is received and expenses are not recorded until they are paid. With the **accrual method,** income is recorded as soon as it is earned, whether or not the payment is received, and expenses are recorded when they are incurred. Whichever way the practice decides to keep its accounts, there are certain essential records that must be carefully kept and maintained. The assistant's task is to enter data accurately the first time on a record and to perform the tasks of **posting** to records, or transferring amounts from one record to another.

The financial records that are used daily in the practice include the following.

- *The daily journal:* The **daily journal** is a record of services rendered, daily fees charged, payments received, and adjustments. It is also called a "general journal," "day sheet," or "daily earnings record."
- *Charge/receipt slips:* **Charge/receipt slips** provide a record of the physician's services and the charges for these. Each slip has a tear-off receipt for the patient.
- *Ledgers:* **Patient ledger cards** contain a patient's name, services rendered, charge, payment, and balance. **Accounts payable** ledgers record expense amounts owed to a supplier or creditor. **Accounts receivable** ledgers record the balance of payments due from patients or others on current accounts.
- *Summaries:* The **monthly summary** shows the daily charges and payments for an entire month. The **annual summary** provides the monthly charges and payments for an entire year. In some practices, quarterly (a three-month period) summaries are prepared.

The assistant is responsible for accurately entering the data and keeping these essential records current. These records are the basis for ongoing decisions about collections and disbursements, and they provide a picture of the financial health of the practice. In all businesses, the managers speak of the importance of the **balance sheet,** the financial statement for a particular date that indicates the total assets (possessions of value, such as equipment), liabilities (debts), and capital (available dollars). Summaries are an important part of the balance sheet.

■ Accounting Software

Many offices keep these records in a paper format. Many other practices use an accounting software package to perform all necessary accounting functions. There are several software applications that have been customized with vocabulary and features specific to medical practices. Software programs require some effort to learn and manipulate. However, they save time by automatically performing routine tasks and most mathematical calculations.

■ Daily Journal

The daily journal is used to record the daily fees charged and payments received. It is, then, the journal used for accounts receivable (fees charged) and cash receipts (payments received). Fees charged, payments received, and adjustments must be recorded promptly in the daily journal.

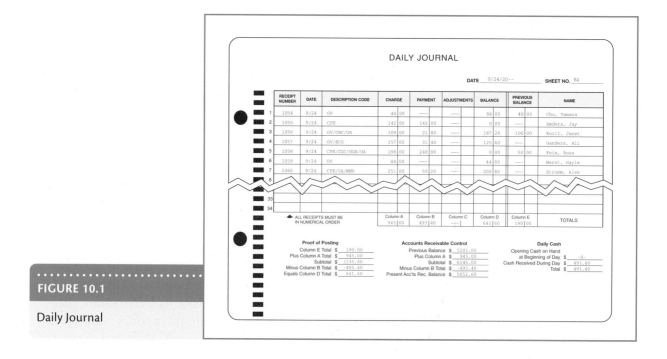

FIGURE 10.1

Daily Journal

FIGURE 10.2

NDCmedisoft™ Day Sheet

Karen Larsen, M.D.
Procedure Code Day Sheet
Ending 9/24/2008

Entry	Date	Chart	Name	Document	POS	Debits	Credits
80048		**SMA-8 Basic metabolic panel**					
	9/24/2008	ROGERCL0	Rogers, Clarence	0309240000		51.00	
		Total of 80048		Quantity:	1	$51.00	$0.00
81001		**UA with microscopy**					
	9/24/2008	MATTHEA1	Matthews, Ardis	0309240000		24.00	
	9/24/2008	DAYTOTH0	Dayton, Theresa	0309240000		24.00	
		Total of 81001		Quantity:	2	$48.00	$0.00
85022		**Hemogram (CBC) with differential**					
	9/24/2008	MATTHEA1	Matthews, Ardis	0309240000		25.00	
	9/24/2008	DAYTOTH0	Dayton, Theresa	0309240000		25.00	
		Total of 85022		Quantity:	2	$50.00	$0.00
87088		**UC**					
	9/24/2008	MATTHEA1	Matthews, Ardis	0309240000		35.00	
		Total of 87088		Quantity:	1	$35.00	$0.00
88150		**Pap**					
	9/24/2008	MENDEAN0	Mendez, Ana	0309240000		33.00	
	9/24/2008	DAYTOTH0	Dayton, Theresa	0309240000		33.00	
		Total of 88150		Quantity:	2	$66.00	$0.00
93000		**Electrocardiogram (ECG)**					
	9/24/2008	ROGERCL0	Rogers, Clarence	0309240000		70.00	
		Total of 93000		Quantity:	1	$70.00	$0.00

It is necessary to have an accurate balance of accounts. The daily journal in Figure 10.1 shows typical entries and balances. Accuracy is obtained by using the section at the bottom of the journal page, in the center, labeled "Accounts Receivable Control." *Accounts Receivable* in the label refers to the balance due from patients on current accounts. By maintaining this section of the daily journal, the practice keeps a "control" on the amount of money it is owed. Every day, the charges are added and the payments are subtracted from the previous day's balance. The result is the current day's accounts receivable balance.

There is also a section, usually in the lower left corner of the page, labeled "Proof of Posting." In this case, *proof* does not mean that the correct amounts were charged. *Proof* means only that the columns balance.

The section labeled "Daily Cash" in the lower right corner is used to account for the daily cash flow, or the amount of cash received during that day.

Computerized Daily Journal. Medical management software provides electronic daily journal forms. The example shown in Figure 10.2 is a feature of NDCmedisoft™. It is called the **procedure day sheet** and lists numerically all procedures performed on a given day. It also provides patient names, document numbers, places of service (POS), and debits and credits.

■ Methods of Bookkeeping

There are three methods of bookkeeping. Only the last will be discussed here because it is the most frequently used manual system in medical practices and other businesses.

- *Single-entry method:* This system requires only one entry for each transaction and is the oldest system. It is, however, a difficult system to use because it is not a self-balancing method; therefore, users find it hard to recognize errors.
- *Double-entry method:* This system requires more knowledge of accounting principles on the part of the user than the other methods do. It is a method based on the accounting equation: assets equal liabilities plus owner equity. In businesses where this method is used, one account must be debited and another account credited after each transaction. Thus, the system takes more time to use than the other methods.
- *Pegboard method:* This most commonly used system is efficient and easy to learn. The pegboard system is discussed below.

■ Pegboard Accounting

The **pegboard accounting** system is also called the "write it once" or "one-write" system. An accurate system and not difficult to learn, this system is widely used in physicians' offices. Pegs on the left or right side of the pegboard hold several forms. These forms are made with holes that line up to fit over the pegs. The holes are placed in such a way that the forms are layered one on top of the other. Information recorded on the form on top is recorded at the same time on the forms underneath. Usually, no-carbon-required (NCR) forms are used. Three forms are required for the pegboard system, and they are layered in this way:

- *Top form, first layer—charge/receipt slip:* Patient's name, services rendered, charge, payment, and balance are recorded here.
- *Next form, second layer—patient's ledger card:* The information recorded on the charge/receipt slip is also recorded here.
- *Third form, bottom layer—daily journal:* The information on fees charged and payment received is recorded on the charge/receipt slip and, at the same time, on the patient's ledger card (the second layer) and in the daily journal (the bottom layer).

Because of the way the system works, postings can be made to the patient ledger cards in the presence of the patient. The patient receives the bill immediately and the ledger card is always up to date and ready for use in preparing a monthly billing statement. In addition, every charge/receipt slip is accounted for because these slips are entered in the daily journal in numeric sequence.

■ Summaries

In many practices, the physician will want to analyze charges, cash receipts, and disbursements at the end of the month, at the end of each quarter, and at the end of the year. The purpose of analyzing summaries is to compare the present financial performance of the practice with performance last year, last quarter, or last month. The physician, and in some cases an accountant, will look at cash receipts from certain kinds of services, the expenses involved in running the office, and other categories. The analysis will help the physician plan for the future of the practice by cutting back on expenses, for example, or by investing in equipment that will enable the practice to offer more patients a particularly profitable service.

Computer Summaries. The use of a software program to provide summaries is an efficient way to assemble and summarize information. The database can be manipulated to provide a summary by procedure code or by number of procedures within a certain time frame. It also can provide a comparative summary over time of payments used to make a deposit. Such software solutions are available in specialized medical accounting software programs.

In NDCmedisoft™, for example, a **practice analysis report** may be generated monthly or for another specified period of time. The purpose of the report is, as its name shows, to analyze the revenue of the practice for a specified period of time. In the report, the description of and revenue for each procedure is shown first, as in Figure 10.3 *(a)* on page 260. A summary page at the end of the report then shows the total charges, patient payments, copayments, adjustments, and so on. The summary page is shown in Figure 10.3 *(b)* on page 260. This report may also be used to generate financial statements for the practice.

In addition, programs such as NDCmedisoft™ provide other useful summaries, such as **aging reports.** This analysis lists the amounts of money owed to the practice, and the report is organized according to the number of days late. In such a report, the "aging" begins on the date of the transaction and will report those debts that are current—or "0 to 30 days"—and several other time frames of past due debts. See the example of an aging report in Figure 10.4 on page 260.

Spreadsheet capabilities in software applications also enhance the physician's ability to analyze the performance of the practice. These spreadsheets may be designed so as to provide profit and loss reports, expense reports, and budget planning documents. To create a program to serve your practice, the designer customizes the spreadsheet by specifying the format and creating formulas that will provide the desired calculations.

GO TO PROJECT 10.1 ON PAGE 273

FIGURE 10.3

(a) Practice Analysis
    Report, Page 1
(b) Practice Analysis
    Report, Summary Page

Karen Larsen, M.D.
Practice Analysis
From September 1, 2008 to September 30, 2008

Code	Modifier	Description	Amount	Units	Average	Cost	Net
80048		SMA-8 Basic metabolic panel	51.00	1	51.00	0.00	51.00
81001		UA with microscopy	48.00	2	24.00	0.00	48.00
85022		Hemogram (CBC) with differential	50.00	2	25.00	0.00	50.00
87088		UC	35.00	1	35.00	0.00	35.00
88150		Pap	66.00	2	33.00	0.00	66.00
93000		Electrocardiogram (ECG)	70.00	1	70.00	0.00	70.00
99212		OV, EP, Focused	44.00	1	44.00	0.00	44.00
99213		OV, EP, Expanded	60.00	1	60.00	0.00	60.00
99221		Initial hospital visit, detailed	121.00	1	121.00	0.00	121.00
99231		Subsequent hospital visit, focused	65.00	1	65.00	0.00	65.00

(a)

Karen Larsen, M.D.
Practice Analysis
From September 1, 2008 to September 30, 2008

Total Procedure Charges	$882.00
Total Product Charges	$0.00
Total Inside Lab Charges	$0.00
Total Outside Lab Charges	$0.00
Total Billing Charges	$0.00
Total Tax Charges	$0.00
Total Insurance Payments	-$543.20
Total Cash Copayments	$0.00
Total Check Copayments	$0.00
Total Credit Card Copayments	$0.00
Total Patient Cash Payments	$0.00
Total Patient Check Payments	-$274.40
Total Credit Card Payments	$0.00
Total Debit Adjustments	$0.00
Total Credit Adjustments	$0.00
Total Insurance Debit Adjustments	$0.00
Total Insurance Credit Adjustments	$0.00
Total Insurance Withholds	$0.00
Net Effect on Accounts Receivable	$64.40

(b)

Karen Larsen, M.D.
Patient Aging
From January 1, 2008 to October 7, 2008

Chart	Name	Birthdate	Current 0 - 30	Past 31 - 60	Past 61 - 90	Past 91 --->	Total Balance
DAYTOTH0	Theresa Dayton	3/13/1986	33.60				33.60
Last Pmt: -68.80	On: 9/24/2008	(312)555-2231					
MENDEAN0	Ana Mendez	3/24/1974	8.45				8.45
Last Pmt: -102.20	On: 10/6/2008	(312)555-3606					
ROBERSU0	Suzanne Roberts	7/7/1986			156.00		156.00
Last Pmt: -50.00	On: 7/25/2008	(312)555-2267					
ROGERCL0	Clarence Rogers	9/25/1980	86.20				86.20
Last Pmt: -100.00	On: 10/3/2008	(312)555-5297					
	Report Aging Totals		$128.25	$0.00	$156.00	$0.00	284.25
	Percent of Aging Total		45.1 %	0.0 %	54.9 %	0.0 %	100.00 %

FIGURE 10.4

Aging Report

It is clear that handling the banking functions of the practice accurately and promptly contributes to the financial health of the practice. The administrative medical assistant is responsible for many of these banking duties, including preparing deposits and reconciling bank statements. Banking tasks require **absolute accuracy,** correctness that is one hundred percent, because the assistant acts as the physician's agent in these matters.

■ Checks and Checking

The practice may have at least two types of checking accounts—one regular business checking account and an account that pays interest. There may also be a savings account in the name of the practice. Money for taxes or expenses that are not immediate will be kept in a checking or savings account where it will earn **interest,** or money paid by the bank to depositors in return for the bank's use of the depositor's money. You will use the regular business account most frequently: to deposit patient payments and to draw checks for the payment of office expenses. Although this account does not pay interest, it allows for availability and flexibility. No interest is lost by the frequent transactions.

Negotiable Checks. A **check** is an order to a bank to pay a specific amount of money. In order for the check to be negotiable, that is, to allow the legal transfer of money, it must meet several requirements. It is important for you to know what these are; you should examine all checks given to you before accepting them. To be negotiable a check must:

- Contain the specific amount to be paid.
- Be made out (made payable) to the payee. The payee may be the title of the practice rather than the physician's name, depending on the title of the account.
- Carry the name of the bank that is making the payment.
- Specify the date on which payment is to be made.
- Be signed by the payer, the person who writes the check and is promising to pay the money.

Be sure that you understand and follow office policies about accepting checks. For example, a patient visiting the office for the first time may be required to present identification before the check is accepted.

The following kinds of checks are usually not acceptable:

- *Postdated checks:* A check dated in the future (postdated) cannot be cashed until that future date.

- *Predated checks:* A check dated in the past (predated) is acceptable only if the date is *within* a six-month period before the date on which you receive it.
- *Third-party checks:* In this case, *third party* refers not to an insurer but to anyone other than the patient. A third-party check is a check written to the patient by a person unknown to the practice.
- *Check with an annotation of "Paid in Full":* When the amount of the check does not correspond to the total, or full, amount due for the services rendered, the office should not accept a check marked "Paid in Full."

Check Endorsements. All checks received should be endorsed as soon as they are accepted. This lessens the chance that they will be lost, stolen, or forgotten. There are three types of endorsements that may be used. These are shown in Figure 10.5.

- *Blank endorsement:* In a **blank endorsement** the signature of the person to whom the check is payable is placed on the back of the check. Once a check is endorsed this way, the check may be cashed by anyone. Blank endorsements are not used in business.
- *Full endorsement:* The **full endorsement** indicates the person, company, account number, or bank to which the check is being transferred, followed by the payee's name.
- *Restrictive endorsement:* A **restrictive endorsement** is the safest and most commonly used endorsement in business. The check is "restricted" by being marked "For Deposit Only." The use of the check is thus limited because the party to whom the money should be paid and the purpose have been stated. The restrictive endorsement is convenient for business use. The assistant may use a "For Deposit Only" rubber stamp and may deposit the check without obtaining the physician's signature.

FIGURE 10.5

(a) Blank Endorsement

(b) Full Endorsement

(c) Restrictive Endorsement

Deposits. The checks and cash placed into the account belonging to the practice are called **deposits.** Once the checks have been accepted and endorsed, a deposit slip is prepared. For a sizable practice, depositing checks daily is important because it improves the cash flow and ensures that checks sent by the practice will not bounce. If the practice is specialized or very small, deposits may be made less often during the week. The bank where the checking account is maintained provides deposit slips. These are preprinted with the title of the account and the account number. A sample deposit slip is shown in Figure 10.6. On the first line, marked "Cash," the amount of currency—bills and coins—is entered. Beneath this entry, each check is listed separately. Some banks prefer to have the check identified by its number or bank name. The total amount, cash and checks, is entered on the appropriate line (usually the last line). The amount of the deposit is then entered on the first unused checkbook stub or in the check register.

It is important to obtain a deposit receipt from the bank. All deposit slips, the checkbooks, and the check register should be kept in a secure and locked place in the office.

Returned Checks. The bank may return a check that has not been completed properly: the check may be missing a date or signature. The check will also be returned if there is not enough money in the account to cover the amount shown on the check. In this case, the check is stamped, or identified "NSF" or "Nonsufficient Funds." When this happens, you will need to contact the person who gave you the check.

■ The Banking Policy of the Practice

The physician must indicate the persons in the practice authorized to sign all checks. One person may be authorized to write checks, and another may be authorized to sign. This is a good system to avoid mistakes and misappropriations. It may be that the physician will require two signatures for each check, or limits may be set on the amounts of money for which anyone other than the physician may write checks.

FIGURE 10.6

Deposit Slip

Each month the bank submits a statement of the checking account, such as the one shown in Figure 10.7. The monthly statement shows the beginning balance, total credits (deposits added to the account during the month), total debits (checks paid out of the account during the month), any service charges that apply, and the resulting new balance.

The new balance on the statement must be compared with the checkbook balance to determine whether there is a difference between the amounts. This process is known as reconciling the bank statement, or **bank reconciliation.** Many banks provide a reconciliation form, such as the one shown in Figure 10.8, on one of the pages of the monthly statement.

The steps you should take in the reconciliation process are:

1. Compare the canceled checks returned by the bank with the items listed on the bank statement. When banks do not provide the actual canceled checks, miniaturized photostats of the checks are usually

---

First National Bank
Chicago, IL 60623-2791

STATEMENT OF
ACCOUNT NUMBER
242 027720

CLOSING DATE	ITEMS
6/25	12

KAREN LARSEN, MD
2235 SOUTH RIDGEWAY AVENUE
CHICAGO, IL 60623-2240

PERSONAL CHECKING ACCOUNT STATEMENT

BEGINNING BALANCE	(+) TOTAL CREDITS	(-) TOTAL DEBITS	(-) SERVICE CHARGE	(=) NEW BALANCE
2,592.74	1,030.00	919.06		2703.68

CHECKS & OTHER DEBITS		DEPOSITS & OTHER CREDITS	DATE	BALANCE
	2.54	165.00	6/2	2,755.20
		100.00	6/4	2,855.20
	97.00		6/5	2,758.20
	450.00		6/6	2,308.20
		120.00	6/9	2,428.20
	29.37		6/11	
	13.00			2,385.83
		85.00	6/12	2,470.83
	7.00	210.00	6/16	2,673.83
	15.62		6/17	2,658.21
		90.00	6/18	2,748.21
	37.98	185.00	6/23	
	65.12			2,830.11
	145.00		6/24	
	15.00			2,670.11
	41.43	75.00	6/25	2,703.68

SYMBOLS

C = CORRECTION	DM = DEBIT MEMO	RI = RETURN ITEM	ST = SAVINGS TRANSFER
CM = CREDIT MEMO	OD = OVERDRAFT	SC = SERVICE CHARGE	

FIGURE 10.7

Bank Statement

provided. These, in addition to the listing of the checks on the statement, may be used for reference.

2. Compare the checks listed on the bank statement with the checkbook stubs to verify that check numbers and amounts agree. Deductions, such as service charges, are explained on the bank statement. These must now be recorded in the checkbook. Checks that were written during the last month but have not yet been paid by the bank are not included with the statement. These are called "outstanding checks" and should be listed on the reconciliation form as shown in Figure 10.8.

3. Compare the deposits recorded in the checkbook with the credits listed on the bank statement. A deposit listed in the checkbook but not recorded by the bank at the time the statement was issued is called a "deposit in transit."

4. If the checking account earns interest, record the interest as a credit, similar to a deposit, in the checkbook.

5. Complete the reconciliation form following the directions.

CHANGE OF ADDRESS ORDER
TO CHANGE YOUR ADDRESS, PLEASE COMPLETE THIS FORM;
THEN CUT ALONG DOTTED LINE, AND MAIL OR BRING TO THE BANK.

NEW ADDRESS

NUMBER AND STREET

CITY — STATE AND ZIP CODE — NEW PHONE NUMBER

DATE — CUSTOMER'S SIGNATURE

OUTSTANDING CHECKS	
NUMBER	AMOUNT
	125 00
	18 65
	22 19
	48 90
TOTAL	214 74

TO RECONCILE YOUR STATEMENT AND CHECKBOOK

1. DEDUCT FROM YOUR CHECKBOOK BALANCE ANY SERVICE OR OTHER CHARGE ORIGINATED BY THE BANK. THESE CHARGES WILL BE IDENTIFIED BY SYMBOLS AS SHOWN ON FRONT.

2. ARRANGE ENDORSED CHECKS BY DATE OR NUMBER AND CHECK THEM OFF AGAINST THE STUBS IN YOUR CHECKBOOK.

3. LIST IN THE OUTSTANDING CHECKS SECTION AT THE LEFT ANY CHECKS ISSUED BY YOU AND NOT YET PAID BY US.

TO RECONCILE YOUR STATEMENT AND CHECKBOOK		
LAST BALANCE SHOWN ON STATEMENT	2,703	68
PLUS: DEPOSITS AND CREDITS MADE AFTER DATE OF LAST ENTRY ON STATEMENT	130	00
SUBTOTAL	2,833	68
MINUS: OUTSTANDING CHECKS	214	74
BALANCE: WHICH SHOULD AGREE WITH YOUR CHECKBOOK	2,618	94

FIGURE 10.8

Reconciliation Section of a Bank Statement

If the final amount on the reconciliation form does not agree with the amount in the checkbook, compare the monthly statement with the checkbook again.

- Recheck the deposits entered on the bank statement with those you have entered in the checkbook.
- Confirm that all service charges shown on the statement are entered in the checkbook and have been properly deducted.
- Make sure no check has been drawn that has not been recorded in the checkbook. Compare all checks with the stubs to make sure the amounts agree.
- Review the list of outstanding checks to see whether an old check is still outstanding.
- Recheck all addition and subtraction.

When the checkbook is reconciled, make a notation to that effect in the checkbook on the last-used stub or register line.

■ Banking Electronically

Banking by computer can contribute to both efficiency and accuracy. The tasks that you have when banking electronically are the same as those you perform when using paper procedures. You are still responsible for recording and physically depositing checks. You will still need to reconcile statements. However, the software will make all the calculations automatically. This not only saves time but also reduces the chances for error. You will no longer need to worry about a secure storage place for the checkbook and deposit slips. The password that you determine in order to access the bank account is the only item you must protect.

The software systems made available by banks require a modem attached to your computer. With a modem in place, the bank makes the following activities possible:

- Checking balances in the accounts.
- Receiving electronic deposits.
- Finding out which checks have cleared.
- Transferring money from one account to another.
- Paying certain monthly bills.

In some cases, banks supply the software at minimal cost or have interfaces with commercial software. The menus are easy to use. Main menus present choices such as "Pay Bills" and "Record Deposits." The directions for transactions are step by step. Reconciling monthly statements may also be done electronically with a computerized version of the reconciliation form.

In June 2000, federal legislation was signed that granted electronic signatures, or e-signatures, the same legal standing as printed signatures. The **e-signature** is a unique identifier, or "signature," created for each person through computer code. It is not a computer image of a person's pen-and-ink signature. Verifying the identities of those doing business in cyberspace is still an issue to be resolved. Although there are very few institutions technologically equipped to do business recognizing e-signatures, this way of check writing, contract signing, transferring of patient releases, and other transactions will grow more popular.

The practice may also authorize a payer to transfer funds electronically. That is, a third-party payer such as the federal government or an insurance company may deposit payment to the practice electronically and directly into the practice's account.

■ Petty Cash

A **petty cash fund** is a fund containing small amounts of cash to be used for small expenses. These expenses are usually so small that checks would not be written to pay for them: cab fares, postage stamps, payments to messengers, and delivery charges.

Each time you make a payment from the petty cash fund, make an entry in the petty cash register or complete a voucher if this is the system used in your office. The register or voucher provides a record of these small expenses and ensures that only authorized payments are made from this fund.

To obtain money for the petty cash fund, the minor expenses for the month are estimated. A check for the estimated amount is drawn, payable to the person in the office authorized to handle the petty cash fund. The check is cashed, and the money is obtained in an assortment of small bills and change. The money is kept in a secure place, such as a locked metal cash box in a drawer.

At the end of the month or when the amount of cash is low, the fund is replenished. First, from the record in the petty cash register, determine the total amount of disbursements made. Count the remaining cash in the fund. Be sure the two amounts add up to the original amount of the check that was last cashed. This procedure is called "proving the petty cash fund." A new check is then drawn to bring the fund back to its original amount.

EXAMPLE

The original amount of the petty cash fund was $100. According to the petty cash register, expenses added up to $89.75. Thus, there should be $10.25 in cash and $89.75 in receipts remaining in the fund. Count the cash to verify that the correct amount remains. Draw a check for $89.75 to bring the amount of petty cash back to $100 once the check has been cashed.

The petty cash expenditures should be recorded in the correct columns on the monthly summary sheet. They may be entered as petty cash.

 GO TO PROJECT 10.2 ON PAGE 273

10.3 PAYROLL

The total earnings of all the employees in the practice is called the **payroll.** If you are responsible for handling the payroll in your office, you will be completing the following tasks:

- Calculate the earnings of employees.
- Subtract the correct amounts of taxes and other **deductions,** or amounts of money withheld from earnings.
- Create employee payroll records.
- Prepare the salary checks.
- Submit payroll taxes.
- Keep current with formulas and regulations issued by the IRS that affect payroll. Many tax tables and other information may be found on the IRS Web site.

■ Creating Employee Payroll Records

Because accurate records are required and because the process is complex, you will want to create a payroll information record for each person employed in the practice. For each employee, list the following information:

- Name, address, social security number, marital status, number of dependents.
- Pay schedule. Show how often the employee is paid: weekly or biweekly, for example.
- Type of payment. Show whether the employee is paid a straight salary or an hourly wage.
- Employee-requested deductions. An employee may have payments to an employer-sponsored insurance plan, contributions to a savings plan sponsored by the practice, or additional tax contributions withheld.

If any employees are not citizens of the United States, they must be authorized to work in the United States. A completed Employment Eligibility Verification Form (Form I-9) should be kept with the payroll records. This document verifies that the person is a legally admitted alien or a person authorized to work in this country.

Employer and Employee Identification Numbers

All employers, whatever the size of the business, are required to have a tax identification number. This **employer identification number (EIN)** enables the IRS to track the financial activity of employers in meeting payroll and tax obligations. The number is obtained by requesting Form SS-4 from the IRS. Employees are required to be identified by social security numbers.

Taxes Deducted From Earnings

Direct earnings are defined as salaries (fixed amounts paid regardless of hours worked) or wages (pay based on an hourly or daily specific rate) paid to employees. **Indirect earnings** may be paid leaves or specific employer-paid benefit programs.

When employees are first hired, they must complete the Employee's Withholding Allowance Certification (Form W-4), on which they state the number of allowances or exemptions to be used when the employer is calculating how much money to withhold from their salaries as deductions. The actual amounts to be withheld from an employee's salary for federal and state taxes are determined from wage-bracket tables supplied by the IRS. The amount withheld depends on the amount of money earned, the number of exemptions claimed, and the current tax rate. The IRS also supplies wage-bracket tables that apply to various payroll cycles: daily, weekly biweekly, semimonthly, monthly. Refer to the state and local tax tables to determine the additional amounts of money to be withheld.

FICA Tax

The Federal Insurance Contributions Act, or **FICA**, governs the social security system. This law requires that a certain amount of money be withheld for social security. The employee pays half the required contribution, and the employer pays the other half. This amount is deducted in two separate payroll taxes: one helps finance Medicare, and the other helps fund social security pension benefits. These amounts, dictated by the IRS, are a percentage of the employee's taxable earnings, considering payroll periods and allowances claimed. Since Congress can change this amount yearly, you must obtain information from the IRS or from the physician's accountant.

■ Calculating Payroll

Spreadsheet programs perform these complex calculations very quickly. It is important for you to understand the formulas used and the process involved.

- *Gross earnings:* Calculate gross earnings. For an employee on salary, the salary amount for the period is the employee's gross earnings, regardless of whether or not the employee worked more than 35 or 40 hours. For an hourly wage worker, the hourly rate multiplied by the number of hours worked yields the employee's gross earnings.
- *Exemptions; state and local tax deductions:* Find the number of exemptions claimed by the employee on Form W-4. Refer to the IRS tax table for the amount to be deducted, based on the gross earnings and the exemptions. State and local taxes are often at a set rate, for example, 5 percent or 2 percent of gross earnings. Subtract these amounts from gross earnings.
- *FICA taxes:* Withhold, and deduct, half the amount due for the pay period from the employee's gross earnings. The other half is paid by the practice. There is one rate for the social security deduction (6.2 percent) and another for the Medicare deduction (1.45 percent).
- *Unemployment taxes:* These taxes vary from state to state. Some states tax only employers. Withhold these taxes as necessary.
- *Voluntary deductions:* Deduct any amounts requested by the employee for insurance, a savings plan, additional tax withholding, and so on.
- *Employer's obligation:* Post the employer's FICA contribution and taxes due to federal and state unemployment funds to the physician's account.
- *Net earnings:* When total deductions are taken from gross earnings, the result is the employee's net earnings.

■ Employers' Tax Responsibilities

Employers are required to help fund a Federal Unemployment Tax Act, or **FUTA,** account, which is used to help those who have been without work for a specified time as they seek new employment. This dollar amount is a percentage of each employee's gross salary but is not to be deducted from the employee's salary. Usually, payments into a state unemployment fund are applied as credit against the amount of FUTA tax.

Unemployment laws in most states require only the employer to contribute to the unemployment insurance fund. There are states that make an exception, and both employers and employees contribute. There are also some states where an employer does not contribute if the company has very few employees.

Employers' Deposit and Tax Return Obligations. The practice must make federal tax withholding payments and FICA payments to a federal deposit account in a Federal Reserve Bank or in some authorized bank. The money must be deposited at least monthly. The IRS imposes a severe penalty for the failure to make these deposits.

The employer is required to file a quarterly tax return, Form 941, to report federal income and FICA taxes withheld from employee paychecks.

■ Payroll Records: Contents and Retention

The practice is required by law to retain payroll data for four years. A typical format for this record is shown in Figure 10.9.

Each employee's earnings record must contain the employee's name, social security number, address, number of exemptions claimed, gross salary earned, net salary paid, income taxes withheld, and FICA, state, and local taxes deducted. The column labeled "Other" is used to record certain other deductions required by law or those voluntary deductions that may be made under an agreement with the employer. For example, many employers will deduct, at the employee's request, amounts for savings bonds, insurance, or union dues. All amounts deducted by the employer are held in trust. The employer must remit the monies to the proper authority in a timely manner.

INDIVIDUAL EMPLOYEE'S EARNINGS RECORD

Name: Molly Benson   Social Security No.: 301-48-7122   Position: M.A. (part-time)
Address: 5985 West Park Ave.   Marital Status: Single   Monthly Rate: _____
City: Chicago, IL 60650   No. of Allowances: 1   Weekly Rate: $528
Telephone: 555-4251   Birthdate: 5/29/1968   Overtime Rate: $25/hour

Period Ending	Hours Worked	Gross Earnings			Deductions								Net Pay	Accumulated Earnings (Gross)
		Regular	Overtime	Total	FICA	Federal Withholding	State Withholding	City Withholding	Insurance	Other	Total			
6-13	24	528 00		528 00	40 40	63 19	15 84					119 43	408 57	12,672 00
6-20	24	528 00		528 00	40 40	63 19	15 84					119 43	408 57	13,200 00
6-27	24	528 00		528 00	40 40	63 19	15 84					119 43	408 57	13,728 00
7-4	24	528 00		528 00	40 40	63 19	15 84					119 43	408 57	14,256 00
7-11	24	528 00		528 00	40 40	63 19	15 84					119 43	408 57	14,784 00
7-18	24	528 00		528 00	40 40	63 19	15 84					119 43	408 57	15,312 00
7-25	24	528 00		528 00	40 40	63 19	15 84					119 43	408 57	15,840 00
8-8	24	528 00		528 00	40 40	63 19	15 84					119 43	408 57	16,368 00
8-15	24	528 00		528 00	40 40	63 19	15 84					119 43	408 57	16,896 00

FIGURE 10.9

Individual Employee's Earnings Record

■ Electronic Payroll: Direct Deposit

Through direct deposit, the employee's net pay is automatically withdrawn from the practice's account and deposited into the employee's account. The physician must contract with the bank for this procedure, known as **EFT** (electronic funds transfer), and employees must give employers their checking account numbers. The employee receives a deposit stub showing the gross pay, net pay, and specific deductions. This aspect of electronic banking has many advantages for both employers and employees in the practice:

1. The loss or theft of paychecks is eliminated. When an employee is on vacation or absent, the check is deposited.
2. Productivity and cost-saving are increased. Time and expense are saved because no paychecks need to be written.
3. Employees have the convenience of eliminating a trip to the bank to deposit a paycheck, and the money is available on the day of deposit.

GO TO PROJECT 10.3 ON PAGE 273

GO TO PROJECT 10.4 ON PAGE 273

Chapter Projects

PROJECT 10.1 Updating Daily Journals

On October 23, you need to complete the daily journals started for October 20 (WP 69), October 21 (WP 70), and October 22 (WP 71).

Note that the patients have been listed for you. Use patient statements to obtain each previous balance. Post each day's transactions onto both the daily journal and the patient statement, computing the current balance. Information for charges has been obtained from each patient's encounter form or from payments received on account.

Total Columns A, B, C, D, and E. Complete the Proof of Posting, the Accounts Receivable Control, and Daily Cash sections. Post the daily ending accounts receivable balance onto the next daily journal.

Note that no deposits were yet made.

Homework

PROJECT 10.2 Internet Research: Discovering Local Banking Services

Find the Web addresses for all of the banks in your town or city. Visit the Web sites, and determine which services are likely to be useful to a small medical practice. Make a list of these services, and be prepared to discuss them in class.

PROJECT 10.3 Internet Research: Using the IRS as a Resource

Using a favorite search engine, key in "internal revenue service." Go to the site for the IRS, and examine the information available. Look especially at the tax forms, the help for small businesses, and the section on payroll tax rules. Determine why this site is helpful to a medical practice. Be prepared to discuss the specific helpful information you find.

PROJECT 10.4 Updating Payments and Deposits

The following payments were received on October 24:

Joseph Castro	$44.00
Suzanne Roberts	$156.00
Gene Sinclair	$44.00

Homework! Here! Needs to be done by Thurs!

Enter and apply the payments. Print a walkout receipt for each patient who made a payment.

Complete a daily journal (WP 72), and post transactions to patient statements. Complete a deposit slip (WP 73) for payments received October 20–24.

CHAPTER SUMMARY

1. Five accounting terms related to the assistant's responsibilities are accounts payable (expense amounts owed to suppliers or creditors), accounts receivable (balance of payments due from patients or others on current accounts), bookkeeping (the part of accounting that is the accurate recording of transactions), daily journal (the record of services rendered, daily fees charged, payments received, and adjustments), and audit (an IRS review of all financial data to ensure the accuracy and completeness of the data).

2. The procedures for maintaining two of the essential financial records follow. *Daily journal:* Record daily the fees charged; record daily the payments received; keep the Accounts Receivable Control section accurate with the record of payments received from patients; balance the columns for the Proof of Posting; and record the amount of cash received during the day in Daily Cash section to account for the cash flow. *Monthly summary:* Summarize the daily charges and payments on a monthly basis.

3. Three banking duties performed by the assistant are accepting valid checks in payment for services rendered, depositing cash and checks in the practice's account, and reconciling bank statements.

4. The assistant's duties related to the payroll process are are follows:
   (a) Calculate gross earnings. Determine the salary amount, or multiply the number of hours worked by the hourly wage amount.
   (b) Determine the proper exemptions, and state and local tax deductions. Subtract these from the gross earnings. *(c) Subtract FICA tax.* Withhold half the specified amount from the employee's paycheck. The employer pays the other half. *(d) Subtract unemployment tax if the state requires payment from the employee.* Some states demand payment only from the employer. *(e) Subtract voluntary deductions.* If the employee has asked that amounts be withheld for insurance, savings, and so on, deduct these amounts. *(f) Subtract the total deductions from the gross earnings.* The result is the employee's net salary. *(g) Remember to post the taxes that are the physician's obligation to the practice account.*

KEY TERMS

The following key terms appear in **boldface** type in this chapter. Administrative medical assistants must know the meaning and the correct use of each of these terms. Can you recall what each term means? Refer to this chapter or to the glossary for any terms you need to review.

absolute accuracy	charge/receipt slips	indirect earnings
accounting	check	interest
accounts payable	daily journal	monthly summary
accounts receivable	deductions	patient ledger cards
accrual method	deposits	payroll
aging reports	direct earnings	pegboard accounting
annual summary	EFT	petty cash fund
audit	employer identifica-	posting
balance sheet	tion number (EIN)	practice analysis
bank reconciliation	e-signature	report
blank endorsement	FICA	procedure day sheet
bookkeeping	full endorsement	restrictive
cash basis	FUTA	endorsement

THINKING IT THROUGH

These questions cover the most important points in this chapter. Using your critical thinking skills, play the role of an administrative medical assistant as you answer each question. Be prepared to present your responses in class.

1. What are the major financial responsibilities that you have as an administrative medical assistant? What are the accounting terms used to describe these responsibilities?

2. You have been asked to help a colleague understand how to deal with the daily journal. How will you explain this?

3. Mr. Thompson is a patient whose insurance company has paid a portion of the fee for the physician's services; Mr. Thompson is responsible for the remaining amount. He is angry and determined to dispute the matter with the insurance company. For this reason, he has given you a postdated check for the amount owed to the doctor, $427.50. The check is dated three weeks from the current date. How will you handle this nonnegotiable check?

4. One of staff members asks you to explain the difference between the terms *gross* and *net* on the paycheck. How do you respond?

CHAPTER 11

Office Management

OBJECTIVES

After studying this chapter, you will be able to:

1. List three qualifications for office management.
2. List four office management tasks.
3. Describe two guidelines for making travel arrangements.
4. Explain the preparations to be made in arranging for a meeting.
5. List four topics to be covered in a patient information brochure.
6. Explain the importance of a policies and procedures manual.

INTRODUCTION

The word *administrative* in the administrative medical assistant's job title refers to more than clerical or office tasks that contribute to the care of patients. The word also describes the management functions that assistants fulfill on a daily basis. In many practices, career advancement to office management may be an outgrowth of skills and abilities used every day on the job.

This chapter deals with **management qualifications**—the skills, abilities, and responsibilities of the medical assistant in the role of office manager, including:

- Helping with editorial research projects.
- Making travel and meeting arrangements.
- Evaluating, updating, and distributing patient information and instruction handouts.
- Creating and maintaining office policies and procedures manuals.

KEY TERMS

Study these important words, which are defined in this chapter, to build your professional vocabulary:

agenda	meeting minutes	patient information	reprints
itinerary	outside services file	brochure	travel agent
management	patient education	policies and procedures	
qualifications	materials	manual	

11.1 THE OFFICE MANAGER'S ROLE

Advancing from the position of administrative medical assistant to office manager requires experience and specific skills and abilities. The experience ensures a broad and deep understanding of the many ways in which the medical practice is a business uniquely designed to serve people's most important and intimate needs. A high level of skill ensures a readiness to exercise initiative and to direct others.

Moving into an office management position sometimes requires a change of duties. It always requires a change of emphasis in job responsibilities. While the employee working as an assistant must have certain planning and management skills, the emphasis is most often on carefully following instructions, implementing plans made by the physician or other managers, and responding skillfully to a variety of situations. Office management requires the exercise of initiative that lets assistants act confidently because they grasp the goals and purposes of the practice.

Office management responsibilities involve the following managerial skills and abilities:

- *Being a team player:* It is important to understand the social fabric of the relationships in the office and to be recognized as someone who helps generously; freely gives credit to other employees for their work; contributes to a pleasant atmosphere; and relates well to colleagues as well as to managers.

FIGURE 11.1

Medical office staff meetings provide an opportunity to share ideas. *What do you think are the most important aspects of effective meetings?*

- *Increasing productivity:* Understanding how to complete tasks more efficiently, actually increasing output, is the mark of a good manager. Directing others so that they are able to get more tasks done more efficiently may be part of the office manager's responsibility. Thus, the manager's own development of time management skills and efficient ways of doing tasks is critical.

- *Planning strategically:* The office manager is expected to see beyond an immediate assignment, to view the whole business of the practice so as to contribute in ways that improve the daily operations of the office. This may involve anything from selecting new software for scheduling patients to recommending the choice of a new supplier because of quality or price.

- *Using problem-solving skills:* The employer counts on the office manager to be able to analyze situations, determine the critical factors, apply knowledge gained in past working experience, and propose and implement solutions.

- *Using available resources:* When physicians delegate the day-to-day management of the office, they may expect the office manager to get help from experts: an accountant, a lawyer, an insurance representative, even a time management expert. Companies specializing in office management, known as medical management consultants, are available to assist the office manager. The consultant will spend time analyzing the accounting system, the appointment scheduling and flow of patients, the filing methods, and the work habits of everyone on staff, including the physicians. The consultant will then make recommendations for changes. Perhaps the appointment system will need to be changed to accommodate physicians or patients better. There may be ways that office expenses can be reduced. A consultant may also provide comprehensive training for office personnel. If the practice can afford the use of such a resource, the help may be very valuable, especially to a newly appointed office manager.

The ability to manage the office on a daily basis demands, above all, the quality of leadership. This quality enables the office manager to choose what to achieve, to plan for complex tasks, to prioritize time and tasks, and to motivate other employees to work effectively and efficiently.

▶ **GO TO PROJECT 11.1 ON PAGE 298** ▶

The physician may be involved with research in a wide variety of areas, including investigating clinical procedures, instruments, or drugs, and conducting experiments. Perhaps the physician needs to prepare a medical case history of particular interest or an article summarizing findings to the scientific community. Whether it is for a lecture, an article, or a book, the assistant may become involved in initial stages of research through obtaining material for the physician's reports at the library. The assistant will also keep copies of medical journals and will obtain and file reprints of articles in the physician's areas of interest or articles the physician has written.

■ Using the Library

In specialized medical libraries, such as those found in large medical centers or universities, librarians have educational qualifications in medical research and are prepared to be helpful to those who need to use the library. Public libraries have large computerized databases of materials in various medical specialties. These databases are quite simple to use because most of them include tips on how to search and are searchable by topic. If the document is located in another library, that information is also usually given. If the physician has given you only a topic and brief description, it may be efficient to print out those entries pertaining to the topic and ask the physician to check off those entries that seem most pertinent to the research. This will give direction to your search and will ensure that the most useful books or articles are provided.

On-line computerized databases are available in medical libraries or through the Internet, and information sites such as the Health Libraries or Health Sciences Resource List are also useful. Other helpful resources are listed here.

- MEDLINE software, developed by the National Library of Medicine in 1966, provides immediate access to abstracts and journals and allows the full text of journal articles to be retrieved on-line.
- Compact disks for use at home or in an office may contain whole medical books, periodicals, journals, or even interactive training (for example, on how to perform a particular surgery, complete with pictures, animations, photographs, and videos).
- Specialized e-mail bulletin boards provide an opportunity for physicians to communicate publicly or privately with other physicians through e-mail messages.

Medical Journals

Most medical societies publish their own journals. The American Medical Association (AMA) publishes about a dozen periodicals on special subjects. In addition, the AMA publishes the official publication of the society, the *Journal of the American Medical Association (JAMA)*. *JAMA* contains articles on all aspects of the field of medicine. Most medical specialties have their own journals. The physician will find it useful to have copies of journals bound and stored. These contain much valuable information for reference and for research. It is useful for you to know that each journal publishes a topical index at the end of a publishing cycle, although this cycle may not correlate exactly to a calendar year. Some research material that you may need may be found in the office storage area where these journals are kept.

Reprints

Physicians may inform their colleagues about their work by lecturing and by writing articles and papers. If a physician presents a paper at a meeting of medical colleagues, the paper is usually published in the proceedings of the conference, in the organization's own publication, or in another medical journal. However, the physician may have submitted the article to a journal without having first presented it at a meeting.

Once the article is published, the author may receive a certain number of free copies of the article, called **reprints.** Additional copies are usually available at cost. The physician sends these reprints to colleagues interested in the same or allied fields. You should keep a record of the names and addresses of those who have received copies of the article and of those who have acknowledged receiving the article.

▸ **GO TO PROJECT 11.2 ON PAGE 298** ▸

11.3 TRAVEL AND MEETING ARRANGEMENTS

When the physician travels for professional or personal reasons, you will be involved in preparing for the trip. You need to know and understand the physician's preferences well in order to handle travel arrangements satisfactorily.

There are two general guidelines for handling travel:

1. Always consult with the physician enough in advance to be sure that the physician's preferences will be honored. Consider preferences in airline and airplane seating; dietary needs or preferences in airplane

meals; lodging requirements and the geographic relationship of the hotel to the meeting or conference site; car rental company of choice or limousine service; times of travel; airport, if there is more than one in the departure or destination city; and any need for information about the city—places of interest or restaurants, for example.

2. Be sure to use the services of a skilled **travel agent** at a reputable agency or Web site. The travel agent does not charge the customer, and it is the agent's job to make all transportation, car rental, and lodging arrangements requested by the traveler. Communicate the physician's preferences to the agent. Many agents require the completion of a written travel profile that states the traveler's needs and preferences. This is a valuable tool because the physician does not have to take time to answer these questions every time a trip is to be planned.

■ Reservations

A request to the travel agent should be made as early as possible so that the agent can research and obtain the best fare rate. Because many airlines now use electronic tickets, called "e-tickets," the airline provides a confirmation of the reservation and purchase rather than a printed ticket. This confirmation may be used at curbside to check luggage, and/or at the ticket counter to obtain a boarding pass. Airlines will provide a printed ticket if there is a specific request for one. Having a printed ticket makes changing airlines easier, should that be necessary during the trip.

Once you have given the agent all relevant information on arrangements, request written confirmation if there is time. In any case, the agent provides multiple copies of an **itinerary,** or daily schedule of events, including flight times, flight numbers, hotel and car arrangements, and all pertinent addresses and phone numbers. A sample of an itinerary is shown in Figure 11.2 on page 282. As soon as you receive the itinerary, check to be sure that every arrangement is the same as what was originally requested or agreed upon. This itinerary, along with the confirmation ticket or airline ticket, should then be placed in a folder until the physician needs the information. However, you should notify the physician as soon as the itinerary arrives so that copies can be sent to the physician's family members and any others whom the physician specifies. One copy for reference should be kept in a convenient place in the office.

■ Changes in Travel Plans

Changes or delays sometimes occur in the physician's travel plans. Ordinarily, the physician will share with you information on how likely it is that the trip will occur. This is important because airplane tickets that are refundable or that may be used at another time are more expensive than nonrefundable tickets. However, it may be cost-effective to purchase a more expensive ticket that allows for some flexibility in the physician's planning.

FIGURE 11.2

Travel Itinerary

ITINERARY

For Karen Larsen, MD

March 10-14, 20—

<u>Friday, March 10</u>

5:00 p.m.   <u>Depart Chicago</u>, O'Hare International Airport,
            American Airlines 104, nonstop, 737

8:00 p.m.   <u>Arrive New York City</u>, JFK International Airport

Hotel: Mariott Marquis
1535 Broadway, Manhattan
212-555-5000
Conf. No.: GX476T02; nonsmoking room requested

<u>Sunday, March 12</u>

7:00 p.m.   <u>Depart New York</u>, LaGuardia Airport, American
            Airlines 526, nonstop, 737

8:01 p.m.   <u>Arrive Boston</u>, Logan International Airport

Hotel: Sheraton-Boston Hotel
Prudential Center, Boston
613-555-6789
Conf. No.: TZE32145, nonsmoking room requested

<u>Monday, March 13</u>

<u>Reminder:</u> Make restaurant reservations.

7:30 p.m.   Dinner with Dr. and Mrs. Lawrence Carley

<u>Tuesday, March 14</u>

6:45 p.m.   <u>Depart Boston</u>, Logan International Airport,
            American Airlines 175, nonstop, 737

8:12 p.m.   <u>Arrive Chicago</u>, O'Hare International Airport

Travel and accommodations arranged by Linda Solomon, Chicago
Travel, 312-555-6777.

Because most hotel reservations are secured with a credit card, it is also important to cancel a room reservation as soon as the travel plan changes. Each hotel has its own rules about cancellation without a financial penalty. The travel agent should be notified immediately, or you should call the hotel yourself to cancel the reservation. Request confirmation from the hotel that the reservation has been cancelled. Confirmation is usually in the form of an e-mail or a cancellation confirmation number. If a charge is made mistakenly to the credit card, it will be easier to deal with the credit card company if there is a verification of cancellation.

■ Duties Related to the Physician's Absence

Be certain that you have instructions about how to handle phone calls, correspondence, and appointments in the physician's absence. Mark the days on the calendar when the physician will be away so that no patients are scheduled. Notify those patients who are already scheduled that the physician will be away and either make new appointments or refer the patient to the physician who will be substituting in the physician's absence. It is also useful to keep a running daily summary of phone calls, incidents, and patient inquiries specifying whatever action was taken while the physician was away.

■ Meeting Arrangements

Many physicians belong to the AMA. In addition, there are organizations related to all of the medical specialties. Most national organizations also have state and local levels, and physicians belong to the association at all three levels. These organizations provide a valuable way for physicians to exchange information, learn about new developments, continue their education, and contribute to their profession.

Participation in organizations may involve simply attending meetings or may involve working on committees or chairing committees. Your responsibilities will vary depending on the physician's responsibilities.

National and state societies hold meetings once or twice a year. The dates, times, and places of a national or state meeting are usually determined a year in advance of the next meeting. This information is printed several months in advance in the state or national journal. Notices of the meeting are sent to members of the organization well in advance of the meeting. Enter meeting information on the physician's appointment calendar as soon as notice of the meeting arrives. It is helpful to put a reminder in the tickler file so that you can meet with the physician well in advance to find out about preferences in travel schedules and arrangements.

Local meetings are usually held on the same day of each month, for example, on the second Tuesday. Meeting dates and programs are published in the journal or newsletter. Mark the dates on the physician's appointment calendar, and send a memo or an e-mail to the physician several days in advance of the meeting each month as a reminder.

Special meetings may be called to discuss important business matters pertaining to the organization. In these cases, an announcement of the meeting is sent to each member. A sample of the announcement for such a meeting is shown in Figure 11.3 on page 284.

■ Preparing for Meetings

A physician who is the chair of a committee or an officer of the organization may be responsible for making the arrangements for the meeting. In many cases, the physician will delegate the responsibility for meeting arrangements to the assistant. If the meeting is to be held locally, arranging for the meeting is simpler. However, contracting for a meeting room, food or other refreshments, and equipment will still be necessary.

FIGURE 11.3

Meeting Announcement

**THE CHICAGO MEDICAL SOCIETY
MONTHLY MEETING**

**Tuesday, October 7, 20--
8:00 p.m.**

**UNIVERSITY HOSPITAL
5500 North Ridgeway Avenue
Room 254C**

The following arrangements need to be made:

- Once you know how many people are expected, contact several conference centers or hotels to price the arrangements. Most conference centers and hotels have catering managers or conference planners available to help you. Know whether or not meals or other refreshment will be required; what kinds of media support—computers, flip charts and pens, overhead transparency machines, microphones, recording equipment, and so on—will be required; the length of time the room will be needed; whether or not a lectern or table should be at the front of the room; and whether chairs alone or chairs and tables will be needed for the audience. If the group is to take notes, the hotel will ordinarily provide pads and pens. The hotel will also supply complimentary pitchers of ice water and glasses for the speaker and guests. Many facilities will fax you a worksheet for specifying all requirements so that you can obtain the total cost.

- If there is to be a speaker, the physician will usually invite the person. However, you may need to confirm the person's attendance and the topic of the presentation. You may also need to make travel and hotel arrangements. The speaker should provide you with a brief *vitae* (biographical and credentialing information) so that the physician can make a proper introduction. The *vitae* should be placed in the physician's travel folder. You may also volunteer to prepare copies of handouts and to mail these to the meeting place.

- The physician may ask you to prepare an **agenda,** or outline of the meeting that specifies the location, time, and major topics to be covered. A sample of an agenda is shown in Figure 11.4. Notice the large amount of white space, which enables attendees to make notes. Agendas are ordinarily sent out well ahead of the meeting to allow members to prepare for the business of the meeting.

- You will need to prepare and mail an invitation to each person who is expected to attend the meeting. Those invited must also be told how and when to return their acceptance of the invitation.

Frequently, travel directions to the meeting site are included as a courtesy. If the meeting is local, invitations should be mailed at least one week, but not more than two weeks, prior to the meeting date. If the meeting is to be held in another city, invitations must be mailed about eight weeks prior to the meeting.

■ Keep a record of the names, addresses, and telephone numbers of all those to whom you have sent invitations. It is also wise to keep a copy of the invitation and agenda in a convenient place. It will be necessary to duplicate copies of the agenda so that they may be handed out again on the day of the meeting.

Last-Minute Meeting Preparations. There may be times when you must personally visit the meeting room just before the start of the meeting to ensure that everything has been provided and that the attendees will be comfortable. You may want to call the representative of the

---

THE CHICAGO MEDICAL SOCIETY

Agenda

Monthly Meeting

Tuesday, October 7, 20-- - 8:00 p.m.

University Hospital, Room 254C

1. Call to order

2. Reading of minutes of previous meeting (approved or changed)

3. Reading of correspondence

4. Reading of treasurer's report

5. Old business

    a. Choice of dates for state-level meeting for next year

    b. Arrangements for meeting room for monthly meetings

6. New business

    a. Reviewing plan for increasing membership

    b. Voting on increase of membership dues

7. Program: Thang Huai, MD, Urban Hospital Medical Center, Department of Oncology, "The Patient's Informed Decision About Radiation and/or Chemotherapy Treatment"

8. Announcements

9. Adjournment

FIGURE 11.4

Meeting Agenda

facility with whom you have dealt and ask that person to be available when you visit the meeting room. If food or other refreshments will be served, it is also a good idea to confirm the times of service and what is to be served. Be sure to check the meeting room for the following:

- Appropriate temperature.
- Correct number of chairs.
- Audiovisual and electronic equipment requested and in working order.
- Lectern or table at the front of the room to accommodate the speaker and chairperson along with the microphone, if necessary.
- Notepads and pens for note taking.
- Pitchers of ice water and glasses.
- Name tags if required.
- Copies of the agenda for each attendee.

THE CHICAGO MEDICAL SOCIETY

Minutes

Monthly Meeting

Tuesday, October 7, 20--

The monthly meeting of the Chicago Medical Society was held on October 7, 20--, in Room 254C of the University Hospital. The meeting was called to order at 8:00 p.m. by Dr. Lee Wentworth.

The following members were present: Drs. Brian Cleary, Ernest Dodson, Jane Gunderson, Michael Pope, Yan Tuo, Lisa Twelvetrees, and Lee Wentworth.

The following members were absent: Drs. Roger Ahmed and Gloria Mahibir.

The reading of the minutes from the last meeting was waived.

The Treasurer reported that the Society's balance, as of October 1, 20--, was $1257.72. There is one outstanding bill of $175.43 payable to the University Hospital Catering Service. A motion was made, seconded, and unanimously passed to pay this bill.

The next matter of business was the announcement of dates during which the state-level meeting will be held. Dr. Wentworth reported that the meeting was scheduled for December 4, 20—.

Dr. Gunderson reported that the University Hospital had renewed its agreement with the Society to allow the Society to use Room 254C for two more years.

A committee was formed to study ways to increase membership and will meet on November 1, 20--. Dr. Twelvetrees volunteered to chair the committee, and Drs. Cleary and Dodson agreed to serve as committee members.

For this month's program, Dr. Thang Huai, Urban Hospital Medical Center, Department of Oncology, gave a talk entitled "The Patient's Informed Decision About Radiation and/or Chemotherapy Treatment." A copy of the presentation is attached.

A motion was made to increase membership dues by $100 for the next year. It was seconded and unanimously carried.

The meeting was adjourned at 9:45 p.m.

_____   _____
Recording Secretary   President

FIGURE 11.5 (a)

Example of Formal Minutes

You may also be called upon to greet the guests upon their arrival, and the physician may have requested that you remain so that you can record the minutes of the meeting.

Recording Minutes. The official record of the proceedings of a meeting is called the **meeting minutes.** Many meetings are conducted according to parliamentary procedure, and the minutes are then formatted in a formal way. Other meetings may proceed less formally. Minutes, therefore, may be formatted formally or informally, as shown in Figure 11.5 *(a)* and Figure 11.5 *(b)*. Whatever the appropriate format, certain information is always included:

- Name of the organization or society holding the meeting.
- Date, time, location of the meeting.
- Purpose of the meeting or indication that it is a monthly (quarterly, and so on) meeting.

```
MEMO TO:   Membership Committee of the
           Chicago Medical Society

FROM:      Lisa Twelvetrees, MD
           Committee Chair

DATE:      November 2, 20--

SUBJECT:   Minutes of the Membership Committee
           Meeting of November 1, 20--


Present:   Drs. Brian Cleary and Ernest Dodson

Absent:    None


1. Discussion of the Committee's objectives. The Committee will explore
   ways to increase membership in the Chicago Medical Society. The
   Committee set a goal of attracting ten new members for the next year.

2. Discussion of courses of action. The Committee discussed acquiring
   hospital mailing lists, sending an informational mailer to potential
   members, advertising in hospital bulletins, holding a hospitality
   evening for potential members, and offering incentives to current
   members who recruit new members.

3. Actions to be taken. Dr. Cleary agreed to research the cost of acquir-
   ing mailing lists and producing an informational mailer. Dr. Dodson
   agreed to get information on advertising and holding a hospitality
   evening. Dr. Twelvetrees agreed to speak with the Treasurer of the
   Society about incentives to current members for recruitment of new
   members. Committee members will report their findings at the next
   meeting of the Committee.

The next meeting of the Membership Committee will be held at 7:30 p.m.,
on December 6, 20--, at the office of Dr. Twelvetrees, University Hospital.

Lisa Twelvetrees, MD

rp


Distribution:

Dr. Brian Cleary
Dr. Ernest Dodson
Dr. Lee Wentworth
```

FIGURE 11.5 *(b)*

Example of Informal Minutes

- Name of the presiding officer.
- Names of the members in attendance and absent.
- Order of business as it is taken up and any departures from the order as shown in the agenda.
- Motions made and whether these were approved or rejected. (Some organizations state the names of the people who motioned and who seconded.)
- Summaries of discussions.

At certain meetings, portions of the minutes may need to be verbatim, that is, exactly as spoken. When this is necessary, the meeting is often taped and later transcribed. However, this is not always necessary.

It is usual for most organizations to have a secretary, sometimes called the "recording secretary." It is this person's responsibility to record the minutes of every meeting. The secretary may request that you transcribe the minutes after the meeting. The minutes are signed by the secretary. Minutes are kept in an official book of minutes and are taken to every meeting.

In the secretary's absence, you may be requested to take the minutes. Be sure to familiarize yourself with the agenda, review the names of the attendees, and concentrate on the meeting. Sit next to the presiding officer if that is possible. Review and refer to the minutes of previous meetings. Do not hesitate to ask for clarification or the repetition of a point if you are unclear about what was said.

GO TO PROJECT 11.3 ON PAGE 298

11.4 INFORMATION AND EDUCATION

Information intended to educate patients about the practice and about their own health care is offered in many formats: brochures, fact sheets, and newsletters. Videotapes, CD-ROMs, and in-person seminars are also used. It may be that the practice in which you are employed has a Web site. In this case, you may work with a Web designer to add pages and to update the site.

Information important to employees is often gathered in an office policies and procedures manual. It contains key procedures about office operation.

■ Patient Information Brochure

A **patient information brochure,** or booklet, provides the patient with vital information that is particularly useful because it is in writing and can be kept in a convenient place in the patient's home. However, the brochure does not take the place of a personal orientation for new patients.

Deciding on the contents of the brochure is the first step that must be taken. Topics to be considered include:

- A description of the services offered by the practice, including special classes and medical testing programs.
- A list of physicians' names, specialties, and qualifications.
- The names, functions, and office telephone numbers of the members of the office staff.
- Instructions for scheduling appointments. Be sure to list office hours and to provide patients with instructions for emergencies, such as: "Use 911 in life-threatening emergencies." Inform patients if the office has a 24-hour telephone service for emergency situations.
- Policies and procedures related to physicians' fees and payment, prescription refills, and medical insurance forms.
- A statement of any other policies that are relevant and that you may be directed to include, such as a statement of patient confidentiality.
- A brief section expressing gratitude to patients for choosing the practice and for taking the time to read about the practice and the services it provides. Include a statement such as: "If you have any questions about our clinic, please telephone us at [phone number] or e-mail us at [address]."

■ Patient Education Materials

In some practices, depending on the size, specialties, and resources available, there may be the opportunity to provide other **patient education materials:** for example, descriptions of frequently ordered testing and surgical procedures along with an account of the restrictions on diet or activity that the procedures impose. A list of resources—agencies, CD-ROMs, Internet sites, specialized libraries in the area—may also be useful to patients. A list of preventive actions or "tips," intended to promote good health, may also be provided: getting regular checkups; limiting alcohol consumption; exercising regularly; avoiding tobacco; reducing stress, for example. Providing a list of safety tips for avoiding injury at home and at work may also be appreciated.

■ Design Considerations

In many offices, the brochure is developed using a desktop publishing program. In others, this job is given to an outside resource.

There are many local businesses that specialize in designing and printing brochures, information sheets, and booklets. You will need to make clear to the professional who is assisting you the basic specifications of the piece you wish to create: length, quality of paper, two-color (black ink and one other color for contrast) or full color. In addition, you will want to give the designer a sense of how you want the piece to look: visual appeal, use of photographs, white (blank) space to make it easy to read. If you have friends who work in other practices, it would help you to evaluate the patient information brochures developed in their offices. This assessment will clarify for you the features you find effective. If this is not possible, you may cut out visually appealing magazine articles to show the designer.

In addition to design considerations, there are issues of ease of understanding to be addressed. Whether you or a professional writer creates the text, it must be easy to understand. The use of technical words should be minimal. In some areas, the brochure may need to be written both in English and in one or more other languages.

■ Policies and Procedures Manual

The **policies and procedures manual,** or employee handbook, is the reference that provides all employees with information about the work environment. Because employees are likely to refer to the manual often, it needs to be kept current and complete. The manual serves as a reminder of tasks to be done and the procedures for doing them. During the office manager's temporary absence due to illness or vacation, the manual helps keep the office running smoothly. It is a great help in training new employees, substitutes, or successors.

Format. A looseleaf binder with tab divisions is an ideal holder for a policies and procedures manual. Pages may easily be added or taken out. New topics only require additional tabs, inserted in a logical place. The only other format that offers as much flexibility is the computer. An electronic format, using the word processing program, would be easy to establish. Copies could be sent to each employee using e-mail. Updates, or instructions about deletions, could be sent the same way. It is important that every page be dated so that the most recent update is easily identifiable.

Contents. Prepare an outline of topics that must be covered. The following suggestions for topics and the order of presentation will not address every situation. However, certain topics are common to almost all practices.

- *Office personnel directory:* This directory should contain the names, positions, physical locations, and telephone or extension numbers, cell phone numbers, and pager numbers of everyone in the office along with the numbers for building services, such as maintenance and security.
- *Job descriptions:* This section lists the major responsibilities and duties of all employees other than the physicians; for example, administrative medical assistants, clerks, receptionist, technicians, and billing specialists. A list of the names of the people currently

holding the positions is often included, along with the name and telephone number of a person to be contacted in case of emergency for each employee. Home addresses and telephone numbers are sometimes also given. Either in this section or in a separate section dealing with procedures, descriptions of how to perform the duties of the position are given. If job duties overlap, or if employees are expected to substitute for each other in case of absence or illness, that should be stated in this section of the manual.

- *Procedures:* Once the duties of the positions have been specified, a section on specific procedures may follow. Appropriate forms may be included with the procedures for which they are used. Figure 11.6 *(a)* and Figure 11.6 *(b)* on pages 292 and 293 show pages designed to describe procedures. Below are examples of entries for the procedures section of the manual:

Daily Routine

1. List the duties to be performed to prepare the office each morning before patients arrive. These include checking the neatness and cleanliness of the office; calling the answering service or checking the answering machine for messages; checking e-mail communications; processing incoming and/or outgoing mail; pulling charts for the day's appointments; preparing the appointment schedule; and checking to see that the examination rooms are ready to be used.
2. List other routine duties, including preparing correspondence and patient records, maintaining financial records, and completing insurance forms.
3. List the duties that must be done at the end of the day: locking desks and files, turning off and covering certain equipment, and programming the answering machine for after-hours calls.

Filing

1. Describe the filing method used, and provide a diagram, if necessary, of the locations of sections—active, inactive, closed, transient.
2. Indicate the length of time for keeping records in active files.
3. If colors are used as a filing aid, explain what each color designates.
4. Describe the preferred order of documents in the patients' medical records, including medication sheets, progress notes, laboratory reports, x-ray reports, special procedures notes, correspondence, and hospital summaries.
5. List the types of medical reports that must be attached to a patient's chart before a physician reviews the chart.
6. Describe follow-up procedures for test results.

Transferring Patients' Records

1. State which staff member is responsible for handling the transfer.
2. List the rules for what can and cannot be transferred.
3. Describe the procedures for copying records to be transferred.

FIGURE 11.6 *(a)*

Page From a Procedures Manual Showing Form for Describing Administrative Procedures

---

Section 4: HANDLING RECORDS

PATIENTS WHO HAVE MOVED

Procedure:

DECEASED PATIENTS

Procedure:

TRANSFER OF RECORDS

Procedure:

SUPERVISION OF FILING SYSTEM

Procedure:

---

4. Describe the procedures for faxing records to be transferred.
5. Describe the procedure for recording when and what information was transferred.
6. Describe the procedure for filing the release-of-information form.

Scheduling Appointments

1. List the schedule commitments for each physician, including office hours, hospital hours, and teaching or research schedule.
2. Note which physicians have special scheduling requests, such as limiting the number of physical examinations to no more than two in the morning or scheduling no physical examinations on Monday mornings or Friday afternoons.
3. List the procedure for canceling and rescheduling appointments, including whether or not patients are called on the day before the appointment for confirmation.

COMMONLY PERFORMED PROCEDURES

NAME OF PROCEDURE _____

USUAL TIME REQUIREMENT _____

SUPPLIES AND INSTRUMENTS:

PATIENT PREPARATION:

SPECIAL INSTRUCTIONS:

4. List the information required from patients for scheduling an appointment.
5. List the standard length of time required for various procedures, such as one hour for a complete physical examination, one-half hour for school physicals, and so forth.

Orientation for New Patients
1. Describe the information to be provided to new patients, including office hours and emergency care procedures.
2. List hospitals affiliated with the practice and their addresses, telephone numbers, and visiting hours.
3. Describe the procedures for obtaining medication refills.

Telephone Procedures
1. Give the preferred greeting for answering the telephone.
2. Explain the triage procedure, covering what calls should be put through to the physician.

3. List the ways in which questions should be phrased when obtaining information about patients over the phone.

4. Provide suggestions for referring a patient to a physician on call, to the hospital emergency room, to another facility, or to sources of financial assistance.

Patient Care

This section may be the most significant portion of the manual, covering everything from the level of the interpersonal skills expected of the office staff to the specific ways to perform a variety of procedures.

Billing

1. Provide a sample patient statement, and explain the method of billing.

2. Note the name, address, and telephone number of any accounting service that is used.

3. If there is a billing specialist in the practice, state the procedures for transferring information.

Collections

1. State and explain the steps established by the practice in the standard collection process.

2. Show sample collection letters, and provide a sample of the form used to track the collection process for a patient.

Processing Insurance Forms

1. Provide detailed instructions for handling each insurance account, for completing each type of form, and for billing patients who have insurance.

2. For each insurance carrier, provide the name of a contact person, the address of the company, and a telephone number.

3. List the approximate turnaround time for processing claims for each insurance carrier.

Forms and Supplies

If samples of forms, with instructions for completing them, have not been included in topical sections, a separate section should be used to familiarize employees with all of the forms used in the practice.

Equipment

Include an inventory of all office equipment. It is also useful to list model and registration numbers of equipment. List the names, addresses, and phone numbers of equipment manufacturers, dealers, and local repair services.

Inventory and Ordering Procedures

1. Describe the rules for taking inventory and reporting on inventory levels. Include the required time line for taking inventory, for example, every week.

2. State who is responsible for certain kinds of inventory. Nursing personnel may be responsible for medications, drugs, surgical gloves,

and examination supplies. Assistants may be responsible for desk and stationery supplies and maintenance supplies. Certain items, such as linens—laboratory coats, examination gowns, and towels—may be the property of the practice or may be rented from a linen supply company. Be sure to address how the linen supply is handled.

3. Provide the forms for ordering supplies and directions for completing them.

Employee Hiring Policies

1. Include a statement of nondiscrimination in hiring.
2. Describe hiring procedures, and indicate whose responsibility it is to interview and to recommend hiring for specific positions.

Employee Evaluation Policies

1. Indicate how often employees are evaluated, and explain the process used.
2. Define the rating system, if one is used, and the relationship of ratings to the amount of salary increase.
3. Include a copy of the blank appraisal form.
4. Describe the procedures related to unsatisfactory performance and the steps leading to job probation and/or termination of employment.
5. Describe the grievance or arbitration procedure in place that employees may need to use if they have a serious complaint.

Employee Benefits Policies

1. State the rules regarding vacations, sick days, personal leaves, and the reporting of sickness or absence.
2. Describe the insurance benefits and the options employees may choose.
3. Describe any savings plans or 401-K plans in place for employees.

Office Dress Code

State the rules related to professional dress established in the practice.

Meeting Schedule

1. List the dates or days of staff meetings and committee meetings established in the office.
2. For each committee, list the members and the purposes of the committee.
3. Describe the role and responsibilities or degree of involvement of the physician with each committee.

Maintenance, Safety, and Office Security

1. Describe the schedule of building maintenance along with the names and telephone numbers of the building maintenance staff or of the janitorial service with which the practice has a contract.
2. If the office staff has specific duties to help keep the office clean and tidy, describe the duties and who is to handle these.
3. The guidelines for office safety should be listed.

4. Describe how building security works: requirements for identification badges and the security system itself—locks, alarms, and so forth. Include the rules for keeping doors locked or using buzzers for admittance. Provide the names of the security staff and their work telephone numbers. Include in this section reminders about securing personal property and demanding proper identification of strangers in the building.

Outside Services File

In addition to referring patients to other physicians, every physician must at times refer patients to agencies or businesses for help of various kinds, including health services and medical supplies. The policies and procedures manual should include an **outside services file** containing the names, addresses, and phone numbers of those to whom the physician may refer patients for services such as:

- Convalescent and nursing homes.
- Dentists and dental specialists.
- Health insurance organizations.
- Home health care agencies and hospices.
- Laboratories.
- Medical specialists for referrals.
- Pharmacies.
- Medical supply companies.
- Social services agencies.
- Human services agencies.
- Temporary agencies for staffing of medical personnel.
- Web site addresses of search engines and sites in your city that provide additional service.

■ Responsibility for Records

As office manager, the assistant may be responsible for the supervision of other staff members and for keeping records relating to their employment. Each employee will have a separate file containing information such as an application form and cover letter, résumé, letter of employment agreement, performance evaluations, and attendance record. These are confidential records and are stored in a locked drawer.

Each physician will want to keep in a personal file additional information regarding licenses—state license, narcotics license, workers' compensation registration, for example. Social security information as well as insurance identification numbers should also be kept in this file. A file listing the physician's affiliations with medical societies, organizations, and hospitals is kept along with a list of continuing education requirements. A list should be kept, related to these files, that contains license and membership renewal dates, fees, and any necessary identifying numbers.

It can easily be seen by the extensive list of topics to be covered in the office policies and procedures manual that the assistant serving as office manager has an enormous amount of responsibility. Even though it is difficult to keep the manual current, the manual can be an extraordinarily useful tool. It makes the task of managing both daily routines and personnel less problematic. The routines are made explicit and directions are given for handling daily tasks. Staff members are able to understand thoroughly their job responsibilities. This knowledge, in turn, helps them to understand the expectations that managers have of them.

Another really useful tool is the computer. The information available on the Internet is a great help. There are a number of search engines designed to assist in locating services, articles and books required for physician's research, travel directions, medical organizations and societies, and contact information on companies and professionals.

Also, standard printed references and resources should be available in every office, including dictionaries (standard and medical); a thesaurus; English language usage references to provide formatting instructions, grammar rules, and writing style guidelines; drug references to provide information on medications, such as brand and generic names, manufacturers, and dosages; state and local medical directories to provide credential information about medical personnel, correct spelling of names, office addresses, and telephone numbers.

Chapter Projects

PROJECT 11.1 Internet Research: Qualifications for Office Management

At the Web site for the American Association of Medical Assistants (AAMA), www.aama-ntl.org, there is a feature on the home page under "Medical Assisting & CMAs" called "Profiles of CMAs" (Certified Medical Assistants). Click this feature and read one or two profiles. Make a list of the qualifications, qualities, and experience required for the position of a Certified Medical Assistant based on the profiles you have read. Be prepared to discuss your list in class.

PROJECT 11.2 Internet Research: Journal Articles

Dr. Larsen has asked you to search the Internet for recent articles (within the last year) on chickenpox (varicella) or mumps (parotiditis). Write a short summary of the articles you locate, including bibliographical data.

PROJECT 11.3 Internet Research: Improving Office Management Skills

It is important to have some good resources for informational and motivational articles. Using your favorite Web browser, find articles on time management, prioritizing, problem solving, initiative, strategic planning, and leadership. Choose at least three articles, and summarize the content. Be prepared to discuss your reading in class.

CHAPTER SUMMARY

1. Three qualifications required for office management are being a team player (contributing generously to getting the work done, giving credit to others, and understanding that the social relationships in the office are very important), planning strategically (looking beyond the immediate assignment to understand how to contribute to the overall improvement of the practice), and increasing productivity (completing tasks more efficiently so as to actually increase the output of work).

2. Four office management tasks are helping with editorial research projects; making travel and meeting arrangements; evaluating, updating, and distributing patient information materials; and creating and maintaining an office policies and procedures manual.

3. Two guidelines for making travel arrangements are to meet with the physician well before the scheduled travel and to use a good travel agent from a reliable travel agency.

4. In preparing for a meeting, the assistant must make sure the room is large enough to accommodate the group. Food and beverage service must be arranged. The speaker's agreement to attend must be acknowledged, and the agenda and an invitation must be prepared and mailed to attendees.

5. Topics that should be covered in a patient information brochure are physicians' names, specialties, and credentials; a description of the services the practice offers; the names, functions, and office telephone numbers of staff members; procedures for scheduling appointments; and policies concerning fees and payment, prescription refills, and insurance forms.

6. The policies and procedures manual is an important resource because it gives employees a clear idea of job responsibilities and of how to perform daily tasks. It thus makes managing the daily office routine less problematic.

KEY TERMS

The following key terms appear in **boldface** type in this chapter. Administrative medical assistants must know the meaning and the correct use of each of these terms. Can you recall what each term means? Refer to this chapter or to the glossary for any terms you need to review.

agenda

itinerary

management qualifications

meeting minutes

outside services file

patient education materials

patient information brochure

policies and procedures manual

reprints

travel agent

THINKING IT THROUGH

These questions cover the most important points in this chapter. Using your critical thinking skills, play the role of an administrative medical assistant as you answer each question. Be prepared to present your responses in class.

1. In the following situation, show how you use these three qualifications for office management—being a team player, planning strategically, and increasing productivity: There are three physicians in the practice where you are employed. Each physician has an administrative medical assistant and a technician, and there is an office receptionist. As office manager, you have just received approval to present a proposal for purchasing new waiting room furniture. How will you use your office management skills to handle this task?

2. Of the four main office management tasks discussed in this chapter, which one appeals to you most? Which task has the least appeal? Discuss reasons for your answers.

3. What are several things you can do to ensure that the physician's travel is as pleasant as possible?

4. The physician who is your employer is responsible for the next meeting of the local chapter of a professional association. What are three major tasks you must accomplish in making the arrangements for this meeting?

5. Prepare a rough draft outline—major points only—for a patient information brochure.

6. Several staff members have asked you why the office policies and procedures manual is such an important document. What is your response?

SIMULATION 3

Today you will begin the third simulation in Dr. Larsen's office. The simulation dates are Monday, October 27; Tuesday, October 28; and Wednesday, October 29.

PROCEDURES

Review the section "Before You Start" in Simulation 1. Note that these procedures also apply to this simulation. Also review the "Procedures," because they apply to this simulation. Pull the patients' charts following the appointment calendar, and put them in the appropriate day folder.

MATERIALS

You will need the following materials to complete Simulation 3. If these materials are not already in the proper folder, obtain them from the sources indicated.

Materials	Source
Appointment calendar	
Diagnostic codes	WP 48
Fee Schedule	WP 50
Supplies folder	

To-Do Items

Day 1 folder:

Place patients' charts for October 27.

Telephone log	WP 74
To-do list	WP 75
Patient encounter forms	WP 76–80
Checks received	WP 81
Daily journal #106	WP 82

Day 2 folder:

Place patients' charts for October 28.

Patient encounter forms	WP 83–85
Checks received	WP 86
Daily journal #107	WP 87

Day 3 folder:

Place patients' charts for October 29.

Patient encounter forms	WP 88–93
Checks received	WP 94
Daily journal #108	WP 95

Patients' folders:

The following items have been added to the patients' folders since the last simulation.

Patient statements for all current patients	(Project 10.1, 10.4)

MEDICAL VOCABULARY

Before working through this simulation's assignments, review the following terms to be familiar with their spelling and meaning.

amoxicillin—antibiotic

ASCVD—arteriosclerotic cardiovascular disease

audiogram—graphic record of hearing results

Augmentin—anti-infective agent

cerumen—earwax

Cortisporin otic—ophthalmic anti-infective agent

costochondral—relating to costal cartilages

creatinine—lab test to diagnose impaired renal function

CVA—costovertebral angle

D&C—dilation (dilatation) and curettage

dentition—natural teeth

dorsalis pedis pulse—pulse in the foot

DTRs—deep tendon reflexes

dyspepsia—gastric indigestion

endocervical—within any cervix

fetor—offensive odor

gravida—number of pregnancies

hepatosplenomegaly—enlargement of liver and spleen

hyperlipidemia—abnormal large amount of lipids in blood

iliac—relating to ilium (broad portion of hip bone)

Lotrisone—antifungal

malaise—general discomfort or uneasiness

malar—relating to the cheek or cheekbone

malleolus—rounded bony prominence such as on side of ankle joint

menometrorrhagia—irregular or excessive bleeding during menstruation and between menstrual periods

Midrin—antipyretic agent

osteoarthritis—degenerative joint disease

para—number of births

popliteal pulse—pulse behind the knee

retro-ocular—behind the eyeball

rhinorrhea—discharge from nose

RTC—return to clinic

scoliosis—lateral curvature of the spine

Septra DS—anti-infective agent

suboccipital—relating to below the back of head

thyromegaly—enlargement of thyroid gland

TIA—transient ischemic attack

TM—tympanic membrane

NDCmedisoft™ INSTRUCTIONS

If your instructor has assigned the use of NDCmedisoft™, you will complete certain parts of Simulation 3 using the software program. Follow these instructions:

To complete this simulation in NDCmedisoft™, you must be able to:

- Schedule appointments
- Print physician's schedule
- Enter charges
- Enter payments
- Print walkout receipts
- Print patient statements
- Print patient day sheets

Enter the new appointments in Office Hours. Then print Dr. Larsen's schedule for October 27, 28, and 29.

Enter all charge and payment transactions. Print walkout receipts for patients who made a payment.

Print patient statements for all patients who had transactions on October 27, 28, and 29.

Print patient day sheet reports for October 27, 28, and 29.

Introduction to NDCmedisoft™

NDCmedisoft™ is a widely used patient accounting program for medical offices. In this text you are studying the administrative tasks of the medical assistant. When you work as an administrative medical assistant, it is likely that you will encounter some sort of patient accounting software. The NDCmedisoft™ program includes the basic operations of all patient accounting software programs. Familiarizing yourself with NDCmedisoft™ will enable you to learn almost any similar software in a very brief period of time.

■ The Student Data Disk

Before a medical office begins using NDCmedisoft™, basic information about the practice and its patients must be entered in the computer. This preliminary work has been done for you. Dr. Karen Larsen's practice information is stored in a backup file on the Student Data Disk located inside the cover of this text. The backup file contains all the data you will need to complete the NDCmedisoft™ projects and simulations in the text.

Before restoring the backup file from the Student Data Disk, follow the instructions below to make a working copy of the disk, so that the original copy can be kept separately in a safe place.

Making a Copy of the Student Data Disk

1. Turn on the computer and monitor.
2. After the Windows desktop is displayed, insert the Student Data Disk into the floppy drive (A:).
3. Click on the Start button on the taskbar, and then click on the My Computer icon. (In earlier versions of Windows, the My Computer icon is located on the desktop itself.) The My Computer window is displayed.
4. Click the icon labeled 3 1/2 Floppy (A:). Then, on the File menu, select Copy Disk.

TIP

Note that the Student Data Disk is supplied in both floppy disk and CD format. For example's sake, the instructions here assume the use of the floppy disk. If you are using the CD, ask your instructor for guidance in substituting these instructions with those specific to your computer's setup.

5. The Copy Disk window appears. Click Start to begin the disk copying process.

6. The computer begins reading the files on the source disk. You can monitor the computer's progress by viewing the bar above the words "Reading source disk."

7. When the system prompts you to insert the disk you want to copy to (the destination disk), eject the Student Data Disk from the drive.

8. Insert a blank disk in the floppy drive, and click the OK button. The files are copied to the destination disk.

9. When the copy is completed, the message "Copy completed successfully" is displayed. Eject the disk from the drive, and label it "Working Copy KLarsen." Store the original disk in a safe place.

10. Close the Copy Disk dialog box.

11. Close the My Computer dialog box.

Starting NDCmedisoft™ and Restoring the Backup File

The following instructions take you through the steps of starting the NDCmedisoft™ program the first time the program is used with this text. These steps start the program, create a new directory and data set name for the Karen Larsen MD files, and restore the backup file to the new directory.

1. While holding down the F7 key, use the Start menu on the Windows desktop to start the NDCmedisoft™ program as follows: Click Start, Programs, NDCmedisoft™, NDCmedisoft™ Advanced

Patient Accounting. When the Find NDCmedisoft™ Database dialog box appears, release the F7 key. This dialog box asks you to enter the NDCmedisoft™ data directory.

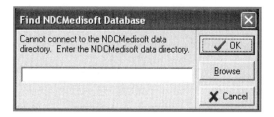

2. Click inside the white data entry box to make it active. Then key C:\MediData in the space provided. The dialog box should now look like this:

Find NDCMedisoft Database

Cannot connect to the NDCMedisoft data directory. Enter the NDCMedisoft data directory.

✓ OK

C:\MediData

Browse

✗ Cancel

3. Click the OK button. An Information dialog box appears with the following message: "This is not an existing root data directory. Do you want to create a new one?"

4. Click Yes.

   (*Note:* If a Warning box appears with information about registering the program, click the Register Later button.) The Create Data dialog box is displayed.

Create Data

Do you want to

Create a <u>n</u>ew set of data

<u>C</u>onvert existing NDCMedisoft Data

☐ <u>A</u>dd tutorial data to list

✗ Cancel

5. Click the Create a New Set of Data button. The Create a New Set of Data dialog box appears. In the upper box, key *Karen Larsen MD.* In the lower box, key *KLarsen.* The dialog box should now look like this:

Create a new set of data

Enter the practice or doctor's name to identify this set of data:

Karen Larsen MD

Enter the data path:

C:\MediData\ KLarsen

Browse

✓ C<u>r</u>eate

✗ Cancel

⚙ <u>H</u>elp

6. Click the Create button. A Confirm dialog box is displayed.

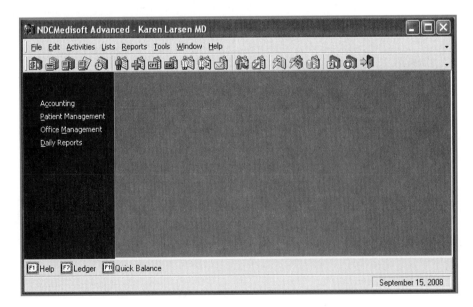

7. Click the Yes button. The Practice Information dialog box appears. In the Practice Name box, key *Karen Larsen MD*. Leave the remaining boxes blank. The dialog box should now look like this:

8. Click the Save button. The main window of the NDCmedisoft™ program is displayed, with the new practice name, Karen Larsen MD, on the title bar. Your screen should look like this:

9. Insert the working copy of the Student Data Disk in the floppy drive (A:). (*Note:* If your computer uses a different letter to represent the floppy drive, or if you are using the CD, substitute the appropriate drive name for A: whenever it appears in these instructions.)
10. Open the File menu, and locate the Restore Data option.
11. Click Restore Data. A Warning dialog box is displayed.

12. Click the OK button. The Restore dialog box is displayed. In the top box, key *A:\KLarsen.mbk* if it is not already displayed. The dialog box should now look like this:

13. Click the Start Restore button. A Confirm dialog box is displayed.

14. Click the OK button. After the program restores the database to the hard drive, an Information dialog box is displayed, indicating that the restore is complete. Click OK.
15. You are returned to the main NDCmedisoft™ window. To open the newly restored data, open the File menu and locate the Open Practice option.

16. Click Open Practice. The Open Practice dialog box is displayed, with the Karen Larsen MD practice name listed.

Open Practice

Karen Larsen MD

- ✓ OK
- ✗ Cancel
- New
- Delete
- Add Tutorial
- Help

17. To open the database files for Karen Larsen MD, click the OK button.
18. The database is now ready for use. (*Hint:* If the main NDCmedisoft™ window does not fill the screen, click the Maximize button to expand it.)
19. To verify that the data has been restored from the Student Data Disk, click Practice Information on the File menu. The Practice Information dialog box should now look like this:

Practice Information

Practice | Billing Service

Practice Name: Karen Larsen, M.D.
Street: 2235 South Ridgeway Avenue

City: Chicago   State: IL
Zip Code: 60623-2240

Phone: (312)555-6022   Extension:
Fax Phone: (312)555-0025
Type: Medical
Federal Tax ID: 99-552340

Extra 1:
Extra 2:

- Save
- ✗ Cancel
- Help

20. Close the Practice Information dialog box.
21. By default, the NDCmedisoft™ displays a sidebar with four options on the left side of the window. As the sidebar is not required for this text, open the Window menu and click the Show Side Bar option to toggle it off.

Note: The NDCmedisoft™ program is designed to open whatever data set it used during the previous session. Therefore, from this point on, when the program is started from the Windows desktop, either by double-clicking the program icon or through the Start menu, the required data set will load automatically.

Backup Procedures

Backing Up Data

By default, whenever the Exit button on the toolbar or the Exit option on the File menu is selected, NDCmedisoft™ displays the Backup Reminder dialog box. This box reminds the user to back up the currently active data set before exiting the program. Other options in the Backup Reminder dialog box include exiting the NDCmedisoft™ program without backing up the data and canceling the Exit command and returning to the main NDCmedisoft™ window.

While working through the NDCmedisoft™ projects in *Medical Office Procedures, always* select the Back Up Data Now option to back up your work to the Student Data Disk whenever you exit the program. The backup procedure is as follows.

1. To end the current session, click the Exit button on the toolbar (the last button on the right) or click Exit on the File menu.
2. The Backup Reminder dialog box appears.

For the purposes of this text, it is recommended that you back up your work to your working copy of the Student Data Disk each time you exit the program. The current backup file will overwrite the previous backup file (A:\KLarsen.mbk) on the disk. To begin the backup, make sure your working copy of the Student Data Disk is inserted in the A: drive. Click the Back Up Data Now button.

3. The Backup dialog box is displayed. Depending on the last time the dialog box was accessed, the Destination File Path and Name box at the top may already contain the entry A:\KLarsen.mbk. If the box is blank, or if it contains something other than this, key *A:\KLarsen.mbk* in the Destination File Path and Name box.

Backup ☒

Destination File Path and Name
A:\KLarsen.mbk   Find

Existing Backup Files
KLarsen.mbk

Password:

Source Path
C:\MediData\KLarsen\   Start Backup

Backup Progress
0%   Close

File Progress
0%   Help

4. NDCmedisoft™ displays the location of the database files to be backed up in the Source Path box in the lower half of the dialog box automatically (C:\MediData\KLarsen). Click the Start Backup button.
5. The program backs up the latest database files to the disk in drive A: and displays an Information dialog box indicating the backup is complete. Click OK to continue.
6. The Backup dialog box disappears, and the NDCmedisoft™ program closes.

If you are not sharing a computer with other students, the backup file serves as an extra copy of your work for safekeeping in the event the data on the hard drive is inadvertently erased or altered, or in the event of a hard disk failure. As in most offices, the extra time it takes to make a backup copy in a medical office can save countless hours later.

If you are sharing a computer with other students, the backup file serves an additional purpose. You will use the backup file to restore your work when you begin the next NDCmedisoft™ session. The steps required to perform a restore are as follows.

Restoring Data

If you are sharing a computer in an instructional environment, you must perform a restore before each new NDCmedisoft™ session to be certain you are working with your own data. The following steps are used to restore the latest data on the backup file.

To restore A:\KLarsen.mbk to C:\MediData\KLarsen:

1. Start NDCmedisoft™.

2. Check the program's title bar at the top of the screen to make sure the Karen Larsen MD data set is the active data set. (If it is not, use the Open Practice option on the File menu to select it.)
3. Insert your working copy of the Student Data Disk in Drive A:.
4. Open the File menu and click Restore Data.
5. When the Warning box appears, click OK.
6. The Restore dialog box appears.

7. In the Backup File Path and Name box at the top of the dialog box, the following filename should already be displayed—A:\KLarsen.mbk. (If it is not, key it now).
8. The Destination Path at the bottom of the box should already say C:\MediData\KLarsen. Leave this as it is.
9. Click the Start Restore button.
10. When the Confirm box appears, click OK.
11. An Information dialog box appears, indicating the restore is complete. Click OK to continue.
12. The Restore dialog box disappears. The latest data has been restored for the next session.

■ NDCmedisoft™ Menus

NDCmedisoft™ offers choices of actions through a series of menus. Commands are issued by clicking an option on the menu bar or by clicking a shortcut button on the toolbar. All data, whether a patient's address or a charge for a procedure, is entered into NDCmedisoft™ through the menus on the menu bar or through the buttons on the toolbar. Selecting an option from the menus or toolbar brings up a dialog box. The Tab key is used to move between text boxes within a dialog box.

File

Open Practice...
New Practice...
Convert Data...

Backup Data...
Backup Scheduler..
View Backup Disks...
Restore Data...

Set Program Date
Practice Information...
Program Options...
Security Setup...

File Maintenance...

Exit   Alt+F4

Edit

Cut
Copy
Paste

Delete

Activities

Enter Transactions
Claim Management
Statement Management
Enter Deposits/Payments

Quick Ledger   F7
Quick Balance   F11

Billing Charges...

Appointment Book
Eligibility Verification...
Credit Card Management...

Lists

Patients/Guarantors and Cases
Patient Recall
Patient Treatment Plans

Procedure/Payment/Adjustment Codes
MultiLink Codes
Diagnosis Codes

Insurance Carriers
Addresses
EDI Receivers
Referring Providers
Providers

Billing Codes
Contact List
Eligibility List

The menu bar lists the names of the menus in NDCmedisoft™: File, Edit, Activities, Lists, Reports, Tools, Window, and Help. Beneath each menu name is a pull-down menu of one or more options.

File Menu. The File menu is used to enter information about the medical office practice when first setting up NDCmedisoft™ (see Figure A.1). It is also used to back up data, maintain files, and set program options.

Edit Menu. The Edit menu contains the basic commands needed to move, change, or delete information (see Figure A.2). These commands are Cut, Copy, Paste, and Delete.

Activities Menu. Most medical office data collected on a day-to-day basis is entered through options on the Activities menu (see Figure A.3). This menu is used to enter financial transactions, including charges and payments; to create insurance claims; and to manage patient statements. Office Hours, NDCmedisoft™'s built-in appointment book, is also accessed via the Activities menu.

Lists Menu. Information on new patients, such as name, address, and employer, is entered through the Lists menu (see Figure A.4). The Lists menu also provides access to lists of codes, insurance carriers, and providers.

Reports Menu. The Reports menu is used to print reports about patients' accounts and other reports about the practice (see Figure A.5).

Tools Menu. The calculator is accessed through the Tools menu (see Figure A.6). Other options on the Tools menu can also be used to view the contents of a file as well as a profile of the computer system.

Window Menu. Using the Window menu, it is possible to switch back and forth among several open windows (see Figure A.7).

Help Menu. The Help menu is used to access NDCmedisoft™'s Help feature (see Figure A.8).

Reports

Day Sheets
Analysis Reports
Aging Reports
Collection Reports
Audit Reports
Patient Ledger

Patient Statements...
Electronic Statements

Superbills...
Custom Report List...
Load Saved Reports...

Design Custom Reports and Bills...

Tools

Calculator
NDCMedisoft Terminal
View File...
Add/Copy User Reports...
Design Custom Patient Data...

Statement Wizard
Customize Menu Bars...
System Information...
Modem Check...

User Information

Window

Close All Windows
Minimize All Windows

Tile Windows Horizontally
Tile Windows Vertically

Show Side Bar   Ctrl+S

Clear Windows Positions
Clear Custom Grid Settings

Help

Table of Contents
How to Use Help
Getting Started
Upgraders from NDCMedisoft for DOS

NDCMedisoft on the Web

Online Updates

✓ Show Hints
✓ Show Shortcut Keys

About NDCMedisoft...

Dates in NDCmedisoft™

NDCmedisoft™ is a date-sensitive program. The dates set in NDCmedisoft™ must be accurate, or the data entered will be of little value to the practice. Many times in medical offices date-sensitive information is not entered into NDCmedisoft™ on the same day that the event or transaction occurs. For example, Friday's office visits may not be entered into NDCmedisoft™ until Monday. If the program date is not changed to Friday's date before entering the data, all the information entered on Monday will be associated with Monday's date. For this reason, it is important to know how to change the NDCmedisoft™ Program Date.

For most of the exercises in this book, you will need to change the NDCmedisoft™ Program Date to the date specified in the project or simulation. The following steps are used to change the NDCmedisoft™ Program Date:

1. Click the Set Program Date on the File menu, or click the date displayed on the status bar. A pop-up calendar is displayed.
2. Click the name of the month that is currently displayed. A pop-up menu appears. Click the desired month on the pop-up menu.
3. Select the desired year by clicking the year that is currently displayed. A pop-up menu appears. Click the desired year on the pop-up menu.
4. Select the desired date by clicking that date in the calendar.
5. The changes to the NDCmedisoft™ Program Date are automatically saved.

> ### Special Note on Office Hours Dates
> Office Hours, NDCmedisoft™'s scheduling program, uses the Windows System Date (the date set in your Windows operating system), not the NDCmedisoft™ Program Date. If you click the Go to Today button in Office Hours, the calendar will jump to the Windows date and not the NDCmedisoft™ date. For this reason, you will need to change the date in the Office Hours calendar regularly to correspond to the dates in the projects and simulations in this text.

In most NDCmedisoft™ dialog boxes, dates are entered in the MMDD CCYY format. The MMDDCCYY format is a specific way in which dates must be keyed. "MM" stands for the month, "DD" stands for the day, "CC" represents century, and "YY" stands for the year. Each day, month, century, and year entry must contain two digits, and no punctuation can be used. For example, the date of February 1, 2008, would be keyed "02012008."

Saving Data

Information entered into NDCmedisoft™ is saved by clicking the Save button that appears in most dialog boxes (those in which data is input).

Deleting Data

In most NDCmedisoft™ dialog boxes, there are buttons for the purpose of deleting data. Data can also be deleted by highlighting an entry or a transaction and then clicking the right mouse button. A shortcut menu is displayed that contains an option to delete the entry. NDCmedisoft™ will ask for confirmation before deleting the data.

Exiting NDCmedisoft™

NDCmedisoft™ is exited by clicking Exit on the File menu or by clicking the Exit button on the toolbar.

Using NDCmedisoft™ Help

NDCmedisoft™ offers users three different types of help.

Hints. As the cursor moves over certain fields, hints appear on the status bar at the bottom of the screen. The hints explain the purpose of the corresponding item.

Built-in Help. For more detailed help, NDCmedisoft™ has an extensive help feature built into the program itself, which is accessed through the Help menu.

Online Help. The Help menu also provides access to NDCmedisoft™ help available on the NDCmedisoft™ corporate Web site, www.medisoft.com. The Web site contains a searchable knowledge base, which is a collection of up-to-date technical information about NDCmedisoft™ products.

■ Entering Patient Information

Patient information is entered in the Patient/Guarantor dialog box. To access this dialog box, first the Patients/Guarantors and Cases option is clicked on the Lists menu. Clicking this option displays the Patient List dialog box, which contains a list of established patients. Information on a new patient is added by clicking the New Patient button at the bottom of the dialog box. When the New Patient button is clicked, the Patient/Guarantor dialog box appears. It contains two tabs for entering information on a new patient: the Name, Address tab and the Other Information tab.

Name, Address Tab

The Name, Address tab (see Figure A.9) is completed with information from a new Patient Information Form. Most of the information is demographic: name, address, e-mail, phone numbers, birth date, sex, and Social Security Number. Phone numbers must be entered without parentheses or hyphens. The birth date is entered using the MMDDCCYY format. The nine-digit Social Security Number should be entered with hyphens. Some of the boxes, such as the e-mail and cell phone number boxes, are optional.

Chart Number. The chart number is a unique number that identifies each patient. The most common method of assigning a number is to use the first five letters of the last name, the first two letters of the first name, and the digit 0, which represents the head of household, or guarantor, in the family. If additional family members are added to the database, the same chart number is used for each member, except that the final digit, 0, changes to 1, 2, 3, and so on. If the person's last name has fewer than five letters, use more letters of the first name and even letters of the middle name, if necessary.

Other Information Tab

The Other Information tab (see Figure A.10 on page 316) contains facts about a patient's employment and other miscellaneous information. The following are the major fields in the Other Information tab.

Type. The Type drop-down list designates whether, for billing purposes, an individual is a patient or guarantor. A guarantor is someone who is responsible for insurance and payment.

Assigned Provider. The code for the specific doctor who provides care to this patient is selected.

Signature on File. A check mark in a Signature on File check box means that the patient's signature is on file for the purpose of submitting insurance claims.

Signature Date. The date keyed in the Signature Date box is the date the patient signed the insurance release form.

Employer. The code for the patient's employer is selected from the drop-down list of employers that are in the database.

■ Cases

Information about a patient's insurance coverage, billing account, diagnosis, and condition are stored in cases. When a patient comes for treatment, a case is created. Cases are set up to contain the transactions that relate to a particular condition. For example, all treatments and procedures for bronchial asthma would be stored in a case called "Bronchial asthma."

Services performed and charges for those services are entered in the system linked to the bronchial asthma case.

In NDCmedisoft™, cases are created, edited, and deleted from within the Patient List dialog box. When the Case radio button in the Patient List dialog box is clicked, the following buttons appear at the bottom of the Patient List dialog box: Edit Case, New Case, Delete Case, Copy Case, Print Grid, and Close. These buttons perform their respective functions on cases. For example, to create a new case, the New Case button is clicked.

Entering Case Information

Information on a patient is entered in nine different tabs within the Case dialog box: Personal, Account, Diagnosis, Condition, Miscellaneous, Policy 1, Policy 2, Policy 3, and Medicaid and Tricare (see Figure A.11). After data is recorded in the appropriate tabs, it is stored by clicking the Save button on the right side of the dialog box.

FIGURE A.11

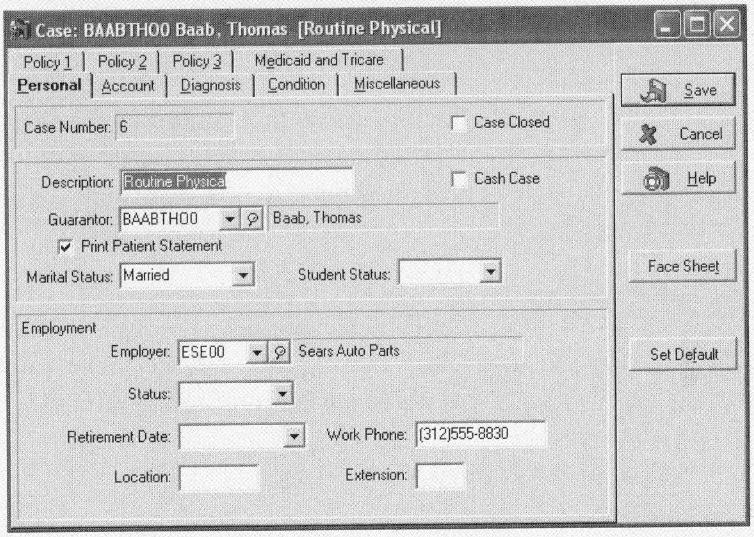

Personal Tab

The Personal tab contains basic information about a patient and his or her employment. The following are the most important boxes that must be completed in the Personal tab.

Description. Information entered in the Description box indicates a patient's complaint, or reason for seeing a physician.

Guarantor. The Guarantor box lists the name of the person responsible for paying the bill.

Account Tab

The Account tab includes information on a patient's assigned provider, referring provider, referral source, and other information that may be used in some medical practices but not others. The following is the most important box that must be completed in the Account tab.

Assigned Provider. The Assigned Provider box is automatically filled in with the code number and name of the assigned provider listed in the Patient/Guarantor dialog box.

Diagnosis Tab

The Diagnosis tab contains a patient's diagnosis, information about allergies, and electronic claim (EDI) notes. The following are the most important boxes that must be completed in the Diagnosis tab.

Default Diagnosis 1, 2, 3, and 4. A patient's diagnosis is selected from the drop-down list of diagnoses. If a patient has more than one diagnosis, the primary diagnosis is entered as diagnosis 1. Up to four diagnoses can be entered for each case.

Condition Tab

The Condition tab stores data about a patient's illness, accident, disability, and hospitalization. This information is used by insurance carriers to process claims.

Miscellaneous Tab

The Miscellaneous tab records a variety of miscellaneous information about the patient and his or her treatment, including outside lab work, prior authorization numbers, and other information.

Policy 1, 2, and 3 Tabs

The Policy tabs are where information about a patient's insurance carrier and coverage is recorded. If a patient has more than one insurance policy, the Policy 2 and 3 tabs are used. The following are the most important boxes that must be completed in the Policy tabs.

Insurance 1. The Insurance 1 box lists the code number and name of the insurance carrier.

Policy Holder 1. This box lists the person who is the policyholder for a particular policy. For example, if the patient is a child covered under his or her parent's insurance plan, the parent's chart number is entered in this box.

Relationship to Insured. This box describes a patient's relationship to the individual listed in the Insured 1 box.

Policy Number. The insurance policy number is entered in the Policy Number box.

Group Number. If there is a group number for the policy, it is entered in the Group Number box.

Assignment of Benefits/Accept Assignment. For physicians who are participating in an insurance plan, a check mark in this box indicates that the provider accepts payment directly from the insurance carrier.

Medicaid and Tricare Tab

For patients covered by Medicaid and Tricare, this tab is used to enter additional information about the government program.

■ Transaction Entry

Transactions are entered in the Transaction Entry dialog box, which is accessed by clicking Enter Transactions on the Activities menu (see Figure A.12). The Transaction Entry dialog box lists existing transactions—both charges and payments—and provides options for editing existing transactions as well as creating new transactions.

Entering Charges

To begin entering a new charge transaction, a patient's chart number is clicked on the drop-down list in the Chart box. After the chart number has been selected, the Case box displays a case number and description for a particular patient. If a patient has more than one open case, the drop-down list displays the full list of cases.

FIGURE A.12

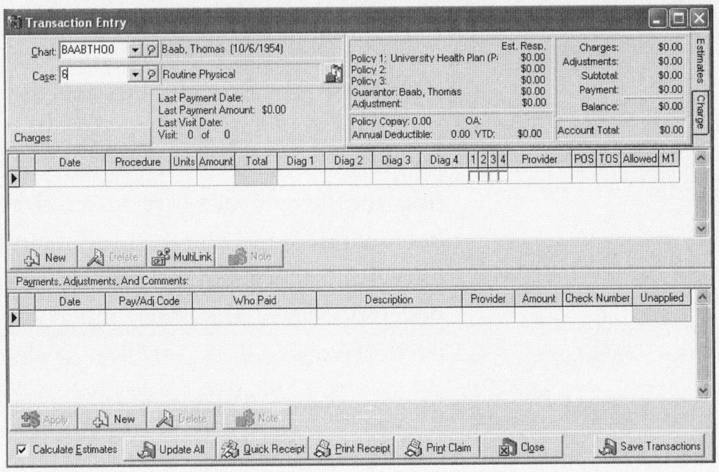

After the chart and case numbers have been entered, a new transaction is created by clicking the New button in the Charges section in the middle of the Transaction Entry dialog box.

Dates. When the New button is clicked, the program automatically enters the current date—that is, the NDCmedisoft™ Program Date—in the Date box. If this date is not the date the procedures were performed, the NDCmedisoft™ Program Date must be reset accordingly using the pop-up calendar inside the Date box. The date can also be changed by keying over the information that is already in the Date box. After the date is selected, the Tab key is pressed to move the cursor to the Procedure box.

Procedure. The procedure code for a service performed is selected from the drop-down list of CPT codes already entered in the system. Clicking inside the Procedure box displays a triangle button. When the triangle button is clicked, the drop-down list of procedure codes stored in the database is displayed. Only one procedure code can be selected for each transaction. If multiple procedures were performed for a patient, each one must be entered as a separate transaction.

After the CPT code is selected from the drop-down list and the Tab key is pressed, the charge for the procedure is displayed in the Amount box automatically.

Units. The Units box defaults to "1," but it can be changed if necessary.

Amount. The amount box lists the charge amount for a procedure performed. The amount is entered automatically once a CPT code is entered.

Total. This field displays the total charges for the procedures performed. The system multiples the number in the Units box by the number in the Amount box.

Diagnosis. The Diag 1, 2, 3, and 4 boxes correspond to the information in the Diagnosis tab of the Case folder. The patient's diagnoses are displayed automatically.

Provider. The Provider box lists the code number for a patient's assigned provider.

The remaining boxes in the Charges section display other information about the procedure selected. When all the charge information has been entered and checked for accuracy, it must be saved by clicking the Save Transactions button at the bottom of the Transaction Entry dialog box. Once saved, the transactions will be shaded gray to indicate they have been saved.

> ### Special Note on Saving Transactions
>
> If the date of the transactions you are saving is later than the current date on your computer system (the Windows System Date), NDCmedisoft™ will display a Date of Service Validation box for each new transaction before it saves the transaction. This box asks you to confirm that you want to save the transaction, even though it has a future date. For the purposes of the projects and simulations in this text, which take place in 2008, click Yes each time this box appears.
>
> **Date of Service Validation**
>
> (i) Date is a future date. Do you want to save this transaction?
>
> [Yes]   [No]

Entering Payments

Payments are entered in the Payments, Adjustments, And Comments section in the lower portion of the Transaction Entry dialog box. Just as when entering charges, a patient's chart number and case number must be selected before a transaction can be entered. A new payment transaction can be created or an existing transaction can be edited. To create a new payment transaction, the New button is clicked at the bottom of the Payments, Adjustments, And Comments section.

Date. When the New button is clicked, the program automatically enters the current date in the Date box. If this date is not the date the payment is being entered in the program, it must be edited. Once the correct date is displayed, the Tab key is pressed to move the cursor to the Pay/Adj Code box.

Pay/Adj Code. From the drop-down list in the Pay/Adj Code box, the type of payment is selected. For purposes of this text, the codes are

INSPAY	Insurance carrier payment
PACPAY	Patient payment, cash
PATPAY	Patient payment, check

Who Paid. After the code is selected and the Tab key is pressed, the program automatically completes the Who Paid box based on information stored in the database. The party that made the payment is selected from a drop-down list of guarantors and insurance carriers that are assigned in the patient case folder.

Description. The Description field can be used to enter a description of the payment received, if desired.

Amount. The amount of a payment is entered in the Amount box.

Check Number. If a payment is made by check, the check number is entered in this box.

After the boxes in the Payments, Adjustments, And Comments section of the Transaction Entry dialog box have been completed and checked for accuracy, the payment must be applied to charges. This is accomplished by clicking the Apply button at the bottom of the dialog box.

Clicking the Apply button displays the Apply Payment to Charges dialog box, which lists information about all unpaid charges for a patient, including the date of the procedure, the document number, the procedure code, the charge, the balance, and the total amount paid. In the top right corner of the dialog box, the amount of payment that has not yet been applied to charges is listed in the Unapplied box. Clicking the zeros in the This Payment box moves the zeros to the top left corner of the box. This indicates that the box is active and ready for entry. The amount of the payment is entered without a decimal point and the Tab key is pressed.

Clicking the Close button exits the Apply Payment to Charges dialog box, and the Transaction Entry dialog box is again displayed. The payment is now listed in the list of transactions at the bottom of the dialog box with the Unapplied box at the end of the transaction line reduced to $0.00.

As with a charge transaction, when all the information on a payment transaction has been entered and checked for accuracy, it must be saved by clicking the Save Transactions button at the bottom of the Transaction Entry dialog box.

Printing Walkout Receipts

After transactions have been entered and saved in the Transaction Entry dialog box, a walkout receipt can be printed for a patient by clicking the Print Receipt button at the bottom of the Transaction Entry dialog box. (*Note:* Although the Quick Receipt button can also be used to print receipts, because of the likely difference in your computer's system date and the date used in the projects and simulations, the Print Receipt button should be used.)

The Open Report dialog box is displayed. Click Walkout Receipt (All Transactions) to select the report title, and then click the OK button.

NDCmedisoft™ then asks whether the report is to be previewed on the screen, sent directly to the printer, or exported to a file. If the report is to be previewed on screen, it can subsequently be printed directly from the Preview Report window. After the preview or print option is selected, the Data Selection Questions dialog box is displayed, confirming the date of the transaction. Clicking the OK button produces the report on screen or on paper.

Editing and Deleting Transactions

Transactions in the Transaction Entry dialog box are edited by clicking inside the appropriate box and then making the desired change. Transactions are deleted by clicking anywhere inside the transaction line and then clicking the Delete button at the bottom of the corresponding section—either the Charges section or the Payments, Adjustments, And Comments section. After changes or deletions are made, the date is saved by clicking the Save Transactions button.

■ Office Hours

The Office Hours scheduling program has its own menu bar and tool-bar (see Figure A.13). The Office Hours menu bar lists the menus available: File, Edit, View, Lists, Reports, Tools, and Help. Under the menu bar is a toolbar with shortcut buttons. The functions of Office Hours are accessed by selecting a choice from one of the menus or by clicking a shortcut button.

FIGURE A.13

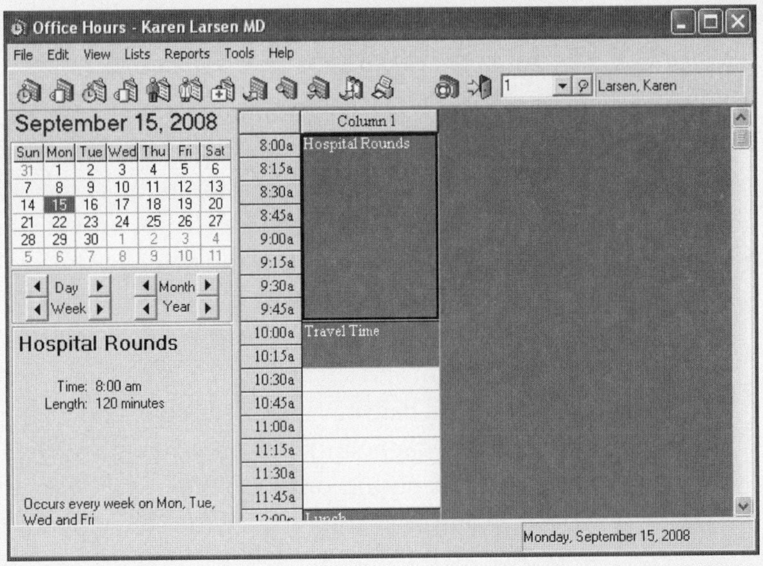

The Office Hours program uses the Windows System Date (rather than the NDCmedisoft™ Program Date) as the default date. Therefore, you will need to change the date in the Office Hours calendar regularly to correspond to the dates in the projects and simulations in this text.

The left half of the Office Hours screen displays the current date and a calendar of the current month. The current date is highlighted on the calendar. Clicking a different date on the calendar switches the schedule on the right side of the screen to the new day. Clicking the Go to Today shortcut button resets the screen to the current date (the Windows System Date).

The Office Hours schedule, shown in the right half of the screen, is a listing of time slots for a particular day for a specific provider.

Starting and Exiting Office Hours

Office Hours can be started from within NDCmedisoft™ or directly from Windows. To access Office Hours from within NDCmedisoft™, Appointment Book is clicked on the Activities menu. Office Hours can also be started by clicking the corresponding shortcut button on the NDCmedisoft™ toolbar.

To start Office Hours without entering NDCmedisoft™ first:

1. Click the Start button on the Windows task bar.
2. Click NDCmedisoft™ on the Program submenu.
3. Click Office Hours on the NDCmedisoft™ submenu.

The Office Hours program is closed by clicking Exit on the Office Hours File menu, or by clicking the Exit button on its toolbar. If Office Hours was started from within NDCmedisoft™, exiting will return you to NDCmedisoft™. If Office Hours was started directly from Windows, clicking Exit will return you to the Windows desktop.

Entering Appointments

Entering an appointment begins with selecting the provider for whom the appointment is being scheduled. The current provider is listed in the Provider box at the top right of the screen. Clicking the triangle button displays a drop-down list of providers in the system. To choose a different provider, click the name of the provider on the drop-down list.

After the provider is selected, the date of the desired appointment must be chosen. Dates are changed by clicking the Day, Week, Month, and Year right and left arrow buttons located under the calendar. After the provider and date have been selected, patient appointments can be entered.

Appointments are entered by clicking the Appointment Entry shortcut button or by double-clicking in a time slot on the schedule. When either action is taken, the New Appointment Entry dialog box is displayed (see Figure A.14). The program automatically enters information in the Length, Date, Time, and Provider fields.

The following are the main fields in the New Appointment Entry dialog box.

Chart. A patient's chart number is chosen from the Chart drop-down list. To select the desired patient, click the name and press Enter. If you are setting up an appointment for a new patient who has not been assigned a chart number, skip this box and key the patient's name in the Name box.

Once a patient's chart is selected from the Chart drop-down list and the Enter or Tab key is pressed, NDCmedisoft™ completes several other fields, including Name, Phone, and Case.

Length. The amount of time an appointment will take (in minutes) is entered in the Length box. The default entry is 15 minutes. To change the time, highlight 15 and key a new number (it must be a 15-minute increment, such as 30, 45, or 60). If an appointment is more than 15 minutes, the time slots below the first 15-minute slot on the schedule will be shaded.

Date. The Date box displays the date that is currently displayed on the calendar. If this is not the desired date, it may be changed by keying in a different date or by clicking the calendar button and selecting a date.

Time. The Time box displays the appointment time that is currently selected on the schedule. If this is not the desired time, it may be changed by keying in a different time.

Provider. The provider who will be treating the patient during this appointment is selected from the drop-down list of providers.

After the boxes in the New Appointment Entry dialog box have been completed, clicking the Save button enters the information on the schedule. The patient's name appears in the time slot corresponding to the appointment time. In addition, information about the appointment appears in the lower left corner of the Office Hours window.

Looking for a Future Date

Often a patient will need a follow-up appointment at a certain time in the future. For example, suppose a physician has seen a certain patient on a particular day and would like a checkup appointment in three weeks. The most efficient way to search for a future appointment in Office Hours is to use the Go to a Date shortcut button on the toolbar. (This feature can also be accessed on the Edit menu.)

Clicking the Go to a Date shortcut button displays the Go to Date dialog box. Within the dialog box, the Date From box indicates the current date in the appointment search. Four other boxes offer options for locating a date a specific number of days, weeks, months, or years in the future from the date indicated in the Date From box. After a number is entered in one of the four boxes, clicking the Go button closes the dialog box and begins the search. The system locates the future date and displays the calendar schedule for that date.

Searching for an Available Appointment Time

Often it is necessary to search for available appointment space on a particular day of the week and at a specific time. For example, a patient needs a 30-minute appointment and would like it to be during his lunch hour, which is from 12:00 p.m. to 1:00 p.m. He can get away from the office only on Mondays and Fridays. Office Hours makes it easy to locate an appointment slot that meets these requirements with the Search for Open Time Slot shortcut button.

Entering Appointments for New Patients

When a new patient phones the office for an appointment, the appointment can be scheduled in Office Hours before the patient information is entered in NDCmedisoft™. Simply key the patient's information in the Name and Phone boxes in the New Appointment Entry dialog box. You do not need to assign a chart number at this time. The rest of the necessary information will be gathered when the patient comes in for the appointment and fills out a patient information form.

Creating Breaks

Office Hours provides features for inserting standard breaks in providers' schedules. The Office Hours break is a block of time when a physician is unavailable for appointments with patients. Examples of breaks include lunch breaks, meetings, surgery, and vacation. To set up a break, the desired provider is selected from the drop-down list in the Office Hours Provider box and then the Break Entry shortcut button is clicked (the second button from the left that looks like a coffee cup in front of an appointment book). When the New Break Entry dialog box appears (see Figure A.15), the Name and Length fields are filled in to define the desired break.

If the break is to be repeated (daily, weekly, monthly, or yearly), the Change button is used to define the frequency. When the Save button is clicked, the dialog box closes and the program enters the break in Office Hours automatically.

Changing or Deleting Appointments

It is often necessary to change a patient's appointment or cancel an appointment. Changing an appointment is accomplished with the Cut and Paste commands on the Office Hours Edit menu.

The following steps are used to reschedule an appointment.

1. Locate the appointment that needs to be changed. Make sure the appointment slot is visible on the schedule.
2. Click on the existing time-slot box. A black border surrounds the slot to indicate that it is selected.
3. Click Cut on the Edit menu. The appointment disappears from the schedule.
4. Click the date on the calendar when the appointment is to be rescheduled.
5. Click the desired time-slot box on the schedule. The slot becomes active.
6. Click Paste on the Edit menu. The patient's name appears in the new time-slot box.

The following steps are used to cancel an appointment without rescheduling.

1. Locate the appointment on the schedule.
2. Click the time-slot box to select the appointment.
3. Click Cut on the Edit menu. The appointment disappears from the schedule.

Previewing and Printing Schedules

In most medical offices, providers' schedules are printed on a daily basis. To view a list of all appointments for a provider for a given day, click Appointment List on the Office Hours Reports menu. The report can be previewed on screen, sent directly to the printer, or exported to a file. If the preview option is selected, the appointment list is displayed in a preview window. Various buttons are used to view the schedule at different sizes, to move from page to page, to print the schedule, and to save the schedule as a file. Clicking the Close button closes the preview window.

The schedule can also be printed by clicking the Print Appointment List shortcut button on the Office Hours toolbar, without using the Preview option. (Office Hours prints the schedule for the provider who is listed in the Provider box. To print the schedule of a different provider, change the entry in the Provider box before printing the schedule.)

■ Reports in the Medical Office

NDCmedisoft™ provides a variety of standard reports, and it has the ability to create custom reports using the Report Designer. Standard and custom reports are accessed through the NDCmedisoft™ Reports menu. Most of the standard NDCmedisoft™ reports use the Windows System Date, not the NDCmedisoft™ Program Date, as a default.

Patient Day Sheet

At the end of the day, many medical practices print a patient day sheet, which is a summary of the patient activity on that day. NDCmedisoft™ 's version of this report lists the procedures for a particular day, grouped by patient, in alphabetical order by chart number. To print a patient day sheet, Day Sheets is clicked on the Reports menu and Patient Day Sheet on the submenu. The Print Report where? dialog box is displayed, asking whether the report should be previewed on the screen, sent directly to the printer, or exported to a file.

When the Start button is clicked, the Data Selection Questions dialog box is displayed. This dialog box provides the opportunity to select the patients, dates, and providers for whom a report is being generated. If any box is left blank, all values are included in the report. When these selection boxes have been completed, the OK button is clicked and NDCmedisoft™ generates the report.

Procedure Day Sheet

A procedure day sheet lists all the procedures performed on a particular day and gives the dates, patients, document numbers, places of service, debits, and credits relating to these procedures. Procedures are listed in numerical order. Procedure day sheets are printed by clicking Day Sheets

Note: Beginning with version 9 of NDCmedi-soft™, patient statements can be printed using the Statement Management feature as well as by using the Reports menu. However, for the purposes of this text, the Reports menu is used.

on the Reports menu and then Procedure Day Sheet on the submenu. The same Print Report Where? dialog box used for a patient day sheet is displayed. Again, the report can be previewed on the screen, printed directly, or exported to a file.

Patient Statements

A patient statement lists the amount of money a patient owes, organized by the amount of time the money has been owed, the procedures performed, and the dates the procedures were performed. For the purposes of this text, the default statement format, known as Patient Statement (30, 60, 90), is used. The bottom of the report lists the total balance due, as well as the amount that is past due 30 days, 60 days, and 90 days.

Custom Reports

Clicking Custom Report List on the Reports menu displays a list of custom reports available in NDCmedisoft™. The custom report list is used to view or print out a large variety of reports, including lists (such as patient lists and insurance carrier lists), insurance forms, and superbills.

HIPAA Overview

HIPAA (the Health Insurance Portability and Accountability Act of 1996) became Public Law 104-191 in 1996. A major provision of HIPAA, known as Administrative Simplification, affects medical practices as well as hospitals, health plans, and health care clearinghouses. Its rules have gradually been passed and then implemented in the health care industry.

Implementing HIPAA has changed administrative, financial, and case management policies and procedures. There are now strict requirements for the uniform transfer of electronic health care data, such as for billing and payment; new patient rights regarding personal health information, including the right to access this information and to limit its disclosure; and broad new security rules that health care organizations must put in place to safeguard the confidentiality of patients' medical information.

There are four parts to HIPAA's Administrative Simplification provisions:

1. **HIPAA Electronic Transaction and Code Set Standards Requirements**
   National standards for electronic formats and data content are the foundation of this requirement. HIPAA requires every provider who does business electronically to use the same health care transactions, code sets, and identifiers.
2. **HIPAA Privacy Requirements**
   The privacy requirements limit the release of patient protected health information without the patient's knowledge and consent beyond that required for patient care.
3. **HIPAA Security Requirements**
   The security regulations outline the maximum administrative, technical, and physical safeguards required to prevent unauthorized access to protected health care information. The security standards help safeguard confidential health information during the electronic interchange of health care transactions.
4. **HIPAA National Identifier Requirements**
   HIPAA will require health care providers, health plans, and employers to have standard national numbers that identify them on the standard transactions. Two of these standards are now law, and the others will be enacted in the future.

■ Who Must Comply?

Covered Entities

There are three categories of what is termed "covered entities"—health providers, health plans, and health care clearinghouses—that must comply with HIPAA.

- *Health care providers.* "Health care provider" includes any person or organization who furnishes, bills, or is paid for health care in the normal course of business. Providers include, among many others, physicians, hospitals, pharmacies, nursing homes, durable medical equipment suppliers, dentists, optometrists, and chiropractors. A health care provider is a covered entity under the HIPAA Privacy Rule only if it conducts any HIPAA standard transactions electronically or if another person or entity conducts the HIPAA standard transactions electronically on its behalf (such as a billing service company and a hospital billing department).

- *Health plans.* A health plan is an individual or a group plan that provides or pays for the cost of medical care. Health plans include employee welfare benefit plans as defined under the Employee Retirement Income Security Act of 1974 (ERISA), including insured and self-insured plans, except plans with fewer than 50 participants that are self-administered by the employer.

- *Health care clearinghouses.* Health care clearinghouses are companies that "translate" or "facilitate" translation of electronic transactions between the "standard" formats and code sets required under HIPAA and nonstandard formats and code sets.

Almost all physician practices are included under the HIPAA standards. A practice is *not* a covered entity only if it does not send any claims (or any other HIPAA transaction) electronically *and* does not employ someone else, such as a billing agency or clearinghouse, to send electronic claims or other electronic transactions to payers or health plans on its behalf. Since the Centers for Medicare and Medicaid Services (CMS) refuse to pay any Medicare claims that are not filed electronically from all but the smallest groups, noncompliance is not practical for physician practices.

Business Associates

HIPAA also indirectly affects many others in the health care field. For instance, software billing vendors and third-party billing services that are not clearinghouses are not required to comply with the law; however, they may need to make changes in order to be able to continue to do business with someone who is a covered entity. Through business associate agreements, health care providers are responsible for making sure that the software they use, or the third-party biller or clearinghouse they use to help process claims, is able to produce HIPAA-compliant transactions. Business associates must also provide the covered entity satisfactory assurances that it will appropriately guard information as required by HIPAA.

■ HIPAA Transaction and Code Set Standards

The HIPAA Transaction and Code Set Standards require standardization in health care e-commerce. These standards enable any provider to fill out a claim for a patient—regardless of the payer—and submit that claim electronically in the same format. Every payer must accept the standard format and standard codes and send electronic messages back to the provider, also in standard formats, advising the provider of claim status, remittance, and other key information necessary for payment to proceed.

Standard Transactions

The HIPAA transactions standards apply to exchanges for the most common provider-to-health plan messages between providers and payers, greatly expanding the amount of health information that is exchanged electronically as well as the types of patient information involved in electronic communications.

Technically described as X12, standards for eight electronic transactions have been adopted:

- Claims or encounters (equivalent to the paper CMS-1500, UB-92, and ADA Dental Claim forms)
- Claim status inquiry and response
- Eligibility inquiry and response
- Enrollment and disenrollment in a health plan
- Referral authorization inquiry and response
- Payment and remittance advice
- Health plan premium payments
- Coordination of Benefits (COB)

In the future, standards for First Report of Injury and claim attachments must be adopted, also due to HIPAA mandate.

Standard Code Sets

Under HIPAA, a code set is any group of codes used for encoding data elements, such as tables of terms, medical concepts, medical diagnosis codes, or medical procedure codes. Medical data code sets used in the health care industry include coding systems for diseases, impairments, other health-related problems, and their manifestations; actions taken to diagnose, treat, or manage diseases, injuries, and impairments; and any substances, equipment, supplies, or other items used to perform these actions.

Code sets for medical data are required for data elements in the administrative and financial health care transaction standards adopted under HIPAA for diagnoses, procedures, and drugs. The HIPAA standard code sets are

- *For diseases, injuries, impairments, and other health-related problems:* International Classification of Diseases, 9th edition, Clinical Modification (ICD-9-CM), Volumes 1 and 2
- *For procedures or other actions taken to prevent, diagnose, treat, or manage diseases, injuries, and impairments:*
  - *Inpatient hospital services:* International Classification of Diseases, 9th edition, Clinical Modification, Volume 3: Procedures
  - *Dental services,* Code on Dental Procedures and Nomenclature (CDT-4)
  - *Physicians' services:* Current Procedural Terminology, 4th edition (CPT)
- *Other hospital-related services:* Healthcare Common Procedures Coding System (HCPCS)

■ HIPAA Privacy Rule

The HIPAA Privacy Rule provides the first comprehensive federal protection for the privacy of health information. It is designed to provide strong privacy protections that do not interfere with patient access to, or the quality of, health care delivery. It creates for the first time national standards to protect individuals' medical records and other personal health information. The privacy rule is intended to

- Give patients more control over their health information.
- Set boundaries on the use and release of health records.
- Establish appropriate safeguards that health care providers and others must achieve to protect the privacy of health information.
- Hold violators accountable, with civil and criminal penalties that can be imposed if they violate patients' privacy rights.
- Strike a balance when public responsibility supports disclosure of some forms of data—for example, to protect public health.

Before the HIPAA Privacy Rule, the personal information that moves across hospitals, doctors' offices, insurers or third-party payers, and state lines fell under a patchwork of federal and state laws. This information could be distributed—without either notice or authorization—for reasons that had nothing to do with a patient's medical treatment or health care reimbursement. For example, unless otherwise forbidden by state or local law, without the privacy rule patient information held by a health plan could, without the patient's permission, be passed on to a lender, who could then deny the patient's application for a home mortgage or a credit card, or to an employer, who could use it in personnel decisions. The privacy rule establishes a federal floor of safeguards to protect the confidentiality of medical information. State laws that provide stronger privacy protections will continue to apply over and above the federal privacy standards.

Protected Health Information (PHI)

The core of the HIPAA Privacy Rule is the protection, use, and disclosure of protected health information (PHI). Health information (HI) means any information, whether oral or recorded in any form or medium, that is created or received by a health care provider, a health plan, a public health authority, an employer, a life insurer, a school or university, or a health care clearinghouse and that relates to the past, present, or future physical or mental health or condition of an individual; the provision of health care to an individual; or the past, present, or future payment for the provision of health care to an individual.

Protected health information (PHI) means individually identifiable health information that is transmitted or maintained by electronic (or other) media. The privacy rule protects all PHI held or transmitted by a covered entity, in any form or media, whether electronic, paper, or oral, including verbal communications among staff members, patients, and/or other providers. Under this definition, a report of the number of people treated by a physician who have diabetes is not PHI, but the names of the patients are protected. PHI includes many facts about people, such as names, addresses, birth dates, employers, telephone numbers, Social Security numbers, and health plan beneficiary numbers, any of which could be used to identify them.

Provider Responsibilities

The Privacy Rule recognizes that medical offices and payers must be able to exchange PHI in the normal course of business. The rule says that there are three everyday situations in which PHI can be released *without* the patient's permission: treatment, payment, and operations (TPO).

- *Treatment* means providing and coordinating the patient's medical care. Physicians and other medical staff members can discuss patients' cases in the office and with other physicians. Laboratory or x-ray technicians may call to clarify requests they cannot read because of the physician's handwriting. This information can be provided by the physician or another medical staff member.
- *Payment* refers to the exchange of information with health plans. Medical office staff members can take the required information from patients' records and prepare health care claims that are transmitted to health plans.
- *Operations* are the general business management functions needed to run the office.

For the average health care provider or health plan, the privacy rule requires activities such as

1. Notifying parents about their privacy rights and how their information can be used
2. Adopting and implementing privacy procedures for its practice, hospital, or plan
3. Training employees so that they understand the privacy procedures
4. Designating an individual to be responsible for seeing that the privacy procedures are adopted and followed
5. Securing patient records containing individually identifiable health information, so that they are not readily available to those who do not need them

Medical office staff should be careful not to discuss patients' cases with anyone outside the office, including family and friends. Avoid talking about cases, too, in the practice's reception areas, where other patients might overhear comments. Close charts on desks when they are not being worked on. A computer screen displaying a patient's records should be positioned so that only the person working with the file can view it. Files should be closed when the computer is not in use.

A covered entity must disclose protected health information in only two situations: (a) to individuals (or their personal representatives) specifically when they request access to, or an accounting of disclosures of, their protected health information and (b) to HHS when it is undertaking a compliance investigation or review or enforcement action.

The privacy rule must be followed by all covered entities—health plans, health care clearinghouses, and health care providers—even if they contract with others to perform some of their essential functions. These outside contractors are called business associates, defined as a person or an organization that performs certain functions or activities for a covered entity that involve the use or disclosure of individually identifiable health information. When a covered entity uses a contractor or other non-workforce member to perform *business associate* services or activities, the rule requires that the covered entity include certain protections for the information in a business associate agreement. In the business associate contract, a covered entity must impose specified written safeguards on the individually identifiable health information used or disclosed by its business associates.

Notice of an Acknowledgment of Receipt of Notice of Privacy Practices

To comply with the Privacy Rule, medical offices, as well as other providers and health plans, must give each patient an explanation of privacy practices at the patient's first contact or encounter. To satisfy this requirement, medical offices give patients a copy of their Notice of Privacy Practices. The notice explains how patients' PHI may be used and describes their rights. The office must also ask patients to review this notice and sign an Acknowledgment of Receipt of Notice of Privacy Practices, showing that they have read and understand the document.

Minimum Necessary

When using or disclosing protected health information, a provider must make reasonable efforts to limit the use or disclosure to the minimum amount of PHI necessary to accomplish the intended purpose. Minimum necessary means taking reasonable safeguards to protect a person's health information from incidental disclosure. State laws may impose more stringent requirements regarding the protection of patient information.

These minimum necessary policies and procedures also reasonably must limit who within the entity has access to protected health information, and under what conditions, based on job responsibilities and the nature of the business. The minimum necessary standard does not apply to disclosures, including oral disclosures, among health care providers for treatment purposes. For example, a physician is not required to apply the minimum necessary standard when discussing a patient's medical chart information with a specialist at another hospital.

Patient Rights

Under HIPAA, patients have an increased awareness of their health information privacy rights, including the following:

- The right to access, copy, and inspect their health information
- The right to request an amendment to their health care information
- The right to obtain an accounting of certain disclosures of their health information
- The right to alternative means of receiving communications from providers
- The right to complain about alleged violations of the regulations and the provider's own information policies

For use or disclosure of PHI other than for treatment, payment, or operations (TPO), the patient must sign an authorization to release the information. For example, information about alcohol and drug abuse may not be released without a specific authorization from the patient. The authorization document must be in plain language and include the following:

- A description of the information to be used or disclosed
- The name or other specific identification of the person(s) authorized to use or disclose the information
- The name of the person(s) or group of people to whom the covered entity may make the disclosure
- A description of the purpose of each requested use or disclosure
- An expiration date
- The signature of the individual (or authorized representative) and date

Patients who observe privacy problems in their providers' offices can complain either to the medical office or to the Department of Health and

Human Services (HHS). Complaints must be put in writing, on paper or electronically, and sent to the Office of Civil Rights (OCR), which is part of HHS, usually within 180 days. The office must cooperate with an HHS investigation and give HHS access to its facilities, books, records, and systems, including relevant protected health information.

Exceptions to the Privacy Rule

There are a number of exceptions to the privacy rule. All these types of disclosures must also be logged, and the release information must be available to the patient who requests it.

- *Release under Court Order.* If the patient's PHI is required as evidence by a court of law, the provider may release it without the patient's approval upon judicial order. In the case of a lawsuit, a court sometimes decides that a physician or medical practice staff member must provide testimony. The court issues a **subpoena,** an order of the court directing a party to appear and testify. If the court requires the witness to bring certain evidence, such as a patient's medical record, it issues a **subpoena *duces tecum,*** which directs the party to appear, to testify, and to bring specified documents or items.
- *Workers' Compensation Cases.* State laws may provide for release of records to employers in workers' compensation cases. The law may also authorize release to the state workers' compensation administration board and to the insurance company that handles these claims for the state.
- *Statutory Reports.* Some specific types of information are required by state law to be released to state health or social services departments. For example, physicians must make such statutory reports for patients' births and deaths and for cases of abuse. Because of the danger of harm to patients or others, communicable diseases such as tuberculosis, hepatitis, and rabies must usually be reported.
- *HIV and AIDS.* A special category of communicable disease control is applied to patients with diagnoses of human immunodeficiency virus (HIV) infection and acquired immunodeficiency syndrome (AIDS). Every state requires AIDS cases to be reported. Most states also require reporting of the HIV infection that causes the syndrome. However, state law varies concerning whether only the fact of a case is to be reported, or if the patient's name must also be reported. The medical office's guidelines will reflect the state laws and must be strictly observed, as all these regulations should be, to protect patients' privacy and to comply with the regulations.
- *Research Data.* PHI may be made available to researchers approved by the practice. For example, if a physician is conducting clinical research on a type of diabetes, the practice may share information

from appropriate records for analysis. When the researcher issues reports or studies based on the information, specific patients' names may not be identified.

- *De-Identified Health Information.* There are no restrictions on the use or disclosure of "de-identified" health information that does not identify an individual.

■ HIPAA Security Rule

The regulations of the Security Rule work in concert with the final privacy standards and require that covered entities establish administrative, physical, and technical safeguards to protect the confidentiality, integrity, and availability of health information covered by HIPAA. The security rule specifies how they must secure such protected health information (PHI) on computer networks, the Internet, disks and magnetic tape, and extranets.

The security rule also mandates that

- A security official must be assigned the responsibility for the entity's security.
- All staff, including management, must receive security awareness training.
- Organizations must implement audit controls that record and examine workers who have logged into information systems that contain PHI.
- Organizations must limit physical access to facilities that contain electronic PHI.
- Organizations must conduct risk analyses to determine information security risks and vulnerabilities.
- Organizations must establish policies and procedures that allow access to electronic PHI on a need-to-know basis.

■ HIPAA National Identifiers

The HIPAA law requires identifiers for

- Providers
- Employers
- Health plans
- Patients

CMS has only issued rules for two: the Employer and National Provider Identifiers.

Employer Identifier

The HIPAA Employer Identifier standard was needed because employers are frequently sponsors of health insurance for their employees. The identifier is used to identify the patient's employer on claims to the plan. In addition, employers must identify themselves in transactions when they enroll or disenroll employees in a health plan or make premium payments to plans on behalf of their employees. The final regulation establishes the Employer Identification Number (EIN) issued by the Internal Revenue Service as the HIPAA standard.

Health Care Provider Identifier

The National Provider Identifier (NPI) rule provides a unique provider identifier for each provider. It is a 10-position numeric identifier with a check digit in the last position to help detect keying errors.

Patient and Health Plan Identifiers Not Issued

Due to the public concern over privacy, a patient identifier standard has not yet been adopted. Because of the central importance of health plans in the provision and administration of health care services, HIPAA requires the development of a Health Plan Identifier. CMS has not proposed such an identifier, and it is not certain when one will be issued.

abandonment The physician's failure to furnish care for a particular illness for as long as it is required unless the patient has been discharged in an appropriate manner.

absolute accuracy Correctness that is 100 percent; correctness without error, required for handling financial transactions.

accepting assignment The agreement by a health care provider who participates in an insurance plan to accept the allowed charge as payment in full for services.

accession book A book containing a list of consecutive numbers used to assign each patient a number in practices where a numeric filing system is used; see *numeric filing.*

accounting A system used to classify, record, and summarize financial transactions.

accounts payable The unpaid amounts of money owed by the practice to creditors and/or suppliers.

accounts receivable The unpaid amounts of money owed to the medical practice by patients and third-party payers.

accrual method The accounting method whereby income is recorded as soon as it is earned, whether or not payment is received; expenses are recorded when they are incurred.

accuracy Correctness, including attention to detail; the trait often ranked most important in assistants by physicians.

active files Those records belonging to patients currently seeing the physician.

administrative medical assistant The title given to medical office professionals who perform administrative tasks in a wide variety of settings.

agenda Outline of a meeting, specifying location, time, date, and major topics to be discussed.

aging report A report that shows the passage of time between the issuing of a request for payment (invoice) and the receipt of payment; used to determine late payments and collect them.

allowed charge The maximum amount that an insurer will pay for a service or procedure; also called "allowable," "maximum."

alphabetic filing A system of filing whereby documents are kept according to names, titles, or classifications in alphabetic order.

AAMA (American Association of Medical Assistants) National association providing continuing education, professional networking opportunities, and certification examinations to its members.

AAMT (American Association for Medical Transcription) National association promoting professional standards and growth; certification available through the association's examination.

AHIMA (American Health Information Management Association) National organization that serves health information management professionals, keeps professionals current with legislation, and provides consumers of health services with topics of interest to them.

AMT (American Medical Technologists) National organization that promotes professional standards and growth; certification available through the association's examination.

annotate The act of making notes that are either helpful or necessary in the margins of communications before forwarding them to the physician.

annual summary A report providing the monthly charges and payments for an entire year.

application software Computer programs that apply the computer's capabilities to specific uses such as word processing, graphics, database management, and spreadsheets.

arbitration The process whereby a neutral third party judges the merits of a complaint by one party against another, with the consent of the parties; serves as an alternative to trial and the judgment is binding.

ARMA (Association of Records Managers and Administrators) An international association that includes among its members information managers, archivists, librarians, and educators; sets standards for filing, record retention, and other aspects of records management.

assault The clear threat of injury to another.

assertiveness The ability to step forward to make a point in a confident, positive manner.

assessment The physician's interpretation of subjective and objective findings as contained in the SOAP record; also called "diagnosis" or "impression."

assignment of benefits The permission given by a policyholder that allows a third-party payer to pay benefits directly to the health care provider.

audit A review of all financial data by an independent party outside the practice—the IRS or an accountant—to ensure the accuracy and completeness of all financial transactions.

authorization Expressed (stated) permission given by the physician and required to convey information about a patient to anyone (including the patient).

balance billing Collecting payment from the insured patient of the difference between a provider's usual fee and a payer's lower allowed charge.

balance sheet A report for a stated period indicating the practice's complete assets, liabilities, and capital.

bank reconciliation The process of comparing the balance on the monthly bank statement with the checkbook balance to determine whether there is agreement or a difference in the amounts.

basic insurance plan A policy that generally includes coverage of hospitalization, laboratory tests, surgery, and x-rays.

battery Any bodily contact without permission; in medicine, interpreted to include procedures performed without the patient's consent or those that go beyond the degree of consent given.

BCBS (Blue Cross and Blue Shield Association) One of the largest private-sector insurers in the United States; offers both indemnity and managed care plans with many variations.

bibliography A list of all references used by an author in the preparation of a manuscript; listed in a separate section at the end of the text.

bioethics The branch of ethics that deals specifically with medical treatment, technology, and procedure; see *ethics*.

birthday rule A guideline for determining which of two parents with medical coverage has the primary insurance for a child; states that the policy held by the insured with the earliest birthday in the calendar year is the primary policy.

blank endorsement The presence of only a signature to enable a check to be cashed or deposited; the most common form of endorsement.

block-style letter Arrangement of a letter so that all lines, including those beginning new paragraphs, begin at the left margin.

bookkeeping The accurate recording of financial transactions.

capitation A form of payment made by the insurance company in advance of medical services received; the prepayment by the insurance carrier of a fixed amount to a physician to cover services for a member of a particular plan.

carrier An insurance company; also known as a third-party payer.

cash basis The system of accounting whereby charges for services are not recorded as income to the practice until payment is received and expenses are not recorded until they are paid.

CC (chief complaint) The reason for the patient's visit to seek the physician's advice.

CD-ROM drive An optical storage medium using a compact disk (CD); read only memory (ROM) means that the disk cannot record information but may be used to copy new programs onto the hard drive or to store information.

certification An essential minimum standard of competence in a particular medical specialty, awarded by The American Board of Specialties; achieved through academic in-hospital training and successful completion of a comprehensive examination.

certified mail A service offered by the US Postal Service whereby the Postal Service keeps a record of delivery and the sender receives a mailing receipt.

CHAMPVA Acronym for The Civilian Health and Medical Program of the Veteran's Administration; the government health insurance program that covers the medical expenses of families of veterans with total, permanent, service-connected disabilities; covers spouses and dependents of veterans who die as a result of injuries sustained in the line of duty.

charge/receipt slip A record of the doctor's services to each patient and the charges, combined with a tear-off receipt for the patient.

check A written order to a bank to pay a specific amount of money.

clearinghouse A service bureau that collects electronic claims from many different medical practices and forwards the claims to the appropriate insurance carriers.

closed files The records of those patients who have moved away from the area, died, or who have terminated their relationship with the physician.

CMS (Centers for Medicare and Medicaid Services) The federal agency responsible for setting up the terms of Medicare and reviewing managed care plans that want to become Medicare-covered providers; part of the Department of Health and Human Services, CMS was called the Health Care Financing Administration (HCFA) before 2001.

CMS-1500 claim form A paper claim for physician services.

COB (coordination of benefits) The clause in insurance policies which states that the insured who has two insurance policies may have only a maximum of 100 percent of the health costs.

code linkage The connection between the diagnostic and procedural information, examined by insurance carriers to evaluate the medical necessity of the reported charges.

coding (1) The placing of a number, letter, color, or underscore beneath a word to indicate where a document should be filed, (2) the process of assigning codes to diagnoses and treatments based on standard code sets.

coinsurance The percentage of each claim that the insured person must pay; the percentage to be paid by the carrier is usually stated first as in "a rate of 80-20."

collection agency A business whose purpose is to collect unpaid debts for the creditor; usually used once other methods of securing payment have failed.

collection at the time of service The payment for services by patients at the time of the visit, by cash, check, or credit card where acceptable; the payment method required for insurance copayments.

color coding Organization of files according to a system of colored file folders.

compliance The act of adhering to legal rules and regulations as well as high ethical standards through practices and procedures within the medical practice, in all aspects of medical care.

confidentiality The legal requirement that a patient's medical information be kept secret except in certain clearly defined instances.

contributory negligence The failure of a patient to follow the advice and/or instructions of the physician, thus contributing to neglect of an outcome that may not be satisfactory.

copayment (or copay) The set charge, required by HMOs and some other insurers, to be paid by patients every time they visit the physician's office; currently between $10 and $20.

CPT The initials used for *Current Procedural Terminology*, a book published by the American Medical Association and updated annually; contains the most commonly used system of procedure codes.

CPU The central processing unit or "brain" of the computer; transforms raw data into organized information.

cross-reference sheet The indication, made on a sheet of paper or card, of other files where a copy of a particular document may be found.

customary fee A physician's charge for a procedure or service determined by what physicians with similar training and experience in a certain geographic area typically charge.

cuts Positions of tabs on folders.

cycle billing A method of billing patients designed to stabilize cash flow and workload; involves dividing patients into groups of a size roughly equal to the number of times that billing will take place during the month.

daily journal A record of services rendered by the physician, daily fees charged, and payments received; also called "general journal" or "daily earnings record."

database A term used for the complete history of a patient as contained in a problem-oriented medical record (POMR): includes the problem, medical, social, and family histories, a review of systems, and the physician's conclusions; also, any collection of related data, sets, or subsets of information.

database management application Software program that helps the user enter data and sort the data into useful subsets of information.

dead storage An area reserved for records that have been closed or that must be stored permanently; usually physically separate from where active files are kept.

deductible A certain amount of medical expense the insured must incur before the insurance carrier will begin paying benefits.

deductions The amounts of money withheld from earnings to cover required taxes, insurance, etc.

defensive medicine Those practices of the physician designed to help him or her avoid incurring law suits, such as ordering additional tests to confirm a diagnosis as well as follow-up visits.

dependability The ability to complete work on schedule, do required tasks without complaint, and always communicate willingness to help; closely related to accuracy and thoroughness.

dependent Person related to a policyholder, such as a spouse or child.

deposition A sworn statement to the court before any trial begins and usually made outside of court.

deposits Checks or cash put into a bank account.

direct earnings Salaries paid to employees; see *indirect earnings.*

disability insurance Plan that provides reimbursement for income lost when the insured person is unable to work because of illness or injury.

diskette A magnetic medium storage device for data; a round, flat disk designed to spin in a circle while being read by or written to the computer.

double-booking appointments The practice used, when the schedule is full, of entering overflow patient appointments in a second column beside regular appointments; in some cases, triple columns are used.

DRGs (diagnostic-related groups) A system used by Medicare to establish payment for hospital stays; based on groupings of diagnostic codes that show the relative value of medical resources used throughout the nation for patients with similar conditions.

Dx (diagnosis) A term used interchangeably with "assessment" or "impression;" gives a name to the condition from which the patient is suffering.

editing The assessment of a document to determine its clarity, consistency, and overall effectiveness.

efficiency The ability to use time and other resources to avoid waste and unnecessary effort.

EFT (electronic funds transfer) The automatic withdrawal of employees' net pays from the practice account and the deposit to each employee's account; arranged for with the bank by the physician.

EIN (employer identification number) A tax identification number that employers are required to have by the Internal Revenue Service (IRS).

electronic claims Those claims that are completed and transmitted to insurance companies by computer, with the assembling of data and completion of claims done using medical billing software.

electronic mail service A service offered by the US Postal Service allowing the secure transmission of documents over the Internet.

e-mail A telecommunications system for exchanging written messages through a computer network; also known as electronic mail.

empathy Sensitivity to the feelings and situations of others that allows one to mentally put oneself in the other person's situation.

endnotes References that the author may have used as background or relevant information, placed on a separate page following the text of the manuscript.

EOB (explanation of benefits) The report sent to the patient and the health care provider by the insurance carrier informing them of the final reimbursement determination, explaining the decision, and appending reimbursement due the provider; used for paper claims.

ERA (electronic remittance advice) The report sent to the patient and health care provider by the insurance carrier informing them of the final reimbursement determination, and containing the same additional information as the EOB; used for electronic claims.

ergonomics The science of designing the work environment to meet the needs of the human body.

e-signature A unique identifier created for each person through computer code; has the same legal standing as a printed signature.

ethics The standards of conduct that grow out of one's understanding of right and wrong.

etiquette Those behaviors and customs that are standards for what is considered good manners.

express consent The patient's approval, which may be given either orally or in writing; required for procedures that are not part of routine care.

Express Mail Service offered by the US Postal Service that provides next day delivery of items.

fee adjustment The reduction of a fee based on the physician's decision of the patient's need; see also *write off.*

fee-for-service A payment method through an insurance carrier whereby the patient (policyholder) pays for medical services at the time of receiving them and is reimbursed by the insurance company once it has reviewed and approved a claim describing the services; alternately, the policyholder's directive that the carrier pay the service provider directly once services are received.

fee schedule A list maintained by each physician or medical practice of the usual procedures the office performs and the corresponding charges.

GLOSSARY

FH (family history) Facts about the health of the patient's parents, siblings, and other blood relatives that might be significant to the patient's condition.

FICA (Federal Insurance Contribution Act) The law that governs the social security system and requires that a certain amount of money be withheld for social security benefits; employer pays half the amount withdrawn and employee pays the other half.

file server A central computer within a computer network, used to store the computer programs and data that must be shared by all the computers in the network; also called, simply, a "server."

first draft The first complete keying of a manuscript.

fixed office hours Designated hours during which the doctor is available for appointments; patients sign in with the receptionist and are seen in the order in which they arrive and sign in.

flexibility Adaptability to new or changing requirements.

folders Containers used to hold those items that are to be filed; frequently made of a sturdy material to withstand handling.

footnotes Notes, usually at the bottom of a page, used to cite sources of information or quotations used in the text.

fraud An intentionally dishonest practice that deprives others of their rights, such as falsifying credentials or submitting false or duplicate insurance claims.

full endorsement The signature on a check indicating the person, account number, or bank to which the check is being transferred, and the payee's name.

FUTA (Federal Unemployment Tax Act) The federal law that requires employers to pay a percentage of each employee's salary; the amount paid provides a fund for employees once they are unemployed and seeking new jobs.

good judgment The ability to use knowledge, experience, and logic to assess all aspects of a situation in order to reach a sound decision.

Good Samaritan Act A law designed to protect a physician who provides emergency care from liabilities for civil damages that may arise from the circumstances.

graphics application Software program that allows the user to manipulate images and to create original images electronically.

guarantor Insurance policyholder for a patient.

guides Rigid dividers placed at the end of a section of files to indicate where a new section or category of files begins.

hard drive Non-removable disk built into the computer that serves as the computer's central "filing cabinet."

HCFA-1500 See *CMS-1500 claim form.*

HCPCS Pronounced "hic-pics;" stands for Health Care Financing Administration's Common Procedure Coding System, for use in coding services for Medicare patients.

Health Insurance Portability and Accountability Act (HIPAA) of 1996 The federal law that protects the security and privacy of health information by regulating how electronic patient information is stored and shared.

HMO (health maintenance organization) Earliest form of managed care; a medical center or designated group of physicians provides medical services to insured persons for a monthly or annual premium.

honesty Truth telling, expressed in words and actions; a quality that enables the person to be trusted at all times and in all situations.

hospital insurance Provides protection against the cost of hospital care and generally provides a room allowance for a maximum number of days per year; provisions exist for operating room charges, x-rays, lab work, drugs, and other necessary items during the patient's hospital stay.

HPI (history of present illness) Information taken from the patient about symptoms: when they began, what factors affect them, what the patient thinks is the cause, remedies tried, and any past treatment for the symptoms.

IAAP (International Association of Administrative Professionals) Worldwide organization that sponsors continuing education and a certification examination with the successful completion earning the designation of Certified Professional Secretary (CPS); also works with employers to promote excellence; formerly known as Professional Secretaries International (PSI).

ICD-9-CM (International Classification of Diseases, 9th Revision, Clinical Modification) A list of codes for diseases and conditions required for use in government health care programs and generally adopted by the health care profession.

implied consent The patient's agreement that is not stated outright but is shown by the patient's having come to the doctor's office for treatment.

impression A term used interchangeably with "assessment" or "diagnosis;" gives a name to the condition from which the patient is suffering.

inactive files The records of those patients who have not seen the doctor for six months or longer.

indemnity plan An insurance plan that provides a percentage of payment to the physician on a fee-for-service basis; the patient assumes responsibility for the remaining portion of the cost.

indexing The process of selecting the name, title, or classification under which a document or item will be filed.

indirect earnings Amounts of money other than salary supplied to the employee, such as paid leave; also benefits such as employer-paid benefit programs that are worth amounts of money.

informed consent The ability of the patient to make a sound decision to agree because the problem has been explained in clear language and the physician has given both treatment options and a prognosis.

initiative The exercise of one's power to act independently.

input Data and instructions from a computer user, provided to the computer through input devices, the most common of which is the keyboard.

inspecting documents The act of checking each item received for filing to be sure that the information is complete and that the item is in good physical condition.

insured May be the person who takes out an insurance policy and is responsible for the payments; may also refer to anyone, such as a spouse or dependent, covered by an insurance policy.

insured mail Articles sent through the US Postal Service or other carriers that are covered against loss or damage through the purchase or provision of insurance.

interest Money paid by the bank to depositors in return for the use of the depositor's money.

Internet A vast worldwide computer network that links millions of computers; enables almost instantaneous sharing of information in various digital forms—text, graphics, sound, video, etc.

itinerary Daily schedule of events for a traveler, containing such information as flight numbers and times, hotel and car arrangements, etc.

keyboard The most common computer input device; consists of a set of keys with numbers, letters, and symbols; used for entering data and instructions into the computer.

labels Oblong pieces of paper, frequently adhesive, used to identify a file by title or subject.

laptop computer Portable model of a computer, designed to fit into a briefcase; able to run on either plug-in current or batteries.

lateral file Drawers or shelves that open horizontally where files are arranged sideways from left to right instead of from front to back.

liability Legal responsibility.

licensure The act of the state whereby health care providers, and those in other professions as well, are granted licenses to practice under certain conditions, including meeting the requirements of education and training.

litigation The bringing of lawsuits against an individual or other entity.

living will Written document providing directions for medical care to be given if a competent adult becomes incapacitated or otherwise unable to make decisions personally; also know as an advance directive.

mainframe computer Designed to store massive databases that many users may all access at the same time.

major medical insurance A policy that offers protection from large medical expenses.

malpractice An act that a reasonable and prudent physician would not do or the failure to do some act that such a physician would do.

managed care A system that combines the financing and delivery of health care services to members.

management qualifications Usually regarded, for the administrative medical assistant, as the ability to be a team player; the ability to do strategic planning; and the ability to increase productivity.

maturity Emotional and psychological integrity composed of many qualities and skills.

Media Mail The rate used by the US Postal Service for the mailing of books, videotapes, looseleaf pages, and binders; also called "Book Rate."

Medicaid A health benefit program, jointly funded by federal and state governments, designed for people with low incomes who cannot afford medical care.

medical insurance Covers benefits for outpatient medical care.

medical practice acts The laws of each state governing who must be licensed to give care, the rules for obtaining licensure, grounds for revoking licenses, and the reports required by state law.

Medicare Federal health plan that provides insurance to citizens and permanent United States residents 65 years and older, people with disabilities (including kidney failure), and dependent widows; divided into Part A, hospitalization insurance, and Part B, medical insurance.

meeting minutes Official record of a meeting, including the major pieces of business conducted, the names and contributions of any attendees who spoke, the date, place, time of the meeting, those present and absent, and the duration of the meeting.

micrographics The process of storing records in miniaturized images, usually in a microfiche sheet or ultrafiche format, viewed on readers that enlarge the image.

minicomputer A computer category having less power than a mainframe; may operate for a single user or along with many terminals.

mobile-aisle files Open-shelf files that are moved manually or by motor.

modem Computer component that allows computers to communicate through telephone lines.

modified-block-style letter The arrangement of a letter whereby the date line, complimentary closing, and signature all begin at the center of the page and all other lines begin at the left margin.

monitor The display screen attached to the computer that shows to the user the results of commands, instructions to the computer, and data input.

monthly billing The system of sending each patient an updated statement of payments made and charges owed to the physician once per month; these are all sent from the office at the same time every month.

monthly summary The report that shows the daily charges and payments for the entire month.

networking A means of communicating, exchanging information, and pooling resources among a group of electronically linked computers.

no shows A term used to refer to patients who, without notifying the physician's office, fail to show up for an appointment.

numeric filing A system of document storage in which each patient is assigned a number; see *accession book*.

objective The physician's examination of the patient contained in the SOAP record; results of the examination may be shown under the heading "Physical Examination (PE)."

on-line A term used to describe a computer user who is connected to a computer network for purposes of communicating, gathering, or exchanging information.

open punctuation No punctuation used outside the body of a letter unless the line ends with an abbreviation.

open-shelf files Shelves that hold files, may be adjustable or fixed, and may extend from floor to ceiling; shelves accept files placed sideways with identifying tabs protruding.

operating system The internal programming that tells the computer how to use its own components by controlling the basic functions of the computer and directing the computer to interact with the user and with input and output devices.

out guide A card placed as a substitute for a file folder; serves to indicate that a file has been removed.

output Processed data sent back to the user by the computer through output devices such as a monitor.

outside services file A list of professional and other resources kept in either a paper or electronic format.

palm computer A version of the personal computer small enough to be held in the palm of the hand; less powerful than other personal computers but usually has e-mail, fax, and other features; also called "palmtop" or, technically, "personal digital assistant (PDA)."

PAR (participating provider) A physician who joins an insurance plan and agrees to provide services according to the rules and payment schedules of the insurance plan.

password A code assigned to a computer user as a security measure; limits access to computer files and safeguards information.

patient education materials Printed materials provided to patients to give information on caring for their health, lists of resources, descriptions of frequently requested tests and procedures, etc.

patient encounter form The list made of procedures, diagnoses, and charges during any particular patient visit.

patient information brochure A booklet that provides vital information about the practice, such as services offered; qualifications of the physicians;

instructions for making appointments; and ordering refills of prescriptions.

patient ledger cards Financial record containing patient's name, services rendered, charges, payments, and balance.

patient medical record The accumulation of all data pertaining to the patient; in addition to medical data, contains patient's personal information and assignment of benefits form.

patient statement The copy provided to the patient of all charges incurred by the patient and all payments made by the patient or the patient's insurance company; also called the "patient bill."

payroll The total earnings of all the employees in the practice.

PCP (primary care provider) The physician who coordinates the patient's overall care and ensures that various medical services are necessary; described as a "gatekeeper" and is often an internist or general practitioner.

PE (physical exam) A complete examination of the patient in which findings for each of the major areas of the body are stated or an examination that covers only the body systems pertinent to that particular visit.

pegboard accounting A simple accounting system widely used in medical practices; uses a pegboard to align several forms on top of each other in such a way that the data recorded on the top form is recorded at the same time on the forms underneath.

personal computer Designed specifically for the single user and may reside on a desktop or may be portable, as laptop and notebook computers are; referred to as "PCs" or, less frequently, as "microcomputers."

petty cash A fund containing small amounts of cash used for expenses so minor that checks would not be written to pay them: postage stamps, cab fares, etc.

PIF (patient information form) Form used to collect patient personal and insurance information; usually updated at least every 12 months.

plan The treatment, as stated in the SOAP record, listing prescribed medication, instructions given to the patient, recommendation for surgery or hospitalization.

PMH (past medical history) A listing of any illnesses the patient may have had in the past; includes treatments and procedures performed.

policies and procedures manual Employee handbook that contains job descriptions, job responsibilities, instructions for completing routine tasks, personnel policies, etc.

POMR (problem-oriented medical record) A patient record organized around a list of the patient's complaints or problems; contains a database of the patient's history, initial plan, and problem list.

posting The activity of transferring an amount from one record to another.

PPO (preferred provider organization) A popular type of managed care plan that contracts to perform services for members at specified rates, usually lower than fees charged to regular patients; also provides members with a list of health care providers from which to receive services at lower PPO rates.

practice analysis report The report used to analyze the revenue of the practice during any specified length of time; contains lab charges, patient payments, co-payments, adjustments, etc.

preauthorization The requirement by HMOs and some other insurance plans that the physician obtain permission from the insurance plan before delivering certain types of services.

premium The rate charged to a person who holds an insurance policy; usually paid on a regular basis, monthly or quarterly.

printer A computer output device that produces a paper, or "hard," copy of electronic information or images.

Priority Mail Service offered by the US Postal Service; two-day delivery service within most domestic destinations.

problem-solving The ability to find solutions through flexibility, seeking advice, information gathering, and using good judgment.

procedure day sheet Numerical listing of all the procedures performed on a given day; includes patient names, document numbers, places of service; may be a computerized journal form.

professional image The appearance, manner, and bearing that reflect health, cleanliness, wholeness; shown by evidence of healthful habits, good grooming, appropriate dress.

proofreading The careful reading and examination of a document for the sole purpose of finding and correcting errors.

provider Physician or other health care professional.

punctuality The ability to be on time.

RAM Random access memory, or the temporary memory function, that the computer requires to process data.

RBRVS (resource-based relative value scale) The payment system used by Medicare; establishes relative value units for services based on what each service costs to provide.

reasonable fee A charge for the physician's service that is a usual and stated charge and/or the charge by physicians in the geographic area with similar experience.

records management The systematic control of the steps in the life of a record, from its creation through its maintenance to its disposition.

referral The recommendation from the primary care provider (PCP) that the patient use a specialist for a specific service; in the referral document the PCP names the provider and states the service.

registered mail Items sent through the US Postal Service where a delivery record is maintained at the mailing post office; receipt is given to sender at the time of mailing.

registration Permit granted by a physician to prescribe and dispense drugs.

release of information Written permission signed by the patient, authorizing the proper transfer of information to those who have made a legitimate request or have a legitimate need; often called simply a "release."

releasing The indication, by initial or by some other agreed upon mark, that a document has been inspected, acted upon, and is ready for filing.

reprints Copies of an already published article; available from the publisher for a small fee or free when the physician is the author.

restricted delivery Direct delivery through the US Postal Service; item delivered only to the addressee or addressee's authorized agent.

restrictive endorsement Signing, or endorsing, a check by writing, or stamping "For Deposit Only," the account number to which the check should be deposited, and the signature.

retention The length of time that records are kept; regulated in many cases by state law; also regulated by Medicare regulations.

return receipt A piece of paper provided by the US Postal Service to give the sender proof of delivery.

ROM (read-only memory) The permanent memory of the computer.

ROS (review of systems) The physician's specific questions to the patient about each of the body's systems.

rotary circular file A small desktop file designed to rotate, thus permitting the use of both sides of an index card.

rule out (R/O) A possible diagnosis that must be proved or "ruled out" by further tests.

RVS (relative value scale) The assignment of values to medical services based on an analysis of the skill and time required to provide them; values are multiplied by a dollar conversion factor to calculate fees.

scanner A computer input device that takes a picture of a printed page or graphic and copies it into the computer's memory.

screening calls The practice of evaluating calls to decide on appropriate appointment action.

self-motivation The quality expressed by willingness to contribute without being asked or required to undertake a task.

settlement Agreement by parties on opposing sides; may be the result of a court decision or agreement arrived at without trial; may involve compensation to the complaining party.

SH (social history) Information that may be pertinent to treatment regarding the patient's marital history, occupation, interests, and eating, drinking, smoking habits.

simplified-style letter The arrangement of a letter in such a way that all lines begin at the left margin, a subject line substitutes for the salutation, the complimentary closing is eliminated; open punctuation is used and the writer's name is in all capital letters on one line.

SOAP An acronym used to refer to the most common system for outlining and structuring notes on a patient's chart; the acronym stands for the headings used: **S**ubjective, **O**bjective, **A**ssessment, and **P**lan.

sorting The arrangement of documents in the order in which they will be filed.

spreadsheet application Software program used for financial planning and budgeting.

standard punctuation The placing of a colon after the salutation of a letter and the placing of a comma after the complimentary closing.

statute of limitations A law made by each state government setting a time limit beyond which the collection of a debt, or the prosecution of many kinds of crimes, is not subject to legal action; varies from three to eight years.

statutory reports Information of a confidential nature that is required by law to be filed with state departments of health or social services.

storing The actual placement of an item in its correct place in a file; also called "filing."

subject filing A system of document storing whereby the placement of related material is alphabetic by subject categories.

subjective The patient's description of the problem or complaint including symptoms, when symptoms began, associated factors, remedies tried, and past medical history.

subpoena A legal document ordering that all materials related to a lawsuit be delivered to court; also, a legal document requiring people to divulge information.

summons Written notice to the person being sued (defendant) ordering the person to answer charges presented in the document.

supercomputer The most powerful computers available.

surgical insurance Provides protection for the cost of the surgeon's fee for performing surgery; generally includes coverage for the cost of anesthesia.

tabs Projections that extend beyond the rest of the file folder so that the folder may be labeled and easily viewed.

tact The ability to speak and act considerately, especially in difficult situations.

team player The phrase used to identify those who are generous with their time, helping other staff members when necessary; who observe both the written and unwritten rules of the office; and who practice professional and personal courtesy.

telephone etiquette Set of skills and attitudes used when answering the phone that allows the assistant to sound alert, interested, and concerned.

template A standard electronic version of a frequently used document; may be altered slightly from one use to the next; saves user time in keying and formatting

terminated account A term used primarily to describe the account of a patient from whom it has not been possible to extract payment; also used to signify the status of accounts at the end of the patient-physician relationship for other reasons.

third-party liability The assumption of responsibility for charges related to a patient by someone other than the patient, for example, children of aged parents.

third-party payer The term used to describe the insurance company when the company agrees to carry the risk of paying for medical services for the insured.

thoroughness The ability to perform tasks with attention to completeness, correctness, and detail.

tickler file An arrangement of index cards by months and by days within the month, used as a reminder for follow-up actions.

title page The first manuscript page, which contains the title of the manuscript, author's name, degree and/or title, and affiliation.

travel agent A professional, often certified by the travel industry, who may work independently or within a travel company; handles all aspects of travel arrangements at no charge to the customer.

triage The determination of how soon a patient needs to be seen by the physician based on whether the patient's condition requires immediate attention.

TRICARE The Department of Defense health insurance plan for military personnel and their families; coverage extends to active or retired members of the Army, Navy, Marines, Air Force, Coast Guard, Public Health Service, National Oceanic and Atmospheric Administration, and dependents of military personnel killed on active duty; formerly called CHAMPUS.

usual fee The health care provider's average charge for a certain procedure or service, usually shown on the physician's fee schedule.

vertical file Drawer files, contained in cabinets of various sizes; files are arranged from front to back.

voice recognition software A program used along with a word processing application to transcribe spoken words into text without the use of a keyboard.

wave scheduling Fixed office hours combined with scheduled office appointments for a specific number of patients.

wireless communication The use of radio waves rather than wires or cables to transmit data through a computer network.

word processing application A software program used to enter, edit, format, and print documents.

work ethic The collective habits and skills that help the worker deal effectively with work tasks and with people.

workers' compensation State law and insurance plan requiring employers to obtain insurance in case of employee accident or injury.

write-off The subtraction of an amount from a patient's bill; entered into the patient ledger as an adjustment.

Zip drive A small disk drive that may be installed inside a PC or operated externally; stores large files or creates archives of files for long-term storage.

PHOTO CREDITS

Page 1: © SuperStock International

Page 7: © Frank Pedrick/Index Stock Imagery

Page 13: © Jeff Greenberg/PhotoEdit

Page 16: © Pete Saloutos/Stock Market/Corbis

Page 22: © Michael Newman/PhotoEdit

Page 56: © David Kelly Crow/PhotoEdit

Page 63: © Vol. 275/Corbis R-F

Page 65: Courtesy of Compaq Computer Corp.

Page 67: Courtesy of Kinesis Corporation

Page 68: © Gary Connor/PhotoEdit

Page 77: © David R. Frazier

Page 79: © Steven Peters/Stone/Getty Images

Page 89: Courtesy of Panasonic Corporation

Page 112: © Jeff Kaufman/FPG International/Getty Images

Page 113 (Top): Elekta Vision/Index Stock Imagery

Page 113 (Bottom): Steelcase Inc.

Page 114: Courtesy of Steelcase Inc.

Page 115: Courtesy of Borroughs Corporation

Page 159: © Robert Brenner/PhotoEdit

Page 163: © B. Busco/Image Bank/Getty Images

Page 169: © Zephyr Picture/Index Stock Imagery

Page 170: © Spencer Grant/PhotoEdit

Page 193: © Picturebank/H. Armstrong Roberts

Page 253: Marc Romanelli/Image Bank/Getty Images

Page 277: Jonathan Nourok/PhotoEdit

A

Abandonment, by physician, 40
Abbreviations
  of patient name, 120
  state, 152
  in transcription, 179, 182–183
Absence of doctor
  duties related to, 282–283
  notifying patients, 40
Absolute accuracy, 261
Abuse of child, 44
Accepting assignment, 202, 240
Accession books, 123
Accounting, 255
Accounting software, 256
Accounts payable, 255
Accounts receivable, 255, 257
Accrual method, 255
Accuracy, 12
Acknowledgment letters, 139, 235
Acronyms, 121
Active files, 126
Administrative duties, 3–5
Administrative medical assistant, 2–26
  billing responsibilities, 60
  defined, 3
  employment opportunities, 9–12
  ethical responsibility of, 29–30
  interpersonal skills, 6–7, 19–24, 48
  personal attributes, 7–8
  professional growth, 6–7, 17–19, 48
  professional image, 16–17
  recording transactions, 223–227
  role in compliance, 47
  skills of, 5–7
  tasks of, 3–5
  work ethic, 12–15
Agenda, meeting, 284, 285, 288
Aging reports, 227, 259, 260
Allowed charge, 202
Alphabetic filing, 119–123
Alphabetic Index (ICD-9-CM), 207–209, 210
American Association of Medical Assistants
    (AAMA), 18
  Code of Ethics and Creed, 29, 31
American Association of Medical Transcription
    (AAMT), 18
American Health Information Management
    Association (AHIMA), record retention
    guidelines, 127–128
American Medical Association (AMA)
  Council on Ethical and Judicial Affairs,
    183–184
  Current Procedural Coding (CPT-4), 211–216
  Journal of the American Medical
    Association, 280
  Manual of Style, 146
  medical assistant tasks and roles, 4–5
  medical specialties, 9
  Principles of Medical Ethics, 29, 30
American Medical Technologists (AMT), 18

Annotation, 151
Annual summary, 255
Answering services, 86
Appealing claims, 230–231
Application software, 69–70
Appointment cards, 103
Appointment schedules, 3, 54, 83,
    93–104, 292–293
  canceling, 102
  emergencies, 97, 100
  extended appointments, 101
  guidelines, 98
  irregular appointments, 100–101
  late patients, 100
  NDCmedisoft™, 316–320
  necessary data, 99
  next appointment, 103
  no shows, 95, 102
  open slots for catching up, 103
  out-of-office appointments, 104
  out-of-office emergencies, 101
  patient preferences in, 98–99
  physician's policy and, 93–94
  registering arrivals, 101–102
  rescheduling, 102
  screening illnesses, 97
  types of scheduling, 94–96, 102
  verifying appointments, 86, 99
Arabic numbers, 122, 180
Arbitration, 42
Assault, 40
Assertiveness, 15
Assessment, 171
Assignment of benefits, 202–204, 240
Association of Records Managers and
    Administrators (ARMA), 111, 119–123
Audit trails, 71
Audits, 255
Automatic speed-dial feature, 88, 89

B

Backup copies, 58, 73
Balance billing, 202
Balance sheet, 256
Bank reconciliation, 264–266
Bank statements, 264–266
Banking, 261–267
  bank reconciliation, 264–266
  checks and checking, 261–263
  electronic banking, 266–267
  petty cash, 267
  policy of practice, 263
Battery, 40
Bibliography, 146
Billing, 294
  computerized, 59–60, 226–227, 234–235
  fee schedule, 224–225
  after insurance claims, 230
  and medical compliance plan, 46
  patient encounter form, 205, 223–224
  patient statements, 225–226, 321
  tasks of administrative medical assistant, 5

Bioethics, 30–32
Birthday rule, 192
Blank endorsement, 262
Block-style letters, 135
Blue Cross and Blue Shield Association (BCBS),
    11, 197
Bookkeeping, 255, 258
Bound Printed Matter, 152
Building numbers, 121
Business names, 121

C

Call letters, 121
Capitalization, 178, 179
Capitation, 194
Care facilities, employment opportunities, 11
Carrier, 191
Cash basis, 255
Cash flow, 263
Cash payments, 237–238
CD (compact disk), 66
CD-ROM (compact-disk—read-only
    memory), 66
CD-ROM drive, 66
Centers for Medicare and Medicaid Services
    (CMS), 201
Centralized files, 111
Certification
  of administrative medical assistants, 17–19
  of medical specialists, 34
  record retention, 127
Certified Administrative Professional (CAP), 19
Certified Mail, 152
Certified Medical Assistant (CMA), 18
Certified Medical Transcriptionists (CMTs), 18
Certified Professional Secretary (CPS), 18–19
CHAMPVA, 199
Charge/receipt slips, 255, 258
Chart notes, 165, 166, 172, 174
Charts, 3. See also Patient medical records
Checks and checking, 261–263
Cheerfulness, 8
Chicago Manual of Style, 146
Chief complaint (CC), 168, 207
Child abuse, 44
CIGNA, 11
City names, 121
Claims. See Insurance claims
Clearinghouse, 235
Clinical forms, 166
Clinical work, computers in, 61
Clinics, employment opportunities, 11
Closed files, 126
CMS-1500 claim form, 228, 231–233
Code linkage, 216–217
Coding, 205–217
  diagnostic, 205, 206–210, 236
  of files, 117
  and medical compliance plan, 46, 216–217
  procedural, 205, 211–216, 236
Coexisting conditions, 207
Coinsurance, 195

Collection agency, 244–245
Collection at the time of service, 237
Collections, 241–245, 294
    communicating with patients, 241
    computers in, 59–60
    course of action, 242–245
    credit arrangements, 245
    guidelines for payment, 241–242
    laws governing, 242
    office collection policy, 242–245
    statute of limitations, 245
    writing off uncollectible
        accounts, 245
Colons (:), 177
Color-coding, 124
Commas (,), 176–177
Commercial answering services, 86
Commission on Accreditation for Allied Health
        Education Programs (CAAHEP), 18
Communication skills, 5
    in billing process, 230
    in collections process, 241
    computer communication and,
        56–59
    language barriers and, 23–24
    See also Appointment schedules;
        Telephone skills
Compact disks, 279
Compliance, 45–47
    administrative medical assistant's
        role in, 47
    audit trails, 71
    coding, 46, 216–217
    medical compliance plan, 46–47
Compliance Program Guidance for Individual
    and Small Group Physician Practices,
    45–47
Compound expressions, 121
Computer skills, 6
Computers, 53–75
    billing process and, 59–60, 226–227,
        234–235
    categories of, 62–63
    confidentiality and, 23, 45, 49, 71–74
    electronic banking, 266–267
    electronic claims, 60–61, 72, 228
    electronic transmission of
        information, 45, 60–61
    e-mail, 6, 45, 57–58, 59, 73, 90–91,
        153, 279
    ergonomics, 67–68
    hardware, 64–67
    Internet, 58–59, 72, 73, 88
    keeping up with technology, 73–74
    proofreading on, 147
    security, 71–73
    software. See Software
    uses in medical offices, 54–61
Confidentiality, 22–23, 42–45, 48–49
    alphabetic filing and, 119
    computer security and, 23, 45, 49, 71–74
    exceptions to, 44–45

fax machines and, 45, 89–90
    helping to ensure, 43
    medical history, 22
    numeric filing and, 123–124
    record, 23, 296
    release of information, 42–43, 72,
        89, 228
    safeguarding, 48–49, 71–74
    in written communications, 134
Consent, 35–38
Consultation letters, 139–141, 166
Consumer Credit Card Protection Act, 245
Continuation pages, 138
Contracts
    medical insurance, 191–192
    in physician's practice, 34–35
Contributory negligence, 41
Conversation, with patients, 20–21
Coordination of benefits (COB), 192
Copayment (copay), 195, 240
Correspondence. See Letters
Council of Biology Editors (CBE), 146
CPT-4, 211–216
    basic steps, 215–216
    coding evaluation and management
        (E/M) services, 212–214, 215
    described, 211
    and HCPCS codes, 215
    immunizations, 214
    laboratory procedures, 214
    modifiers, 212, 216, 217
    notes, 212
    organization of, 212
    surgical procedures, 214
CPU (central processing unit), 64
Credit agreements, 245
Credit rating, 243
Cross-reference sheets, 116
Cross-references, 122
Cultural diversity, 23–24
Custom reports, 321
Customary fees, 204
Cuts, 114–115
Cycle billing, 238

D

DACUM competencies, 18
Daily journal, 255, 256–257, 258
Daily reports, 227
Daily routine, 291
Database management software, 60, 62, 70,
        172–173, 279
Dead storage, 128
Deaf patients, 24
Decentralized files, 111
Decimal points, 180
Deductibles, 195
Deductions, 265, 268–270
Defendant, 41
Defensive medicine, 39
Dental insurance, 193
Dependability, 13

Dependent children, 240
Deposition, 41
Deposits, 263, 266, 272
DHL Worldwide Express, 154
Diagnosis (Dx), 171
Diagnostic coding, 205, 206–210, 236
    basic steps, 210
    ICD-9-CM, 206–210
Diagnostic procedures, information needed
        for, 104
Diagnostic-related groups (DRGs), 205
Difficult patients, 21
Direct earnings, 269
Directories
    office personnel, 290
    telephone, 88
Disability insurance, 193
Discounted fee-for-service payment
        schedule, 194
Diskettes, 66
Disposition of records, 128
Diversity, cultural, 23–24
DME (durable medical equipment), 215
Doctors
    abandonment of patients, 40
    absence of, 40, 282–283
    policies for appointments, 93–94
    research by, 61, 279–280
    response to litigation, 41
    specialties, medical, 10
    substitute, 40
    termination of patients, 39, 244
    travel by, 280–283
    See also Physician practice
Double-booking appointments, 95, 96
Double-entry bookkeeping, 258
Drafts
    final, 143–146
    first, 143
Dress code, 295
Drug Enforcement Administration (DEA), 34
Durable medical equipment (DME), 215
DVD (digital video disk), 66

E

Editing
    defined, 147
    techniques, 150
Editorial research projects, 279–280
    library and, 279
    medical journals, 280
    reprints, 280
Efficiency, 13
EFT (electronic funds transfer), 272
Electronic banking, 266–267
Electronic claims, 60–61, 72, 228
Electronic mail service, 153
Electronic medical records, 23, 45, 49, 55–56,
        71–74
Electronic monthly calendars, 118
Electronic remittance advice (ERA), 229–230,
        235–236, 240

Electronic signature systems, 72, 266–267
E-mail, 6, 45, 57–58, 59, 73, 90–91, 153, 279
Emergencies
    coding for emergency patients, 213
    office visits, 97, 100
    out-of-office, 101
    telephone calls, 83, 84, 86
Empathy, 8
Employees
    employee benefits policies, 295
    evaluation policies, 295
    hiring policies, 295
    payroll records, 268–272
Employee's Withholding Allowance
    Certification (Form W-4), 269
Employer identification number (EIN), 269
Employer's obligation, 270
Employment Eligibility Verification
    Form, 268
Employment opportunities, 9–12
    care facilities, 11
    clinics, 11
    hospitals, 11
    insurance companies, 11–12
    list of medical specialties, 10
    medical centers, 11
    physician practice, 9
Encounter form, 223–224
Encryption, 72, 153
Endnotes, in reports, 146
Endorsement
    check, 262
    in licensing process, 33
EOB (explanation of benefits), 229–230,
    235–236, 240
Equipment
    computer hardware, 64–67
    filing, 112–114
    inventory of, 294
    telephone, 88, 89
    transcription, 175
ERA (electronic remittance advice), 229–230,
    235–236, 240
Ergonomics, 67–68
Errors
    accurate documentation, 47
    coding, 210, 217
    in filing, 119, 124, 125–126
    in patient medical records, 168
    proofreading, 147–148, 149
    reporting, 47
E-signature, 266–267
Established patients, *CPT* codes, 213–214
Ethics, 29–32
    administrative medical assistant and,
        29–30
    bioethics, 30–32
    defined, 29
    principles of, 29
Etiquette
    defined, 32
    greeting patients, 19, 80–81

    saying good-bye to patients, 21, 80
    telephone, 79–81
Evaluation and management (E/M) services,
    212–214, 215
Exemptions, 270
Explanation of benefits (EOB), 229–230,
    235–236, 240
Express consent, 35
Express Mail, 152
Extended appointments, 101

F

Fair Debt Collection Practices Act of 1977, 242
Familiarity with patients, 19–20
Family history (FH), 169
Fax machines, electronic transmission of
    information, 45, 89–90
Federal Express (FedEx), 154
Federal government, 122
Federal Insurance Contributions Act (FICA),
    269, 270, 271
Federal Reserve Bank, 271
Federal Unemployment Tax Act (FUTA),
    270–271
Fee adjustments, 239
Fee-for-service payment, 194
Fee schedules
    for billing, 224–225
    for insurance, 201, 204–205
File servers, 58
Files and filing. *See* Patient medical records;
    Records management
Filing cabinets, 112–114
Final manuscript, 143–146
Final privacy rule, 42
Financial records, 61, 254–274
    accounting software, 256
    accounts payable, 255
    accounts receivable, 255, 257
    annual summary, 255
    banking, 261–267
    bookkeeping methods, 255, 258
    charge receipt/slips, 255, 258
    daily journal, 255, 256–257, 258
    monthly summary, 255
    patient ledger cards, 255, 258
    payroll, 268–272
    pegboard accounting, 258
    retention of, 127
    summaries, 259–260
    See also Billing; Collections
Firewalls, 72
First-class mail, 152, 153
First draft, 143
Fixed office hours, 94–95, 96
Flexibility, 13
Folders, 114–115
Follow-up
    insurance claim, 235–236
    letters, 141
    telephone calls, 91–92, 103
    tickler file, 117–118, 151

Foot pedal, 175
Footnotes, 146
"For Deposit Only" annotation, 262
Foreign government, 123
Format
    of interoffice memorandums, 141–142
    of letters, 134–137
    of patient medical records, 168–174
    of policies and procedures manual, 290
    of professional reports, 143–146
Forms, clinical, 166
Fractions, 180
Fraud, 40–41
Front desk tasks, 3
Full disclosure policy, 72–73
Full endorsement, 262

G

Good-bye, saying, 21, 80
Good judgment, 14
Good Samaritan act, 42
Government names, 122–123
Grammar checkers, 147–148, 149
Graphics applications, 69–70
Greetings, telephone, 80–81
Gregg Reference Manual, The, 138
Grooming, 16–17
Gross earnings, 270
Guarantor, 124, 240
Guides, 115

H

Hard drive, 66
Hardware components, 64–67
HCFA-1500 claim form, 228
HCPCS codes, 215–216
Headings
    report, 145
    in SOAP format, 168–171
Headphones, 175
Health Care Financing Administration
    (HCFA), 201
Health Care Financing Administration
    Common Procedure Coding System
    (HCPCS), 215–216
Health habits, 16–17
Health insurance. *See* Insurance
Health Insurance Portability and
    Accountability Act (HIPAA), 45
    330–339
Hippocrates, 29
Hippocratic oath, 29
Hiring policies, 295
History and physical (H&P), 166
History of present illness (HPI), 169
HMOs (health maintenance organizations),
    195, 237, 239
Honesty, 14
Hospital insurance, 193
Hospitals
    employment opportunities, 11
    information needed for admissions, 104

House numbers, 121
Hyphenated names, 120
Hyphens (-), 178–179

I

ICD-9-CM, 206–210
  Alphabetic Index, 207–209, 210
  basic steps, 210
  described, 206–207
  E codes, 208–209
  Tabular List, 207–209, 210
  using, 207–209
  V codes, 208–209
Illustrations, 146
Immunizations, CPT codes, 214
Implied consent, 35
Impression, 171
Inactive files, 126
Incoming mail, 150–151
Incoming telephone calls, 79–86
Indemnity plans, 194–195
Indexing, of files, 116–117, 118, 120–121
Indirect earnings, 269
Inducements, 46
Information letters, 139
Informed consent, 35–38
Initiative, 14
Input devices, 64–65, 69
Inspecting documents, 116
Insurance, 190–221, 294
  Blue Cross and Blue Shield
    Association (BCBS), 11, 197
  CHAMPVA, 199
  claims. See Insurance claims
  fee schedules, 201, 204–205
  Medicaid, 198
  medical insurance contract, 191–192
  Medicare. See Medicare
  payment concepts, 202–204
  payment types, 194
  plan participation, 200–201
  plan types, 194–197
  tasks of administrative medical
    assistant, 5
  TRICARE, 198–199
  types of coverage, 192–193
  workers' compensation, 199–200
  See also Coding
Insurance claims, 228–236, 294
  appealing, 230–231
  completing claim forms, 231–234
  copayment, 195, 240
  electronic transmission of, 60–61, 72, 228
  electronic versus paper, 234–235
  following up on claims, 235–236
  HCFA-1500 claim form, 228, 231–233
  overview, 228–231
  verifying information, 231
Insurance companies, employment
    opportunities, 11–12
Insurance policies, retention of, 127
Insured, 191

Insured mail, 153
Interest, 261
Internal Revenue Service (IRS), 255
International Association of Administrative
    Professionals (IAAP), 18–19
Internet, 58–59, 72, 73, 88
Interoffice memorandums, 141–142, 181
Interpersonal skills, 6–7, 19–24, 48
Inventory, 294–295
Italics, 146
Itinerary, 281–282

J

Job descriptions, 290–291
Journals, medical, 151, 280

K

Keyboards, 65, 67, 68
Kickbacks, 46

L

Labels, 115
Laboratory procedures
  CPT codes, 214
  lab reports, 166
Language barriers, 23–24
Laptops, 63
Late patients, 100
Lateral files, 114
Legal issues
  in collections, 245
  in retention of files, 126–127
  See also Medical law
Letter of agreement, 241
Letters
  of acknowledgment, 139, 235
  collection, 243
  consultation, 139–141, 166
  continuation pages, 138
  filing of, 111, 166
  follow-up, 141
  formatting, 134–137
  of information, 139
  punctuation, 137
  referral, 139–141, 166
  transcribing, 181
Liability, 38–42
  abandonment, 40
  assault and battery, 40
  defined, 38
  fraud, 40–41
  malpractice, 39, 41, 48, 165
  termination, 39
  third-party, 240
Libraries, 279
Licenses, professional, 33, 127, 296
Licensure, 33, 127
Listening techniques, 175
Listings, 180
Litigation, 41–42, 165
  alternatives to trial, 42
  Good Samaritan act, 42
  malpractice, 39, 41, 48, 165

  physician's response to, 41
  safeguards against, 48–49
  statute of limitations, 42, 245
  steps in, 41
Local government, 122

M

Magnetic media, 66–67
Mail, 150–154
  incoming, 150–151
  outgoing, 151–154
  "Personal," 151
Mainframes, 62
Maintenance, 295–296
Major medical insurance, 193
Malpractice, 39, 41, 48, 165
Managed care, 195–197, 237
Managed care organizations, 12
Management qualifications, 276
Mathematics skills, 5
Maturity, 17
Media Mail, 152, 153
Medicaid, 12, 198, 201
Medical centers, employment
    opportunities, 11
Medical ethics. See Ethics
Medical histories, confidentiality of, 22
Medical insurance. See Insurance
Medical journals, 151, 280
Medical labs, 61, 166, 214
Medical law, 33–37
  compliance plans, 45–47
  confidentiality, 22–23, 42–45, 48–49
  liability, 38–42
  litigation safeguards, 48–49
  patient medical records as legal
    documents, 165
  of physician's practice, 34–38
  record retention requirements,
    126–127
  right to practice, 33–34
Medical management consultants, 278
Medical practice acts, 33
Medical records. See Patient medical
    records
Medical samples, 151
Medical Transcription Certification
    Commission (MTCC), 18
Medicare, 12, 126, 198, 269
  Advance Notice of Uncovered
    Services, 241
  fee schedules, 201, 204–205
  HCPCS coding, 215
  ICD-9-CM coding, 206–210
Medication list, 166
MEDLINE software, 279
Meeting arrangements, 283–288, 295
  basic preparation, 283–285
  last-minute preparation, 285–287
  minutes, 287–288
Meeting minutes, 287–288
Memorandums, interoffice, 141–142, 181

Message-taking, telephone, 82, 84–86, 89–90, 91
  answering services, 86
  follow-through, 91–92, 103
  message slips, 85–86
  patient medical records and, 85, 92
  verifying information, 86
Micrographics, 128
Microsoft Word, 69
Minicomputers, 62
Minors
  guarantors for dependent, 240
  legal consent form, 37
Minutes of meetings, 287–288
Missing files, 125–126
Mistakes. *See* Errors
Mobile-aisle files, 114
Modems, 66, 234, 266
Modified-block-style letters, 136
Modifiers, *CPT*, 212, 216, 217
Monitors, 65, 67, 71
Monthly billing, 238
Monthly reports, 227
Monthly summary, 255
Moral values, 31–32
Mouse, 65, 68

N

Narcotics registration, 34
National Board of Medical Examiners (NBME), 18, 33
NDCmedisoft™, 55, 59–61, 70, 97, 123, 124, 226–227, 234–235, 257, 259, 303–329
  backing up data, 309–310
  cases, 316–319
  dates in, 313
  deleting data, 314
  entering patient information, 314–316
  exiting, 314
  Help, 314
  menus, 311–312
  Office Hours, 95, 97, 323–328
  reports, 328–329
  restoring data, 310–311
  saving data, 314
  starting, 304–308
  student data disk, 303–304
  transaction entry, 319–323
Negotiable checks, 261–262
Net earnings, 270
Networking, 58, 73
New patients
  CPT codes, 213–214
  fee schedules and, 225
  orientation, 293
No shows, 95, 102
Nonparticipating provider (nonPAR), 200, 203–204
Nonpatients, 24
"Nonsufficient Funds" (NSF) notation, 263

Notes, 146
  chart, 165, 166, 172, 174
  CPT, 212
Numbers, 180
Numeric filing, 123–124

O

Objective findings, 170–171
Office hours, 93
Office management, 276–299
  editorial research projects, 279–280
  meeting arrangements, 283–288, 295
  office manager role, 277–278
  office manager's resources, 297
  patient information brochure, 288–290
  policies and procedures manual, 290–296
  responsibility for records, 296
  travel arrangements, 280–283
Office of the Inspector General (OIG), 45–47
Office personnel directory, 290
Office policy
  banking, 263
  collections, 242–245
  for scheduling appointments, 93–94
  transcription, 175
Office security, 295–296
One-write systems, 258
On-line, 58
Open punctuation, 137
Open-shelf files, 112
Operating system, 69
Optical storage media, 66–67
Oral communication, written communication versus, 134
Ordering procedures, 294–295
Ordinal numbers, 180
Organizational names, 121
Organizational skills, 5–6
Out guides, 115
Outgoing mail, 151–154
  classifications, 152
  electronic mail services, 153
  mail services, 152–153
Outgoing telephone calls, 87–92
Out-of-office emergencies, 101
Out-of-office appointments, 104
Output devices, 64–65, 69
Outside services file, 296
Outstanding checks, 265

P

"Paid in Full" annotation, 262
Palm computer, 63
Parcel Post, 152, 153
Part A, Medicare, 198
Part B, Medicare, 198
Participating provider (PAR), 200–201, 203–204
Passwords, 71–72, 153, 266
Past medical history (PMH), 169

Patient(s)
  abandonment by physician, 40
  billing. *See* Billing
  collections. *See* Collections
  conversation with, 20–21
  cultural diversity and, 23–24
  difficult, 21
  familiarity with, 19–20
  greeting, 19, 80–81
  language problems and, 23–24
  medical records of. *See* Patient medical records
  saying good-bye, 21, 80
  scheduling. *See* Appointment schedules
  social relationships with, 20
  terminally ill, 21
  termination of, 39, 244
Patient day sheet, 321
Patient education materials, 289
Patient encounter form, 205, 223–224
Patient information brochure, 288–290
  contents of, 289
  design considerations, 289–290
Patient information form, 228
Patient ledger cards, 255, 258
Patient medical records, 164–187
  confidentiality of, 23, 296
  contents of, 165–166
  corrections, 168
  electronic, 23, 45, 49, 55–56, 71–74
  filing, 111
  indexing, 118
  as legal documents, 165
  letters and, 151, 166
  nature of, 55
  NDCmedisoft™, 309–312
  ownership of, 183–184
  problem-oriented medical records (POMR), 172–174
  quality assurance, 184
  reasons for maintaining, 167–168
  recording transactions, 223–227
  retention of, 127
  SOAP format, 168–171, 173, 174
  telephone messages in, 85, 92
  transcription guidelines, 175–183
  transferring, 291–292
Patient names
  indexing, 120–121
  verifying, 86, 99, 101
Patient statements, 225–226, 321
Payment plans, 239
Payment types, 237–240
  cash, 237–238
  fee adjustment, 239
  health insurance, 240
  payment plans, 239
  from statements, 238
  third-party liability, 240
Payroll, 268–272
  calculating, 270
  creating employee records, 268

Payroll, *Continued*
  deductions, 268–270
  electronic, 272
  employer's tax responsibilities, 270–271
  FICA tax, 269, 270
  identification numbers, 269
  retention of records, 271
Pegboard accounting, 258
Periods (.), 176, 179
Personal computers, 63
Personal digital assistant (PDA), 63
"Personal" notation, 151
Personal telephone calls, 82, 84
Personal titles, 20, 121
Personality
  components of, 7–8
  defined, 7
Petty cash fund, 267
Physical exam (PE), 170–171
Physician-patient relationship
  abandonment by physician, 40
  confidentiality in, 22–23, 42–45,
    48–49, 71–74
  consent in, 35–38
  requirements of patient, 35
  requirements of physician, 34–35
  termination of patient, 39, 244
Physician practice
  employment opportunities, 9
  medical law in, 34–38
  records of. *See* Practice management
    records
Physician research, 61, 279–280
Physicians. *See* Doctors
Plaintiff, 41
Plan, 171
Planning
  meeting, 283–287
  telephone call, 87
  travel, 280–283
Pointers, 65
Policies and procedures manual, 290–296
  contents of, 290–296
  format of, 290
Post Electronic Courier Service
    (PosteCS), 153
Postdated checks, 261
Posting, 255
PPO (preferred provider organization),
    197, 225
Practice analysis report, 259, 260
Practice management records
  fee schedules, 224–225
  nature of, 111
  retention of, 127
Preauthorization, 195, 196
Predated checks, 262
Preferred provider organizations (PPOs),
    197, 225
Prefixes, 120
Premium, 191

Prepositions, 121
Prescriptions
  narcotic, 34
  refills, 82
Presentation software, 69–70
Primary care providers (PCPs), 196
Primary diagnosis, 207
Primary procedure, 216
Printers, 65, 90
Priority Mail, 152, 153
Private-sector payers, 197
Problem list, 173
Problem-oriented medical records (POMR),
    172–174
Problem-solving, 14, 230, 278
Procedural coding, 205, 211–216, 236
  basic steps, 215–216
  CPT-4, 211–216
Procedure day sheet, 257, 321
Professional growth, 17–19
Professional image, 16–17
  maturity, 17
  physical attributes, 16–17
Professional licenses, 33, 127, 296
Professional Secretaries International (PSI),
    18–19
Professional suffixes, 121
Professional titles, 20, 121
Proof, 257
Proofreading, 147–149
  of coding, 210
  common errors, 149
  defined, 147
  insurance claim forms, 231
  methods, 147–148
  symbols, 148
  techniques, 149
Provider, 191
*Publication Manual of the American
    Psychological Association*, 146
Punctuality, 14–15
Punctuation, 137

Q

Quadrants, 121
Quality assurance, 184
Quotation marks ("), 176
Quotations, 146

R

RAM (random-access memory), 64
Read-only memory (ROM), 64
Reasonable and necessary service, 46
Reasonable fees, 204
Rebundling, 214
Recalls, 103
Receipts
  charge/receipt slips, 255, 258
  retention of, 127
  return, 153
Recording secretary, 288

Records management, 3, 110–131
  confidentiality of records, 23, 296
  defined, 111
  filing equipment, 112–114
  filing supplies, 114–116
  filing systems, 118–126, 291
  ownership of medical records, 183–184
  retention of records, 126–128
  steps in filing, 116–118
  See also Financial records; Patient
    medical records
Referral letters, 139–141, 166
Referrals, 46, 139–141, 166, 196, 214
Registered mail, 153
Registered Medical Assistant (RMA), 18
Registration
  of narcotics, 34
  registering arrivals, 101–102
Registry, 267
Reimbursement details, 230
Relative subject index, 124, 125
Relative value scale (RVS), 204
Release of information, 42–43, 72, 89, 228
Releasing, 116
Reports, 143–146
  draft manuscripts, 143
  final manuscripts, 143–146
  medical, 166
  statutory, 44–45
Reprints, 280
Reservations, 281
Residents, 34
Resource-based relative value scale
    (RBRVS), 205
Responsibility
  employer tax, 270–271
  of office manager, 297
  for records, 296
  for referrals, 214
Restricted delivery, 153
Restrictive endorsement, 262
Retention of files, 126–128
  disposition of records, 128
  legal requirements, 126–127
  paper versus electronic files, 128
  payroll records, 271
  time frames for, 127
Return receipt, 153
Returned checks, 263
Review of systems (ROS), 169
ROM (read-only memory), 64
Roman numerals, 122, 180
Rotary circular file, 112
Rule out (R/O), 171

S

Safety, 295–296
Sales representatives, 24
Same-day appointments (SDA), 98
Samples, medical, 151
Scanners, 65, 146, 234

Scheduled appointments, 94, 96
Scheduling, 3, 54
Scientific Style and Format (Council of Biology Editors), 146
Screen savers, 71
Screening telephone calls, 81–84
SDA (same-day appointments), 98
Self-motivation, 15
Self-referrals, 46
Semicolons (;), 177
Seniority designations, 121
Servers, 58
Settlement, 42
Sign language, 24
Signature confirmation, 153
Signatures
    electronic, 72, 266–267
    e-signature, 72, 266–267
    on interoffice memorandums, 142
    on letters, 139
    on release of information, 42–43, 72, 89, 228
Simplified-style letter, 136–137
Single-entry bookkeeping, 258
SOAP format, 168–171, 173, 174
Social history (SH), 169
Social relationships, with patients, 20
Social Security benefits, 198
Social security numbers, 269, 271, 296
Software, 69–70
    accounting, 256, 259
    database, 60, 62, 70, 172–173, 279
    NDCmedisoft™, 55, 59–61, 70, 97, 123, 124, 226–227, 234–235, 257, 259, 303–321
    scheduling, 95, 97, 102
    spell checkers, 69, 147–148, 149
    spreadsheet, 70, 259
    utilities, 70, 73
    virus checkers, 73
    voice recognition, 6, 18, 57
    word processing, 56–57, 69, 119, 147–148
SonicAir BestFlight, 153–154
Sorting, of files, 117
Specialties, medical
    for administrative medical assistants, 10
    certification requirements, 34
    list of, 10
    referral and consultation letters, 139–141
    referrals, 46, 196, 214
Spell checkers, 69, 147–148, 149
Spreadsheet programs, 70, 259
Standard punctuation, 137
Stat, 97, 98
State government, 122
State names, 121
Statements, 225–226, 238
Statute of limitations, 42, 245
Statutory reports, 44–45
Storage devices and media, 66–67
Storing, of files, 117
Straight-numeric filing, 123
Street names, 121

Style manuals, 146, 181
Subject filing, 124
Subjective findings, 168
Subpoena, 41
Suffixes, professional, 121
Summaries, 259–260
Summons, 41
Supercomputers, 62
Supplies, filing, 114–116
Surgical procedures
    CPT codes, 214
    information needed for, 104
    insurance for, 193
Symbols
    filing rules for, 121
    proofreading, 148
    transcription, 181

T
Tabs, 114–115
Tabular List (*ICD-9-CM*), 207–209, 210
Tact, 15
Tax records
    payroll, 269, 270–271
    retention of, 127
Team player, 15
Telephone Consumer Protection Act of 1991, 242
Telephone skills, 6, 79–92, 293–294
    answering calls, 79–86
    answering services, 86
    automated features, 88, 89
    collection, 243
    directories, 88
    e-mail, 90–91
    emergency calls, 83, 84, 86
    etiquette, 79–81
    fax machines, 45, 89–90
    follow-through, 91–92, 103
    greetings, 80–81
    identification, 80–81, 89
    incoming calls, 79–86
    message-taking, 82, 84–86, 89–90, 91
    outgoing calls, 87–92
    personal calls, 82, 84
    placing calls, 89
    planning calls, 87
    prescription refills, 82
    screening calls, 81–84
    transferring calls, 84
    See also Appointment schedules
Templates, 69
Terminal-digit filing, 123
Terminally ill patients, 21
Terminated account, 244
Termination, 39, 244
Third-party checks, 262
Third-party liability, 240
Third-party payers, 191–192, 228–229, 267
Thoroughness, 12
Tickler file, 117–118, 151

Title page, 144, 145
Titles
    of doctors, 20
    of patients, 20, 121
Today appointments, 97, 98
Trackballs, 65
Transcription, 175–183
    guidelines, 176–181
    listening techniques, 175
    office policy, 175
Transferring
    patient medical records, 291–292
    telephone calls, 84
Travel agents, 281–282
Travel arrangements, 280–283
    changes in travel plans, 281–282
    duties related to physician's absence, 282–283
    guidelines, 280–281
    reservations, 281
Triage, 97
TRICARE, 198–199
Truth in Lending Act of 1960, 245

U
UCR fees, 204
Unbundling, 214, 217
Uncollectible accounts, 245
Underscoring, 146
Unemployment taxes, 270
United Parcel Service (UPS), 153–154
U.S. Department of Health and Human Services (HHS), 201
    Office of the Inspector General (OIG), 45–47
U.S. Department of Labor, 9
United States Postal Service (USPS), 152–153
Units of measure, 180
University of Chicago, 146
Upcoding, 217
UPS (United Parcel Service), 153–154
Usual fees, 204
Utilities software, 70, 73

V
Verifying information, 86, 99, 101, 231
Vertical files, 113
Virus checkers, 73
Voice-recognition software, 6, 18, 57
Voluntary deductions, 270
Voucher, 267

W
Wave scheduling, 95, 96
Wireless technologies, 6, 59
Withdrawal letter, 39
Withholding, 269, 271
Word processing programs, 56–57, 69, 119, 147–148
WordPerfect, 69
Work ethic, 12–15
Workers' compensation, 199–200

Write-offs, 239
Written communications, 133–157
    continuation pages, 138
    editing, 147, 150
    formatting, 134–137, 141–146,
        168–174, 290
    interoffice memorandums,
        141–142, 181

    letters, 134–141, 166
    oral communication versus, 134
    processing mail, 150–154
    professional reports, 143–146
    proofreading, 147–149
    punctuation, 137
    statutory reports, 44–45

X
X-ray reports, 166

Z
ZIP Codes, 152
Zip drive, 66

Working Papers

WORKING PAPERS

WP Number	Title
1	Medical Specialists
2	Work Ethic and Interpersonal Relationships
3	Physician's Obligations and Medical Law
4	Medical Liability and Communications
5	Legal Terms
6	Computer Terms
7	Computer Technology
8–15	Taking Messages
16	Scheduling Decision Making
17–33	Setting Up Dr. Larsen's Practice
34	Rescheduling Appointments
35	Out-of-Office Scheduling
36–37	Composing a Referral Letter
38–39	Proofing and Editing Reports
40	Communications Terms
41–42	Patient Information Forms
43	Records Release Form
44	Telephone Log
45	To-Do List
46	Insurance Terminology
47	Insurance Plan, Payers, and Payment Methods
48–49	Identifying Diagnostic and Procedure Codes
50	Updating Patient Statements
51	Telephone Log
52	To-Do List
53	Letter from Dr. Tai
54	Receipts
55	Florence Sherman's Patient Encounter Form
56	Stephen Villano's Patient Encounter Form
57	Gary Robertson's Patient Encounter Form
58	Monica Armstrong's Patient Encounter Form
59	Doris Casagranda's Patient Encounter Form
60	Cheng Sun's Patient Encounter Form

WP Number	Title
61	Charles Jonanthan III's Patient Encounter Form
62	Sara Babcock's Patient Encounter Form
63	Gene Sinclair's Patient Encounter Form
64	Laura Lund's Patient Encounter Form
65	Ana Mendez's Patient Encounter Form
66	Donald Mitchell's Patient Encounter Form
67	Theresa Dayton's Patient Encounter Form
68	Raymond Murrary's Patient Encounter Form
69–72	Updating Daily Journals
73	Deposits
74	Telephone Log
75	To-Do List
76	Marc Phan's Patient Encounter Form
77	Sarah Morton's Patient Encounter Form
78	Doris Casagranda's Patient Encounter Form
79	Randy Burton's Patient Encounter Form
80	Gary Robertson's Patient Encounter Form
81	Checks received
82	Daily journal #106
83	Monica Armstrong's Patient Encounter Form
84	Jeffrey Kramer's Patient Encounter Form
85	Cheng Sun's Patient Encounter Form
86	Checks received
87	Daily journal #107
88	Thomas Baab's Patient Encounter Form
89	Theresa Dayton's Patient Encounter Form
90	Ardis Matthew's Patient Encounter Form
91	Ana Mendez's Patient Encounter Form
92	Gary Robertson's Patient Encounter Form
93	Florence Sherman's Patient Encounter Form
94	Checks received
95	Daily journal #108

MEDICAL SPECIALISTS

Directions: Match the term in Column 2 with its definition in Column 1.

Column 1

q   1. Uses surgery to diagnose and treat diseases of the chest.

p   2. Cares for the eyes and the vision.

g   3. Provides total health care for the family.

q   4. Specializes in jaw surgery and extractions.

e   5. Specializes in diseases of the digestive tract and related organs.

s   6. Provides treatment for the musculoskeletal system.

b   7. Maintains pain relief and stable body functions of patients during surgical procedures.

n   8. Diagnoses and treats cancer.

e   9. Specializes in root canal work.

i   10. Diagnoses and treats urinary tract disease.

u   11. Treats the process and problems of aging.

a   12. Evaluates and treats all types of diseases through physical means.

a   13. Diagnoses and treats adverse reactions to foods, drugs, and other substances.

l   14. Specializes in disorders of the kidneys and related functions.

____ 15. Specializes in straightening teeth.

n   16. Provides care during pregnancy and childbirth.

w   17. Diagnoses and treats mental, emotional, and behavioral disorders.

m   18. Specializes in disorders of the nervous system.

c   19. Diagnoses and treats diseases of the skin and related tissues.

t   20. Specializes in comprehensive treatment of children.

f   21. Specializes in the diagnosis and treatment of illnesses of the ears, nose, and throat.

f   22. Provides immediate treatment for patient trauma in accidents and illnesses.

____ 23. Diagnoses and treats symptoms of immunity, induced sensitivity, and allergies.

____ 24. Specializes in dentures and artificial teeth.

j   25. Diagnoses and treats diseases of the blood.

Column 2

a. allergist
b. anesthesiologist
c. dermatologist
d. emergency room physician
e. endodontist
f. ENT specialist
g. family practice physician
h. gastroenterologist
i. gerontologist
j. hematologist
k. immunologist
l. nephrologist
m. neurologist
n. obstetrician
o. oncologist
p. ophthalmologist
q. oral surgeon
r. orthodontist
s. orthopedist
t. pediatrician
u. physiatrist
v. prosthodontist
w. psychiatrist
x. thoracic surgeon
y. urologist

homework

WORK ETHIC AND INTERPERSONAL RELATIONSHIPS

Directions: Match the term in Column 2 with its definition in Column 1.

Column 1

k 1. On time and ready to work.

b 2. Inspired to increase knowledge and to advance.

a 3. Able to produce work with few or no errors.

f 4. Able to understand how a patient feels.

o 5. Careful to pay attention to detail.

h 6. Truthful; trustworthy.

d 7. Privacy for all patient information.

i 8. Ability to take independent action.

j 9. The correct appearance for the job.

m 10. Able to present ideas and information without offending.

n 11. A person who works well with associates and pitches in when needed.

n 12. Able to make good use of time and materials and to be organized.

l 13. Able to present ideas to others with confidence.

c 14. Pleasant and friendly.

g 15. Able to adapt to new conditions; willing to try new ideas.

Column 2

a. accurate

b. assertive

c. cheerful

d. confidentiality

e. efficient

f. empathetic

g. flexible

h. honest

i. initiative

j. professional image

k. punctual

l. self-motivated

m. tactful

n. team player

o. thorough

homework

PHYSICIAN'S OBLIGATIONS AND MEDICAL LAW

Directions: The following items refer to the obligations of the physician and/or medical law. Mark each statement with either "T" for *true* or "F" for *false*. Be prepared to discuss your answers in class.

_T_   1. The Principles of Medical Ethics states that the physician may refuse to accept a new patient.

_F_   2. A license to practice is good for the life of the physician.

_T_   3. A physician must obtain an annual permit for narcotic registration.

_F_   4. The physician is legally obligated to inform a patient of all possible reactions to a medication.

_F_   5. A physician must obtain a written consent before seeing a new patient.

_T_   6. A physician is legally obligated to seek a referral if the conditions are beyond the physician's scope of knowledge.

_T_   7. A physician's license to practice medicine is valid in all fifty states.

_T_   8. Medical practice acts, established by law, govern the practice of medicine.

_F_   9. The physician cannot refuse to perform a procedure on a patient because of that physician's moral beliefs.

_F_   10. The Drug Education Administration issues narcotic registration and annual renewals.

_F_   11. When a patient visits a physician for an appointment, he or she is establishing implied consent.

_T_   12. A physician must obtain the maximum amount of education in a particular medical specialty before becoming certified in that specialty.

_T_   13. The adult age as defined by law is known as *majority*.

_T_   14. Express consent is not required in an emergency situation.

_F_   15. A physician must sign a consent form before performing any procedure.

MEDICAL LIABILITY AND COMMUNICATIONS

Directions: The following items refer to medical liability and communications. Mark each statement with either "T" for *true* or "F" for *false*. Be prepared to discuss your answers in class.

F **1.** The charge of battery exists when there is a clear threat of injury to another.

T **2.** A subpoena orders the defendant to answer the stated charges.

F **(3.)** Contributory negligence may exist if the patient has failed to follow the physician's advice and treatment.

T **4.** Access to health records is the form that contains written permission to release patient information.

T **5.** Defensive medicine means the physician is dissolving legal responsibility.

F **6.** An authorization for release of information does not have the physician's signature.

T **7.** A statute of limitations controls the time limit for starting a lawsuit.

F **8.** Using e-mail to transmit medical documents is preferred over faxing documents.

F **9.** In a lawsuit, the burden of proof that malpractice exists rests on the patient.

T **10.** The physician may be charged with abandonment if the physician discontinues care without sending proper notification to the patient.

T **11.** Statutory reports require that the patient's condition be reported to the patient's insurance.

T **12.** Operating beyond the patient's expressed consent may establish a charge of battery.

F **(13.)** A deposition is sent to the defendant requiring the defendant's appearance in court.

F **14.** A Good Samaritan act states that a patient may start a lawsuit upon reaching majority.

T **15.** HIPAA is a federal law that protects the security and privacy of a patient's electronic health information.

LEGAL TERMS

Directions: Match the term in Column 2 with its definition in Column 1.

Column 1

_g_ 1. Standards of right and wrong conduct.
_e_ 2. Adherence to rules and regulations.
_l_ 3. Patient's permission for treatment when he or she enters a doctor's office.
_m_ 4. Legal responsibility.
_f_ 5. Testimony under oath, usually outside of court.
_h_ 6. Behavior and customs that are considered good manners.
_q_ 7. Time limit for a lawsuit to start.
_a_ 8. Physician's leaving a case before the patient is recovered.
_o_ 9. State law that governs the state's practice of medicine.
_i_ 10. Patient's written agreement to have a procedure performed.
_c_ 11. Clear threat of injury.
_j_ 12. Depriving others of their rights by dishonest means.
_n_ 13. A lawsuit.
_s_ 14. Legal document ordering all relevant documents to be submitted to the court.
_p_ 15. Authorization to send the patient's information to another physician.
_d_ 16. Operating beyond the patient's given consent.
_t_ 17. Written notice sent to the defendant asking for an answer to the charges.
_b_ 18. Resolution of a case brought about by an unbiased third party.
_k_ 19. Protection for the physician from liability of civil damages in emergency care.
_r_ 20. Confidential information that must be submitted to the state department.

Column 2

a. abandonment
b. arbitration
c. assault
d. battery
e. compliance
f. deposition
g. ethics
h. etiquette
i. express consent
j. fraud
k. Good Samaritan act
l. implied consent
m. liability
n. litigation
o. medical practice act
p. release of information
q. statute of limitations
r. statutory report
s. subpoena
t. summons

COMPUTER TERMS

Directions: Match the term in Column 2 with its definition in Column 1.

Column 1

a **1.** Software that relates to specific tasks such as word processing.

c **2.** Communications system for exchanging messages written on a computer over telephone lines.

d **3.** Portable, notebook-sized computers.

a **4.** The brain of a computer.

o **5.** Software that allows a person to edit a printed document.

f **6.** A display screen.

t **7.** Software that transcribes spoken words into text without using a keyboard.

j **8.** A system that allows a group of computers to communicate, exchange information, or pool resources.

t **9.** A personal computer small enough to fit in a person's hand.

e **10.** Software that allows the creation of images on the computer.

m **11.** A collection of related data.

d **12.** A removable storage medium.

o **13.** Temporary computer memory.

l **14.** Software that allows numerical data to be tabulated according to mathematical formulas.

b **15.** A device to input data.

Column 2

a. application software
b. CPU
c. database
d. diskette
e. e-mail
f. graphics application
g. keyboard
h. monitor
i. networking
j. palm computer
k. laptops
l. RAM
m. spreadsheet program
n. voice-recognition software
o. word processing program

COMPUTER TECHNOLOGY

Directions: The following items refer to computer technology. Mark each statement with either "T" for *true* or "F" for *false*. Be prepared to discuss your answers in class.

T   **1.** It is easier to locate open time slots for appointments on an electronic scheduler than on a paper schedule.

F   **2.** Only one user at a time can access a file on a network.

T   **3.** A mainframe computer is necessary to operate any doctor's office.

T   **4.** A firewall prevents outsider parties from access to the office's particular files.

T   **5.** ROM is temporary; everything in ROM disappears when the computer is shut down.

F   **6.** When you are on-line, you are connected to a network.

T   **7.** An electronic medical record must be backed up with a paper medical record.

F   **8.** E-mail systems do not allow you to print the message.

T   **9.** A transaction database contains data on a specific patient's visit, including such items as services rendered during that visit, necessary diagnosis and procedure codes, and so forth.

T   **10.** The cost of filing an electronic insurance claim is higher than that of filing a paper copy.

T   **11.** A scanner allows you to enter information into the computer's memory without keying it.

T   **12.** Designing the work environment to conform to the physical needs of a user is ergonomics.

F   **13.** A firewall turns data into unrecognizable information during transmission.

F   **14.** Wireless communication transmits data through telephone wires.

T   **15.** The most powerful computer available is the supercomputer.

T   **16.** Virus checkers do not need to be updated.

T   **17.** A screen saver protects data from being seen by others.

T   **18.** Everyone in the medical office will be performing audit trails on computer usage.

T   **19.** Passwords are designed to limit access to computer files.

F   **20.** An office does not need a signed release-of-information form for use with electronic medical records.

MESSAGE

TO _____

DATE _____ TIME _____

FROM _____

PHONE _____

☐ PLEASE CALL ☐ RETURNED YOUR CALL ☐ WILL CALL AGAIN

REGARDING _____

_____

_____

_____

TAKEN BY _____

MESSAGE

TO _____

DATE _____ TIME _____

FROM _____

PHONE _____

☐ PLEASE CALL ☐ RETURNED YOUR CALL ☐ WILL CALL AGAIN

REGARDING _____

_____

_____

_____

TAKEN BY _____

MESSAGE

TO _____

DATE _____ TIME _____

FROM _____

PHONE _____

☐ PLEASE CALL ☐ RETURNED YOUR CALL ☐ WILL CALL AGAIN

REGARDING _____

_____

_____

_____

TAKEN BY _____

MESSAGE

TO _____

DATE _____ TIME _____

FROM _____

PHONE _____

☐ PLEASE CALL ☐ RETURNED YOUR CALL ☐ WILL CALL AGAIN

REGARDING _____

_____

_____

_____

TAKEN BY _____

MESSAGE

TO _____
DATE _____ TIME _____
FROM _____
PHONE _____
☐ PLEASE CALL ☐ RETURNED YOUR CALL ☐ WILL CALL AGAIN
REGARDING _____
_____
_____
_____
TAKEN BY _____

MESSAGE

TO _____
DATE _____ TIME _____
FROM _____
PHONE _____
☐ PLEASE CALL ☐ RETURNED YOUR CALL ☐ WILL CALL AGAIN
REGARDING _____
_____
_____
_____
TAKEN BY _____

MESSAGE

TO _____
DATE _____ TIME _____
FROM _____
PHONE _____
☐ PLEASE CALL ☐ RETURNED YOUR CALL ☐ WILL CALL AGAIN
REGARDING _____
_____
_____
_____
TAKEN BY _____

MESSAGE

TO _____
DATE _____ TIME _____
FROM _____
PHONE _____
☐ PLEASE CALL ☐ RETURNED YOUR CALL ☐ WILL CALL AGAIN
REGARDING _____
_____
_____
_____
TAKEN BY _____

MESSAGE

TO _____ DATE _____ TIME _____

FROM _____

PHONE _____

☐ PLEASE CALL   ☐ RETURNED YOUR CALL   ☐ WILL CALL AGAIN

REGARDING _____

_____

_____

_____

TAKEN BY _____

MESSAGE

TO _____ DATE _____ TIME _____

FROM _____

PHONE _____

☐ PLEASE CALL   ☐ RETURNED YOUR CALL   ☐ WILL CALL AGAIN

REGARDING _____

_____

_____

_____

TAKEN BY _____

MESSAGE

TO _____ DATE _____ TIME _____

FROM _____

PHONE _____

☐ PLEASE CALL   ☐ RETURNED YOUR CALL   ☐ WILL CALL AGAIN

REGARDING _____

_____

_____

_____

TAKEN BY _____

MESSAGE

TO _____ DATE _____ TIME _____

FROM _____

PHONE _____

☐ PLEASE CALL   ☐ RETURNED YOUR CALL   ☐ WILL CALL AGAIN

REGARDING _____

_____

_____

_____

TAKEN BY _____

MESSAGE

TO _____
DATE _____ TIME _____

FROM _____

PHONE _____

☐ PLEASE CALL   ☐ RETURNED YOUR CALL   ☐ WILL CALL AGAIN

REGARDING _____
_____
_____
_____

TAKEN BY _____

MESSAGE

TO _____
DATE _____ TIME _____

FROM _____

PHONE _____

☐ PLEASE CALL   ☐ RETURNED YOUR CALL   ☐ WILL CALL AGAIN

REGARDING _____
_____
_____
_____

TAKEN BY _____

MESSAGE

TO _____
DATE _____ TIME _____

FROM _____

PHONE _____

☐ PLEASE CALL   ☐ RETURNED YOUR CALL   ☐ WILL CALL AGAIN

REGARDING _____
_____
_____
_____

TAKEN BY _____

MESSAGE

TO _____
DATE _____ TIME _____

FROM _____

PHONE _____

☐ PLEASE CALL   ☐ RETURNED YOUR CALL   ☐ WILL CALL AGAIN

REGARDING _____
_____
_____
_____

TAKEN BY _____

MESSAGE

TO _____

DATE _____ TIME _____

FROM _____

PHONE _____

☐ PLEASE CALL   ☐ RETURNED YOUR CALL   ☐ WILL CALL AGAIN

REGARDING _____

_____

_____

_____

TAKEN BY _____

MESSAGE

TO _____

DATE _____ TIME _____

FROM _____

PHONE _____

☐ PLEASE CALL   ☐ RETURNED YOUR CALL   ☐ WILL CALL AGAIN

REGARDING _____

_____

_____

_____

TAKEN BY _____

MESSAGE

TO _____

DATE _____ TIME _____

FROM _____

PHONE _____

☐ PLEASE CALL   ☐ RETURNED YOUR CALL   ☐ WILL CALL AGAIN

REGARDING _____

_____

_____

_____

TAKEN BY _____

MESSAGE

TO _____

DATE _____ TIME _____

FROM _____

PHONE _____

☐ PLEASE CALL   ☐ RETURNED YOUR CALL   ☐ WILL CALL AGAIN

REGARDING _____

_____

_____

_____

TAKEN BY _____

MESSAGE

TO _____

DATE _____ TIME _____

FROM _____

PHONE _____

☐ PLEASE CALL   ☐ RETURNED YOUR CALL   ☐ WILL CALL AGAIN

REGARDING _____

_____

_____

_____

TAKEN BY _____

MESSAGE

TO _____

DATE _____ TIME _____

FROM _____

PHONE _____

☐ PLEASE CALL   ☐ RETURNED YOUR CALL   ☐ WILL CALL AGAIN

REGARDING _____

_____

_____

_____

TAKEN BY _____

MESSAGE

TO _____

DATE _____ TIME _____

FROM _____

PHONE _____

☐ PLEASE CALL   ☐ RETURNED YOUR CALL   ☐ WILL CALL AGAIN

REGARDING _____

_____

_____

_____

TAKEN BY _____

MESSAGE

TO _____

DATE _____ TIME _____

FROM _____

PHONE _____

☐ PLEASE CALL   ☐ RETURNED YOUR CALL   ☐ WILL CALL AGAIN

REGARDING _____

_____

_____

_____

TAKEN BY _____

MESSAGE

TO _____ DATE _____ TIME _____

FROM _____

PHONE _____

☐ PLEASE CALL   ☐ RETURNED YOUR CALL   ☐ WILL CALL AGAIN

REGARDING _____

_____

_____

_____

TAKEN BY _____

MESSAGE

TO _____ DATE _____ TIME _____

FROM _____

PHONE _____

☐ PLEASE CALL   ☐ RETURNED YOUR CALL   ☐ WILL CALL AGAIN

REGARDING _____

_____

_____

_____

TAKEN BY _____

MESSAGE

TO _____ DATE _____ TIME _____

FROM _____

PHONE _____

☐ PLEASE CALL   ☐ RETURNED YOUR CALL   ☐ WILL CALL AGAIN

REGARDING _____

_____

_____

_____

TAKEN BY _____

MESSAGE

TO _____ DATE _____ TIME _____

FROM _____

PHONE _____

☐ PLEASE CALL   ☐ RETURNED YOUR CALL   ☐ WILL CALL AGAIN

REGARDING _____

_____

_____

_____

TAKEN BY _____

MESSAGE

TO _____

DATE _____ TIME _____

FROM _____

PHONE _____

☐ PLEASE CALL ☐ RETURNED YOUR CALL ☐ WILL CALL AGAIN

REGARDING _____

_____

_____

_____

TAKEN BY _____

MESSAGE

TO _____

DATE _____ TIME _____

FROM _____

PHONE _____

☐ PLEASE CALL ☐ RETURNED YOUR CALL ☐ WILL CALL AGAIN

REGARDING _____

_____

_____

_____

TAKEN BY _____

MESSAGE

TO _____

DATE _____ TIME _____

FROM _____

PHONE _____

☐ PLEASE CALL ☐ RETURNED YOUR CALL ☐ WILL CALL AGAIN

REGARDING _____

_____

_____

_____

TAKEN BY _____

MESSAGE

TO _____

DATE _____ TIME _____

FROM _____

PHONE _____

☐ PLEASE CALL ☐ RETURNED YOUR CALL ☐ WILL CALL AGAIN

REGARDING _____

_____

_____

_____

TAKEN BY _____

SCHEDULING DECISION MAKING

Directions: The following calls in Column 1 are for a family practice physician. The physician does see emergencies in the office. Choose the appropriate response from Column 2 to indicate when an appointment should be made for *STAT, Today, Tomorrow, Later,* or a message taken—*Take message.*

Column 1

d **1.** Loni Kayen desires weight control, 312-555-9834.

c **2.** North Lab's report on prothrombin time for Walter Boone; control was 11.6; patient, 18, 312-555-6757.

b **3.** Hank Holm at 312-555-4432 wants to talk to the doctor about his left leg cast; it seems too tight, feels numbness in his toes.

d **4.** Brian Verk at 312-555-2389 needs diabetes recheck.

c **5.** Kay Frank, bee sting, left face check, swelling and a hard spot in the middle; she has no allergies; 312-555-6734.

e **6.** Beth Cater has a urinary problem, hurts to urinate, no blood in urine, 312-555-9823.

A **7.** True Value Drug, 312-555-9877, prescription refill Diane Yvon, Coumadin 5 mg q.d., #60, last filled two months ago.

c **8.** Hu Grangdon, rash over abdomen times 2 days, itching, no new foods or meds, 312-555-3341.

a **9.** Ben Jones, BP recheck, 312-555-3478.

d **10.** Dana Lund, annual Pap smear, 312-555-0043.

e **11.** Donna Kelly, son Alex got hit in head with a bat, bleeding, swelling, 312-555-9823.

A **12.** North X-ray, 312-555-6757, chest x-ray on Ann Tyn is negative.

b **13.** Pamela Bond, 6-week checkup for baby Keith, 312-555-5636.

c **14.** Rein Los Ames, age 2 months, cranky, pulling right ear, slight temperature, 312-555-3223.

d **15.** Tom Urness, 312-555-5574, age 47, noticed blood in stools, very concerned, read about colon cancer in recent magazine.

d **16.** Karin Olsson, age 72, infected hangnail with green pus, hurts, swollen, 312-555-9966.

c **17.** Wendy Rinke, age 8, something in her eye, red, watering. Father was sanding where she was playing, 312-555-7845.

Column 2

a. STAT

b. Today

c. Tomorrow

d. Later

e. Take message

KAREN LARSEN, MD, OFFICE SCHEDULE
2235 South Ridgeway Avenue
Chicago, IL 60623-2240
312-555-6022
Fax: 312-555-0025

Monday, Tuesday, and Wednesday

Hospital rounds	8:00 a.m. – 10:00 a.m.
Travel time	10:00 a.m. – 10:30 a.m.
Patient appointments	10:30 a.m. – 12 noon
Lunch	12 noon – 1:00 p.m.
Teach and work at University Hospital	1:00 p.m. – 5:00 p.m.

Thursday

Teach and work at University Hospital	8:00 a.m. – 5:00 p.m.

Friday

Hospital rounds	8:00 a.m. – 10:00 a.m.
Travel time	10:00 a.m. – 10:30 a.m.
Office for dictation, messages, writing, and course preparation	10:30 a.m. – 12 noon
Office closed	12 noon – 5:00 p.m.

Length of Appointments

Complete physical examination	1 hour
All other appointments, unless designated	15 minutes

Appointment Abbreviations

abd	abdominal
BP	blood pressure
✓	checkup
Dx	diagnosis
ECG	electrocardiogram
F/U	follow-up visit
FX	fracture
GI	gastrointestinal
N & V	nausea and vomiting
NP	new patient
CPE, PE	physical examination
preop	preoperative
postop	postoperative

Monday, October 13

Time	
8:00	
8:15	
8:30	
8:45	
9:00	
9:15	
9:30	
9:45	
10:00	
10:15	
10:30	
10:45	
11:00	Seminar
11:15	
11:30	University
11:45	
12:00	
12:15	
12:30	
12:45	
1:00	
1:15	
1:30	
1:45	
2:00	
2:15	
2:30	
2:45	
3:00	
3:15	
3:30	
3:45	
4:00	
4:15	
4:30	
4:45	
5:00	

Tuesday, October 14

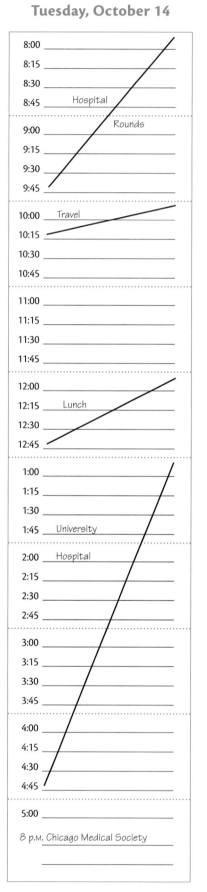

Time	
8:00	
8:15	
8:30	
8:45	Hospital
9:00	Rounds
9:15	
9:30	
9:45	
10:00	Travel
10:15	
10:30	
10:45	
11:00	
11:15	
11:30	
11:45	
12:00	
12:15	Lunch
12:30	
12:45	
1:00	
1:15	
1:30	
1:45	University
2:00	Hospital
2:15	
2:30	
2:45	
3:00	
3:15	
3:30	
3:45	
4:00	
4:15	
4:30	
4:45	
5:00	

8 p.m. Chicago Medical Society

Wednesday, October 15

Time	
8:00	
8:15	
8:30	
8:45	Hospital
9:00	Rounds
9:15	
9:30	
9:45	
10:00	Travel
10:15	
10:30	
10:45	
11:00	
11:15	
11:30	
11:45	
12:00	
12:15	Lunch
12:30	
12:45	
1:00	
1:15	
1:30	
1:45	University
2:00	Hospital
2:15	
2:30	
2:45	
3:00	
3:15	
3:30	
3:45	
4:00	
4:15	
4:30	
4:45	
5:00	

Thursday, October 16

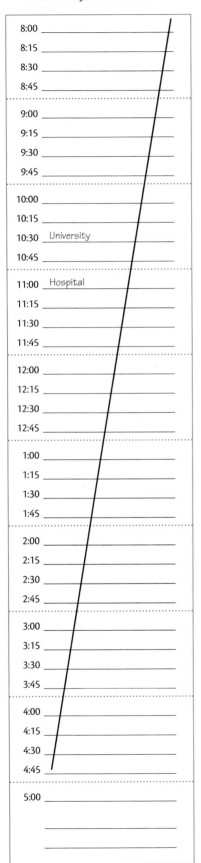

8:00 _____
8:15 _____
8:30 _____
8:45 _____

9:00 _____
9:15 _____
9:30 _____
9:45 _____

10:00 _____
10:15 _____
10:30 University _____
10:45 _____

11:00 Hospital _____
11:15 _____
11:30 _____
11:45 _____

12:00 _____
12:15 _____
12:30 _____
12:45 _____

1:00 _____
1:15 _____
1:30 _____
1:45 _____

2:00 _____
2:15 _____
2:30 _____
2:45 _____

3:00 _____
3:15 _____
3:30 _____
3:45 _____

4:00 _____
4:15 _____
4:30 _____
4:45 _____

5:00 _____

_____

_____

Friday, October 17

8:00 _____
8:15 _____
8:30 _____
8:45 Hospital _____

9:00 _____
9:15 Rounds _____
9:30 _____
9:45 _____

10:00 Travel _____
10:15 _____
10:30 _____
10:45 _____

11:00 Office _____
11:15 _____
11:30 _____
11:45 _____

12:00 _____
12:15 _____
12:30 _____
12:45 _____

1:00 Office _____
1:15 _____
1:30 Closed _____
1:45 _____

2:00 _____
2:15 _____
2:30 _____
2:45 _____

3:00 _____
3:15 _____
3:30 _____
3:45 _____

4:00 _____
4:15 _____
4:30 _____
4:45 _____

5:00 _____

_____

_____

October

S	M	T	W	T	F	S
			1	2	3	4
5	6	7	8	9	10	11
12	13	14	15	16	17	18
19	20	21	22	23	24	25
26	27	28	29	30	31	

November

S	M	T	W	T	F	S
						1
2	3	4	5	6	7	8
9	10	11	12	13	14	15
16	17	18	19	20	21	22
23	24	25	26	27	28	29
30						

December

S	M	T	W	T	F	S
	1	2	3	4	5	6
7	8	9	10	11	12	13
14	15	16	17	18	19	20
21	22	23	24	25	26	27
28	29	30	31			

Monday, October 20

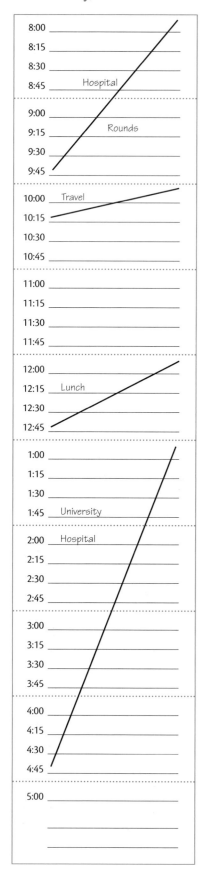

8:00 _____
8:15 _____
8:30 _____
8:45 ___ Hospital _____

9:00 _____
9:15 ____ Rounds _____
9:30 _____
9:45 _____

10:00 __ Travel _____
10:15 _____
10:30 _____
10:45 _____

11:00 _____
11:15 _____
11:30 _____
11:45 _____

12:00 _____
12:15 __ Lunch _____
12:30 _____
12:45 _____

1:00 _____
1:15 _____
1:30 _____
1:45 ___ University ___

2:00 ___ Hospital _____
2:15 _____
2:30 _____
2:45 _____

3:00 _____
3:15 _____
3:30 _____
3:45 _____

4:00 _____
4:15 _____
4:30 _____
4:45 _____

5:00 _____

_____
_____

Tuesday, October 21

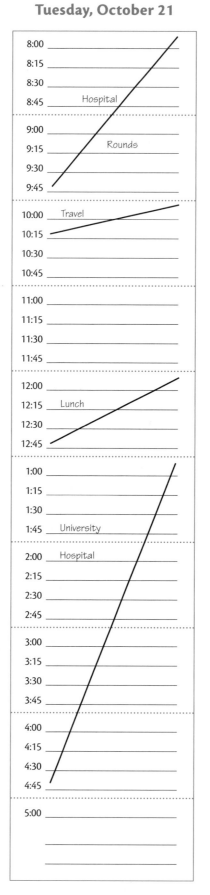

8:00 _____
8:15 _____
8:30 _____
8:45 ___ Hospital _____

9:00 _____
9:15 ____ Rounds _____
9:30 _____
9:45 _____

10:00 __ Travel _____
10:15 _____
10:30 _____
10:45 _____

11:00 _____
11:15 _____
11:30 _____
11:45 _____

12:00 _____
12:15 __ Lunch _____
12:30 _____
12:45 _____

1:00 _____
1:15 _____
1:30 _____
1:45 ___ University ___

2:00 ___ Hospital _____
2:15 _____
2:30 _____
2:45 _____

3:00 _____
3:15 _____
3:30 _____
3:45 _____

4:00 _____
4:15 _____
4:30 _____
4:45 _____

5:00 _____

_____
_____

Wednesday, October 22

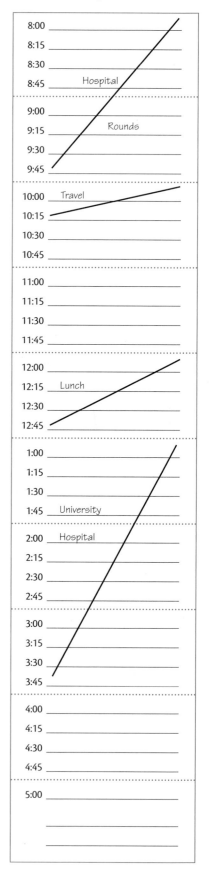

8:00 _____
8:15 _____
8:30 _____
8:45 ___ Hospital _____

9:00 _____
9:15 ____ Rounds _____
9:30 _____
9:45 _____

10:00 __ Travel _____
10:15 _____
10:30 _____
10:45 _____

11:00 _____
11:15 _____
11:30 _____
11:45 _____

12:00 _____
12:15 __ Lunch _____
12:30 _____
12:45 _____

1:00 _____
1:15 _____
1:30 _____
1:45 ___ University ___

2:00 ___ Hospital _____
2:15 _____
2:30 _____
2:45 _____

3:00 _____
3:15 _____
3:30 _____
3:45 _____

4:00 _____
4:15 _____
4:30 _____
4:45 _____

5:00 _____

Thursday, October 23

Time	
8:00	
8:15	
8:30	
8:45	
9:00	
9:15	
9:30	
9:45	
10:00	
10:15	
10:30	University
10:45	
11:00	Hospital
11:15	
11:30	
11:45	
12:00	
12:15	
12:30	
12:45	
1:00	
1:15	
1:30	
1:45	
2:00	
2:15	
2:30	
2:45	
3:00	
3:15	
3:30	
3:45	
4:00	
4:15	
4:30	
4:45	
5:00	

Friday, October 24

Time	
8:00	
8:15	
8:30	
8:45	Hospital
9:00	
9:15	Rounds
9:30	
9:45	
10:00	Travel
10:15	
10:30	
10:45	
11:00	Office
11:15	
11:30	
11:45	
12:00	
12:15	
12:30	
12:45	
1:00	Office
1:15	
1:30	Closed
1:45	
2:00	
2:15	
2:30	
2:45	
3:00	
3:15	
3:30	
3:45	
4:00	
4:15	
4:30	
4:45	
5:00	

October

S	M	T	W	T	F	S
			1	2	3	4
5	6	7	8	9	10	11
12	13	14	15	16	17	18
19	20	21	22	23	24	25
26	27	28	29	30	31	

November

S	M	T	W	T	F	S
						1
2	3	4	5	6	7	8
9	10	11	12	13	14	15
16	17	18	19	20	21	22
23	24	25	26	27	28	29
30						

December

S	M	T	W	T	F	S
	1	2	3	4	5	6
7	8	9	10	11	12	13
14	15	16	17	18	19	20
21	22	23	24	25	26	27
28	29	30	31			

Monday, October 27

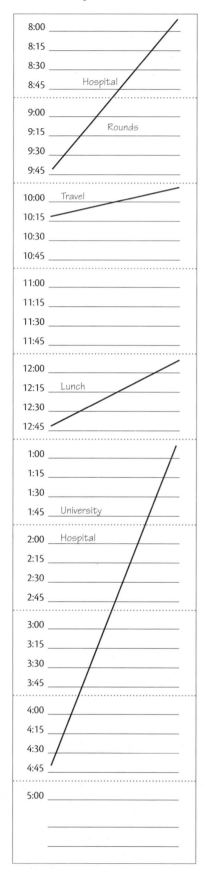

8:00
8:15
8:30
8:45 ____ Hospital

9:00
9:15 _____ Rounds
9:30
9:45

10:00 ___ Travel
10:15
10:30
10:45

11:00
11:15
11:30
11:45

12:00
12:15 ___ Lunch
12:30
12:45

1:00
1:15
1:30
1:45 ___ University

2:00 ___ Hospital
2:15
2:30
2:45

3:00
3:15
3:30
3:45

4:00
4:15
4:30
4:45

5:00

Tuesday, October 28

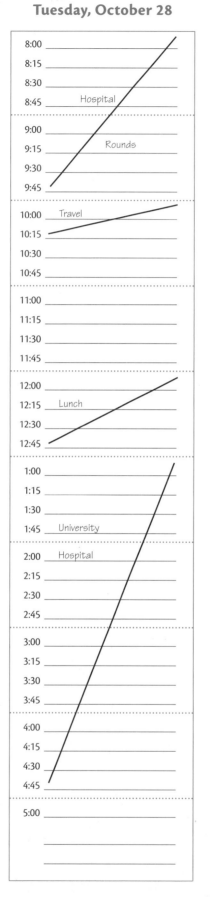

8:00
8:15
8:30
8:45 ____ Hospital

9:00
9:15 _____ Rounds
9:30
9:45

10:00 ___ Travel
10:15
10:30
10:45

11:00
11:15
11:30
11:45

12:00
12:15 ___ Lunch
12:30
12:45

1:00
1:15
1:30
1:45 ___ University

2:00 ___ Hospital
2:15
2:30
2:45

3:00
3:15
3:30
3:45

4:00
4:15
4:30
4:45

5:00

Wednesday, October 29

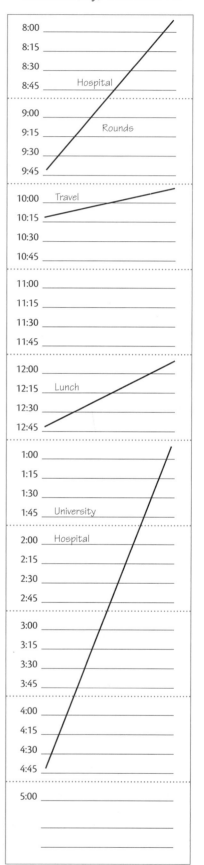

8:00
8:15
8:30
8:45 ____ Hospital

9:00
9:15 _____ Rounds
9:30
9:45

10:00 ___ Travel
10:15
10:30
10:45

11:00
11:15
11:30
11:45

12:00
12:15 ___ Lunch
12:30
12:45

1:00
1:15
1:30
1:45 ___ University

2:00 ___ Hospital
2:15
2:30
2:45

3:00
3:15
3:30
3:45

4:00
4:15
4:30
4:45

5:00

Thursday, October 30

8:00	
8:15	
8:30	
8:45	
9:00	
9:15	
9:30	
9:45	
10:00	
10:15	
10:30	University
10:45	
11:00	Hospital
11:15	
11:30	
11:45	
12:00	
12:15	
12:30	
12:45	
1:00	
1:15	
1:30	
1:45	
2:00	
2:15	
2:30	
2:45	
3:00	
3:15	
3:30	
3:45	
4:00	
4:15	
4:30	
4:45	
5:00	

Friday, October 31

8:00	
8:15	
8:30	
8:45	Hospital
9:00	
9:15	Rounds
9:30	
9:45	
10:00	Travel
10:15	
10:30	
10:45	
11:00	Office
11:15	
11:30	
11:45	
12:00	
12:15	
12:30	
12:45	
1:00	Office
1:15	
1:30	Closed
1:45	
2:00	
2:15	
2:30	
2:45	
3:00	
3:15	
3:30	
3:45	
4:00	
4:15	
4:30	
4:45	
5:00	

October

S	M	T	W	T	F	S
			1	2	3	4
5	6	7	8	9	10	11
12	13	14	15	16	17	18
19	20	21	22	23	24	25
26	27	28	29	30	31	

November

S	M	T	W	T	F	S
						1
2	3	4	5	6	7	8
9	10	11	12	13	14	15
16	17	18	19	20	21	22
23	24	25	26	27	28	29
30						

December

S	M	T	W	T	F	S
	1	2	3	4	5	6
7	8	9	10	11	12	13
14	15	16	17	18	19	20
21	22	23	24	25	26	27
28	29	30	31			

Monday, November 3

Time	
8:00	
8:15	
8:30	
8:45	Hospital
9:00	
9:15	Rounds
9:30	
9:45	
10:00	Travel
10:15	
10:30	
10:45	
11:00	Joseph Castro, CPE
11:15	555-1020
11:30	
11:45	
12:00	
12:15	Lunch
12:30	
12:45	
1:00	
1:15	
1:30	
1:45	University
2:00	Hospital
2:15	
2:30	
2:45	
3:00	
3:15	
3:30	
3:45	
4:00	
4:15	
4:30	
4:45	
5:00	

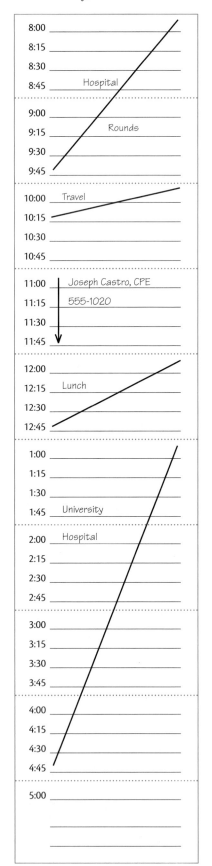

Tuesday, November 4

Time	
8:00	
8:15	
8:30	
8:45	Hospital
9:00	
9:15	Rounds
9:30	
9:45	
10:00	Travel
10:15	
10:30	
10:45	
11:00	
11:15	
11:30	
11:45	
12:00	
12:15	Lunch
12:30	
12:45	
1:00	
1:15	
1:30	
1:45	University
2:00	Hospital
2:15	
2:30	
2:45	
3:00	
3:15	
3:30	
3:45	
4:00	
4:15	
4:30	
4:45	
5:00	

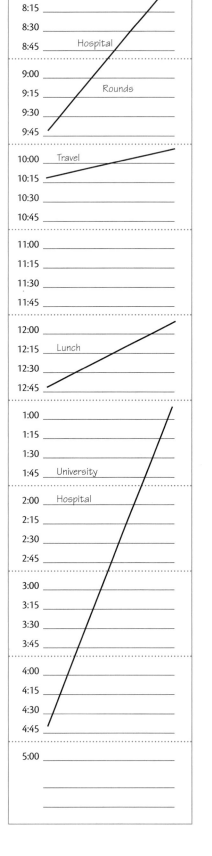

Wednesday, November 5

Time	
8:00	
8:15	
8:30	
8:45	Hospital
9:00	
9:15	Rounds
9:30	
9:45	
10:00	Travel
10:15	
10:30	Clarence Rogers, CPE
10:45	555-5297
11:00	
11:15	
11:30	
11:45	
12:00	
12:15	Lunch
12:30	
12:45	
1:00	
1:15	
1:30	
1:45	University
2:00	Hospital
2:15	
2:30	
2:45	
3:00	
3:15	
3:30	
3:45	
4:00	
4:15	
4:30	
4:45	
5:00	

Thursday, November 6

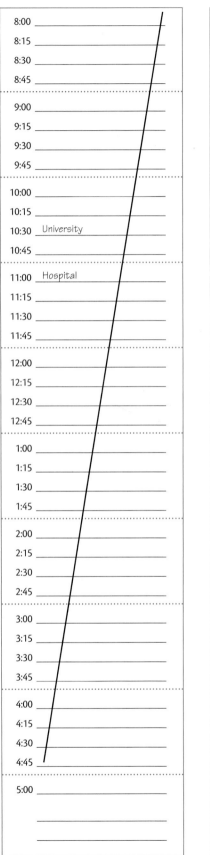

8:00 _____
8:15 _____
8:30 _____
8:45 _____

9:00 _____
9:15 _____
9:30 _____
9:45 _____

10:00 _____
10:15 _____
10:30 University _____
10:45 _____

11:00 Hospital _____
11:15 _____
11:30 _____
11:45 _____

12:00 _____
12:15 _____
12:30 _____
12:45 _____

1:00 _____
1:15 _____
1:30 _____
1:45 _____

2:00 _____
2:15 _____
2:30 _____
2:45 _____

3:00 _____
3:15 _____
3:30 _____
3:45 _____

4:00 _____
4:15 _____
4:30 _____
4:45 _____

5:00 _____

_____
_____

Friday, November 7

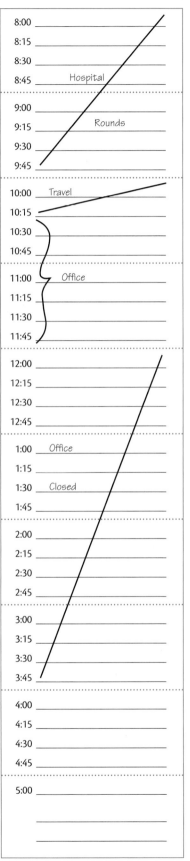

8:00 _____
8:15 _____
8:30 _____
8:45 Hospital _____

9:00 _____
9:15 Rounds _____
9:30 _____
9:45 _____

10:00 Travel _____
10:15 _____
10:30 _____
10:45 _____

11:00 Office _____
11:15 _____
11:30 _____
11:45 _____

12:00 _____
12:15 _____
12:30 _____
12:45 _____

1:00 Office _____
1:15 _____
1:30 Closed _____
1:45 _____

2:00 _____
2:15 _____
2:30 _____
2:45 _____

3:00 _____
3:15 _____
3:30 _____
3:45 _____

4:00 _____
4:15 _____
4:30 _____
4:45 _____

5:00 _____

_____

October

S	M	T	W	T	F	S
			1	2	3	4
5	6	7	8	9	10	11
12	13	14	15	16	17	18
19	20	21	22	23	24	25
26	27	28	29	30	31	

November

S	M	T	W	T	F	S
						1
2	3	4	5	6	7	8
9	10	11	12	13	14	15
16	17	18	19	20	21	22
23	24	25	26	27	28	29
30						

December

S	M	T	W	T	F	S
	1	2	3	4	5	6
7	8	9	10	11	12	13
14	15	16	17	18	19	20
21	22	23	24	25	26	27
28	29	30	31			

Monday, November 10

8:00	
8:15	
8:30	
8:45	Hospital
9:00	
9:15	Rounds
9:30	
9:45	
10:00	Travel
10:15	
10:30	
10:45	
11:00	
11:15	
11:30	
11:45	
12:00	
12:15	Lunch
12:30	
12:45	
1:00	
1:15	
1:30	
1:45	University
2:00	Hospital
2:15	
2:30	
2:45	
3:00	
3:15	
3:30	
3:45	
4:00	
4:15	
4:30	
4:45	
5:00	

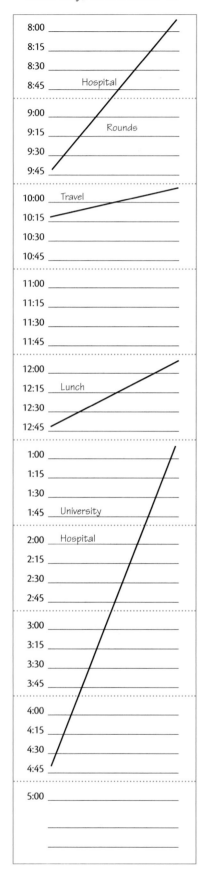

Tuesday, November 11

8:00	
8:15	
8:30	
8:45	Hospital
9:00	
9:15	Rounds
9:30	
9:45	
10:00	Travel
10:15	
10:30	
10:45	Raymond Murrary, CPE
11:00	555-6343
11:15	
11:30	
11:45	
12:00	
12:15	Lunch
12:30	
12:45	
1:00	
1:15	
1:30	
1:45	University
2:00	Hospital
2:15	
2:30	
2:45	
3:00	
3:15	
3:30	
3:45	
4:00	
4:15	
4:30	
4:45	
5:00	

8 p.m. Chicago Medical Society

Wednesday, November 12

8:00	
8:15	
8:30	
8:45	Hospital
9:00	
9:15	Rounds
9:30	
9:45	
10:00	Travel
10:15	
10:30	
10:45	
11:00	
11:15	
11:30	
11:45	
12:00	
12:15	Lunch
12:30	
12:45	
1:00	
1:15	
1:30	
1:45	University
2:00	Hospital
2:15	
2:30	
2:45	
3:00	
3:15	
3:30	
3:45	
4:00	
4:15	
4:30	
4:45	
5:00	

Thursday, November 13

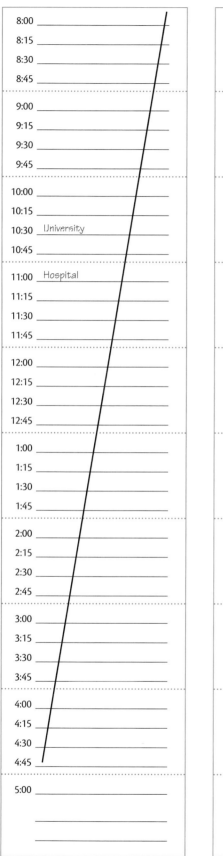

8:00 _____
8:15 _____
8:30 _____
8:45 _____

9:00 _____
9:15 _____
9:30 _____
9:45 _____

10:00 _____
10:15 _____
10:30 University
10:45 _____

11:00 Hospital
11:15 _____
11:30 _____
11:45 _____

12:00 _____
12:15 _____
12:30 _____
12:45 _____

1:00 _____
1:15 _____
1:30 _____
1:45 _____

2:00 _____
2:15 _____
2:30 _____
2:45 _____

3:00 _____
3:15 _____
3:30 _____
3:45 _____

4:00 _____
4:15 _____
4:30 _____
4:45 _____

5:00 _____

_____
_____

Friday, November 14

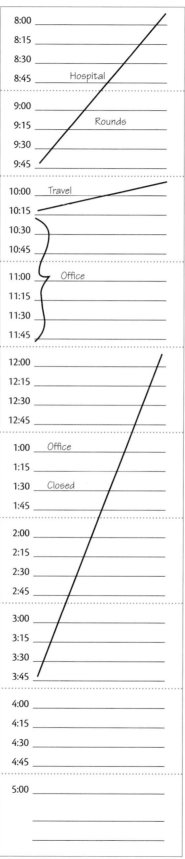

8:00 _____
8:15 _____
8:30 _____
8:45 Hospital

9:00 _____
9:15 Rounds
9:30 _____
9:45 _____

10:00 Travel
10:15 _____
10:30 _____
10:45 _____

11:00 Office
11:15 _____
11:30 _____
11:45 _____

12:00 _____
12:15 _____
12:30 _____
12:45 _____

1:00 Office
1:15 _____
1:30 Closed
1:45 _____

2:00 _____
2:15 _____
2:30 _____
2:45 _____

3:00 _____
3:15 _____
3:30 _____
3:45 _____

4:00 _____
4:15 _____
4:30 _____
4:45 _____

5:00 _____

_____
_____

October

S	M	T	W	T	F	S
			1	2	3	4
5	6	7	8	9	10	11
12	13	14	15	16	17	18
19	20	21	22	23	24	25
26	27	28	29	30	31	

November

S	M	T	W	T	F	S
						1
2	3	4	5	6	7	8
9	10	11	12	13	14	15
16	17	18	19	20	21	22
23	24	25	26	27	28	29
30						

December

S	M	T	W	T	F	S
	1	2	3	4	5	6
7	8	9	10	11	12	13
14	15	16	17	18	19	20
21	22	23	24	25	26	27
28	29	30	31			

Monday, November 17

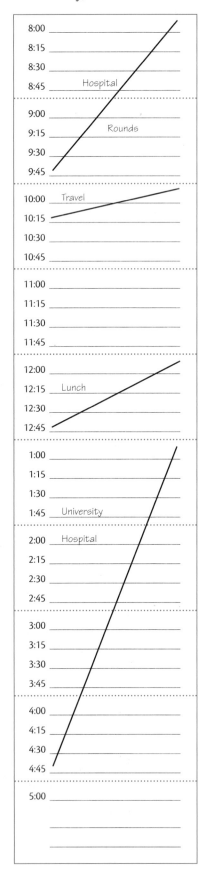

8:00	
8:15	
8:30	
8:45	Hospital
9:00	
9:15	Rounds
9:30	
9:45	
10:00	Travel
10:15	
10:30	
10:45	
11:00	
11:15	
11:30	
11:45	
12:00	
12:15	Lunch
12:30	
12:45	
1:00	
1:15	
1:30	
1:45	University
2:00	Hospital
2:15	
2:30	
2:45	
3:00	
3:15	
3:30	
3:45	
4:00	
4:15	
4:30	
4:45	
5:00	

Tuesday, November 18

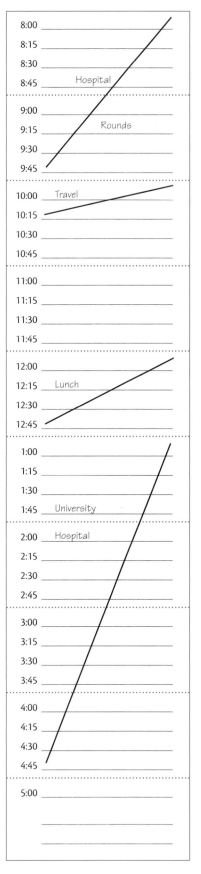

8:00	
8:15	
8:30	
8:45	Hospital
9:00	
9:15	Rounds
9:30	
9:45	
10:00	Travel
10:15	
10:30	
10:45	
11:00	
11:15	
11:30	
11:45	
12:00	
12:15	Lunch
12:30	
12:45	
1:00	
1:15	
1:30	
1:45	University
2:00	Hospital
2:15	
2:30	
2:45	
3:00	
3:15	
3:30	
3:45	
4:00	
4:15	
4:30	
4:45	
5:00	

Wednesday, November 19

8:00	
8:15	
8:30	
8:45	Hospital
9:00	
9:15	Rounds
9:30	
9:45	
10:00	Travel
10:15	
10:30	
10:45	
11:00	
11:15	
11:30	
11:45	
12:00	
12:15	Lunch
12:30	
12:45	
1:00	
1:15	
1:30	
1:45	University
2:00	Hospital
2:15	
2:30	
2:45	
3:00	
3:15	
3:30	
3:45	
4:00	
4:15	
4:30	
4:45	
5:00	

Thursday, November 20

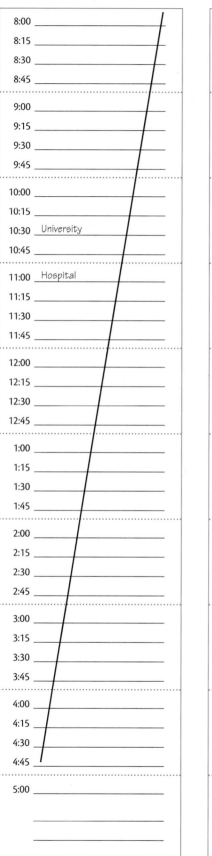

Time	
8:00	
8:15	
8:30	
8:45	
9:00	
9:15	
9:30	
9:45	
10:00	
10:15	
10:30	University
10:45	
11:00	Hospital
11:15	
11:30	
11:45	
12:00	
12:15	
12:30	
12:45	
1:00	
1:15	
1:30	
1:45	
2:00	
2:15	
2:30	
2:45	
3:00	
3:15	
3:30	
3:45	
4:00	
4:15	
4:30	
4:45	
5:00	

Friday, November 21

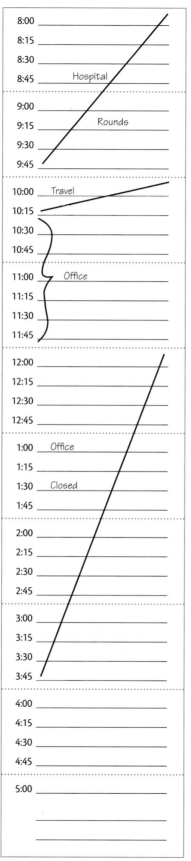

Time	
8:00	
8:15	
8:30	
8:45	Hospital
9:00	
9:15	Rounds
9:30	
9:45	
10:00	Travel
10:15	
10:30	
10:45	
11:00	Office
11:15	
11:30	
11:45	
12:00	
12:15	
12:30	
12:45	
1:00	Office
1:15	
1:30	Closed
1:45	
2:00	
2:15	
2:30	
2:45	
3:00	
3:15	
3:30	
3:45	
4:00	
4:15	
4:30	
4:45	
5:00	

October

S	M	T	W	T	F	S
			1	2	3	4
5	6	7	8	9	10	11
12	13	14	15	16	17	18
19	20	21	22	23	24	25
26	27	28	29	30	31	

November

S	M	T	W	T	F	S
						1
2	3	4	5	6	7	8
9	10	11	12	13	14	15
16	17	18	19	20	21	22
23	24	25	26	27	28	29
30						

December

S	M	T	W	T	F	S
	1	2	3	4	5	6
7	8	9	10	11	12	13
14	15	16	17	18	19	20
21	22	23	24	25	26	27
28	29	30	31			

Monday, November 24

8:00	
8:15	
8:30	
8:45	Hospital
9:00	
9:15	Rounds
9:30	
9:45	
10:00	Travel
10:15	
10:30	
10:45	
11:00	
11:15	
11:30	
11:45	
12:00	
12:15	Lunch
12:30	
12:45	
1:00	
1:15	
1:30	
1:45	University
2:00	Hospital
2:15	
2:30	
2:45	
3:00	
3:15	
3:30	
3:45	
4:00	
4:15	
4:30	
4:45	
5:00	

Tuesday, November 25

8:00	
8:15	
8:30	
8:45	Hospital
9:00	
9:15	Rounds
9:30	
9:45	
10:00	Travel
10:15	
10:30	
10:45	
11:00	
11:15	
11:30	
11:45	
12:00	
12:15	Lunch
12:30	
12:45	
1:00	
1:15	
1:30	
1:45	University
2:00	Hospital
2:15	
2:30	
2:45	
3:00	
3:15	
3:30	
3:45	
4:00	
4:15	
4:30	
4:45	
5:00	

Wednesday, November 26

8:00	
8:15	
8:30	
8:45	Hospital
9:00	
9:15	Rounds
9:30	
9:45	
10:00	Travel
10:15	
10:30	
10:45	
11:00	
11:15	
11:30	
11:45	
12:00	
12:15	Lunch
12:30	
12:45	
1:00	
1:15	
1:30	
1:45	University
2:00	Hospital
2:15	
2:30	
2:45	
3:00	
3:15	
3:30	
3:45	
4:00	
4:15	
4:30	
4:45	
5:00	

Thursday, November 27

8:00 _____
8:15 _____
8:30 _____
8:45 _____

9:00 _____
9:15 _____
9:30 _____
9:45 _____

10:00 _____
10:15 _____
10:30 _____
10:45 *Office* _____

11:00 *Closed* _____
11:15 *Thanksgiving* _____
11:30 _____
11:45 _____

12:00 _____
12:15 _____
12:30 _____
12:45 _____

1:00 _____
1:15 _____
1:30 _____
1:45 _____

2:00 _____
2:15 _____
2:30 _____
2:45 _____

3:00 _____
3:15 _____
3:30 _____
3:45 _____

4:00 _____
4:15 _____
4:30 _____
4:45 _____

5:00 _____

_____

_____

Friday, November 28

8:00 _____
8:15 _____
8:30 _____
8:45 _____

9:00 _____
9:15 _____
9:30 _____
9:45 _____

10:00 _____
10:15 _____
10:30 _____
10:45 *Office* _____

11:00 *Closed* _____
11:15 *Thanksgiving* _____
11:30 _____
11:45 _____

12:00 _____
12:15 _____
12:30 _____
12:45 _____

1:00 _____
1:15 _____
1:30 _____
1:45 _____

2:00 _____
2:15 _____
2:30 _____
2:45 _____

3:00 _____
3:15 _____
3:30 _____
3:45 _____

4:00 _____
4:15 _____
4:30 _____
4:45 _____

5:00 _____

_____

_____

October

S	M	T	W	T	F	S
			1	2	3	4
5	6	7	8	9	10	11
12	13	14	15	16	17	18
19	20	21	22	23	24	25
26	27	28	29	30	31	

November

S	M	T	W	T	F	S
						1
2	3	4	5	6	7	8
9	10	11	12	13	14	15
16	17	18	19	20	21	22
23	24	25	26	27	28	29
30						

December

S	M	T	W	T	F	S
	1	2	3	4	5	6
7	8	9	10	11	12	13
14	15	16	17	18	19	20
21	22	23	24	25	26	27
28	29	30	31			

Monday, December 1

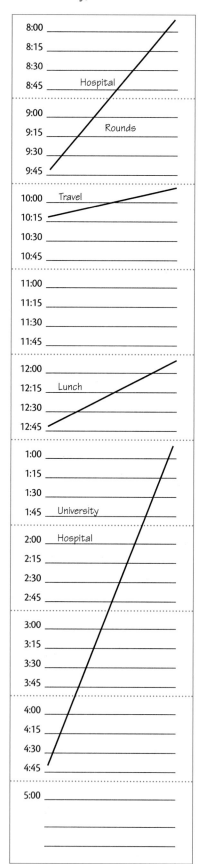

8:00	
8:15	
8:30	
8:45	Hospital
9:00	
9:15	Rounds
9:30	
9:45	
10:00	Travel
10:15	
10:30	
10:45	
11:00	
11:15	
11:30	
11:45	
12:00	
12:15	Lunch
12:30	
12:45	
1:00	
1:15	
1:30	
1:45	University
2:00	Hospital
2:15	
2:30	
2:45	
3:00	
3:15	
3:30	
3:45	
4:00	
4:15	
4:30	
4:45	
5:00	

Tuesday, December 2

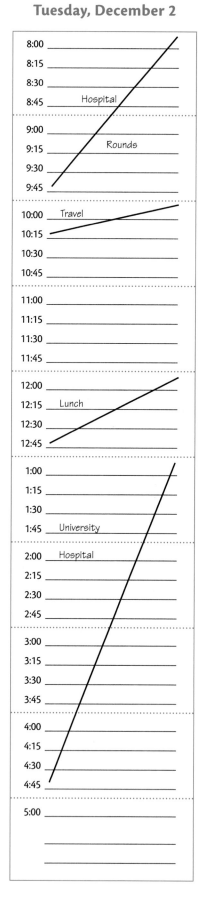

8:00	
8:15	
8:30	
8:45	Hospital
9:00	
9:15	Rounds
9:30	
9:45	
10:00	Travel
10:15	
10:30	
10:45	
11:00	
11:15	
11:30	
11:45	
12:00	
12:15	Lunch
12:30	
12:45	
1:00	
1:15	
1:30	
1:45	University
2:00	Hospital
2:15	
2:30	
2:45	
3:00	
3:15	
3:30	
3:45	
4:00	
4:15	
4:30	
4:45	
5:00	

Wednesday, December 3

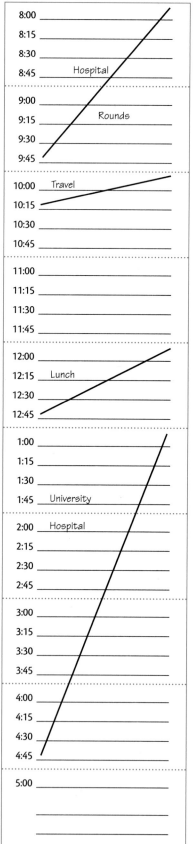

8:00	
8:15	
8:30	
8:45	Hospital
9:00	
9:15	Rounds
9:30	
9:45	
10:00	Travel
10:15	
10:30	
10:45	
11:00	
11:15	
11:30	
11:45	
12:00	
12:15	Lunch
12:30	
12:45	
1:00	
1:15	
1:30	
1:45	University
2:00	Hospital
2:15	
2:30	
2:45	
3:00	
3:15	
3:30	
3:45	
4:00	
4:15	
4:30	
4:45	
5:00	

Thursday, December 4

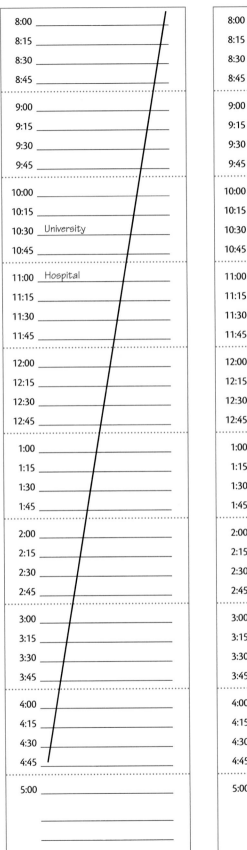

Time	
8:00	
8:15	
8:30	
8:45	
9:00	
9:15	
9:30	
9:45	
10:00	
10:15	
10:30	University
10:45	
11:00	Hospital
11:15	
11:30	
11:45	
12:00	
12:15	
12:30	
12:45	
1:00	
1:15	
1:30	
1:45	
2:00	
2:15	
2:30	
2:45	
3:00	
3:15	
3:30	
3:45	
4:00	
4:15	
4:30	
4:45	
5:00	

Friday, December 5

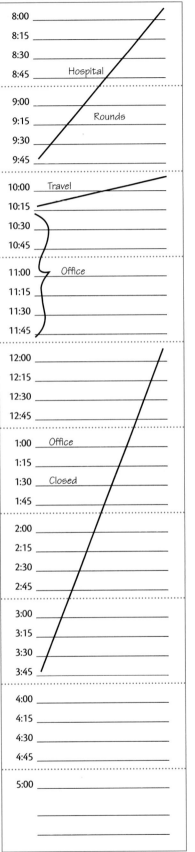

Time	
8:00	
8:15	
8:30	
8:45	Hospital
9:00	
9:15	Rounds
9:30	
9:45	
10:00	Travel
10:15	
10:30	
10:45	
11:00	Office
11:15	
11:30	
11:45	
12:00	
12:15	
12:30	
12:45	
1:00	Office
1:15	
1:30	Closed
1:45	
2:00	
2:15	
2:30	
2:45	
3:00	
3:15	
3:30	
3:45	
4:00	
4:15	
4:30	
4:45	
5:00	

October

S	M	T	W	T	F	S
			1	2	3	4
5	6	7	8	9	10	11
12	13	14	15	16	17	18
19	20	21	22	23	24	25
26	27	28	29	30	31	

November

S	M	T	W	T	F	S
						1
2	3	4	5	6	7	8
9	10	11	12	13	14	15
16	17	18	19	20	21	22
23	24	25	26	27	28	29
30						

December

S	M	T	W	T	F	S
	1	2	3	4	5	6
7	8	9	10	11	12	13
14	15	16	17	18	19	20
21	22	23	24	25	26	27
28	29	30	31			

YOUR APPOINTMENT IS:
_____ AT _____
SPECIAL INSTRUCTIONS:
_____
_____

KAREN LARSEN, MD
2235 South Ridgeway Avenue
Chicago, IL 60623-2240
312-555-6022
PLEASE CALL IF YOU CANNOT KEEP THIS APPOINTMENT.

YOUR APPOINTMENT IS:
_____ AT _____
SPECIAL INSTRUCTIONS:
_____
_____

KAREN LARSEN, MD
2235 South Ridgeway Avenue
Chicago, IL 60623-2240
312-555-6022
PLEASE CALL IF YOU CANNOT KEEP THIS APPOINTMENT.

YOUR APPOINTMENT IS:
_____ AT _____
SPECIAL INSTRUCTIONS:
_____
_____

KAREN LARSEN, MD
2235 South Ridgeway Avenue
Chicago, IL 60623-2240
312-555-6022
PLEASE CALL IF YOU CANNOT KEEP THIS APPOINTMENT.

YOUR APPOINTMENT IS:
_____ AT _____
SPECIAL INSTRUCTIONS:
_____
_____

KAREN LARSEN, MD
2235 South Ridgeway Avenue
Chicago, IL 60623-2240
312-555-6022
PLEASE CALL IF YOU CANNOT KEEP THIS APPOINTMENT.

YOUR APPOINTMENT IS:
_____ AT _____
SPECIAL INSTRUCTIONS:
_____
_____

KAREN LARSEN, MD
2235 South Ridgeway Avenue
Chicago, IL 60623-2240
312-555-6022
PLEASE CALL IF YOU CANNOT KEEP THIS APPOINTMENT.

YOUR APPOINTMENT IS:
_____ AT _____
SPECIAL INSTRUCTIONS:
_____
_____

KAREN LARSEN, MD
2235 South Ridgeway Avenue
Chicago, IL 60623-2240
312-555-6022
PLEASE CALL IF YOU CANNOT KEEP THIS APPOINTMENT.

YOUR APPOINTMENT IS:
_____ AT _____
SPECIAL INSTRUCTIONS:
_____
_____

KAREN LARSEN, MD
2235 South Ridgeway Avenue
Chicago, IL 60623-2240
312-555-6022
PLEASE CALL IF YOU CANNOT KEEP THIS APPOINTMENT.

YOUR APPOINTMENT IS:
_____ AT _____
SPECIAL INSTRUCTIONS:
_____
_____

KAREN LARSEN, MD
2235 South Ridgeway Avenue
Chicago, IL 60623-2240
312-555-6022
PLEASE CALL IF YOU CANNOT KEEP THIS APPOINTMENT.

YOUR APPOINTMENT IS:
_____ AT _____
SPECIAL INSTRUCTIONS:
_____
_____

KAREN LARSEN, MD
2235 South Ridgeway Avenue
Chicago, IL 60623-2240
312-555-6022
PLEASE CALL IF YOU CANNOT KEEP THIS APPOINTMENT.

YOUR APPOINTMENT IS:
_____ AT _____
SPECIAL INSTRUCTIONS:
_____
_____

KAREN LARSEN, MD
2235 South Ridgeway Avenue
Chicago, IL 60623-2240
312-555-6022
PLEASE CALL IF YOU CANNOT KEEP THIS APPOINTMENT.

YOUR APPOINTMENT IS:
_____ AT _____
SPECIAL INSTRUCTIONS:
_____
_____

KAREN LARSEN, MD
2235 South Ridgeway Avenue
Chicago, IL 60623-2240
312-555-6022
PLEASE CALL IF YOU CANNOT KEEP THIS APPOINTMENT.

YOUR APPOINTMENT IS:
_____ AT _____
SPECIAL INSTRUCTIONS:
_____
_____

KAREN LARSEN, MD
2235 South Ridgeway Avenue
Chicago, IL 60623-2240
312-555-6022
PLEASE CALL IF YOU CANNOT KEEP THIS APPOINTMENT.

YOUR APPOINTMENT IS:
_____ AT _____
SPECIAL INSTRUCTIONS:
_____
_____

KAREN LARSEN, MD
2235 South Ridgeway Avenue
Chicago, IL 60623-2240
312-555-6022
PLEASE CALL IF YOU CANNOT KEEP THIS APPOINTMENT.

YOUR APPOINTMENT IS:
_____ AT _____
SPECIAL INSTRUCTIONS:
_____
_____

KAREN LARSEN, MD
2235 South Ridgeway Avenue
Chicago, IL 60623-2240
312-555-6022
PLEASE CALL IF YOU CANNOT KEEP THIS APPOINTMENT.

YOUR APPOINTMENT IS:
_____ AT _____
SPECIAL INSTRUCTIONS:
_____
_____

KAREN LARSEN, MD
2235 South Ridgeway Avenue
Chicago, IL 60623-2240
312-555-6022
PLEASE CALL IF YOU CANNOT KEEP THIS APPOINTMENT.

OUT-OF-OFFICE SCHEDULING

Directions: You are working for several physicians: Dr. R. Gain, a cardiologist; Dr. J. Brent, a family practice physician; and Dr. E. Oren, a general surgeon. Determine what element is missing in the situations in Column 1. Choose the appropriate response from Column 2.

Column 1

b **1.** Dr. Gain asks you to admit the patient, age 72, with a recent myocardial infarction to University Hospital today for controlled cardiovascular monitoring.

c **2.** Dr. Oren asks you to schedule a gastrectomy for Les Weiner, age 65, at University Hospital next Monday or Tuesday morning.

d **3.** Dr. Brent asks you to schedule Mary Maye for a bone marrow aspiration at University Hospital Lab because of her iron deficiency anemia.

e **4.** Peter Nu fractured his right wrist playing racquetball. Dr. Brent wants you to schedule an appointment with an orthopedic surgeon as soon as possible for possible surgery.

a **5.** Dr. Brent asks you to refer a 4-year-old patient, Jan Davis, with acute lymphocytic leukemia to an oncologist next week to start a program of chemotherapy.

e **6.** Dr. Oren wants you to schedule a short-stay surgery room at University Hospital for Tina Messer next Tuesday morning. Tina has a nodule in her right breast.

e **7.** Dr. Gain wants you to admit Ian Wenth to University Hospital. Ian has pulmonary insufficiency caused by pneumonia and will need intensive oxygen therapy.

a **8.** Patient Larry Phen has been diagnosed with emphysema. Dr. Gain now wants to refer Larry to a pulmonary specialist as soon as possible for therapeutic management.

b **9.** Dr. Brent wants to refer this patient as soon as possible to Dr. Henri Wilson, a neurologist. The patient's migraines have increased in frequency and in severity; her therapeutic program needs to be reevaluated.

d **10.** Dr. Oren wants you to admit Jane Hanson with appendicitis to University Hospital this morning.

Column 2

a. Specialist's name
b. Patient's name
c. Diagnosis or problem
d. When to be seen
e. Procedure to be performed

OUTSIDE SERVICES

Hugh Arnold, MD 2785 South Ridgeway Avenue, Suite 440 Chicago, IL 60647-2700 312-555-6800 **Internist**	Martinez Transcription Service 2200 South Ridgeway Avenue Chicago, IL 60623-2000 312-555-2424 **Betze Martinez**
Jason Berger, MD 5000 North Oak Park Drive Chicago, IL 60634-0005 312-555-7050 **Personal Friend**	Elizabeth Miller-Young, MD 2901 West Fifth Avenue, Suite 205 Chicago, IL 60612-9002 312-555-3500 **OB/GYN**
Consumer Pharmacy Pharmacists: Dale Geddal, MD 312-555-1252 Joy Rishard, MD **Pharmacy in medical center**	Mark Newman, MD 2785 South Ridgeway Avenue Chicago, IL 60647-2700 312-555-2700 **On-call doctor**
Lynn Corbett, MD Professional Buildng 8672 South Ridgeway Avenue, Suite 300 Chicago, IL 60623-2240 312-555-2300 **Cardiologist**	Margery Pierce, MD 6452 North Ridgeway Avenue, Suite 209 Chicago, IL 60626-5462 312-555-4880 **Pediatrician**
Richard Diangelis, MD 2785 South Ridgeway Avenue, Suite 280 Chicago, IL 60647-2700 312-555-1575 **Ophthalmologist**	Laura Sinn, MD 2901 West Fifth Avenue, Suite 100 Chicago, IL 60612-9002 312-555-7850 **Urologist**
Greg Koski, MD Professional Building 8672 South Ridgeway Avenue, Suite 350 Chicago, IL 60623-2240 312-555-4500 **Orthopedic Surgeon**	Theresa Townsend, MD 500 South Dearborn Street Chicago, IL 60605-0005 **Chairperson** 312-555-2200 **Chicago Medical Society**
University Hospital 5500 North Ridgeway Avenue Chicago, IL 60625-1200 312-555-2500	**Education services:** Juanita Yates 312-555-2950 **Human Resources:** 312-555-1200 **Resident services:** Lee Eaton 312-555-3043

CHART NOTE

Sherman, Florence   312-555-1217
DOB: 05/22/19--   Age: 65

10/08/20--
CHIEF COMPLAINT: Trouble with vision.

SUBJECTIVE: Patient is a 65-year-old female who had two episodes during the last week of jagged lights occurring in central visual field. These lasted 15-20 minutes; no other symptoms. Patient has long history of migraines.

OBJECTIVE: Within normal limits; specifically, no evidence of tear or hole in the retina.

ASSESSMENT: Migraine equivalent vs. posterior vitreous detachment.

PLAN: 1. Discussed with ophthalmologist, Richard Diangelis, MD. Patient advised about signs and symptoms of detachment of the retina and told to seek immediate medical attention should any of these signs appear.
         2. Trial of Midrin for migraines.
         3. Recheck in one to two months.
         4. Patient requests referral to Dr. Diangelis.

Karen Larsen, MD/ls

Doublespace body.
Page numbers on upper
right starting on page 2.

RUBELLA (GERMAN MEASLES)

DEFINITION

Rubella (german measles) is a highly communicable viral disease characterized by
diffuse, punctate, macular rash. Rubella is a relatively benign viral illness
unless there is transplacental transmision. (Define the following terms:
communicable, diffuse, punctate, transplacental, and *macular.*)

ETIOLOGY

Rubella is caused by rubella virus *(Rubivirus)* that is spread by air borne
direct contact with nasopharyngeal secretions. This disease is communicable from
one week before the rash appears to five days after the rash disappears. Rubella is
most common in children but may also affect adults who were not infected during
childhood. (Define the following terms: <u>airborne</u>, <u>direct contact</u>, and <u>nasopharyngeal</u>.)

INCIDENCE

Rubella occurs most often in the spring, but there are major epidemics occurring
in 6 to 9 year cycles. (Investigate recent epidemics vs. the use of the vaccine.)

PATHOPHYSIOLOGY

The virus invades the nasopharynx and travels to the lymph glands, causing
lymphadenopathy. Then in 5 to seven days it enters the blood stream stimulating
an immune response causing the skin rash. This rash lasts about three days.
(Define <u>lymphadenopathy</u>.)

CLINICAL SYSTEMS

The first Clinical symptoms of rubella include swollen gands, fever, sorethroat, cough,
and fatigue. The often pruritic rash generally starts in 1 to 5 days after the prodrome.
The rash begins on the face and the trunk and spreads to the upper and lower extremities. Symptoms of headache and conjunctivitis may occur after the rash. (Define
<u>conjunctivitis</u>, <u>pruritic,</u> and <u>swollen glands</u>.)

ADDITIONAL ASSIGNMENT:

Investigate what complications may occur to a fetsu and a child with rubella,
describing each complication plus its incidence.
Investigate what complications may occur in adults with rubella, describing each
complication plus its incidence.
Investigate what diagnostic testing can done for the occurrence of rubella.
Investigate treatment options.

MUMPS (INFECTIOUS PAROTITIS)

DEFINITION

Mumps is an acute viral disease that may include myalgia, anorexia, malaise, headache, low-grade fever, and parotid gland tenderness and unilateral or bilateral swelling, although many other organs can be involved. (Define the following terms: *myalgia, anorexia,* and *malaise*.)

ETIOLOGY

Mumps is caused by paramyxovirus transmitted in saliva droplets or direct contact. The virus lives in the saliva six to 9 days before the parotid gland swelling. The highest communicable period is 48 hours before the on set of swelling but continue until swelling is decreased. Incubation period ranges from 14 to 25 days.

INCIDENCE

(Investigate the incidence in the past 10 years.)

PATHOPHYSIOLOGY

During the incubation period, the virus invades the salivary glands which cause tissue edema and and infiltration of lymphocytes. Degeneration of cells inthe glandular tissue produces necrotic debris that plugs the ducts.

CLINICAL SYMPTOMS

The prodrome of mumps generally begins with ~~generally begins~~ myalgia, anorexia, malaise, headache, and low-grade fever. Next the patient may have an ear ache aggravated by chewing, temperature of 101° to 104° F, and pain from chewing food or drinking acidic liquid. Both the parotid gland and other salivary glands may become swollen. (Define *prodrome*).

ADDITIONAL ASSIGNMENT:

Investigate what complications may occur with mumps in both children and adults.

Summarize how mumps would be diagnosed.

Summarize out patient and inpatient complications of treatment.

COMMUNICATIONS TERMS

Directions: Match the term in Column 2 with its definition in Column 1.

Column 1

_b_ **1.** Letter that begins all parts of the letter at the left margin.

_c_ **2.** Manuscript sources at the bottom of the page on which the source is cited.

_e_ **3.** Careful reading and examination of document to find and correct errors.

_f_ **4.** Style that has a colon after the salutation and a comma after the complimentary closing.

_i_ **5.** To skim a document and write notes in the margin.

_n_ **6.** Letter that begins the date line, complimentary closing, and signature line at the center point.

_f_ **7.** Fastest way to send heavier mail items less than 70 pounds.

_k_ **8.** Mail service providing the greatest security for valuables.

_j_ **9.** Style without punctuation after the salutation and complimentary closing.

_m_ **10.** Assessing a document to determine its clarity, consistency, and overall effectiveness.

_g_ **11.** Mail service that provides the sender with a mailing receipt.

_n_ **12.** Letter without a salutation or complimentary closing.

_a_ **13.** Rate used for books or film.

_d_ **14.** Fastest mail service, available 365 days a year.

_o_ **15.** Manuscript sources placed on a separate page following the last page of text.

Column 2

a. annotate
b. block-style letter
c. certified mail
d. editing
e. endnotes
f. Express Mail
g. footnotes
h. Media Mail
i. modified-block-style letter
j. open punctuation
k. Priority Mail
l. proofreading
m. registered mail
n. simplified-style letter
o. standard punctuation

Welcome

Please complete this form completely in ink. This information will remain confidential.

PATIENT INFORMATION

Last name:	First name:	Initial:	Date of birth:	Home phone:

Address:	Marital status: (check appropriate box) S ☐ M ☐ D ☐ W ☐	Sex M F

City:	State:	ZIP:	Social Security number:

Patient's employer: (If student, name of school.)	Employment address: Business phone:

Bill to:	Relationship:

Address:	City:	State:	ZIP:

NOTIFY IN CASE OF EMERGENCY

Name:	Relationship:

Address:	Phone:

City:	State:	ZIP:	

INSURANCE INFORMATION

Primary insurance company:	Secondary insurance company:

Subscriber's name:	DOB:	Subscriber's name:	DOB:

Policy #:	Group #:	Policy #:	Group #:

OTHER INFORMATION

Reason for visit:	Name of referring physician:

_____ Patient's signature/Parent or guardian's signature	Today's date

Welcome

Please complete this form completely in ink. This information will remain confidential.

PATIENT INFORMATION

Last name:	First name:	Initial:	Date of birth:	Home phone:

Address:	Marital status: (check appropriate box) S ☐ M ☐ D ☐ W ☐	Sex M F

City:	State:	ZIP:	Social Security number:

Patient's employer: (If student, name of school.)	Employment address: Business phone:

Bill to:	Relationship:

Address:	City:	State:	ZIP:

NOTIFY IN CASE OF EMERGENCY

Name:	Relationship:

Address:	Phone:

City:	State:	ZIP:	

INSURANCE INFORMATION

Primary insurance company:	Secondary insurance company:

Subscriber's name:	DOB:	Subscriber's name:	DOB:

Policy #:	Group #:	Policy #:	Group #:

OTHER INFORMATION

Reason for visit:	Name of referring physician:

Patient's signature/Parent or guardian's signature	Today's date

WP 42

RECORDS RELEASE

TO: _____ Health care provider

_____ Address

_____ City, State, ZIP

I authorize the above-named health care provider to release the specified information listed below to the following physician:

Karen Larsen, MD
2235 South Ridgeway Avenue
Chicago, IL 60623-2240

312-555-6022
Fax: 312-555-0025

PATIENT: _____ DOB: _____

_____ Address

_____ City, State, ZIP

Please include _____ specific records.

Signed _____ Date _____

RECORDS RELEASE

TO: _____ Health care provider

_____ Address

_____ City, State, ZIP

I authorize the above-named health care provider to release the specified information listed below to the following physician:

Karen Larsen, MD
2235 South Ridgeway Avenue
Chicago, IL 60623-2240

312-555-6022
Fax: 312-555-0025

PATIENT: _____ DOB: _____

_____ Address

_____ City, State, ZIP

Please include _____ specific records.

Signed _____ Date _____

TELEPHONE LOG

Date _____

TIME	CALLER	TELEPHONE NUMBER	REASON	DONE

TO-DO LIST

Date _____

RUSH	ITEMS TO DO	DONE

WP 46

INSURANCE TERMINOLOGY

Directions: Match the term in Column 2 with its definition in Column 1.

Column 1

h 1. Insurance through employment with all employees having one master policy.

m 2. Person who is covered by an insurance policy.

i 3. Insurance company that provides insurance benefits.

t 4. Provides reimbursement for income lost because of insured's illness.

l 5. Rate charged for policy.

x 6. Health care professional who supplies the health care.

k 7. Ensures that payment for medical expenses will not exceed 100 percent of the medical expenses.

n 8. Generally covers hospitalization, lab tests, surgery, and x-rays.

e 9. A term used to describe an insurance company in the context of the doctor's and patient's relationship.

d 10. Covers medically necessary services while insured is an inpatient.

b 11. Covers physician's services for office visits.

a 12. Covers medical expenses in a catastrophic situation.

c 13. In a family with two family insurance contracts, determines which policy will be the primary carrier for the children.

o 14. Covers physician's fee for surgery.

g 15. Person in whose name the policy is written.

Column 2

a. basic insurance plan
b. birthday rule
c. carrier
d. COB
e. disability insurance
f. group insurance
g. hospital insurance
h. insured
i. major medical insurance
j. medical insurance
k. policyholder
l. premium
m. provider
n. surgical insurance
o. third-party payer

INSURANCE PLANS, PAYERS, AND PAYMENT METHODS

Directions: The following items refer to insurance plans and processing claims. Mark each statement with either "T" for *true* or "F" for *false*. Be prepared to discuss your answers in class.

_F_ 1. Coinsurance is the amount of medical expense that the insured must pay before the insurance carrier begins paying benefits.

_T_ 2. A government agency called the Centers for Medicare and Medicaid Services (CMS) administers the Medicare and Medicaid programs.

_F_ 3. In an indemnity plan, patients receive medical services from a primary care physician who coordinates the patient's overall care.

_T_ 4. Coinsurance is the percentage of each claim that the insured must pay, according to the terms of the insurance policy.

_F_ 5. Everyone eligible for Medicare Part A (hospitalization insurance) automatically receives Medicare Part B (medical insurance).

_T_ 6. *Balance billing* refers to billing the patient for any amount due on a provider's bill after the insurance company has taken care of its responsibility.

_F_ 7. The customary fee, in insurance terms, is the most the insurance company will pay any provider for a given procedure.

_T_ 8. Every time HMO and PPO members visit their physician, they pay a set charge called a copayment.

_F_ 9. A PAR provider who agrees to accept the allowed charge set forth by the insurance company as payment in full is accepting assignment.

_T_ 10. In a capitated plan, a physician may receive $35 per month for each patient assigned to him or her, even if the patient receives no care during that month.

_T_ 11. A Medicare participating provider decides whether to accept assignment on a claim-by-claim basis.

_F_ 12. RBRVS is the payment system used by Medicare for determining how much it will pay for inpatient care.

_T_ 13. When the amount the physician charges is more than the insurance company's allowed charge, the difference must be absorbed by the insurance company or the provider.

ICD-9-CM DIAGNOSTIC CODES

Codes	Description	Codes	Description
626.0	Amenorrhea	785.6	Lymphadenopathy
285.9	Anemia	627.9	Menopausal symptom
413.9	Angina	626.9	Menstrual disorder
427.9	Arrhythmia	787.02	Nausea
716.90	Arthritis, NOS	278.00	Obesity
714.0	Arthritis, rheumatoid	733.0	Osteoporosis
715.90	Arthritis/DJD/Osteo	380.10	Otitis externa
493.90	Asthma	382.9	Otitis media
791.9	Bacteruria	789.00	Pain, abdominal
373.00	Blepharitis	724.9	Pain, back, NOS
490	Bronchitis	729.1	Pain, muscular
682.9	Cellulitis/Abscess	785.1	Palpitations
437.9	Cerebrovascular disease	625.9	Pelvic pain, female
786.50	Chest pain	462	Pharyngitis/Sore throat
428.0	CHF	486	Pneumonia
575.1	Cholecystitis	783.5	Polydipsia
372.30	Conjunctivitis	788.42	Polyuria
786.2	Cough	V72.4	Pregnancy test
692.9	Dermatitis	V72.83	Pre-op
V18.0	Diabetes family history	V70.0	Preventive, adult
250.01	Diabetes I—IDDM	V72.3	Preventive including GYN exam
250.00	Diabetes II—NIDDM	V20.2	Preventive, pediatric
787.91	Diarrhea	V70.3	Preventive, school admission
562.1	Diverticulitis	600	Prostatic hypertrophy, benign
780.4	Dizziness/Lightheadedness	601.9	Prostatitis
536.8	Dyspepsia	791.0	Proteinuria
788.1	Dysuria	790.93	PSA, elevated
782.3	Edema	782.1	Rash/Skin eruption
V70.5	Employment exam	786.09	Shortness of breath
784.7	Epistaxis	461.9	Sinusitis, acute
780.79	Fatigue	785.0	Tachycardia
780.6	Fever	795.3	Throat culture, positive
535.50	Gastritis	388.30	Tinnitus
558.9	Gastroenteritis	463	Tonsillitis, acute
008.8	Gastroenteritis, viral	556.2	Ulcerative colitis/Proctitis
530.1	Gastroesophageal reflux	465.9	URI
784.0	Headache	788.41	Urinary frequency
346.90	Headache, migraine	788.30	Urinary incontinence
V17.4	Heart disease family history	599.0	UTI
272.0	Hypercholesterolemia	616.10	Vaginitis
272.4	Hyperlipidema	079.99	Viral infection
401.9	Hypertension	V73.99	Viral screening, unspecified
487.1	Influenza	787.03	Vomiting
780.52	Insomnia	288.8	wbc high
564.1	Irritable bowel	288.0	wbc low
719.40	Joint pain	783.2	Weight loss

No.	Date	Description	Charge	Credit Payment	Credit Adjustment	Current Balance
	03/11/20--	Annual exam/CBC/UA	185.00	25.00	-------	160.00

Patient Information

7921 W. 42d Street
Address

Chicago, IL 60632-1426
City, State Zip

312-555-4279   312-555-6264
Home phone   **Work phone**

same   self
Responsible Person   **Relationship**

Blue Cross/Blue Shield   407-55-1275
Insurance   **Contract numbers**

Patient _Provost, Janet_

Date: 03/11/20--   **Chart #**

Karen Larsen, MD
2235 S. Ridgeway Avenue
Chicago, IL 60623-2240

312-555-6022

Fax: 312-555-0025

Diagnoses:

1. _V70.0_

2. _____

3. _____

4. _____

OFFICE VISITS

New Patient	Established Patient

Preventive Medicine

	New Patient		Preventive Medicine		Established		Established
		_____ 99381	under 1 year	_____ 99391			
_____ 99201		_____ 99382	1–4	_____ 99392		_____ 99211	
_____ 99202		_____ 99383	5–11	_____ 99393		_____ 99212	
_____ 99203		_____ 99384	12–17	_____ 99394		_____ 99213	
_____ 99204		_____ 99385	18–39	_136_ 99395		_____ 99214	
_____ 99205		_____ 99386	40–64	_____ 99396		_____ 99215	
		_____ 99387	65+	_____ 99397			

Hospital Visits

Initial:
_____ 99221
_____ 99222
_____ 99223
Subsequent:
_____ 99231
_____ 99232
_____ 99233

Nursing Facility
Subsequent:
_____ 99311
_____ 99312
_____ 99313

Other
_____

Lab:
_____ 80048 Basic metabolic panel (SMA-8)
_____ 87110 Chlamydia culture
_____ 85651 ESR; nonautomated
_____ 83001 FSH
_____ 82947 Glucose, blood
_25_ 85022 Hemogram (CBC) with differential
_____ 80076 Hepatic function panel
_____ 85018 HGB
_____ 86701 HIV-1
_____ 83002 LH
_____ 80061 Lipid panel
_____ 86617 Lyme antibody

_____ 86308 Monospot test
_____ 88150 Pap
_____ 85610 Prothrombin time
_____ 84152 PSA
_____ 86430 Rheumatoid factor
_____ 82270 Stool hemoccult x 3
_____ 87430 Strep screen
_____ 84478 Triglycerides
_____ 84443 TSH
_24_ 81001 UA with microscopy
_____ 87088 UC
_____ 84550 Uric acid, blood
_____ 81025 Urine pregnancy test
_____
_____

Injections:
_____ 90471 admin 1 vac
_____ 90472 each add'l vac
_____ 90716 Chickenpox
_____ 90702 DT
_____ 90701 DTP
_____ 90657 Influenza 6-35 months
_____ 90658 Influenza 3 years +
_____ 90665 Lyme disease
_____ 90707 MMR
_____ 90704 Mumps
_____ 90713 Polio vac inactivated (IPV)
_____ 90703 Tetanus Tox

ECG: _____ 93000 ECG

Other
_____
_____

Chap 8

WP 49

Fee Schedule—Karen Larsen, MD

New Patient	Established Patient

Preventive Medicine

New Patient				Established Patient			
		_139_ 99381	under 1 year	_110_ 99391			
_54_ 99201		_145_ 99382	1–4	_123_ 99392		_29_ 99211	
_73_ 99202		_142_ 99383	5–11	_128_ 99393		_44_ 99212	
_100_ 99203		_177_ 99384	12–17	_148_ 99394		_60_ 99213	
_147_ 99204		_165_ 99385	18–39	_136_ 99395		_87_ 99214	
_190_ 99205		_178_ 99386	40–64	_148_ 99396		_134_ 99215	
		_199_ 99387	65+	_119_ 99397			

Hospital Visits

Initial:

_121_ 99221

_172_ 99222

_217_ 99223

Subsequent:

_65_ 99231

_90_ 99232

_132_ 99233

Nursing Facility

Subsequent:

_53_ 99311

_77_ 99312

_109_ 99313

Other

_____

_____

Lab:

_51_ 80048 Basic metabolic panel (SMA-8)

_74_ 87110 Chlamydia culture

_21_ 85651 ESR; nonautomated

_97_ 83001 FSH

_21_ 82947 Glucose, blood

_25_ 85022 Hemogram (CBC) with differential

_55_ 80076 Hepatic function panel

_13_ 85018 HGB

_77_ 86701 HIV-1

_97_ 83002 LH

_72_ 80061 Lipid panel

_86_ 86617 Lyme antibody

_33_ 86308 Monospot test

_33_ 88150 Pap

_23_ 85610 Prothrombin time

_91_ 84152 PSA

_30_ 86430 Rheumatoid factor

_15_ 82270 Stool hemoccult x 3

_39_ 87430 Strep screen

_21_ 84478 Triglycerides

_69_ 84443 TSH

_24_ 81001 UA with microscopy

_35_ 87088 UC

_20_ 84550 Uric acid, blood

_23_ 81025 Urine pregnancy test

_____

_____

_____

Injections:

_10_ 90471 admin 1 vac

_8_ 90472 each add'l vac

_133_ 90716 Chickenpox

_31_ 90702 DT

_78_ 90701 DTP

_30_ 90657 Influenza 6-35 months

_35_ 90658 Influenza 3 years +

_40_ 90665 Lyme disease

_104_ 90707 MMR

_51_ 90704 Mumps

_52_ 90713 Polio vac inactivated (IPV)

_26_ 90703 Tetanus Tox

ECG: _70_ 93000 ECG

Other

_____

_____

_____

TELEPHONE LOG

Date _____

TIME	CALLER	TELEPHONE NUMBER	REASON	DONE

TO-DO LIST

Date _____

RUSH	ITEMS TO DO	DONE

TAI CLINIC, INC.
Grace Tai, MD
100 Sun Valley Road, Lisle, IL 60532
312-555-9300

October 20, 20--

Karen Larsen, MD
2235 South Ridgeway Avenue
Chicago, IL 60623-2240

Dear Dr. Larsen:

RE: David Kramer   DOB: 4/28/20--

David is up to date on his immunizations. His immunization
record is as follows:

```
DTP: 3 months (7/26/20--)    Oral polio: 3 months (7/26/20--)
     6 months (10/22/20--)               6 months (10/22/20--)
     9 months (1/29/20--)                9 months (1/29/20--)

MMR: 2 years (5/2/20--)
```

David is due for a booster DTP before starting kindergarten.

If you have any questions, please contact our office.

Sincerely,

Grace Tai, MD

Grace Tai, MD

jz

KL
Please file.

No. __1214__

To _____

Date _____

For _____

Amount _____

_____

No. __1214__   _____ 20 _____

Received from _____

_____ *Dollars*

For _____

_____

$ _____

No. _____

To _____

Date _____

For _____

Amount _____

_____

No. _____   _____ 20 _____

Received from _____

_____ *Dollars*

For _____

_____

$ _____

No. _____

To _____

Date _____

For _____

Amount _____

_____

No. _____   _____ 20 _____

Received from _____

_____ *Dollars*

For _____

_____

$ _____

No. _____

To _____

Date _____

For _____

Amount _____

_____

No. _____   _____ 20 _____

Received from _____

_____ *Dollars*

For _____

_____

$ _____

No.	Date	Description	Charge	Credit		Current Balance
				Payment	Adjustment	

Patient Information

6111 N. Lincoln Avenue
Address

Chicago, IL 60608-3173
City, State Zip

312-555-1217
Home phone   **Work phone**

self
Responsible Person   **Relationship**

Medicare   669-35-2244
Insurance   **Contract numbers**

Patient _____ Florence Sherman _____

Date: 10/20/20--   **Chart #**

Karen Larsen, MD
2235 S. Ridgeway Avenue
Chicago, IL 60623-2240

312-555-6022

Fax: 312-555-0025

Diagnoses:

1. _____
2. _____
3. _____
4. _____

OFFICE VISITS

New Patient	Established Patient

Preventive Medicine

		under 1 year	_____ 99391
_____ 99201	_____ 99382	1–4	_____ 99392
_____ 99202	_____ 99383	5–11	_____ 99393
_____ 99203	_____ 99384	12–17	_____ 99394
_____ 99204	_____ 99385	18–39	_____ 99395
_____ 99205	_____ 99386	40–64	_____ 99396
	_____ 99387	65+	_____ 99397

_____ 99211
(99212)
_____ 99213
_____ 99214
_____ 99215

_____ 99381

Hospital Visits
Initial:
_____ 99221
_____ 99222
_____ 99223
Subsequent:
_____ 99231
_____ 99232
_____ 99233
Nursing Facility
Subsequent:
_____ 99311
_____ 99312
_____ 99313
Other
_____

Lab:
_____ 80048 Basic
     metabolic panel
     (SMA-8)
_____ 87110 Chlamydia
     culture
_____ 85651 ESR;
     nonautomated
_____ 83001 FSH
_____ 82947 Glucose,
     blood
_____ 85022 Hemogram
     (CBC) with
     differential
_____ 80076 Hepatic
     function panel
_____ 85018 HGB
_____ 86701 HIV-1
_____ 83002 LH
_____ 80061 Lipid panel
_____ 86617 Lyme
     antibody

_____ 86308 Monospot
     test
_____ 88150 Pap
_____ 85610 Prothrombin
     time
_____ 84152 PSA
_____ 86430 Rheumatoid
     factor
_____ 82270 Stool
     hemoccult x 3
_____ 87430 Strep screen
_____ 84478 Triglycerides
_____ 84443 TSH
_____ 81001 UA with
     microscopy
_____ 87088 UC
_____ 84550 Uric acid,
     blood
_____ 81025 Urine
     pregnancy test
_____
_____

Injections:
_____ 90471 admin 1 vac
_____ 90472 each add'l
     vac
_____ 90716 Chickenpox
_____ 90702 DT
_____ 90701 DTP
_____ 90657 Influenza
     6-35 months
_____ 90658 Influenza
     3 years +
_____ 90665 Lyme
     disease
_____ 90707 MMR
_____ 90704 Mumps
_____ 90713 Polio vac
     inactivated (IPV)
_____ 90703 Tetanus Tox
ECG: _____ 93000 ECG

Other
_____
_____

No.	Date	Description	Charge	Credit		Current Balance
				Payment	Adjustment	

Patient Information

3518 South 23d Street
Address

Chicago, IL 60623-7355
City, State Zip

	father
312-555-3493	312-555-8842
Home phone	**Work phone**

Juan Villano	father
Responsible Person	**Relationship**

Employee Benefit Plan, 200-97-4811-02,35A Grp
Insurance   **Contract numbers**

Patient _____ Stephen Villano _____

Date: 10/20/20--   **Chart #**

Karen Larsen, MD
2235 S. Ridgeway Avenue
Chicago, IL 60623-2240

312-555-6022

Fax: 312-555-0025

Diagnoses:

1. ___034.0___

2. _____

3. _____

4. _____

OFFICE VISITS

New Patient	Established Patient

Preventive Medicine

	_____ 99381	under 1 year	_____ 99391	
_____ 99201	_____ 99382	1–4	_____ 99392	_____ 99211
_____ 99202	_____ 99383	5–11	_____ 99393	⟨99212⟩
_____ 99203	_____ 99384	12–17	_____ 99394	_____ 99213
_____ 99204	_____ 99385	18–39	_____ 99395	_____ 99214
_____ 99205	_____ 99386	40–64	_____ 99396	_____ 99215
	_____ 99387	65+	_____ 99397	

Hospital Visits
Initial:
_____ 99221
_____ 99222
_____ 99223
Subsequent:
_____ 99231
_____ 99232
_____ 99233
Nursing Facility
Subsequent:
_____ 99311
_____ 99312
_____ 99313
Other
_____

Lab:
_____ 80048 Basic
          metabolic panel
          (SMA-8)
_____ 87110 Chlamydia
          culture
_____ 85651 ESR;
          nonautomated
_____ 83001 FSH
_____ 82947 Glucose,
          blood
_____ 85022 Hemogram
          (CBC) with
          differential
_____ 80076 Hepatic
          function panel
_____ 85018 HGB
_____ 86701 HIV-1
_____ 83002 LH
_____ 80061 Lipid panel
_____ 86617 Lyme
          antibody

_____ 86308 Monospot
          test
_____ 88150 Pap
_____ 85610 Prothrombin
          time
_____ 84152 PSA
_____ 86430 Rheumatoid
          factor
_____ 82270 Stool
          hemoccult x 3
⟨87430⟩ Strep screen
_____ 84478 Triglycerides
_____ 84443 TSH
_____ 81001 UA with
          microscopy
_____ 87088 UC
_____ 84550 Uric acid,
          blood
_____ 81025 Urine
          pregnancy test
_____
_____

Injections:
_____ 90471 admin 1 vac
_____ 90472 each add'l
          vac
_____ 90716 Chickenpox
_____ 90702 DT
_____ 90701 DTP
_____ 90657 Influenza
          6-35 months
_____ 90658 Influenza
          3 years +
_____ 90665 Lyme
          disease
_____ 90707 MMR
_____ 90704 Mumps
_____ 90713 Polio vac
          inactivated (IPV)
_____ 90703 Tetanus Tox
ECG: _____ 93000 ECG

Other
_____

No.	Date	Description	Charge	Credit		Current Balance
				Payment	**Adjustment**	

Patient Information

3449 W. Foster Avenue

Address

Chicago, IL 60625-2377

City, State Zip

312-555-9565   312-555-8857

Home phone   **Work phone**

self

Responsible Person   **Relationship**

Prudential Group Health 255-74-1021

Insurance   **Contract numbers**

Patient _____ Gary Robertson _____

Date: 10/20/20--   **Chart #**

Karen Larsen, MD
2235 S. Ridgeway Avenue
Chicago, IL 60623-2240

312-555-6022

Fax: 312-555-0025

Diagnoses:

1. _____ 590.10 _____

2. _____

3. _____

4. _____

OFFICE VISITS

New Patient	Established Patient

Preventive Medicine

New Patient				Established Patient
_____ 99201	_____ 99381	under 1 year	_____ 99391	_____ 99211
_____ 99202	_____ 99382	1–4	_____ 99392	(99212)
_____ 99203	_____ 99383	5–11	_____ 99393	_____ 99213
_____ 99204	_____ 99384	12–17	_____ 99394	_____ 99214
_____ 99205	_____ 99385	18–39	_____ 99395	_____ 99215
	_____ 99386	40–64	_____ 99396	
	_____ 99387	65+	_____ 99397	

Hospital Visits

Initial:

_____ 99221

_____ 99222

_____ 99223

Subsequent:

_____ 99231

_____ 99232

_____ 99233

Nursing Facility

Subsequent:

_____ 99311

_____ 99312

_____ 99313

Other

_____

_____

Lab:

_____ 80048 Basic metabolic panel (SMA-8)

_____ 87110 Chlamydia culture

_____ 85651 ESR; nonautomated

_____ 83001 FSH

_____ 82947 Glucose, blood

_____ 85022 Hemogram (CBC) with differential

_____ 80076 Hepatic function panel

_____ 85018 HGB

_____ 86701 HIV-1

_____ 83002 LH

_____ 80061 Lipid panel

_____ 86617 Lyme antibody

_____ 86308 Monospot test

_____ 88150 Pap

_____ 85610 Prothrombin time

_____ 84152 PSA

_____ 86430 Rheumatoid factor

_____ 82270 Stool hemoccult x 3

_____ 87430 Strep screen

_____ 84478 Triglycerides

_____ 84443 TSH

_____ 81001 UA with microscopy

_____ 87088 UC

_____ 84550 Uric acid, blood

_____ 81025 Urine pregnancy test

_____

_____

Injections:

_____ 90471 admin 1 vac

_____ 90472 each add'l vac

_____ 90716 Chickenpox

_____ 90702 DT

_____ 90701 DTP

_____ 90657 Influenza 6-35 months

_____ 90658 Influenza 3 years +

_____ 90665 Lyme disease

_____ 90707 MMR

_____ 90704 Mumps

_____ 90713 Polio vac inactivated (IPV)

_____ 90703 Tetanus Tox

ECG: _____ 93000 ECG

Other

_____

_____

No.	Date	Description	Charge	Credit		Current Balance
				Payment	**Adjustment**	

Patient Information

5518 Monroe Street
Address

Chicago, IL 60644-5519
City, State Zip

312-555-4413   312-555-8825
Home phone   **Work phone**

self
Responsible Person   **Relationship**

Blue Cross/Blue Shield, 486-29-3789-1, 2458 Grp
Insurance   **Contract numbers**

Patient _____ Monica Armstrong _____

Date: 10/20/20--   **Chart #**

Karen Larsen, MD
2235 S. Ridgeway Avenue
Chicago, IL 60623-2240

312-555-6022

Fax: 312-555-0025

Diagnoses:

1. _____

2. _____

3. _____

4. _____

OFFICE VISITS

New Patient		**Established Patient**	

Preventive Medicine

New Patient			Preventive Medicine	Established	Established
_____ 99201	_____ 99381	under 1 year	_____ 99391		_____ 99211
_____ 99202	_____ 99382	1–4	_____ 99392		(99212)
_____ 99203	_____ 99383	5–11	_____ 99393		_____ 99213
_____ 99204	_____ 99384	12–17	_____ 99394		_____ 99214
_____ 99205	_____ 99385	18–39	_____ 99395		_____ 99215
	_____ 99386	40–64	_____ 99396		
	_____ 99387	65+	_____ 99397		

Hospital Visits
Initial:
_____ 99221
_____ 99222
_____ 99223
Subsequent:
_____ 99231
_____ 99232
_____ 99233
Nursing Facility
Subsequent:
_____ 99311
_____ 99312
_____ 99313
Other
_____
_____

Lab:
_____ (80048) Basic metabolic panel (SMA-8)
_____ 87110 Chlamydia culture
_____ 85651 ESR; nonautomated
_____ (83001) FSH
_____ 82947 Glucose, blood
_____ (85022) Hemogram (CBC) with differential
_____ 80076 Hepatic function panel
_____ 85018 HGB
_____ 86701 HIV-1
_____ 83002 LH
_____ 80061 Lipid panel
_____ 86617 Lyme antibody

_____ 86308 Monospot test
_____ 88150 Pap
_____ 85610 Prothrombin time
_____ 84152 PSA
_____ 86430 Rheumatoid factor
_____ 82270 Stool hemoccult x 3
_____ 87430 Strep screen
_____ 84478 Triglycerides
_____ 84443 TSH
_____ (81001) UA with microscopy
_____ 87088 UC
_____ 84550 Uric acid, blood
_____ 81025 Urine pregnancy test
_____
_____

Injections:
_____ 90471 admin 1 vac
_____ 90472 each add'l vac
_____ 90716 Chickenpox
_____ 90702 DT
_____ 90701 DTP
_____ 90657 Influenza 6-35 months
_____ 90658 Influenza 3 years +
_____ 90665 Lyme disease
_____ 90707 MMR
_____ 90704 Mumps
_____ 90713 Polio vac inactivated (IPV)
_____ 90703 Tetanus Tox
ECG: _____ 93000 ECG

Other
_____
_____

No.	Date	Description	Charge	Credit		Current Balance
				Payment	Adjustment	

Patient Information

3132 W. 42d Street
Address

Chicago, IL 60632-1406
City, State Zip

	father
312-555-1200	312-555-1245
Home phone	**Work phone**

George Casagranda	father
Responsible Person	**Relationship**

National Insurance	497-27-3367-05
Insurance	**Contract numbers**

Patient _____ Doris Casagranda _____

Date: 10/20/20--   **Chart #**

Karen Larsen, MD
2235 S. Ridgeway Avenue
Chicago, IL 60623-2240

312-555-6022

Fax: 312-555-0025

Diagnoses:

1. _____ 705.83 _____
2. _____
3. _____
4. _____

OFFICE VISITS

New Patient	Established Patient

Preventive Medicine

New Patient				Established Patient
	_____ 99381	under 1 year	_____ 99391	
_____ 99201	_____ 99382	1–4	_____ 99392	_____ 99211
_____ 99202	_____ 99383	5–11	_____ 99393	(99212)
_____ 99203	_____ 99384	12–17	_____ 99394	_____ 99213
_____ 99204	_____ 99385	18–39	_____ 99395	_____ 99214
_____ 99205	_____ 99386	40–64	_____ 99396	_____ 99215
	_____ 99387	65+	_____ 99397	

Hospital Visits
Initial:
_____ 99221
_____ 99222
_____ 99223
Subsequent:
_____ 99231
_____ 99232
_____ 99233
Nursing Facility
Subsequent:
_____ 99311
_____ 99312
_____ 99313
Other
_____
_____

Lab:
_____ 80048 Basic metabolic panel (SMA-8)
_____ 87110 Chlamydia culture
_____ 85651 ESR; nonautomated
_____ 83001 FSH
_____ 82947 Glucose, blood
_____ 85022 Hemogram (CBC) with differential
_____ 80076 Hepatic function panel
_____ 85018 HGB
_____ 86701 HIV-1
_____ 83002 LH
_____ 80061 Lipid panel
_____ 86617 Lyme antibody

_____ 86308 Monospot test
_____ 88150 Pap
_____ 85610 Prothrombin time
_____ 84152 PSA
_____ 86430 Rheumatoid factor
_____ 82270 Stool hemoccult x 3
_____ 87430 Strep screen
_____ 84478 Triglycerides
_____ 84443 TSH
_____ 81001 UA with microscopy
_____ 87088 UC
_____ 84550 Uric acid, blood
_____ 81025 Urine pregnancy test
_____
_____

Injections:
_____ 90471 admin 1 vac
_____ 90472 each add'l vac
_____ 90716 Chickenpox
_____ 90702 DT
_____ 90701 DTP
_____ 90657 Influenza 6-35 months
_____ 90658 Influenza 3 years +
_____ 90665 Lyme disease
_____ 90707 MMR
_____ 90704 Mumps
_____ 90713 Polio vac inactivated (IPV)
_____ 90703 Tetanus Tox
ECG: _____ 93000 ECG

Other

No.	Date	Description	Charge	Credit		Current Balance
				Payment	Adjustment	

Patient Information	Patient _____ Cheng Sun _____

2235 W. School Street
Address

Chicago, IL 60618-5785
City, State Zip

312-555-3750   312-555-8149
Home phone   **Work phone**

Billings, Inc. Worker's Comp, employer
Responsible Person   **Relationship**

Insurance   **Contract numbers**

Date: 10/21/20--

Chart #

Karen Larsen, MD
2235 S. Ridgeway Avenue
Chicago, IL 60623-2240

312-555-6022

Fax: 312-555-0025

Diagnoses:

1. _____ 915 _____

2. _____

3. _____

4. _____

OFFICE VISITS

New Patient	Established Patient

Preventive Medicine

	_____ 99381	under 1 year	_____ 99391	
_____ 99201	_____ 99382	1–4	_____ 99392	_____ 99211
_____ 99202	_____ 99383	5–11	_____ 99393	(99212)
_____ 99203	_____ 99384	12–17	_____ 99394	_____ 99213
_____ 99204	_____ 99385	18–39	_____ 99395	_____ 99214
_____ 99205	_____ 99386	40–64	_____ 99396	_____ 99215
	_____ 99387	65+	_____ 99397	

Hospital Visits
Initial:
_____ 99221
_____ 99222
_____ 99223
Subsequent:
_____ 99231
_____ 99232
_____ 99233
Nursing Facility
Subsequent:
_____ 99311
_____ 99312
_____ 99313
Other
_____
_____

Lab:
_____ 80048 Basic
    metabolic panel
    (SMA-8)
_____ 87110 Chlamydia
    culture
_____ 85651 ESR;
    nonautomated
_____ 83001 FSH
_____ 82947 Glucose,
    blood
_____ 85022 Hemogram
    (CBC) with
    differential
_____ 80076 Hepatic
    function panel
_____ 85018 HGB
_____ 86701 HIV-1
_____ 83002 LH
_____ 80061 Lipid panel
_____ 86617 Lyme
    antibody

_____ 86308 Monospot
    test
_____ 88150 Pap
_____ 85610 Prothrombin
    time
_____ 84152 PSA
_____ 86430 Rheumatoid
    factor
_____ 82270 Stool
    hemoccult x 3
_____ 87430 Strep screen
_____ 84478 Triglycerides
_____ 84443 TSH
_____ 81001 UA with
    microscopy
_____ 87088 UC
_____ 84550 Uric acid,
    blood
_____ 81025 Urine
    pregnancy test
_____
_____

Injections:
_____ 90471 admin 1 vac
_____ 90472 each add'l
    vac
_____ 90716 Chickenpox
_____ 90702 DT
_____ 90701 DTP
_____ 90657 Influenza
    6-35 months
_____ 90658 Influenza
    3 years +
_____ 90665 Lyme
    disease
_____ 90707 MMR
_____ 90704 Mumps
_____ 90713 Polio vac
    inactivated (IPV)
_____ 90703 Tetanus Tox
ECG: _____ 93000 ECG

Other
_____
_____

No.	Date	Description	Charge	Credit		Current Balance
				Payment	**Adjustment**	

Patient Information

5708 W. 63d Place
Address

Chicago, IL 60638-3391
City, State Zip

312-555-3097   312-555-8850
Home phone   **Work phone**

self
Responsible Person   **Relationship**

Kaiser Insurance   444-02-4422,991A Grp
Insurance   **Contract numbers**

Patient _____ Charles Jonathan III _____

Date: 10/21/20--   **Chart #**

Karen Larsen, MD
2235 S. Ridgeway Avenue
Chicago, IL 60623-2240

312-555-6022

Fax: 312-555-0025

Diagnoses:

1. _____ 719.46 _____

2. _____

3. _____

4. _____

OFFICE VISITS

New Patient	**Established Patient**

Preventive Medicine

		_____ 99381	under 1 year	_____ 99391	
_____ 99201	_____ 99382	1–4	_____ 99392	_____ 99211
_____ 99202	_____ 99383	5–11	_____ 99393	(99212)
_____ 99203	_____ 99384	12–17	_____ 99394	_____ 99213
_____ 99204	_____ 99385	18–39	_____ 99395	_____ 99214
_____ 99205	_____ 99386	40–64	_____ 99396	_____ 99215
	_____ 99387	65+	_____ 99397	

Hospital Visits
Initial:
_____ 99221
_____ 99222
_____ 99223
Subsequent:
_____ 99231
_____ 99232
_____ 99233
Nursing Facility
Subsequent:
_____ 99311
_____ 99312
_____ 99313
Other
_____
_____

Lab:
_____ 80048 Basic metabolic panel (SMA-8)
_____ 87110 Chlamydia culture
_____ 85651 ESR; nonautomated
_____ 83001 FSH
_____ 82947 Glucose, blood
_____ 85022 Hemogram (CBC) with differential
_____ 80076 Hepatic function panel
_____ 85018 HGB
_____ 86701 HIV-1
_____ 83002 LH
_____ 80061 Lipid panel
_____ 86617 Lyme antibody

_____ 86308 Monospot test
_____ 88150 Pap
_____ 85610 Prothrombin time
_____ 84152 PSA
_____ 86430 Rheumatoid factor
_____ 82270 Stool hemoccult x 3
_____ 87430 Strep screen
_____ 84478 Triglycerides
_____ 84443 TSH
_____ 81001 UA with microscopy
_____ 87088 UC
_____ 84550 Uric acid, blood
_____ 81025 Urine pregnancy test
_____
_____

Injections:
_____ 90471 admin 1 vac
_____ 90472 each add'l vac
_____ 90716 Chickenpox
_____ 90702 DT
_____ 90701 DTP
_____ 90657 Influenza 6-35 months
_____ 90658 Influenza 3 years +
_____ 90665 Lyme disease
_____ 90707 MMR
_____ 90704 Mumps
_____ 90713 Polio vac inactivated (IPV)
_____ 90703 Tetanus Tox
ECG: _____ 93000 ECG

Other
_____
_____

No.	Date	Description	Charge	Credit		Current Balance
				Payment	**Adjustment**	

### Patient Information	**Patient** _____ Sara Babcock _____
131 N. Mason Avenue	
Address	**Date:** 10/21/20-- **Chart #**
Chicago, IL 60644-4455	**Karen Larsen, MD**
City, State Zip	**2235 S. Ridgeway Avenue**
312-555-5441 312-555-9966	**Chicago, IL 60623-2240**
Home phone **Work phone**	
self	**312-555-6022**
Responsible Person **Relationship**	
Kaiser Insurance 987-87-3759	**Fax: 312-555-0025**
Insurance **Contract numbers**	

Diagnoses:

1. _____ V72.3 _____
2. _____ 112.1 _____
3. _____ V25.41 _____
4. _____ 625.6 _____

OFFICE VISITS

New Patient	**Established Patient**

Preventive Medicine

	_____ 99381	under 1 year	_____ 99391	
_____ 99201	_____ 99382	1–4	_____ 99392	_____ 99211
_____ 99202	_____ 99383	5–11	_____ 99393	_____ 99212
_____ 99203	_____ 99384	12–17	_____ 99394	_____ 99213
_____ 99204	_____ 99385	18–39	_____ (99395)	_____ 99214
_____ 99205	_____ 99386	40–64	_____ 99396	_____ 99215
	_____ 99387	65+	_____ 99397	

Hospital Visits
Initial:
_____ 99221
_____ 99222
_____ 99223
Subsequent:
_____ 99231
_____ 99232
_____ 99233
Nursing Facility
Subsequent:
_____ 99311
_____ 99312
_____ 99313
Other
_____
_____

Lab:
_____ 80048 Basic metabolic panel (SMA-8)
_____ 87110 Chlamydia culture
_____ 85651 ESR; nonautomated
_____ 83001 FSH
_____ 82947 Glucose, blood
_____ 85022 Hemogram (CBC) with differential
_____ 80076 Hepatic function panel
_____ (85018) HGB
_____ 86701 HIV-1
_____ 83002 LH
_____ (80061) Lipid panel
_____ 86617 Lyme antibody

_____ 86308 Monospot test
_____ (88150) Pap
_____ 85610 Prothrombin time
_____ 84152 PSA
_____ 86430 Rheumatoid factor
_____ 82270 Stool hemoccult x 3
_____ 87430 Strep screen
_____ 84478 Triglycerides
_____ 84443 TSH
_____ (81001) UA with microscopy
_____ 87088 UC
_____ 84550 Uric acid, blood
_____ 81025 Urine pregnancy test
_____
_____

Injections:
_____ 90471 admin 1 vac
_____ 90472 each add'l vac
_____ 90716 Chickenpox
_____ 90702 DT
_____ 90701 DTP
_____ 90657 Influenza 6-35 months
_____ 90658 Influenza 3 years +
_____ 90665 Lyme disease
_____ 90707 MMR
_____ 90704 Mumps
_____ 90713 Polio vac inactivated (IPV)
_____ 90703 Tetanus Tox
ECG: _____ 93000 ECG

Other
_____
_____

No.	Date	Description	Charge	Credit		Current Balance
				Payment	Adjustment	

| Patient Information | Patient ___ Gene Sinclair ___ |

2721 W. 18th Street
Address

Chicago, IL 60608-6260
City, State Zip

312-555-4381
Home phone   **Work phone**

self
Responsible Person   **Relationship**

Medicare   322-91-7722A
Insurance   **Contract numbers**

Date: 10/22/20--   **Chart #**

Karen Larsen, MD
2235 S. Ridgeway Avenue
Chicago, IL 60623-2240

312-555-6022

Fax: 312-555-0025

Diagnoses:

1. ___ 709.9 ___

2. _____

3. _____

4. _____

OFFICE VISITS

| New Patient | Established Patient |

Preventive Medicine

New Patient			Established Patient
___ 99201	___ 99381	under 1 year	___ 99391	
___ 99202	___ 99382	1–4	___ 99392	___ 99211
___ 99203	___ 99383	5–11	___ 99393	(99212)
___ 99204	___ 99384	12–17	___ 99394	___ 99213
___ 99205	___ 99385	18–39	___ 99395	___ 99214
	___ 99386	40–64	___ 99396	___ 99215
	___ 99387	65+	___ 99397	

Hospital Visits
Initial:
___ 99221
___ 99222
___ 99223
Subsequent:
___ 99231
___ 99232
___ 99233
Nursing Facility
Subsequent:
___ 99311
___ 99312
___ 99313
Other
_____
_____

Lab:
___ 80048 Basic metabolic panel (SMA-8)
___ 87110 Chlamydia culture
___ 85651 ESR; nonautomated
___ 83001 FSH
___ 82947 Glucose, blood
___ 85022 Hemogram (CBC) with differential
___ 80076 Hepatic function panel
___ 85018 HGB
___ 86701 HIV-1
___ 83002 LH
___ 80061 Lipid panel
___ 86617 Lyme antibody

___ 86308 Monospot test
___ 88150 Pap
___ 85610 Prothrombin time
___ 84152 PSA
___ 86430 Rheumatoid factor
___ 82270 Stool hemoccult x 3
___ 87430 Strep screen
___ 84478 Triglycerides
___ 84443 TSH
___ 81001 UA with microscopy
___ 87088 UC
___ 84550 Uric acid, blood
___ 81025 Urine pregnancy test
_____
_____

Injections:
___ 90471 admin 1 vac
___ 90472 each add'l vac
___ 90716 Chickenpox
___ 90702 DT
___ 90701 DTP
___ 90657 Influenza 6-35 months
___ 90658 Influenza 3 years +
___ 90665 Lyme disease
___ 90707 MMR
___ 90704 Mumps
___ 90713 Polio vac inactivated (IPV)
___ 90703 Tetanus Tox
ECG: ___ 93000 ECG

Other
_____
_____

Name: _____ **Date:** _____

No.	Date	Description	Charge	Credit		Current Balance
				Payment	**Adjustment**	

Patient Information

13419 S. Buffalo Avenue
Address

Chicago, IL 60633-2010
City, State Zip

312-555-4106   father   312-555-8840
Home phone   **Work phone**

Lawrence Lund   father
Responsible Person   **Relationship**

Employee Benefit Plan   200-66-3980-01
Insurance   **Contract numbers**

Patient _____ Laura Lund _____

Date: 10/22/20--   **Chart #**

Karen Larsen, MD
2235 S. Ridgeway Avenue
Chicago, IL 60623-2240

312-555-6022

Fax: 312-555-0025

Diagnoses:

1. _____ 847.0 _____

2. _____

3. _____

4. _____

OFFICE VISITS

New Patient	Established Patient

Preventive Medicine

New Patient				Established Patient	
	_____ 99381	under 1 year	_____ 99391		
_____ 99201	_____ 99382	1–4	_____ 99392	_____ 99211	
_____ 99202	_____ 99383	5–11	_____ 99393	(99212)	
_____ 99203	_____ 99384	12–17	_____ 99394	_____ 99213	
_____ 99204	_____ 99385	18–39	_____ 99395	_____ 99214	
_____ 99205	_____ 99386	40–64	_____ 99396	_____ 99215	
	_____ 99387	65+	_____ 99397		

Hospital Visits
Initial:
_____ 99221
_____ 99222
_____ 99223
Subsequent:
_____ 99231
_____ 99232
_____ 99233
Nursing Facility
Subsequent:
_____ 99311
_____ 99312
_____ 99313
Other
_____
_____

Lab:
_____ 80048 Basic metabolic panel (SMA-8)
_____ 87110 Chlamydia culture
_____ 85651 ESR; nonautomated
_____ 83001 FSH
_____ 82947 Glucose, blood
_____ 85022 Hemogram (CBC) with differential
_____ 80076 Hepatic function panel
_____ 85018 HGB
_____ 86701 HIV-1
_____ 83002 LH
_____ 80061 Lipid panel
_____ 86617 Lyme antibody

_____ 86308 Monospot test
_____ 88150 Pap
_____ 85610 Prothrombin time
_____ 84152 PSA
_____ 86430 Rheumatoid factor
_____ 82270 Stool hemoccult x 3
_____ 87430 Strep screen
_____ 84478 Triglycerides
_____ 84443 TSH
_____ 81001 UA with microscopy
_____ 87088 UC
_____ 84550 Uric acid, blood
_____ 81025 Urine pregnancy test
_____
_____

Injections:
_____ 90471 admin 1 vac
_____ 90472 each add'l vac
_____ 90716 Chickenpox
_____ 90702 DT
_____ 90701 DTP
_____ 90657 Influenza 6-35 months
_____ 90658 Influenza 3 years +
_____ 90665 Lyme disease
_____ 90707 MMR
_____ 90704 Mumps
_____ 90713 Polio vac inactivated (IPV)
_____ 90703 Tetanus Tox
ECG: _____ 93000 ECG
Other
_____
_____

WP 64

No.	Date	Description	Charge	Credit Payment	Credit Adjustment	Current Balance

Patient Information

3457 W. 63d Place
Address

Chicago, IL 60629-4270
City, State Zip

312-555-3606
Home phone   **Work phone**

self
Responsible Person   **Relationship**

Blue Cross & Blue Shield   295-99-3325,354 Grp
Insurance   **Contract numbers**

Patient _____ Ana Mendez _____

Date: 10/22/20--   **Chart #**

Karen Larsen, MD
2235 S. Ridgeway Avenue
Chicago, IL 60623-2240

312-555-6022

Fax: 312-555-0025

Diagnoses:

1. _____ 463 _____

2. _____ 289.3 _____

3. _____

4. _____

OFFICE VISITS

New Patient	Established Patient

Preventive Medicine

New Patient				Established Patient
	_____ 99381	under 1 year	_____ 99391	
_____ 99201	_____ 99382	1–4	_____ 99392	_____ 99211
_____ 99202	_____ 99383	5–11	_____ 99393	(99212)
_____ 99203	_____ 99384	12–17	_____ 99394	_____ 99213
_____ 99204	_____ 99385	18–39	_____ 99395	_____ 99214
_____ 99205	_____ 99386	40–64	_____ 99396	_____ 99215
	_____ 99387	65+	_____ 99397	

Hospital Visits
Initial:
_____ 99221
_____ 99222
_____ 99223
Subsequent:
_____ 99231
_____ 99232
_____ 99233
Nursing Facility
Subsequent:
_____ 99311
_____ 99312
_____ 99313
Other
_____
_____

Lab:
_____ 80048 Basic metabolic panel (SMA-8)
_____ 87110 Chlamydia culture
_____ 85651 ESR; nonautomated
_____ 83001 FSH
_____ 82947 Glucose, blood
_____ 85022 Hemogram (CBC) with differential
_____ 80076 Hepatic function panel
_____ 85018 HGB
_____ 86701 HIV-1
_____ 83002 LH
_____ 80061 Lipid panel
_____ 86617 Lyme antibody

_____ 86308 Monospot test
_____ 88150 Pap
_____ 85610 Prothrombin time
_____ 84152 PSA
_____ 86430 Rheumatoid factor
_____ 82270 Stool hemoccult x 3
_____ 87430 Strep screen
_____ 84478 Triglycerides
_____ 84443 TSH
_____ 81001 UA with microscopy
_____ 87088 UC
_____ 84550 Uric acid, blood
_____ 81025 Urine pregnancy test
_____
_____

Injections:
_____ 90471 admin 1 vac
_____ 90472 each add'l vac
_____ 90716 Chickenpox
_____ 90702 DT
_____ 90701 DTP
_____ 90657 Influenza 6-35 months
_____ 90658 Influenza 3 years +
_____ 90665 Lyme disease
_____ 90707 MMR
_____ 90704 Mumps
_____ 90713 Polio vac inactivated (IPV)
_____ 90703 Tetanus Tox
ECG: _____ 93000 ECG

Other
_____
_____

No.	Date	Description	Charge	Credit		Current Balance
				Payment	Adjustment	

Patient Information

5231 W. School Street
Address

Chicago, IL 60651-2248
City, State Zip

312-555-8153	father 312-555-6141
Home phone	**Work phone**

Alan Mitchell	father
Responsible Person	**Relationship**

New York Mutual	304253, 5245 Grp
Insurance	**Contract numbers**

Patient _____ Donald Mitchell _____

Date: 10/22/20--   **Chart #**

Karen Larsen, MD
2235 S. Ridgeway Avenue
Chicago, IL 60623-2240

312-555-6022

Fax: 312-555-0025

Diagnoses:

1. _____
2. _____
3. _____
4. _____

OFFICE VISITS

New Patient	**Established Patient**

Preventive Medicine

	_(99381)_	under 1 year	_____ 99391		
_____ 99201	_____ 99382	1–4	_____ 99392	_____ 99211	
_____ 99202	_____ 99383	5–11	_____ 99393	_____ 99212	
_____ 99203	_____ 99384	12–17	_____ 99394	_____ 99213	
_____ 99204	_____ 99385	18–39	_____ 99395	_____ 99214	
_____ 99205	_____ 99386	40–64	_____ 99396	_____ 99215	
	_____ 99387	65+	_____ 99397		

Hospital Visits
Initial:
_____ 99221
_____ 99222
_____ 99223
Subsequent:
_____ 99231
_____ 99232
_____ 99233
Nursing Facility
Subsequent:
_____ 99311
_____ 99312
_____ 99313
Other
_____
_____

Lab:
_____ 80048 Basic metabolic panel (SMA-8)
_____ 87110 Chlamydia culture
_____ 85651 ESR; nonautomated
_____ 83001 FSH
_____ 82947 Glucose, blood
_____ 85022 Hemogram (CBC) with differential
_____ 80076 Hepatic function panel
_____ 85018 HGB
_____ 86701 HIV-1
_____ 83002 LH
_____ 80061 Lipid panel
_____ 86617 Lyme antibody

_____ 86308 Monospot test
_____ 88150 Pap
_____ 85610 Prothrombin time
_____ 84152 PSA
_____ 86430 Rheumatoid factor
_____ 82270 Stool hemoccult x 3
_____ 87430 Strep screen
_____ 84478 Triglycerides
_____ 84443 TSH
_____ _(81001)_ UA with microscopy
_____ 87088 UC
_____ 84550 Uric acid, blood
_____ 81025 Urine pregnancy test
_____
_____

Injections:
_____ 90471 admin 1 vac
_____ 90472 each add'l vac
_____ 90716 Chickenpox
_____ 90702 DT
_____ 90701 DTP
_____ 90657 Influenza 6-35 months
_____ 90658 Influenza 3 years +
_____ 90665 Lyme disease
_____ 90707 MMR
_____ 90704 Mumps
_____ 90713 Polio vac inactivated (IPV)
_____ 90703 Tetanus Tox
ECG: _____ 93000 ECG

Other
_____
_____

No.	Date	Description	Charge	Credit		Current Balance
				Payment	**Adjustment**	

Patient Information

105 W. Chestnut Street
Address

Chicago, IL 60610-2816
City, State Zip

312-555-2231   312-555-2583
Home phone   **Work phone**

self
Responsible Person   **Relationship**

University Health Plan, 797-90-1128, S357C Grp.
Insurance   **Contract numbers**

Patient _____ Theresa Dayton

Date: 10/22/20--   **Chart #**

Karen Larsen, MD
2235 S. Ridgeway Avenue
Chicago, IL 60623-2240

312-555-6022

Fax: 312-555-0025

Diagnoses:

1. ____ 610.0 ____

2. ____ V25.9 ____

3. _____

4. _____

OFFICE VISITS

New Patient		**Established Patient**

Preventive Medicine

New Patient				Established Patient	
	_____ 99381	under 1 year	_____ 99391		
_____ 99201	_____ 99382	1–4	_____ 99392		_____ 99211
_____ 99202	_____ 99383	5–11	_____ 99393		(99212)
_____ 99203	_____ 99384	12–17	_____ 99394		_____ 99213
_____ 99204	_____ 99385	18–39	_____ 99395		_____ 99214
_____ 99205	_____ 99386	40–64	_____ 99396		_____ 99215
	_____ 99387	65+	_____ 99397		

Hospital Visits
Initial:
_____ 99221
_____ 99222
_____ 99223
Subsequent:
_____ 99231
_____ 99232
_____ 99233
Nursing Facility
Subsequent:
_____ 99311
_____ 99312
_____ 99313
Other
_____
_____

Lab:
_____ 80048 Basic metabolic panel (SMA-8)
_____ 87110 Chlamydia culture
_____ 85651 ESR; nonautomated
_____ 83001 FSH
_____ 82947 Glucose, blood
_____ 85022 Hemogram (CBC) with differential
_____ 80076 Hepatic function panel
_____ 85018 HGB
_____ 86701 HIV-1
_____ 83002 LH
_____ 80061 Lipid panel
_____ 86617 Lyme antibody

_____ 86308 Monospot test
_____ 88150 Pap
_____ 85610 Prothrombin time
_____ 84152 PSA
_____ 86430 Rheumatoid factor
_____ 82270 Stool hemoccult x 3
_____ 87430 Strep screen
_____ 84478 Triglycerides
_____ 84443 TSH
_____ 81001 UA with microscopy
_____ 87088 UC
_____ 84550 Uric acid, blood
_____ 81025 Urine pregnancy test
_____
_____

Injections:
_____ 90471 admin 1 vac
_____ 90472 each add'l vac
_____ 90716 Chickenpox
_____ 90702 DT
_____ 90701 DTP
_____ 90657 Influenza 6-35 months
_____ 90658 Influenza 3 years +
_____ 90665 Lyme disease
_____ 90707 MMR
_____ 90704 Mumps
_____ 90713 Polio vac inactivated (IPV)
_____ 90703 Tetanus Tox
ECG: _____ 93000 ECG
Other
_____
_____

No.	Date	Description	Charge	Credit		Current Balance
				Payment	Adjustment	

Patient Information

3908 N. Central Avenue
Address

Chicago, IL 60634-3276
City, State Zip

312-555-6343
Home phone   **Work phone**

self
Responsible Person   **Relationship**

Medicare   555-88-3822B
Insurance   **Contract numbers**

Patient _____ Raymond Murrary _____

Date: 10/22/20--   **Chart #**

Karen Larsen, MD
2235 S. Ridgeway Avenue
Chicago, IL 60623-2240

312-555-6022

Fax: 312-555-0025

Diagnoses:

1. _____ 491.21 _____

2. _____ 490 _____

3. _____

4. _____

OFFICE VISITS

New Patient	Established Patient

Preventive Medicine

New Patient		Preventive Medicine	Established Patient	
	_____ 99381	under 1 year	_____ 99391	
_____ 99201	_____ 99382	1–4	_____ 99392	_____ 99211
_____ 99202	_____ 99383	5–11	_____ 99393	_____ 99212
_____ 99203	_____ 99384	12–17	_____ 99394	_____ 99213
_____ 99204	_____ 99385	18–39	_____ 99395	_____ 99214
_____ 99205	_____ 99386	40–64	_____ 99396	_____ 99215
	_____ 99387	65+	_____ 99397	

Hospital Visits
Initial:
_____ 99221
_____ 99222
_____ 99223
Subsequent:
_____ 99231
_____ 99232
_____ 99233
Nursing Facility
Subsequent:
_____ (99311)
_____ 99312
_____ 99313
Other
_____
_____

Lab:
_____ 80048 Basic metabolic panel (SMA-8)
_____ 87110 Chlamydia culture
_____ 85651 ESR; nonautomated
_____ 83001 FSH
_____ 82947 Glucose, blood
_____ 85022 Hemogram (CBC) with differential
_____ 80076 Hepatic function panel
_____ 85018 HGB
_____ 86701 HIV-1
_____ 83002 LH
_____ 80061 Lipid panel
_____ 86617 Lyme antibody

_____ 86308 Monospot test
_____ 88150 Pap
_____ 85610 Prothrombin time
_____ 84152 PSA
_____ 86430 Rheumatoid factor
_____ 82270 Stool hemoccult x 3
_____ 87430 Strep screen
_____ 84478 Triglycerides
_____ 84443 TSH
_____ 81001 UA with microscopy
_____ 87088 UC
_____ 84550 Uric acid, blood
_____ 81025 Urine pregnancy test
_____
_____

Injections:
_____ 90471 admin 1 vac
_____ 90472 each add'l vac
_____ 90716 Chickenpox
_____ 90702 DT
_____ 90701 DTP
_____ 90657 Influenza 6-35 months
_____ 90658 Influenza 3 years +
_____ 90665 Lyme disease
_____ 90707 MMR
_____ 90704 Mumps
_____ 90713 Polio vac inactivated (IPV)
_____ 90703 Tetanus Tox
ECG: _____ 93000 ECG

Other
_____
_____

DAILY JOURNAL

DATE ___10/20/20--___   SHEET NO. ___102___

	RECEIPT NUMBER	DATE	DESCRIPTION CODE	CHARGE	PAYMENT	ADJUSTMENTS	BALANCE	PREVIOUS BALANCE	NAME
1	1090	10/20	OV	44 00	—	—	44 00	—	Sherman
2	1091	10/20	OV/Strep screen	83 00	16 60	—	66 40	—	Villano
3	1092	10/20	OV	44 00	—	—	147 00	103 00	Robertson
4	1093	10/20	OV/LAB	241 00	48 20	—	192 80	—	Armstrong
5	1094	10/20	OV	44 00	—	—	44 00	—	Casagranda
6									
7									
32									
33									
34			Column A	Column B	Column C	Column D	Column E		TOTALS

◄ ALL RECEIPTS MUST BE
IN NUMERICAL ORDER

Proof of Posting

Column E Total	$ _____
Plus Column A Total	$ _____
Subtotal	$ _____
Minus Column B Total	$ _____
Equals Column D Total	$ _____

Accounts Receivable Control

Previous Balance	$ 6260.40
Plus Column A	$ _____
Subtotal	$ _____
Minus Column B Total	$ _____
Present Acc'ts Rec. Balance	$ _____

Daily Cash

Opening Cash on Hand at Beginning of Day	$ _____
Cash Received During Day	$ —0—
Total	$ _____

DAILY JOURNAL

DATE ___10/21/20-___   SHEET NO. 103

	RECEIPT NUMBER	DATE	DESCRIPTION CODE	CHARGE	PAYMENT	ADJUSTMENTS	BALANCE	PREVIOUS BALANCE	NAME
1	1095	10/21	OV (WC)	44 00	—	—	44 00	—	Sun, Cheng
2	1096	10/21	OV	44 00	—	—	44 00	—	Jonathan
3	1097	10/21	CPE/LAB	278 00			278 00	—	Babcock
4									
5									
6									
7									
32									
33									
34									
				Column A	Column B	Column C	Column D	Column E	TOTALS

◄ ALL RECEIPTS MUST BE
   IN NUMERICAL ORDER

Proof of Posting

Column E Total $ _____
Plus Column A Total $ _____
Subtotal $ _____
Minus Column B Total $ _____
Equals Column D Total $ _____

Accounts Receivable Control

Previous Balance $ _____
Plus Column A $ _____
Subtotal $ _____
Minus Column B Total $ _____
Present Acc'ts Rec. Balance $ _____

Daily Cash

Opening Cash on Hand
at Beginning of Day $ _____
Cash Received During Day $ _____
Total $ _____

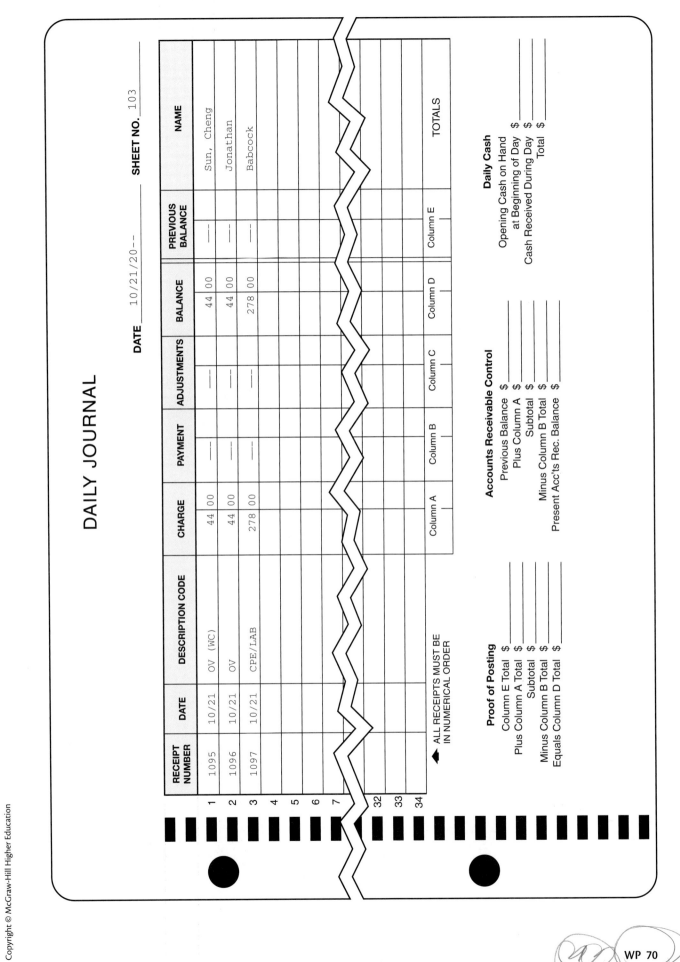

WP 70

DAILY JOURNAL

DATE 10/22/20--   SHEET NO. 104

	RECEIPT NUMBER	DATE	DESCRIPTION CODE	CHARGE	PAYMENT	ADJUSTMENTS	BALANCE	PREVIOUS BALANCE	NAME
1	1098	10/22	OV	44 00	—	—			Sinclair
2	1099	10/22	OV	44 00	—	—			Lund
3	1100	10/22	OV	44 00	8 80	—			Mendez
4	1101	10/22	CPE/UA	163 00					Mitchell, D.
5	1102	10/22	OV	44 00	—	—			Dayton
6	1103	10/22	Nursing home visit	53 00	—	—			Murrary
7									
32									
33									
34			Column A	Column B	Column C	Column D	Column E		TOTALS

◀ ALL RECEIPTS MUST BE IN NUMERICAL ORDER

Proof of Posting

Column E Total $ _____
Plus Column A Total $ _____
Subtotal $ _____
Minus Column B Total $ _____
Equals Column D Total $ _____

Accounts Receivable Control

Previous Balance $ _____
Plus Column A $ _____
Subtotal $ _____
Minus Column B Total $ _____
Present Acc'ts Rec. Balance $ _____

Daily Cash

Opening Cash on Hand
at Beginning of Day $ _____
Cash Received During Day $ _____
Total $ _____

DAILY JOURNAL

DATE _____   SHEET NO. _____

RECEIPT NUMBER	DATE	DESCRIPTION CODE	CHARGE	PAYMENT	ADJUSTMENTS	BALANCE	PREVIOUS BALANCE	NAME
1								
2								
3								
4								
5								
6								
7								
32								
33								
34								
TOTALS			Column A	Column B	Column C	Column D	Column E	

◄ ALL RECEIPTS MUST BE IN NUMERICAL ORDER

Proof of Posting

Column E Total $ _____
Plus Column A Total $ _____
Subtotal $ _____
Minus Column B Total $ _____
Equals Column D Total $ _____

Accounts Receivable Control

Previous Balance $ _____
Plus Column A $ _____
Subtotal $ _____
Minus Column B Total $ _____
Present Acc'ts Rec. Balance $ _____

Daily Cash

Opening Cash on Hand
at Beginning of Day $ _____
Cash Received During Day $ _____
Total $ _____

WP 72

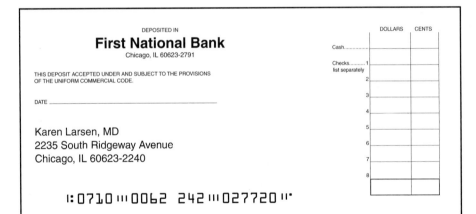

DEPOSITED IN

First National Bank
Chicago, IL 60623-2791

THIS DEPOSIT ACCEPTED UNDER AND SUBJECT TO THE PROVISIONS
OF THE UNIFORM COMMERCIAL CODE.

DATE _____

Karen Larsen, MD
2235 South Ridgeway Avenue
Chicago, IL 60623-2240

I: 0710 III 0062 242 III 027720 II.

	DOLLARS	CENTS
Cash..................		
Checks..........1		
list separately		
2		
3		
4		
5		
6		
7		
8		

DEPOSITED IN

First National Bank
Chicago, IL 60623-2791

THIS DEPOSIT ACCEPTED UNDER AND SUBJECT TO THE PROVISIONS
OF THE UNIFORM COMMERCIAL CODE.

DATE _____

Karen Larsen, MD
2235 South Ridgeway Avenue
Chicago, IL 60623-2240

I: 0710 III 0062 242 III 027720 II.

	DOLLARS	CENTS
Cash..................		
Checks..........1		
list separately		
2		
3		
4		
5		
6		
7		
8		

DEPOSITED IN

First National Bank
Chicago, IL 60623-2791

THIS DEPOSIT ACCEPTED UNDER AND SUBJECT TO THE PROVISIONS
OF THE UNIFORM COMMERCIAL CODE.

DATE _____

Karen Larsen, MD
2235 South Ridgeway Avenue
Chicago, IL 60623-2240

I: 0710 III 0062 242 III 027720 II.

	DOLLARS	CENTS
Cash..................		
Checks..........1		
list separately		
2		
3		
4		
5		
6		
7		
8		

DEPOSITED IN

First National Bank
Chicago, IL 60623-2791

THIS DEPOSIT ACCEPTED UNDER AND SUBJECT TO THE PROVISIONS
OF THE UNIFORM COMMERCIAL CODE.

DATE _____

Karen Larsen, MD
2235 South Ridgeway Avenue
Chicago, IL 60623-2240

I: 0710 III 0062 242 III 027720 II.

	DOLLARS	CENTS
Cash..................		
Checks..........1		
list separately		
2		
3		
4		
5		
6		
7		
8		

TELEPHONE LOG

Date _____

TIME	CALLER	TELEPHONE NUMBER	REASON	DONE

TO-DO LIST

Date _____

RUSH	ITEMS TO DO	DONE

No.	Date	Description	Charge	Credit		Current Balance
				Payment	**Adjustment**	

Patient Information

9340 S. Green Street
Address

Chicago, IL 60620-8129
City, State Zip

	father
312-555-3344	312-555-2577
Home phone	**Work phone**

Tam Phan	father
Responsible Person	**Relationship**

University Health Plan, 888-90-8229 A287-05
Insurance   **Contract numbers**

Patient _____ Marc Phan _____

Date: 10/27/20--   **Chart #**

Karen Larsen, MD
2235 S. Ridgeway Avenue
Chicago, IL 60623-2240

312-555-6022

Fax: 312-555-0025

Diagnoses:

1. ____ 490 ____
2. ____ 691.0 ____
3. _____
4. _____

OFFICE VISITS

New Patient	Established Patient

Preventive Medicine

	_____ 99381	under 1 year	_____ 99391	
_____ 99201	_____ 99382	1–4	_____ 99392	_____ 99211
_____ 99202	_____ 99383	5–11	_____ 99393	(99212)
_____ 99203	_____ 99384	12–17	_____ 99394	_____ 99213
_____ 99204	_____ 99385	18–39	_____ 99395	_____ 99214
_____ 99205	_____ 99386	40–64	_____ 99396	_____ 99215
	_____ 99387	65+	_____ 99397	

Hospital Visits
Initial:
____ 99221
____ 99222
____ 99223
Subsequent:
____ 99231
____ 99232
____ 99233
Nursing Facility
Subsequent:
____ 99311
____ 99312
____ 99313
Other
_____
_____

Lab:
____ 80048 Basic metabolic panel (SMA-8)
____ 87110 Chlamydia culture
____ 85651 ESR; nonautomated
____ 83001 FSH
____ 82947 Glucose, blood
____ 85022 Hemogram (CBC) with differential
____ 80076 Hepatic function panel
____ 85018 HGB
____ 86701 HIV-1
____ 83002 LH
____ 80061 Lipid panel
____ 86617 Lyme antibody

____ 86308 Monospot test
____ 88150 Pap
____ 85610 Prothrombin time
____ 84152 PSA
____ 86430 Rheumatoid factor
____ 82270 Stool hemoccult x 3
____ 87430 Strep screen
____ 84478 Triglycerides
____ 84443 TSH
____ 81001 UA with microscopy
____ 87088 UC
____ 84550 Uric acid, blood
____ 81025 Urine pregnancy test
_____
_____

Injections:
____ 90471 admin 1 vac
____ 90472 each add'l vac
____ 90716 Chickenpox
____ 90702 DT
____ 90701 DTP
____ 90657 Influenza 6-35 months
____ 90658 Influenza 3 years +
____ 90665 Lyme disease
____ 90707 MMR
____ 90704 Mumps
____ 90713 Polio vac inactivated (IPV)
____ 90703 Tetanus Tox
ECG: ____ 93000 ECG

Other
_____
_____

No.	Date	Description	Charge	Credit Payment	Credit Adjustment	Current Balance

Patient Information

723 W. Sixth Place
Address

Chicago, IL 60621-2314
City, State Zip

	mother
312-555-2324	312-555-8876
Home phone	**Work phone**

Esther Morton	mother
Responsible Person	**Relationship**

Northstar Insurance,	300-29-1874 255-03
Insurance	**Contract numbers**

Patient ___Sarah Morton___

Date: 10/27/20--   **Chart #**

Karen Larsen, MD
2235 S. Ridgeway Avenue
Chicago, IL 60623-2240

312-555-6022

Fax: 312-555-0025

Diagnoses:

1. ___737.30___
2. ___736.81___
3. _____
4. _____

OFFICE VISITS

New Patient	Established Patient

Preventive Medicine

	_____ 99381	under 1 year	_____ 99391		
_____ 99201	_____ 99382	1–4	_____ 99392	_____ 99211	
_____ 99202	_____ 99383	5–11	_____ 99393	(99212)	
_____ 99203	_____ 99384	12–17	_____ 99394	_____ 99213	
_____ 99204	_____ 99385	18–39	_____ 99395	_____ 99214	
_____ 99205	_____ 99386	40–64	_____ 99396	_____ 99215	
	_____ 99387	65+	_____ 99397		

Hospital Visits
Initial:
_____ 99221
_____ 99222
_____ 99223
Subsequent:
_____ 99231
_____ 99232
_____ 99233
Nursing Facility
Subsequent:
_____ 99311
_____ 99312
_____ 99313
Other
_____
_____

Lab:
_____ 80048 Basic metabolic panel (SMA-8)
_____ 87110 Chlamydia culture
_____ 85651 ESR; nonautomated
_____ 83001 FSH
_____ 82947 Glucose, blood
_____ 85022 Hemogram (CBC) with differential
_____ 80076 Hepatic function panel
_____ 85018 HGB
_____ 86701 HIV-1
_____ 83002 LH
_____ 80061 Lipid panel
_____ 86617 Lyme antibody

_____ 86308 Monospot test
_____ 88150 Pap
_____ 85610 Prothrombin time
_____ 84152 PSA
_____ 86430 Rheumatoid factor
_____ 82270 Stool hemoccult x 3
_____ 87430 Strep screen
_____ 84478 Triglycerides
_____ 84443 TSH
_____ 81001 UA with microscopy
_____ 87088 UC
_____ 84550 Uric acid, blood
_____ 81025 Urine pregnancy test
_____
_____

Injections:
_____ 90471 admin 1 vac
_____ 90472 each add'l vac
_____ 90716 Chickenpox
_____ 90702 DT
_____ 90701 DTP
_____ 90657 Influenza 6-35 months
_____ 90658 Influenza 3 years +
_____ 90665 Lyme disease
_____ 90707 MMR
_____ 90704 Mumps
_____ 90713 Polio vac inactivated (IPV)
_____ 90703 Tetanus Tox
ECG: _____ 93000 ECG

Other
_____
_____

No.	Date	Description	Charge	Credit		Current Balance
				Payment	**Adjustment**	

Patient Information

3132 W. 42d Street

Address

Chicago, IL 60632-1406

City, State Zip

	father
312-555-1200	312-555-1245
Home phone	**Work phone**

George Casagranda   father

Responsible Person   **Relationship**

National Insurance   497-27-3367-05

Insurance   **Contract numbers**

Patient _____ Doris Casagranda _____

Date: 10/27/20--   **Chart #**

Karen Larsen, MD
2235 S. Ridgeway Avenue
Chicago, IL 60623-2240

312-555-6022

Fax: 312-555-0025

Diagnoses:

1. _____ 705.83 _____

2. _____

3. _____

4. _____

OFFICE VISITS

New Patient	Established Patient

Preventive Medicine

New Patient			Established Patient	
	_____ 99381	under 1 year	_____ 99391	
_____ 99201	_____ 99382	1–4	_____ 99392	_____ 99211
_____ 99202	_____ 99383	5–11	_____ 99393	(99212)
_____ 99203	_____ 99384	12–17	_____ 99394	_____ 99213
_____ 99204	_____ 99385	18–39	_____ 99395	_____ 99214
_____ 99205	_____ 99386	40–64	_____ 99396	_____ 99215
	_____ 99387	65+	_____ 99397	

Hospital Visits

Initial:
_____ 99221
_____ 99222
_____ 99223

Subsequent:
_____ 99231
_____ 99232
_____ 99233

Nursing Facility

Subsequent:
_____ 99311
_____ 99312
_____ 99313

Other

_____
_____

Lab:
_____ 80048 Basic metabolic panel (SMA-8)
_____ 87110 Chlamydia culture
_____ 85651 ESR; nonautomated
_____ 83001 FSH
_____ 82947 Glucose, blood
_____ 85022 Hemogram (CBC) with differential
_____ 80076 Hepatic function panel
_____ 85018 HGB
_____ 86701 HIV-1
_____ 83002 LH
_____ 80061 Lipid panel
_____ 86617 Lyme antibody

_____ 86308 Monospot test
_____ 88150 Pap
_____ 85610 Prothrombin time
_____ 84152 PSA
_____ 86430 Rheumatoid factor
_____ 82270 Stool hemoccult x 3
_____ 87430 Strep screen
_____ 84478 Triglycerides
_____ 84443 TSH
_____ 81001 UA with microscopy
_____ 87088 UC
_____ 84550 Uric acid, blood
_____ 81025 Urine pregnancy test

_____
_____

Injections:
_____ 90471 admin 1 vac
_____ 90472 each add'l vac
_____ 90716 Chickenpox
_____ 90702 DT
_____ 90701 DTP
_____ 90657 Influenza 6-35 months
_____ 90658 Influenza 3 years +
_____ 90665 Lyme disease
_____ 90707 MMR
_____ 90704 Mumps
_____ 90713 Polio vac inactivated (IPV)
_____ 90703 Tetanus Tox

ECG: ____ 93000 ECG

Other

_____
_____

| No. | Date | Description | Charge | Credit | | Current Balance |
				Payment	Adjustment	

Patient Information

4345 W. Grace Street
Address

Chicago, IL 60641-6730
City, State Zip

312-555-7292
Home phone   **Work phone**

Paul Burton   father
Responsible Person   **Relationship**

No insurance
Insurance   **Contract numbers**

Patient _____ Randy Burton _____

Date: 10/27/20--   **Chart #**

Karen Larsen, MD   **Diagnoses:**
2235 S. Ridgeway Avenue
Chicago, IL 60623-2240   1. _____

                              2. _____
312-555-6022
                              3. _____

Fax: 312-555-0025   4. _____

OFFICE VISITS

New Patient	Established Patient

Preventive Medicine

New Patient			Established Patient	
	_____ 99381	under 1 year	_____ 99391	
_____ 99201	_____ 99382	1–4	(99392)	_____ 99211
_____ 99202	_____ 99383	5–11	_____ 99393	_____ 99212
_____ 99203	_____ 99384	12–17	_____ 99394	_____ 99213
_____ 99204	_____ 99385	18–39	_____ 99395	_____ 99214
_____ 99205	_____ 99386	40–64	_____ 99396	_____ 99215
	_____ 99387	65+	_____ 99397	

Hospital Visits
Initial:
_____ 99221
_____ 99222
_____ 99223
Subsequent:
_____ 99231
_____ 99232
_____ 99233
Nursing Facility
Subsequent:
_____ 99311
_____ 99312
_____ 99313
Other
_____
_____

Lab:
_____ 80048 Basic metabolic panel (SMA-8)
_____ 87110 Chlamydia culture
_____ 85651 ESR; nonautomated
_____ 83001 FSH
_____ 82947 Glucose, blood
_____ 85022 Hemogram (CBC) with differential
_____ 80076 Hepatic function panel
_____ 85018 HGB
_____ 86701 HIV-1
_____ 83002 LH
_____ 80061 Lipid panel
_____ 86617 Lyme antibody

_____ 86308 Monospot test
_____ 88150 Pap
_____ 85610 Prothrombin time
_____ 84152 PSA
_____ 86430 Rheumatoid factor
_____ 82270 Stool hemoccult x 3
_____ 87430 Strep screen
_____ 84478 Triglycerides
_____ 84443 TSH
_____ 81001 UA with microscopy
_____ 87088 UC
_____ 84550 Uric acid, blood
_____ 81025 Urine pregnancy test
_____
_____

Injections:
_____ (90471) admin 1 vac
_____ (90472) each add'l vac
_____ 90716 Chickenpox
_____ 90702 DT
_____ (90701) DTP
_____ 90657 Influenza 6-35 months
_____ 90658 Influenza 3 years +
_____ 90665 Lyme disease
_____ 90707 MMR
_____ 90704 Mumps
_____ (90713) Polio vac inactivated (IPV)
_____ 90703 Tetanus Tox
ECG: _____ 93000 ECG

Other
_____
_____

No.	Date	Description	Charge	Credit		Current Balance
				Payment	**Adjustment**	

Patient Information

3449 W. Foster Avenue

Address

Chicago, IL 60625-2377

City, State Zip

312-555-9565   312-555-8857

Home phone   **Work phone**

self

Responsible Person   **Relationship**

Prudential Group Health   255-74-1021

Insurance   **Contract numbers**

Patient _____ Gary Robertson _____

Date: 10/27/20--   **Chart #**

Karen Larsen, MD
2235 S. Ridgeway Avenue
Chicago, IL 60623-2240

312-555-6022

Fax: 312-555-0025

Diagnoses:

1. _____ 590.10 _____

2. _____

3. _____

4. _____

OFFICE VISITS

New Patient	Established Patient

Preventive Medicine

New Patient				Established Patient	
	_____ 99381	under 1 year	_____ 99391		
_____ 99201	_____ 99382	1–4	_____ 99392	_____ 99211	
_____ 99202	_____ 99383	5–11	_____ 99393	_____ 99212	
_____ 99203	_____ 99384	12–17	_____ 99394	_____ 99213	
_____ 99204	_____ 99385	18–39	_____ 99395	_____ 99214	
_____ 99205	_____ 99386	40–64	_____ 99396	_____ 99215	
	_____ 99387	65+	_____ 99397		

Hospital Visits

Initial:
_____ 99221
_____ 99222
_____ 99223

Subsequent:
x 3 (99231)
_____ 99232
_____ 99233

Nursing Facility

Subsequent:
_____ 99311
_____ 99312
_____ 99313

Other

_____

_____

Visits:
10/21
10/23
10/25

Lab:
_____ 80048 Basic metabolic panel (SMA-8)
_____ 87110 Chlamydia culture
_____ 85651 ESR; nonautomated
_____ 83001 FSH
_____ 82947 Glucose, blood
_____ 85022 Hemogram (CBC) with differential
_____ 80076 Hepatic function panel
_____ 85018 HGB
_____ 86701 HIV-1
_____ 83002 LH
_____ 80061 Lipid panel
_____ 86617 Lyme antibody

_____ 86308 Monospot test
_____ 88150 Pap
_____ 85610 Prothrombin time
_____ 84152 PSA
_____ 86430 Rheumatoid factor
_____ 82270 Stool hemoccult x 3
_____ 87430 Strep screen
_____ 84478 Triglycerides
_____ 84443 TSH
_____ 81001 UA with microscopy
_____ 87088 UC
_____ 84550 Uric acid, blood
_____ 81025 Urine pregnancy test

_____

_____

Injections:
_____ 90471 admin 1 vac
_____ 90472 each add'l vac
_____ 90716 Chickenpox
_____ 90702 DT
_____ 90701 DTP
_____ 90657 Influenza 6-35 months
_____ 90658 Influenza 3 years +
_____ 90665 Lyme disease
_____ 90707 MMR
_____ 90704 Mumps
_____ 90713 Polio vac inactivated (IPV)
_____ 90703 Tetanus Tox
ECG: _____ 93000 ECG

Other

_____

_____

NO. 5321   20 – 62
            710

October 24 20 --

PAY
TO THE
ORDER OF Karen Larsen, MD $ 44 00/100

Forty-four and no/100 _____ DOLLARS

First National Bank
Chicago, IL 60623-2791

FOR _____   *Charles Jonathan*

I:0710 III0062 242 III046580 II'

NO. 10082   20 – 62
            710

October 24 20 --

PAY
TO THE
ORDER OF Karen Larsen, MD $ 44 and no/100

Forty-four and no/100 _____ DOLLARS

First National Bank
Chicago, IL 60623-2791

FOR *Cheng Sun Worker's Comp*   *Billings, Inc.*

I:0710 III0062 202 III056232 II'

NO. 152462   20 – 62
             710

October 24 20 --

PAY
TO THE
ORDER OF Karen Larsen, MD $ 143 and 20/100

One hundred forty-three and 20/100 _____ DOLLARS

Chicago Bank
Chicago, IL 60621

FOR *David Kramer*   *New York Mutual*

I:0710 III0155 262 III025592 II'

NO. 152463   20 – 62
             710

October 24 20 --

PAY
TO THE
ORDER OF Karen Larsen, MD $ 90 and 40/100

Ninety and 40/100 _____ DOLLARS

Chicago Bank
Chicago, IL 60621

FOR *Erin Mitchell*   *New York Mutual*

I:0710 III0155 262 III025592 II'

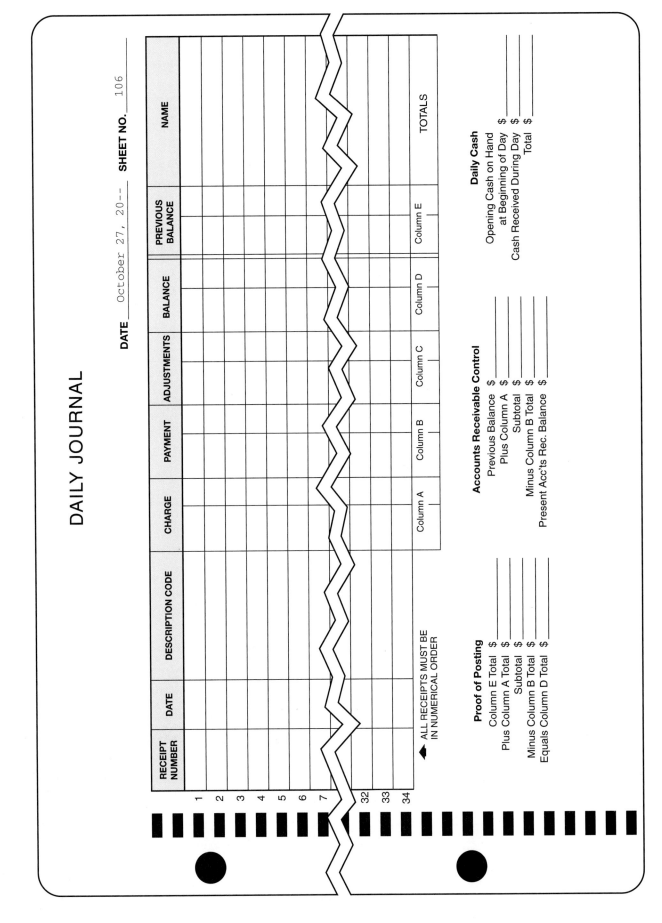

DAILY JOURNAL

DATE _____October 27, 20-- ___ SHEET NO. ___106___

RECEIPT NUMBER	DATE	DESCRIPTION CODE	CHARGE	PAYMENT	ADJUSTMENTS	BALANCE	PREVIOUS BALANCE	NAME
1								
2								
3								
4								
5								
6								
7								
32								
33								
34								
		TOTALS	Column A	Column B	Column C	Column D	Column E	

◀ ALL RECEIPTS MUST BE IN NUMERICAL ORDER

Proof of Posting

Column E Total	$ _____
Plus Column A Total	$ _____
Subtotal	$ _____
Minus Column B Total	$ _____
Equals Column D Total	$ _____

Accounts Receivable Control

Previous Balance	$ _____
Plus Column A	$ _____
Subtotal	$ _____
Minus Column B Total	$ _____
Present Acc'ts Rec. Balance	$ _____

Daily Cash

Opening Cash on Hand at Beginning of Day	$ _____
Cash Received During Day	$ _____
Total	$ _____

No.	Date	Description	Charge	Credit		Current Balance
				Payment	Adjustment	

Patient Information

5518 Monroe Street
Address

Chicago, IL 60644-5519
City, State Zip

312-555-4413   312-555-8825
Home phone   **Work phone**

self
Responsible Person   **Relationship**

Blue Cross/Blue Shield, 486-29-3789-1, 2458 Grp
Insurance   **Contract numbers**

Patient _____ Monica Armstrong

Date: 10/28/20--   **Chart #**

Karen Larsen, MD
2235 S. Ridgeway Avenue
Chicago, IL 60623-2240

312-555-6022

Fax: 312-555-0025

Diagnoses:

1. _____ 626.2 _____

2. _____ 622.7 _____

3. _____ 785.2 _____

4. _____

OFFICE VISITS

New Patient	Established Patient

Preventive Medicine

		_____ 99381	under 1 year	_____ 99391	
_____ 99201		_____ 99382	1–4	_____ 99392	_____ 99211
_____ 99202		_____ 99383	5–11	_____ 99393	_____ 99212
_____ 99203		_____ 99384	12–17	_____ 99394	_____ 99213
_____ 99204		_____ 99385	18–39	_____ 99395	_____ 99214
_____ 99205		_____ 99386	40–64	(99396)	_____ 99215
		_____ 99387	65+	_____ 99397	

Hospital Visits

Initial:
_____ 99221
_____ 99222
_____ 99223

Subsequent:
_____ 99231
_____ 99232
_____ 99233

Nursing Facility

Subsequent:
_____ 99311
_____ 99312
_____ 99313

Other
_____
_____

Lab:
_____ 80048 Basic metabolic panel (SMA-8)
_____ 87110 Chlamydia culture
_____ 85651 ESR; nonautomated
_____ 83001 FSH
_____ 82947 Glucose, blood
_____ 85022 Hemogram (CBC) with differential
_____ 80076 Hepatic function panel
_____ 85018 HGB
_____ 86701 HIV-1
_____ 83002 LH
_____ 80061 Lipid panel
_____ 86617 Lyme antibody

_____ 86308 Monospot test
(88150 Pap)
_____ 85610 Prothrombin time
_____ 84152 PSA
_____ 86430 Rheumatoid factor
_____ 82270 Stool hemoccult x 3
_____ 87430 Strep screen
_____ 84478 Triglycerides
_____ 84443 TSH
_____ 81001 UA with microscopy
_____ 87088 UC
_____ 84550 Uric acid, blood
_____ 81025 Urine pregnancy test
_____
_____

Injections:
_____ 90471 admin 1 vac
_____ 90472 each add'l vac
_____ 90716 Chickenpox
_____ 90702 DT
_____ 90701 DTP
_____ 90657 Influenza 6-35 months
_____ 90658 Influenza 3 years +
_____ 90665 Lyme disease
_____ 90707 MMR
_____ 90704 Mumps
_____ 90713 Polio vac inactivated (IPV)
_____ 90703 Tetanus Tox
ECG: _____ 93000 ECG

Other
_____
_____

No.	Date	Description	Charge	Credit		Current Balance
				Payment	Adjustment	

Patient Information

510 N. Marine Drive

Address

Chicago, IL 60640-5607

City, State Zip

312-555-1913   father
                                              312-555-8820

Home phone   **Work phone**

Andrew Kramer   father

Responsible Person   **Relationship**

Northstar Premium Insurance,
                              747-22-3401-02, Grp 411

Insurance   **Contract numbers**

Patient _____ Jeffrey Kramer _____

Date: 10/28/20--   Chart #

Karen Larsen, MD
2235 S. Ridgeway Avenue
Chicago, IL 60623-2240

312-555-6022

Fax: 312-555-0025

Diagnoses:

1. _____ 382.00 _____

2. _____ 380.10 _____

3. _____

4. _____

OFFICE VISITS

New Patient	Established Patient

Preventive Medicine

		under 1 year		99391		99211
_____ 99201	_____ 99381	1–4	_____ 99392		_____ 99212 (circled)
_____ 99202	_____ 99382	5–11	_____ 99393		_____ 99213
_____ 99203	_____ 99383	12–17	_____ 99394		_____ 99214
_____ 99204	_____ 99384	18–39	_____ 99395		_____ 99215
_____ 99205	_____ 99385	40–64	_____ 99396		
	_____ 99386	65+	_____ 99397		
	_____ 99387				

Hospital Visits

Initial:
_____ 99221
_____ 99222
_____ 99223

Subsequent:
_____ 99231
_____ 99232
_____ 99233

Nursing Facility

Subsequent:
_____ 99311
_____ 99312
_____ 99313

Other

_____

_____

Lab:
_____ 80048 Basic metabolic panel (SMA-8)
_____ 87110 Chlamydia culture
_____ 85651 ESR; nonautomated
_____ 83001 FSH
_____ 82947 Glucose, blood
_____ 85022 Hemogram (CBC) with differential
_____ 80076 Hepatic function panel
_____ 85018 HGB
_____ 86701 HIV-1
_____ 83002 LH
_____ 80061 Lipid panel
_____ 86617 Lyme antibody

_____ 86308 Monospot test
_____ 88150 Pap
_____ 85610 Prothrombin time
_____ 84152 PSA
_____ 86430 Rheumatoid factor
_____ 82270 Stool hemoccult x 3
_____ 87430 Strep screen
_____ 84478 Triglycerides
_____ 84443 TSH
_____ 81001 UA with microscopy
_____ 87088 UC
_____ 84550 Uric acid, blood
_____ 81025 Urine pregnancy test

_____

_____

Injections:
_____ 90471 admin 1 vac
_____ 90472 each add'l vac
_____ 90716 Chickenpox
_____ 90702 DT
_____ 90701 DTP
_____ 90657 Influenza 6-35 months
_____ 90658 Influenza 3 years +
_____ 90665 Lyme disease
_____ 90707 MMR
_____ 90704 Mumps
_____ 90713 Polio vac inactivated (IPV)
_____ 90703 Tetanus Tox

ECG: _____ 93000 ECG

Other

_____

_____

No.	Date	Description	Charge	Credit		Current Balance
				Payment	**Adjustment**	

Patient Information

2235 W. School Street
Address

Chicago, IL 60618-5785
City, State Zip

312-555-3750   312-555-8149
Home phone   **Work phone**

self
Responsible Person   **Relationship**

Metro State Plan, 285-90-9125,35A Grp.
Insurance   **Contract numbers**

Patient _____ Cheng Sun _____

Date: 10/28/20--   **Chart #**

Karen Larsen, MD   **Diagnoses:**
2235 S. Ridgeway Avenue
Chicago, IL 60623-2240   1. _____

                              2. _____
312-555-6022
                              3. _____

Fax: 312-555-0025   4. _____

OFFICE VISITS

New Patient	**Established Patient**

Preventive Medicine

	_____ 99381	under 1 year	_____ 99391	
_____ 99201	_____ 99382	1–4	_____ 99392	_____ 99211
_____ 99202	_____ 99383	5–11	_____ 99393	_____ 99212
_____ 99203	_____ 99384	12–17	_____ 99394	_____ 99213
_____ 99204	_____ 99385	18–39	_____ 99395	_____ 99214
_____ 99205	_____ 99386	40–64	_____ (99396)	_____ 99215
	_____ 99387	65+	_____ 99397	

Hospital Visits
Initial:
_____ 99221
_____ 99222
_____ 99223
Subsequent:
_____ 99231
_____ 99232
_____ 99233
Nursing Facility
Subsequent:
_____ 99311
_____ 99312
_____ 99313
Other
_____
_____

Lab:
_____ (80048) Basic
    metabolic panel
    (SMA-8)
_____ 87110 Chlamydia
    culture
_____ 85651 ESR;
    nonautomated
_____ 83001 FSH
_____ 82947 Glucose,
    blood
_____ 85022 Hemogram
    (CBC) with
    differential
_____ 80076 Hepatic
    function panel
_____ 85018 HGB
_____ 86701 HIV-1
_____ 83002 LH
_____ (80061) Lipid panel
_____ 86617 Lyme
    antibody

_____ 86308 Monospot
    test
_____ 88150 Pap
_____ 85610 Prothrombin
    time
_____ (84152) PSA
_____ 86430 Rheumatoid
    factor
_____ (82270) Stool
    hemoccult x 3
_____ 87430 Strep screen
_____ 84478 Triglycerides
_____ 84443 TSH
_____ (81001) UA with
    microscopy
_____ 87088 UC
_____ 84550 Uric acid,
    blood
_____ 81025 Urine
    pregnancy test
_____
_____

Injections:
_____ 90471 admin 1 vac
_____ 90472 each add'l
    vac
_____ 90716 Chickenpox
_____ 90702 DT
_____ 90701 DTP
_____ 90657 Influenza
    6-35 months
_____ 90658 Influenza
    3 years +
_____ 90665 Lyme
    disease
_____ 90707 MMR
_____ 90704 Mumps
_____ 90713 Polio vac
    inactivated (IPV)
_____ 90703 Tetanus Tox
ECG: _____ 93000 ECG

Other
_____
_____

NO. 1532106   20 – 62 / 710

October 24 20 --

PAY TO THE ORDER OF Karen Larsen, MD $ 192 and 80/100

One hundred ninety-two and 80/100 ——————————— **DOLLARS**

First National Bank
Chicago, IL 60623-2791

FOR Monica Armstrong   *BC/BS*

1: 0710 111 0062 242 111 046580 11'

NO. 1909242   20 – 62 / 710

October 24 20 --

PAY TO THE ORDER OF Karen Larsen, MD $ 93 and no/100

Ninety-three and no/100 ——————————— **DOLLARS**

First National Bank
Chicago, IL 60623-2791

FOR Laura Lund   *Employee Benefit*

1: 0710 111 0062 202 111 056232 11'

NO. 19646482   20 – 62 / 710

October 24 20 --

PAY TO THE ORDER OF Karen Larsen, MD $ 222 and 40/100

Two hundred twenty-two and 40/100 ——————————— **DOLLARS**

Chicago Bank
Chicago, IL 60621

FOR Sara Babcock   *Kaiser Insurance*

1: 0710 111 0155 262 111 025592 11'

NO. 1227847   20 – 62 / 710

October 23 20 --

PAY TO THE ORDER OF Karen Larsen, MD $ 147 and 00/100

One hundred forty-seven and 00/100 ——————————— **DOLLARS**

First National Bank
Chicago, IL 60623-2791

FOR Gary Robertson   *Prudential Group Health*

1: 0710 111 0062 081 111 502249 11'

DAILY JOURNAL

DATE ___October 28, 20-- ___ **SHEET NO.** __107__

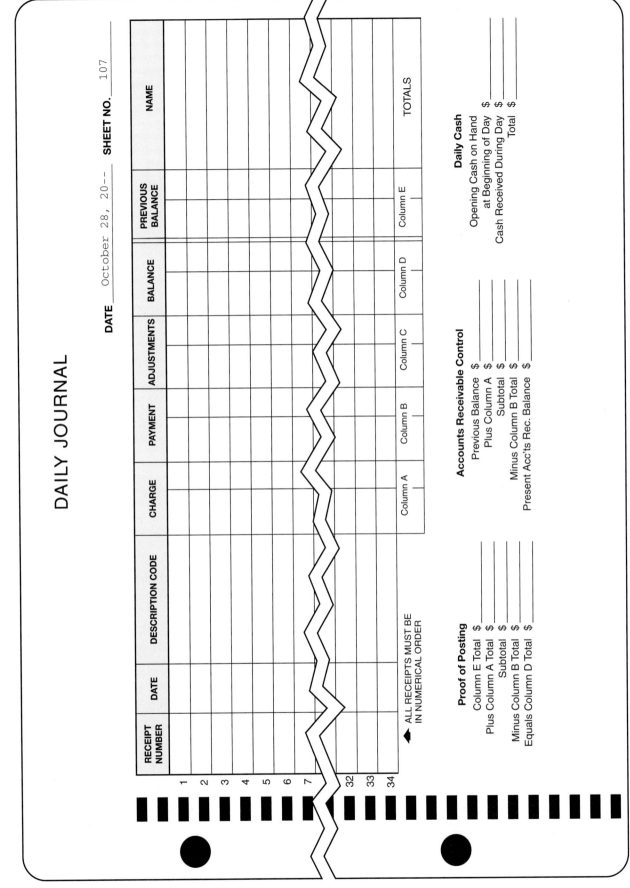

RECEIPT NUMBER	DATE	DESCRIPTION CODE	CHARGE	PAYMENT	ADJUSTMENTS	BALANCE	PREVIOUS BALANCE	NAME
1								
2								
3								
4								
5								
6								
7								
32								
33								
34								
		TOTALS	Column A	Column B	Column C	Column D	Column E	

◄ ALL RECEIPTS MUST BE IN NUMERICAL ORDER

Proof of Posting

Column E Total $ _____
Plus Column A Total $ _____
Subtotal $ _____
Minus Column B Total $ _____
Equals Column D Total $ _____

Accounts Receivable Control

Previous Balance $ _____
Plus Column A $ _____
Subtotal $ _____
Minus Column B Total $ _____
Present Acc'ts Rec. Balance $ _____

Daily Cash

Opening Cash on Hand
at Beginning of Day $ _____
Cash Received During Day $ _____
Total $ _____

WP 87

No.	Date	Description	Charge	Credit		Current Balance
				Payment	Adjustment	

Patient Information

5015 N. Ridgeway Avenue
Address

Chicago, IL 60625-1220
City, State Zip

312-555-3478   312-555-8830
Home phone   **Work phone**

self
Responsible Person   **Relationship**

University Health Plan,
          581-57-0376-59, A87 Grp
Insurance   **Contract numbers**

Patient _____ Thomas Baab

Date: 10/29/20--   **Chart #**

Karen Larsen, MD
2235 S. Ridgeway Avenue
Chicago, IL 60623-2240

312-555-6022

Fax: 312-555-0025

Diagnoses:

1. _____

2. _____

3. _____

4. _____

OFFICE VISITS

New Patient		**Established Patient**	

Preventive Medicine

New Patient	Preventive	Age	Established	Established
	___ 99381	under 1 year	___ 99391	
___ 99201	___ 99382	1–4	___ 99392	___ 99211
___ 99202	___ 99383	5–11	___ 99393	(99212)
___ 99203	___ 99384	12–17	___ 99394	___ 99213
___ 99204	___ 99385	18–39	___ 99395	___ 99214
___ 99205	___ 99386	40–64	___ 99396	___ 99215
	___ 99387	65+	___ 99397	

Hospital Visits
Initial:
___ 99221
___ 99222
___ 99223
Subsequent:
___ 99231
___ 99232
___ 99233
Nursing Facility
Subsequent:
___ 99311
___ 99312
___ 99313
Other
_____
_____

Lab:
___ 80048 Basic
    metabolic panel
    (SMA-8)
___ 87110 Chlamydia
    culture
___ 85651 ESR;
    nonautomated
___ 83001 FSH
___ 82947 Glucose,
    blood
___ 85022 Hemogram
    (CBC) with
    differential
___ 80076 Hepatic
    function panel
___ 85018 HGB
___ 86701 HIV-1
___ 83002 LH
___ 80061 Lipid panel
___ 86617 Lyme
    antibody

___ 86308 Monospot
    test
___ 88150 Pap
___ 85610 Prothrombin
    time
___ 84152 PSA
___ 86430 Rheumatoid
    factor
___ 82270 Stool
    hemoccult x 3
___ 87430 Strep screen
___ 84478 Triglycerides
___ 84443 TSH
___ 81001 UA with
    microscopy
___ 87088 UC
___ 84550 Uric acid,
    blood
___ 81025 Urine
    pregnancy test
_____
_____

Injections:
___ 90471 admin 1 vac
___ 90472 each add'l
    vac
___ 90716 Chickenpox
___ 90702 DT
___ 90701 DTP
___ 90657 Influenza
    6-35 months
___ 90658 Influenza
    3 years +
___ 90665 Lyme
    disease
___ 90707 MMR
___ 90704 Mumps
___ 90713 Polio vac
    inactivated (IPV)
___ 90703 Tetanus Tox
ECG: ___ 93000 ECG

Other
_____
_____

No.	Date	Description	Charge	Credit Payment	Credit Adjustment	Current Balance

Patient Information

105 W. Chestnut Street
Address

Chicago, IL 60610-2816
City, State Zip

312-555-2231   312-555-2583
Home phone   **Work phone**

self
Responsible Person   **Relationship**

University Health Plan,
          797-90-1128, S357C Grp.
Insurance   **Contract numbers**

Patient _____ Theresa Dayton _____

Date: 10/29/20--   **Chart #**

Karen Larsen, MD
2235 S. Ridgeway Avenue
Chicago, IL 60623-2240

312-555-6022

Fax: 312-555-0025

Diagnoses:

1. _____ 307.81 _____

2. _____

3. _____

4. _____

OFFICE VISITS

New Patient		Established Patient	

Preventive Medicine

New Patient				Established Patient	
	_____ 99381	under 1 year	_____ 99391		
_____ 99201	_____ 99382	1–4	_____ 99392		_____ 99211
_____ 99202	_____ 99383	5–11	_____ 99393		(99212)
_____ 99203	_____ 99384	12–17	_____ 99394		_____ 99213
_____ 99204	_____ 99385	18–39	_____ 99395		_____ 99214
_____ 99205	_____ 99386	40–64	_____ 99396		_____ 99215
	_____ 99387	65+	_____ 99397		

Hospital Visits
Initial:
_____ 99221
_____ 99222
_____ 99223
Subsequent:
_____ 99231
_____ 99232
_____ 99233
Nursing Facility
Subsequent:
_____ 99311
_____ 99312
_____ 99313
Other
_____
_____

Lab:
_____ 80048 Basic
metabolic panel
(SMA-8)
_____ 87110 Chlamydia
culture
_____ 85651 ESR;
nonautomated
_____ 83001 FSH
_____ 82947 Glucose,
blood
_____ 85022 Hemogram
(CBC) with
differential
_____ 80076 Hepatic
function panel
_____ 85018 HGB
_____ 86701 HIV-1
_____ 83002 LH
_____ 80061 Lipid panel
_____ 86617 Lyme
antibody

_____ 86308 Monospot
test
_____ 88150 Pap
_____ 85610 Prothrombin
time
_____ 84152 PSA
_____ 86430 Rheumatoid
factor
_____ 82270 Stool
hemoccult x 3
_____ 87430 Strep screen
_____ 84478 Triglycerides
_____ 84443 TSH
_____ 81001 UA with
microscopy
_____ 87088 UC
_____ 84550 Uric acid,
blood
_____ 81025 Urine
pregnancy test
_____
_____

Injections:
_____ 90471 admin 1 vac
_____ 90472 each add'l
vac
_____ 90716 Chickenpox
_____ 90702 DT
_____ 90701 DTP
_____ 90657 Influenza
6-35 months
_____ 90658 Influenza
3 years +
_____ 90665 Lyme
disease
_____ 90707 MMR
_____ 90704 Mumps
_____ 90713 Polio vac
inactivated (IPV)
_____ 90703 Tetanus Tox
ECG: _____ 93000 ECG

Other
_____
_____

No.	Date	Description	Charge	Credit		Current Balance
				Payment	**Adjustment**	

Patient Information

105 W. Chestnut Street

Address

Chicago, IL 60610-2816

City, State Zip

312-555-2231   312-555-2583

Home phone   **Work phone**

self

Responsible Person   **Relationship**

University Health Plan,
                    797-90-1128, S357C Grp.

Insurance   **Contract numbers**

Patient _____ Theresa Dayton _____

Date: 10/29/20--   **Chart #**

Karen Larsen, MD
2235 S. Ridgeway Avenue
Chicago, IL 60623-2240

312-555-6022

Fax: 312-555-0025

Diagnoses:

1. _____ 307.81 _____

2. _____

3. _____

4. _____

OFFICE VISITS

New Patient	Established Patient

Preventive Medicine

New Patient				Established Patient	
	____ 99381	under 1 year	____ 99391		
____ 99201	____ 99382	1–4	____ 99392		____ 99211
____ 99202	____ 99383	5–11	____ 99393		____ (99212)
____ 99203	____ 99384	12–17	____ 99394		____ 99213
____ 99204	____ 99385	18–39	____ 99395		____ 99214
____ 99205	____ 99386	40–64	____ 99396		____ 99215
	____ 99387	65+	____ 99397		

Hospital Visits
Initial:
____ 99221
____ 99222
____ 99223
Subsequent:
____ 99231
____ 99232
____ 99233
Nursing Facility
Subsequent:
____ 99311
____ 99312
____ 99313
Other
_____
_____

Lab:
____ 80048 Basic
     metabolic panel
     (SMA-8)
____ 87110 Chlamydia
     culture
____ 85651 ESR;
     nonautomated
____ 83001 FSH
____ 82947 Glucose,
     blood
____ 85022 Hemogram
     (CBC) with
     differential
____ 80076 Hepatic
     function panel
____ 85018 HGB
____ 86701 HIV-1
____ 83002 LH
____ 80061 Lipid panel
____ 86617 Lyme
     antibody

____ 86308 Monospot
     test
____ 88150 Pap
____ 85610 Prothrombin
     time
____ 84152 PSA
____ 86430 Rheumatoid
     factor
____ 82270 Stool
     hemoccult x 3
____ 87430 Strep screen
____ 84478 Triglycerides
____ 84443 TSH
____ 81001 UA with
     microscopy
____ 87088 UC
____ 84550 Uric acid,
     blood
____ 81025 Urine
     pregnancy test
_____
_____

Injections:
____ 90471 admin 1 vac
____ 90472 each add'l
     vac
____ 90716 Chickenpox
____ 90702 DT
____ 90701 DTP
____ 90657 Influenza
     6-35 months
____ 90658 Influenza
     3 years +
____ 90665 Lyme
     disease
____ 90707 MMR
____ 90704 Mumps
____ 90713 Polio vac
     inactivated (IPV)
____ 90703 Tetanus Tox
ECG: ____ 93000 ECG

Other
_____
_____

No.	Date	Description	Charge	Credit		Current Balance
				Payment	**Adjustment**	

Patient Information

4443 W. Monroe Street
Address

Chicago, IL 60624-8966
City, State Zip

312-555-3178   312-555-8848
Home phone   **Work phone**

Earl Matthews   husband
Responsible Person   **Relationship**

Arling Employee Plan,
          294-82-8099-02, 33A Grp
Insurance   **Contract numbers**

Patient _____ Ardis Matthews _____

Date: 10/29/20--   **Chart #**

Karen Larsen, MD
2235 S. Ridgeway Avenue
Chicago, IL 60623-2240

312-555-6022

Fax: 312-555-0025

Diagnoses:

1. _____
2. _____
3. _____
4. _____

OFFICE VISITS

New Patient	Established Patient

Preventive Medicine

New Patient			Established Patient	
	_____ 99381	under 1 year	_____ 99391	
_____ 99201	_____ 99382	1–4	_____ 99392	_____ 99211
_____ 99202	_____ 99383	5–11	_____ 99393	(99212)
_____ 99203	_____ 99384	12–17	_____ 99394	_____ 99213
_____ 99204	_____ 99385	18–39	_____ 99395	_____ 99214
_____ 99205	_____ 99386	40–64	_____ 99396	_____ 99215
	_____ 99387	65+	_____ 99397	

Hospital Visits
Initial:
_____ 99221
_____ 99222
_____ 99223
Subsequent:
_____ 99231
_____ 99232
_____ 99233
Nursing Facility
Subsequent:
_____ 99311
_____ 99312
_____ 99313
Other
_____
_____

Lab:
_____ 80048 Basic
          metabolic panel
          (SMA-8)
_____ 87110 Chlamydia
          culture
_____ 85651 ESR;
          nonautomated
_____ 83001 FSH
_____ 82947 Glucose,
          blood
_____ 85022 Hemogram
          (CBC) with
          differential
_____ 80076 Hepatic
          function panel
_____ 85018 HGB
_____ 86701 HIV-1
_____ 83002 LH
_____ 80061 Lipid panel
_____ 86617 Lyme
          antibody

_____ 86308 Monospot
          test
_____ 88150 Pap
_____ 85610 Prothrombin
          time
_____ 84152 PSA
_____ 86430 Rheumatoid
          factor
_____ 82270 Stool
          hemoccult x 3
_____ 87430 Strep screen
_____ 84478 Triglycerides
_____ 84443 TSH
_____ 81001 UA with
          microscopy
_____ 87088 UC
_____ 84550 Uric acid,
          blood
_____ 81025 Urine
          pregnancy test
_____
_____

Injections:
_____ 90471 admin 1 vac
_____ 90472 each add'l
          vac
_____ 90716 Chickenpox
_____ 90702 DT
_____ 90701 DTP
_____ 90657 Influenza
          6-35 months
_____ 90658 Influenza
          3 years +
_____ 90665 Lyme
          disease
_____ 90707 MMR
_____ 90704 Mumps
_____ 90713 Polio vac
          inactivated (IPV)
_____ 90703 Tetanus Tox
ECG: _____ 93000 ECG

Other
_____
_____

| No. | Date | Description | Charge | Credit | | Current Balance |
				Payment	Adjustment	

Patient Information

3457 W. 63d Place
Address

Chicago, IL 60629-4270
City, State Zip

312-555-3606
Home phone   **Work phone**

self
Responsible Person   **Relationship**

Blue Cross & Blue Shield,
         295-99-3325, 354 Grp.
Insurance   **Contract numbers**

Patient _____ Ana Mendez _____

Date: 10/29/20--   **Chart #**

Karen Larsen, MD
2235 S. Ridgeway Avenue
Chicago, IL 60623-2240

312-555-6022

Fax: 312-555-0025

Diagnoses:

1. _____

2. _____

3. _____

4. _____

OFFICE VISITS

New Patient	Established Patient

Preventive Medicine

New Patient		Established Patient	
_____ 99201	_____ 99381 under 1 year	_____ 99391	_____ 99211
_____ 99202	_____ 99382 1–4	_____ 99392	⦿ 99212
_____ 99203	_____ 99383 5–11	_____ 99393	_____ 99213
_____ 99204	_____ 99384 12–17	_____ 99394	_____ 99214
_____ 99205	_____ 99385 18–39	_____ 99395	_____ 99215
	_____ 99386 40–64	_____ 99396	
	_____ 99387 65+	_____ 99397	

Hospital Visits

Initial:
_____ 99221
_____ 99222
_____ 99223

Subsequent:
_____ 99231
_____ 99232
_____ 99233

Nursing Facility

Subsequent:
_____ 99311
_____ 99312
_____ 99313

Other

_____

_____

Lab:
_____ 80048 Basic metabolic panel (SMA-8)
_____ 87110 Chlamydia culture
_____ 85651 ESR; nonautomated
_____ 83001 FSH
_____ 82947 Glucose, blood
_____ 85022 Hemogram (CBC) with differential
_____ 80076 Hepatic function panel
_____ 85018 HGB
_____ 86701 HIV-1
_____ 83002 LH
_____ 80061 Lipid panel
_____ 86617 Lyme antibody

_____ 86308 Monospot test
_____ 88150 Pap
_____ 85610 Prothrombin time
_____ 84152 PSA
_____ 86430 Rheumatoid factor
_____ 82270 Stool hemoccult x 3
_____ 87430 Strep screen
_____ 84478 Triglycerides
_____ 84443 TSH
_____ 81001 UA with microscopy
_____ 87088 UC
_____ 84550 Uric acid, blood
_____ 81025 Urine pregnancy test

_____

_____

Injections:
_____ 90471 admin 1 vac
_____ 90472 each add'l vac
_____ 90716 Chickenpox
_____ 90702 DT
_____ 90701 DTP
_____ 90657 Influenza 6-35 months
_____ 90658 Influenza 3 years +
_____ 90665 Lyme disease
_____ 90707 MMR
_____ 90704 Mumps
_____ 90713 Polio vac inactivated (IPV)
_____ 90703 Tetanus Tox
ECG: _____ 93000 ECG

Other

_____

_____

Copyright © McGraw-Hill Higher Education

WP 91

No.	Date	Description	Charge	Credit		Current Balance
				Payment	Adjustment	

Patient Information

3449 W. Foster Avenue
Address

Chicago, IL 60625-2377
City, State Zip

312-555-9565   312-555-8857
Home phone   **Work phone**

self
Responsible Person   **Relationship**

Prudential Group Health, 255-74-1021
Insurance   **Contract numbers**

Patient _____ Gary Robertson _____

Date: 10/29/20--   **Chart #**

Karen Larsen, MD
2235 S. Ridgeway Avenue
Chicago, IL 60623-2240

312-555-6022

Fax: 312-555-0025

Diagnoses:

1. ____ 590.80 ____

2. _____

3. _____

4. _____

OFFICE VISITS

New Patient	Established Patient

Preventive Medicine

	____ 99381	under 1 year	____ 99391	
____ 99201	____ 99382	1–4	____ 99392	____ 99211
____ 99202	____ 99383	5–11	____ 99393	(99212)
____ 99203	____ 99384	12–17	____ 99394	____ 99213
____ 99204	____ 99385	18–39	____ 99395	____ 99214
____ 99205	____ 99386	40–64	____ 99396	____ 99215
	____ 99387	65+	____ 99397	

Hospital Visits

Initial:
____ 99221
____ 99222
____ 99223
Subsequent:
____ 99231
____ 99232
____ 99233

Nursing Facility

Subsequent:
____ 99311
____ 99312
____ 99313

Other

_____

Lab:
____ 80048 Basic metabolic panel (SMA-8)
____ 87110 Chlamydia culture
____ 85651 ESR; nonautomated
____ 83001 FSH
____ 82947 Glucose, blood
____ 85022 Hemogram (CBC) with differential
____ 80076 Hepatic function panel
____ 85018 HGB
____ 86701 HIV-1
____ 83002 LH
____ 80061 Lipid panel
____ 86617 Lyme antibody

____ 86308 Monospot test
____ 88150 Pap
____ 85610 Prothrombin time
____ 84152 PSA
____ 86430 Rheumatoid factor
____ 82270 Stool hemoccult x 3
____ 87430 Strep screen
____ 84478 Triglycerides
____ 84443 TSH
____ 81001 UA with microscopy
____ 87088 UC
____ 84550 Uric acid, blood
____ 81025 Urine pregnancy test

_____

Injections:
____ 90471 admin 1 vac
____ 90472 each add'l vac
____ 90716 Chickenpox
____ 90702 DT
____ 90701 DTP
____ 90657 Influenza 6-35 months
____ 90658 Influenza 3 years +
____ 90665 Lyme disease
____ 90707 MMR
____ 90704 Mumps
____ 90713 Polio vac inactivated (IPV)
____ 90703 Tetanus Tox
ECG: ____ 93000 ECG

Other

No.	Date	Description	Charge	Credit		Current Balance
				Payment	**Adjustment**	

Patient Information

6111 N. Lincoln Avenue
Address

Chicago, IL 60608-3173
City, State Zip

312-555-1217
Home phone   **Work phone**

self
Responsible Person   **Relationship**

Medicare   669-35-2244B
Insurance   **Contract numbers**

Patient _____ Florence Sherman _____

Date: 10/29/20--   **Chart #**

Karen Larsen, MD
2235 S. Ridgeway Avenue
Chicago, IL 60623-2240

312-555-6022

Fax: 312-555-0025

Diagnoses:

1. _____ 920 _____

2. _____ 923.03 _____

3. _____

4. _____

OFFICE VISITS

New Patient	Established Patient

Preventive Medicine

New Patient				Established Patient	
	_____ 99381	under 1 year	_____ 99391		
_____ 99201	_____ 99382	1–4	_____ 99392	_____ 99211	
_____ 99202	_____ 99383	5–11	_____ 99393	(99212)	
_____ 99203	_____ 99384	12–17	_____ 99394	_____ 99213	
_____ 99204	_____ 99385	18–39	_____ 99395	_____ 99214	
_____ 99205	_____ 99386	40–64	_____ 99396	_____ 99215	
	_____ 99387	65+	_____ 99397		

Hospital Visits
Initial:
_____ 99221
_____ 99222
_____ 99223
Subsequent:
_____ 99231
_____ 99232
_____ 99233
Nursing Facility
Subsequent:
_____ 99311
_____ 99312
_____ 99313
Other
_____
_____

Lab:
_____ 80048 Basic
   metabolic panel
   (SMA-8)
_____ 87110 Chlamydia
   culture
_____ 85651 ESR;
   nonautomated
_____ 83001 FSH
_____ 82947 Glucose,
   blood
_____ 85022 Hemogram
   (CBC) with
   differential
_____ 80076 Hepatic
   function panel
_____ 85018 HGB
_____ 86701 HIV-1
_____ 83002 LH
_____ 80061 Lipid panel
_____ 86617 Lyme
   antibody

_____ 86308 Monospot
   test
_____ 88150 Pap
_____ 85610 Prothrombin
   time
_____ 84152 PSA
_____ 86430 Rheumatoid
   factor
_____ 82270 Stool
   hemocult x 3
_____ 87430 Strep screen
_____ 84478 Triglycerides
_____ 84443 TSH
_____ 81001 UA with
   microscopy
_____ 87088 UC
_____ 84550 Uric acid,
   blood
_____ 81025 Urine
   pregnancy test
_____
_____

Injections:
_____ 90471 admin 1 vac
_____ 90472 each add'l
   vac
_____ 90716 Chickenpox
_____ 90702 DT
_____ 90701 DTP
_____ 90657 Influenza
   6-35 months
_____ 90658 Influenza
   3 years +
_____ 90665 Lyme
   disease
_____ 90707 MMR
_____ 90704 Mumps
_____ 90713 Polio vac
   inactivated (IPV)
_____ 90703 Tetanus Tox
ECG: _____ 93000 ECG

Other
_____
_____

NO. 439205   20 – 62
              710

October 22 20 --

PAY
TO THE
ORDER OF Karen Larsen, MD $ 114 and no/100

One hundred fourteen and 00/100 ————————————— DOLLARS

First National Bank
Chicago, IL 60623-2791

FOR Todd Grant   Prudential Plan

I:0710 III 0062 081 III 502249 II·

NO. 1983425   20 – 62
               710

October 20 20 --

PAY
TO THE
ORDER OF Karen Larsen, MD $ 42 and 40/100

Forty-two and 40/100 ————————————— DOLLARS

First National Bank
Chicago, IL 60623-2791

FOR Raymond Murrary   Medicare

I:0710 III 0062 242 III 046580 II·

NO. 475   20 – 62
           710

October 23 20 --

PAY
TO THE
ORDER OF Karen Larsen, MD $ 86 and 20/100

Eighty-six and 20/100 ————————————— DOLLARS

First National Bank
Chicago, IL 60623-2791

FOR ————————————   Clarence Rogers

I:0710 III 0062 202 III 056232 II·

NO. 704382   20 – 62
              710

October 22 20 --

PAY
TO THE
ORDER OF Karen Larsen, MD $ 66 and 40/100

Sixty-six and 40/100 ————————————— DOLLARS

Chicago Bank
Chicago, IL 60621

FOR Stephen Villano   Employee Benefit Plan

I:0710 III 0155 262 III 025592 II·

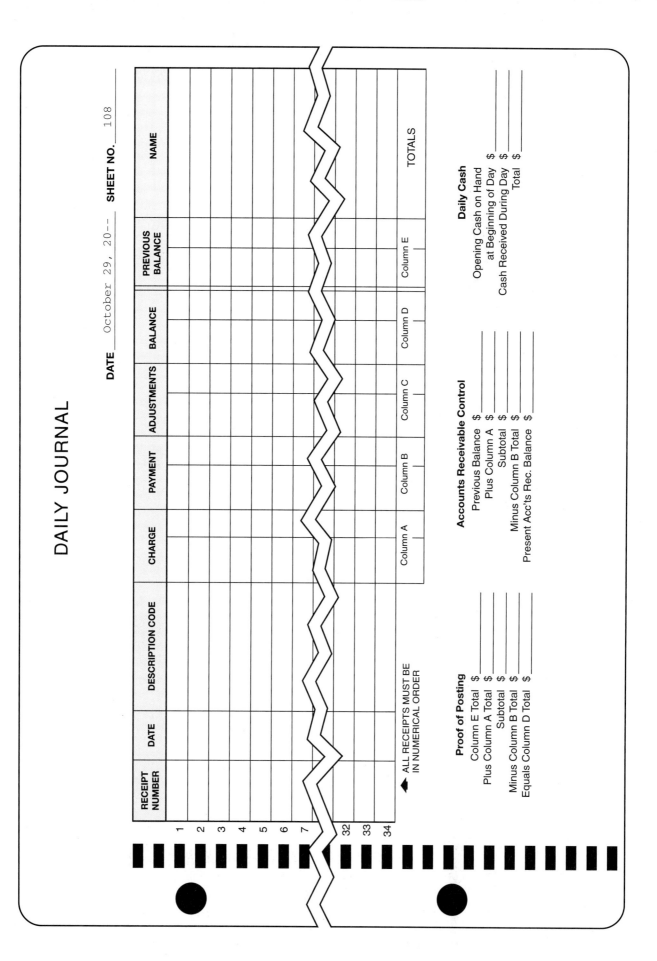

DAILY JOURNAL

DATE October 29, 20-- SHEET NO. 108

RECEIPT NUMBER	DATE	DESCRIPTION CODE	CHARGE	PAYMENT	ADJUSTMENTS	BALANCE	PREVIOUS BALANCE	NAME
1								
2								
3								
4								
5								
6								
7								
32								
33								
34								
		TOTALS	Column A	Column B	Column C	Column D	Column E	

◄ ALL RECEIPTS MUST BE
  IN NUMERICAL ORDER

Proof of Posting

Column E Total	$ _____
Plus Column A Total	$ _____
Subtotal	$ _____
Minus Column B Total	$ _____
Equals Column D Total	$ _____

Accounts Receivable Control

Previous Balance	$ _____
Plus Column A	$ _____
Subtotal	$ _____
Minus Column B Total	$ _____
Present Acc'ts Rec. Balance	$ _____

Daily Cash

Opening Cash on Hand at Beginning of Day	$ _____
Cash Received During Day	$ _____
Total	$ _____